Olena Palko, Manuel Férez Gil (eds.)
Ukraine's Many Faces

New Europes | Volume 1

Die freie Verfügbarkeit der E-Book-Ausgabe dieser Publikation wurde ermöglicht durch **POLLUX – Informationsdienst Politikwissenschaft**

und die Open Library Community Politik 2023 – einem Netzwerk wissenschaftlicher Bibliotheken zur Förderung von Open Access in den Sozial- und Geisteswissenschaften:

Hauptsponsor: Fachinformationsdienst Politikwissenschaft – POLLUX
Vollsponsoren: Technische Universität Braunschweig | Carl von Ossietzky-Universität Oldenburg | Universiätsbibliothek der FernUniversität Hagen | Freie Universität Berlin – Universitätsbibliothek | Niedersächsische Staats- und Universitätsbibliothek Göttingen | Goethe-Universität Frankfurt am Main | Gottfried Wilhelm Leibniz Bibliothek – Niedersächsische Landesbibliothek | TIB – Leibniz-Informationszentrum Technik und Naturwissenschaften und Universitätsbibliothek | Humboldt-Universität zu Berlin | Justus-Liebig-Universität Gießen | Universitätsbibliothek Eichstätt-Ingolstadt | Ludwig-Maximilians-Universität München | Max Planck Digital Library (MPDL) | Rheinische Friedrich-Wilhelms-Universität Bonn | Ruhr-Universität Bochum | Staats- und Universitätsbibliothek Carl von Ossietzky, Hamburg | SLUB Dresden | Staatsbibliothek zu Berlin | Universitätsbibliothek Chemnitz | Universitäts- und Landesbibliothek Darmstadt | Universitätsbibliothek „Georgius Agricola" der TU Bergakademie Freiberg | Universitätsbibliothek Kiel (CAU) | Universitätsbibliothek Leipzig | Universität Wien | Universitäts- und Landesbibliothek Düsseldorf | Universitäts- und Landesbibliothek Münster | Universitäts- und Stadtbibliothek Köln | Universitätsbibliothek Bielefeld | Universitätsbibliothek der Bauhaus-Universität Weimar | Universitätsbibliothek Kassel | Universitätsbibliothek Osnabrück | Universitätsbibliothek St. Gallen | Universitätsbibliothek Vechta | Vorarlberger Landesbibliothek | Zentral- und Hochschulbibliothek Luzern | Zentralbibliothek Zürich | ZHAW Zürcher Hochschule für Angewandte Wissenschaften, Hochschulbibliothek
Sponsoring Light: Bundesministerium der Verteidigung | Bibliothek der Hochschule für Technik und Wirtschaft Dresden | Bibliothek der Hochschule für Technik, Wirtschaft und Kultur Leipzig | Bibliothek der Westsächsischen Hochschule Zwickau | Bibliothek der Hochschule Zittau/Görlitz | Hochschulbibliothek der Hochschule Mittweida | Institut für Auslandsbeziehungen (IfA) | Landesbibliothek Oldenburg | Österreichische Parlamentsbibliothek
Mikrosponsoring: Bibliothek der Berufsakademie Sachsen | Bibliothek der Evangelische Hochschule Dresden | Bibliothek der Hochschule für Musik und Theater „Felix Mendelssohn Bartholdy" Leipzig | Bibliothek der Hochschule für Bildende Künste Dresden | Bibliothek der Hochschule für Musik „Carl Maria von Weber" Dresden | Bibliothek der Hochschule für Grafik und Buchkunst Leipzig | Bibliothek der Palucca-Hochschule für Tanz Dresden | Leibniz-Institut für Europäische Geschichte | Stiftung Wissenschaft und Politik (SWP) – Deutsches Institut für Internationale Politik und Sicherheit

Olena Palko, Manuel Férez Gil (eds.)
Ukraine's Many Faces
Land, People, and Culture Revisited

[transcript]

Funding: The publication of this volume has been supported by the BASEES Study Group for Minority History and URIS Ukrainian Research in Switzerland Initiative.

Bibliographic information published by the Deutsche Nationalbibliothek
The Deutsche Nationalbibliothek lists this publication in the Deutsche Nationalbibliografie; detailed bibliographic data are available in the Internet at http://dnb.d-nb.de

This work is licensed under the Creative Commons Attribution-Non Commercial 4.0 (BY-NC) license, which means that the text may be may be remixed, build upon and be distributed, provided credit is given to the author, but may not be used for commercial purposes.
For details go to: https://creativecommons.org/licenses/by-nc/4.0/
Permission to use the text for commercial purposes can be obtained by contacting rights@transcript-publishing.com
Creative Commons license terms for re-use do not apply to any content (such as graphs, figures, photos, excerpts, etc.) not original to the Open Access publication and further permission may be required from the rights holder. The obligation to research and clear permission lies solely with the party re-using the material.

First published in 2023 by transcript Verlag, Bielefeld
© Olena Palko, Manuel Férez Gil (eds.)

Cover layout: Maria Arndt, Bielefeld
Translation: Olga Chyzmar
Proofread: Samuel Foster
Printed by Majuskel Medienproduktion GmbH, Wetzlar
Print-ISBN 978-3-8376-6664-9
PDF-ISBN 978-3-8394-6664-3
EPUB-ISBN 978-3-7328-6664-9
https://doi.org/10.14361/9783839466643
ISSN of series: 2941-3079
eISSN of series: 2941-3087

Printed on permanent acid-free text paper.

To all those in Ukraine fighting for freedom

Contents

Illustrations 13

Timeline of Ukrainian History 17

Foreword. Where is Ukraine?
How a Western Outlook Perpetuates Myths about Europe's Largest Country
Olesya Khromeychuk 21

Introduction. Ukraine's Many Faces
Olena Palko and Manuel Férez Gil 29

I. Modernity at the Crossroads of Empires

Primary Sources

Ukrainian Draft Treaty of 1654
A Byelorussian Copy of the Articles sent by the Cossack Envoys Samoylo
Bohdanov and Pavlo Teterya on the 14th day of May, 7162 (A.D. 1654) 41

To My Fellow-Countrymen, In Ukraine and Not in Ukraine, Living, Dead and as Yet Unborn
My Friendly Epistle
Taras Shevchenko 45

Bohdan Khmelnytsky's Entry to Kyiv in 1649 (1912)
Mykola Ivasiuk 51

Conversation Pieces

Revealing Pan-Slavic Russian Imperialism
Ewa Thompson, in conversation with Manuel Férez Gil 55

Ukrainian History through Literature
Tamara Hundorova, in conversation with Manuel Férez Gil 61

Analytical Articles

Between East and West: Understanding Early Modern Ukraine
Oleksii Sokyrko 73

Between Empires: Ukraine in the Nineteenth Century
Fabian Baumann 83

Jews in Habsburg Galicia: Challenges of Modernity
Vladyslava Moskalets 91

Grain, Coal, and Gas. Ukraine's Economy since the Eighteenth Century
Boris Belge 101

II. Ukrainian Selfhood in the Soviet Era

Primary Sources

Ukrainian Declaration of Independence (1918)
January 9th, 1918 123

Letter from the Collective Farmer Mykola Reva to Joseph Stalin about the Famine of 1933 in Ukraine 129

Fedir Krychevsky, Life Triptych (1925) 131

Conversation Pieces

Ukraine: Between Empires and National Self-Determination
Olena Palko, in conversation with Manuel Férez Gil 135

Analytical Articles

The Ukrainian Revolution, the Bolsheviks, and the Inertia of Empire
Hanna Perekhoda 149

The Territory of Ukraine and Its History
Stephan Rindlisbacher 165

Constructing Ethnic Identities in Early Soviet Ukraine
Olena Palko and Roman Korshuk 175

Street Children in Early Soviet Odesa
Matthew D. Pauly 191

Selfhood and Statehood in Interwar Ukraine: Inventing the "New Man"
Oksana Klymenko and Roman Liubavskyi 205

Stalinism and The Holodomor
Daria Mattingly 221

Ukrainian Greek Catholics in Search of Ancestry, Belonging, and Identity
Iuliia Buyskykh 233

Crimean Tatars: Claiming the Homeland
Martin-Oleksandr Kisly 247

III. Sovereignty Regained: Ukraine in the Post-Soviet Age

Primary Sources

Declaration of State Sovereignty of Ukraine (1990)
Passed by the Verkhovna Rada of the Ukrainian Soviet Socialist Republic 267

Home is still possible there...
Kateryna Kalytko 273

Matvey Vaisberg, The Wall [Stina] (2014) 275

Conversation Pieces

**Between the Holodomor and Euromaidan:
In Search of Contemporary Ukrainian National Identity**
David Marples, in conversation with Manuel Férez Gil 279

Ukraine: Between National Security and the Rule of Law
Maria Popova, in conversation with Manuel Férez Gil 291

Analytical Articles

Society in Turbulent Times: The Impact of War on Ukraine
Anna Chebotarova 299

Competing Identities of Ukraine's Russian Speakers
Volodymyr Kulyk 315

The Donbas: A Region and a Myth
Oleksandr Zabirko 331

Towards Gender Equality in the Ukrainian Society
Tamara Martsenyuk 345

The Art of Misunderstanding
Kateryna Botanova 357

The Territory Resists the Map
Geolocating Reality and Hyperreality in the Russo-Ukrainian War
Roman Horbyk 365

Afterword. Let Ukraine Speak

Integrating Scholarship on Ukraine into Classroom Syllabi
John Vsetecka 375

Contributing Authors 393

Illustrations

Image 1.	Mykola Ivasiuk, *The Entry of Bohdan Khmelnytsky into Kyiv in 1649* (1912). National Art Museum of Ukraine, Kyiv. Public Domain, p. 51.
Image 2.	Fedir Krychevsky, *Life: Triptych (Love, Family, and Return)* (1925–7). National Art Museum of Ukraine, Kyiv. Public Domain, p. 131.
Image 3.	Matvey Vaisberg, Painting from *The Wall Cycle* (2014). Reprinted with the artist's permission, p. 275.
Fig. 0–1.	Map of Ukraine, 1993. © Dmytro Vortman, p. 15.
Fig. 1–1.	Ukrainian Economy, 2006. Wikipedia Commons, p. 103.
Fig. 1–2.	Soil Map of Ukraine. Source: General Directorate of Surveying and Cartography of the Soviet Ministry, GUGK, SSSR, 1977. Downloaded from the European Soil Data Centre (ESDAC), p. 104.
Fig. 1–3.	"Wheat Exports of the Russian Empire (including Ukraine), 1861–1913", Source: Falkus, M.E., Russia and the International Wheat Trade, 1861–1814, New Series, Vol. 33, No. 132 (Nov., 1966), p. 417, p. 108.
Fig. 1–4.	"Donbass – serdtse Rossii." The New York Public Library Digital Collections. 1921, p. 111.
Fig. 2–1.	The formation of the Russo-Ukrainian border between 1919 and 1928. Courtesy of Stephan Rindlisbacher, p. 168.
Fig. 2–2.	A prospective plan of the apartment block for Traktorobud 3. 1930. TsDAML Ukraïny. F.8, op. 1, spr. 261. Reprinted with permission, p. 207.
Fig. 2–3.	Workers club of Shestopark Theatre. New Year's Eve, 1924. Kharkiv Historical Museum. Reprinted with permission, p. 210.
Fig. 2–4.	Workers from the Kholodnohirs'kyi raion on 1 May 1923. Kharkiv Historical Museum. Reprinted with permission, p. 212.

Fig. 2–5. Father playing the violin, while his son is performing a traditional Crimean Tatar dance Haytarma. Uzbekistan, the 1950s. Photo by Mustafa Tomak. Courtesy of Nizami Ibraimov archive, p. 250.

Fig. 2–6. The Karabash family in the central park of Simferopol, 1968. From the family archive, p. 254.

Fig. 2–7. Forced eviction from Crimea, the 1970s. From Gulnara Bekirova archive, p. 255.

Fig. 2–8. Musa Mamut funeral. From the book Reshat Dzhemilev, ed., Zhivoy fakel: samosozhzhenie Musy Mamuta (New York: Fond Krym, 1986), p. 257.

Fig. 2–9. "Homeland or Death". Crimea, 1990. Photo by Valeriy Miloserdov, p. 258.

Fig. 2–10. "Here will be our home, son!". Crimea, 1991. Photo by Rifat Yakupov, p. 259.

Fig. 3–1. Distribution of desirable solutions for the Donbas Conflict ("Ukrainian Regionalism" Survey, University of St. Gallen, 2015–2017), p. 302.

Fig. 3–2. Results of the second ballot for the Ukrainian presidential elections by winning candidate per oblast (2010; 2019), p. 304.

Fig. 3–3. The dynamics of feeling proud for being a Ukrainian citizen, 2002–2020, Ukrainian Society: Sociological Monitoring Survey, p. 305.

Fig. 3–4. Predominant language of communication with various groups, 2017 ("Ukrainian Regionalism" Survey, University of St. Gallen), p. 306.

Fig. 3–5. Preferable geopolitical choice, 2013–2017, Ukrainian Regionalism Survey, p. 307.

Fig. 0–1: Map of Ukraine, 1993. © Dmytro Vortman

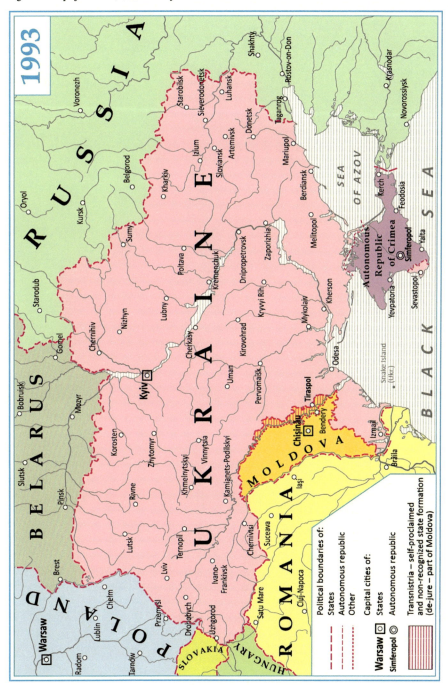

Timeline of Ukrainian History

482:	Founding of Kyiv, the future capital of Ukraine.
Late 9th century:	Founding of the eastern Slavic proto state of Kyivan Rus.
1037:	Construction of the Cathedral of Saint Sophia in Kyiv, which, still stands today.
1240:	A Mongol army captures Kyiv, bringing most of present-day Ukraine under the control of the Golden Horde, a segment of the vast Mongol Empire.
1476:	Ivan III of Muscovy declares independence from the Golden Horde and lays claims to a portion of present-day Ukraine.
1569:	Lithuania and Poland officially complete their political merger, forming the Polish-Lithuanian Commonwealth.
1648:	Hetman Bohdan Khmelnytsky launches a major Cossack rebellion against Polish-Lithuanian rule.
1654:	The Cossack Hetmanate turns to the Tsardom of Russia for assistance and protection in their war against the Polish-Lithuanian Commonwealth leading to the signing of the Treaty of Pereiaslav.
1667:	The Tsardom of Russia and the Polish-Lithuanian Commonwealth sign a truce dividing Ukraine between them with the Dnieper River as the boundary.
1709:	Following Sweden's defeat at Poltava during the Great Northern War, Russia cements its control over the eastern half of Ukraine.
1764:	The Cossack Hetmanate is politically dissolved.
1783:	The Russian Empress Catherine the Great annexes Crimea from the Ottoman Empire.
1795:	As a result of the three partitions of the Polish-Lithuanian Commonwalth, the territory of today's Ukraine is divided

	between the Habsburg Monarchy and Romanov Empire with Russia gaining the vast majority of the Ukrainian lands.
1800s:	Various national movements gradually spread throughout the Ukrainian lands.
1863:	The Valuev Circular is issued, forbidding the use of the Ukrainian language, claiming that "A Little Russian [Ukrainian] language never existed, does not exist, and never shall exist. Its dialects as spoken by the masses are the same as the Russian language".
1876:	The *Ems Ukaz* bans the right to publish in the Ukrainian language.
1917:	The Ukrainian Central Rada, the legislative authority of the future Ukraine's People's Republic is founded. Ukraine is also proclaimed as an autonomous state within a federative Russia, whose people should "have the right to order their own lives in their own land."
1918, January:	Ukraine is proclaimed a fully independent state following the signing of a separate peace treaty between the Ukrainian People's Republic and the Central Powers.
1918, December:	The Ukrainian Soviet Republic is proclaimed in Kharkiv.
1919:	Following the end of the First World War, the territory of present-day Ukraine is partitioned between Poland, Romania, Czechoslovakia and the Russian Soviet Federative Socialist Republic.
1921:	The Russian Civil War in Ukraine culminates in a Bolshevik victory.
1922:	The Soviet Union is established with Soviet Ukraine as a founding member.
1932–33:	The great famine in Ukraine, known as the Holodomor, claims the lives of an estimated 3.9 million people.
1936–38:	Stalin's purges include a number of national operations targeting Ukraine's minority communities.
1939:	Under the Nazi-Soviet Pact, the Soviet Union invades western Ukraine and proclaims it as part of Soviet Ukraine
1941–42:	Nazi Germany invades the Soviet Union and establishes a military occupation across most of Ukraine's territory by 1942. During the Second World War, Ukraine suffers an

	estimated 5 million to 7 million deaths, or roughly 16 percent of its pre-war population with an estimated 1 million Ukrainian Jews believed to have perished in the Holocaust.
1944:	The Soviet authorities launch the mass deportation of the Crimean Tatars. Altogether, some 200,000 people are relocated from Crimea to Soviet Central Asia. The Crimean Tatars were permitted to return during the late 1980s.
1954:	Crimea is transferred to Ukraine.
1986, April:	The Chernobyl nuclear disaster.
1991, August:	Ukraine declares independence from the Soviet Union.
2004:	The Orange Revolution breaks out as a response to election fraud.
2005, January:	Victor Yushchenko is elected President of Ukraine and launches a series of reforms.
2010, February:	The pro-Russian Viktor Yanukovych is elected President of Ukraine.
2014:	The Revolution of Dignity takes place in Kyiv, resulting in the ousting of Victor Yanukovych, who flees to the Russian Federation. Moscow annexes the Crimean Peninsula in response while also lending support to pro-Russian separatists in Donetsk and Luhansk. This marks the beginning of an ongoing war against Ukraine, which would claim some 14,000 lives by 2022.
2022, February:	The Russian Federation launches a full-fledged invasion of Ukraine.

Foreword. Where is Ukraine?
How a Western Outlook Perpetuates Myths about Europe's Largest Country

Olesya Khromeychuk

Let's perform an experiment, the same one I do with my students of modern European history at the start of the academic year. Visualise the map of Europe. And now visualise the easternmost border of what you think of as Europe. Where is this border? Will it stretch as far as the Urals? If it runs along the eastern side of Estonia, Latvia and Lithuania, what does it do when it reaches Belarus? Is Belarus in, or is it out? Once the line gets to northern Ukraine, where does it go from there? Does it go farther east to encompass the whole of Ukraine? Kharkiv? Donbas? Will it run along the western border of Ukraine, leaving Lviv and Uzhhorod outside of Europe? Or do you visualise the easternmost border of your mental map of Europe, as do most of my students of modern European history, running along the Dnipro River, splitting Ukraine in half? And, if so, what does it do when it gets to the Black Sea? Where does Crimea fit on the map inside your mind?

Our mental maps are formed from the places we visit, the languages we understand, the literature we read, the culture we appreciate, the people we meet and care about. Our mental maps are just as important as those used in classrooms and war rooms. Ukraine has existed on the official map of Europe for at least 30 years. Placenames were misspelled, the definitive article added before the name for no good reason. But it was there, printed and coloured. The largest country in Europe. Yet it was mostly missing from our mental maps.

Are we able to name a 'Ukrainian Shostakovich', a 'Ukrainian Solzhenitsyn', a 'Ukrainian Akhmatova'? Can we tell when someone presented as a Russian avant-garde artist, or a Russian filmmaker, or a Russian playwright, is actually Ukrainian? Did we spot that Degas' 'Russian Dancers' were actually wearing Ukrainian outfits before the National Gallery renamed the drawing in April

2022, finally releasing them from the Russian imperial embrace? The gallery itself seems only to have spotted it in the context of Russia's full-scale invasion of Ukraine and the pressure to decolonise its art collection.

Russia's attack on Ukraine on 24 February 2022 demonstrated that understanding of the region among politicians, journalists and societies more widely was lacking. As the Director of the Ukrainian Institute London and a historian, I received numerous requests for commentary in the context of Russia's war against Ukraine. Most began with a question asking me to elaborate on the actual difference between Russia and Ukraine. The question was well meant; it was intended to debunk Putin's weaponised mythology. But the interviewers were oblivious to their own entrapment in the imperialist framework even as they attempted to give Ukraine a voice. This framework has been cultivated by years of uncritical reading of Russia and, more recently, aggressively propagated by Putin. Weary of giving a 'proper' answer (starting with Volodymyr the Great and ending with Volodymyr Zelenskyi) for the umpteenth time, I asked one journalist a question in return: "What, exactly, is the difference between Ireland and England?" Instead of an answer, I heard a nervous giggle. We have mostly figured out the inappropriateness of asking such questions related to western empires. But we are not yet as skilled at seeing the same inappropriateness when it comes to other empires.

It soon became obvious that, even in the middle of a full-scale attack, western observers viewed Ukraine simply as a pawn in a geopolitical game being played by Russia and the collective West. Some were beating their chests and saying "Yes, Ukraine's agency has been overlooked. We will have no more conversations about Ukraine without Ukraine." And yet, many panels went ahead with no in-house Ukraine experts or no Ukraine experts at all.

The question we need to ask ourselves in the curatorial rooms of galleries and museums, in academia, in think tanks, on political advisory boards, is why, until Ukraine was attacked, had we not thought of securing mandatory in-house expertise on the largest country in Europe? Why had we thought of a nation of over 40 million as small and insignificant? Why had we chosen to dismiss its culture as minor? Why had we decided that learning the Ukrainian language was pointless because 'they all speak Russian there anyway'? The answers to these questions are likely to be uncomfortable. They are likely to speak to our own prejudices, and conscious and unconscious biases.

The uncritical reading of Russian history and culture made many observers blind to Putin's neo-imperialism. They were thus shocked by the invasion, by the fabricated reasons the Kremlin chose to justify the attack, and the brutality of the Russian military campaign, including war crimes of which we are learning more and more every day. The experiential knowledge of Russian imperialism and resistance to it possessed by Ukrainians and others in the region – for instance, the Baltic States, Poland and Finland – if taken seriously, could have better prepared 21st-century Europe for Russia's full-scale invasion of a sovereign state. Maybe it could have even prevented it altogether. At the least, it might have awakened us from our slumber of inaction in 2014, when Crimea and Donbas were occupied.

In 2014, we watched the 'Russian world' brought to life in Crimea, where Crimean Tatars were targeted *en masse*, in a way reminiscent of the persecution they suffered in 1944. The 'Russian world' where all, including ethnic Russians, could be sent to jail on fabricated charges simply for disagreeing with the occupation. We watched the 'Russian world' unfold in Donbas, too, where a gallery was overtaken by the Russian proxies, modern art executed, literally, with guns, and the space turned into a concentration camp where civilians were illegally kept, tortured and deprived of all rights.

How many of us responded to the creation of this 'Russian world' by introducing a discussion on the culture of Crimean Tatars and its repression by Russian imperial or Soviet power? How many proposed to curate an exhibition or a talk by the artists exiled from Donbas? How many, after visiting one of numerous exhibitions on the centenary of the Russian Revolution, left a critical entry in the visitor's book about a Ukrainian filmmaker presented as Russian? How many reviewed a book by an author who witnessed war crimes in the Russian-occupied territories of eastern Ukraine for an English-language outlet? And as we reviewed the growing number of books on what was termed the 'Ukraine crisis' penned by western scholars, how many commented that such books should really try to reference Ukrainian sources?

Scholars of Ukraine have been doing all this for years. And, for years, we have been viewed as killjoys spoiling the party. Being a vocal Ukrainianist meant being perceived like an angry woman who will not stop screeching about the patriarchy. Suddenly, though, there is a desire to hear Ukrainian voices, even if just to figure out how to pronounce the name of the capital of Ukraine: we all now know it shouldn't be 'Kiev', but how on earth are you meant to say 'Kyiv'?

Hearing Ukrainian voices is good, but it is not enough. Just as it is good, but not enough, to set up emergency funds for Ukrainian scholars and artists. 'Emergency' implies temporary. For the duration of the war only. A systemic change would require setting up centres for the study of the region, including

Ukraine. And if the funding was to be found for such a centre, some imagination would be required when coming up with a name for it. 'Russian and Eurasian' will no longer work if the centre wishes to study the entire region in a meaningful way. Here is a suggestion: how about the Lesia Ukraïnka Centre for the Study of Europe? After all, Ukraïnka is one of Ukraine's foremost writers; best known for her poems and plays, she knew nine languages in addition to Ukrainian and translated works from English, German, French and Greek. What better patron for a new centre than a *fin-de-siecle* modernist, feminist writer who rewrote European classical myths from the point of view of a woman in the language of the subaltern?

What we need is a permanent alteration – de-colonisation, de-imperialisation – of our knowledge. We need to equip ourselves with appropriate terminology to discuss the region not just as 'post-Soviet', but in ways that will reflect the different trajectories taken by the former republics in the three decades since the collapse of the USSR and how each tackled the legacy of the Russian as well as Soviet empire over this time.

Knowledge is not only about power; it is also a matter of security. The mental maps our students form in their classrooms will be carried with them into galleries, newsrooms, boardrooms, parliaments, military barracks and, of course, back into classrooms by the next generation of educators. If Ukraine does not exist on these mental maps, its existence on the actual map of the world will continue to be at risk.

Self-reflection and the expansion of our knowledge is a good start. But that, too, is not enough. I have seen Russia experts who wish to improve their understanding of Ukraine lament that they cannot become Ukraine experts overnight. But that is not what they are asked to do. In fact, they are asked to do the opposite: to not try to explain Ukraine. To not speak on panels on Ukraine unless those panels have Ukraine experts. And not just one expert tucked on at the end to tick the box of a 'Ukrainian voice', like a woman scholar who discusses gender on the last panel scheduled on the last day of a conference. Inclusivity is not about adding all subjects to the list. It is about making sure that the discussion is fair. And that means using our expertise in a politically responsible way.

It is the Russia experts who were well placed to warn us that widespread support of Putin's annexation of Crimea meant that the Russians could be expected to show the same widespread support, and not condemnation, of Putin's so-called 'special operation' of shelling civilians, looting and pillaging in Ukraine. It is these experts who could have warned us that annual Victory

Day parades – which included driving around in cars with stickers that said, "To Berlin for German women!" or "We can do it again!" – were not just a peculiar Russian way of commemorating the Second World War. That there was a chance that they would do it again. Not taking seriously the Russian *pobedobesie* – a violent Victory Day frenzy complete with rape culture, hate speech and glorification of violence – is the result of our acceptance of the vision of Russia not as a perpetrator, but as an ally of the West, a victor in and a victim of the Second World War, and thus not obliged to face up to the crimes committed by its own government and its own army.

The Russians' choice to reject the term 'Second World War' in favour of the anachronistic 'Great Patriotic War' should have set off alarm bells, as it highlights that, for Russia, the war began in 1941, when Hitler attacked the USSR, not in 1939, when the USSR attacked Europe together with Hitler. The Russian army continued the legacy of the Soviet armed forces with its cult of violence, bullying, acceptance of war crimes and disregard for human life, not only that of the enemy – whether military or civilian – but of its own personnel. It perfected this criminal behaviour in Chechnya and Syria and, for the last eight years, in Ukraine.

Yet, somehow, it is the Ukrainian armed forces that are being dissected by journalists and scholars today: does the Azov regiment hold far-right views or does it not? This discussion is being had in a great many articles I have read about Russia's war in Ukraine. However, few of these texts point out that, in 2019, after Putin had already attacked Ukraine and long after the formation of Azov and its incorporation into the National Guard, all the Ukrainian nationalist parties put together received just above 2% of the vote in Ukraine, meaning that they did not meet the 5% threshold for admission to parliament. Few point out that, at the same time, in France, Italy and Germany the far right won between 10% and 17% of the vote. Not to mention the popularity of a certain presidential candidate who delivered the biggest ever share of the French vote to the far right in her race against President Emmanuel Macron in France's recent (April 2022) general election.

Even fewer contemplate what ideology drives the Russian soldiers who are sent on the mission to 'de-nazify' Ukraine and kill the very Russophone civilians they are meant to 'liberate' from their Jewish, Russophone president. The same ideology that drives them not only to kill Ukrainians by shelling their cities, claiming they had been aiming to kill the Azov fighters, but by shooting civilians with their hands tied behind their backs in the back of their heads.

Could the 'great Russian culture' have anything to do with this ideology? Have we done enough to critically examine the imperialism inherent in the often-aggressive attitude towards Ukraine that we find in poets from Pushkin to Brodsky? But surely it is the fault of Putin, not Pushkin. Many in the West are reluctant to boycott Russia, especially Russian culture. It seems too violent a move to many. Let me make a different suggestion: let us boycott the remnants of our own imperialist view of the world and focus our energies on getting to know the culture that doesn't seem to be there: Ukrainian culture.

Where is the 'Ukrainian Pushkin' after all? If he doesn't exist on our bookshelves, does it mean that he doesn't exist at all? And if he is to be found on our bookshelves, is he there by accident? I once got excited in a London bookshop when I spotted a book with Taras Shevchenko, the 19th-century Ukrainian Romantic poet, the 'father of the nation', on the cover. I thought a badly needed new translation of Shevchenko's Kobzar must finally have been published. When I picked it up, it turned out to be Dostoyevsky's The Brothers Karamazov. The publisher must have thought that any moustached man in a big coat and furry hat would do for the cover of a book about the mysterious Russian soul.

Taras Shevchenko. Lesia Ukraïnka. Ivan Franko. Olha Kobylianska. Maik Iohansen. Mykola Kulish. Vasyl Stus. Lina Kostenko. Oksana Zabuzhko. Boris Khersonskyi. Serhy Zhadan. Olena Stiazhkina. Iryna Shuvalova. The vast majority of those reading this will not know these names. This literature is absent from our shelves not because it is not worthy, but because its existence has been systematically undermined through political repression, as well as scarce linguistic knowledge and chronic lack of funding for translations. Another uncomfortable truth is that these authors do not live on our shelves because our cultural appetite for the whole of eastern Europe is easily satisfied by Dostoyevsky.

The sudden appearance of Ukraine in the limelight has not yet brought about a better understanding of the country. Paradoxically, western admiration of and surprise at Ukrainian bravery in the face of Russian aggression merely emphasise the limited knowledge we possess about Ukraine. When we admire the resilience of Ukrainians, let us think of what turns ordinary people into heroes. What would it take for us, civilians, perhaps pacifists, to pick up arms or at least to donate all we can to the army? I do not know what drove my brother, Volodya, a civilian, an artist, a reader, to enlist in the Ukrainian Armed Forces in 2015, but I know it was not the desire to become a hero. Especially a dead hero.

Glorifying Ukrainian resilience without understanding its roots is another form of misunderstanding the country and its people. The root of that resilience is the intolerance of imperialist oppression, both historic and recent. It is the knowledge that, although Ukraine is the largest country in Europe, people still do not see it and might not even notice if it disappeared from the map. It is thus up to Ukrainians, all 40 million of them, to make sure that their country stays on the map with its borders intact. It is up to all of us to make sure that it appears on our mental maps. And that it stays there. With its borders intact.

This article first appeared as: Olesya Khromeychuk, "Where is Ukraine? How a western outlook perpetuates myths about Europe's largest country," Royal Society for Arts Journal (Issue 2, 2022): https://www.thersa.org/globalassets/pdfs/journals/rsa-journal-issue-2-2022.pdf. *Reprinted with permission.*

Introduction. Ukraine's Many Faces

Olena Palko and Manuel Férez Gil

Ever since the start of Russia's war on Ukraine in 2014, western commentators have attempted to explain events in the country through the lens of linguistic and regional divide. Maps of Ukraine split between a presumably Russian-speaking south-east and Ukrainian-speaking north-west inundated the Internet and were used by political analysts across the ideological spectrum.[1] Moreover, this linguistic heterogeneity was also used to justify Moscow's occupation of Crimea and Russia's support for the two breakaway regions in Ukraine's east. As such, the ongoing war in Ukraine had been framed as a confrontation, or competition, between the Ukrainian majority and the large Russian minority, to which Russian-speaking Ukrainians would often be uncritically ascribed.

Ukraine's heterogeneity fed into Vladimir Putin's aspirations to recreate the might of the Russian Empire. It is no surprise than that immediately prior to Russia's unprovoked full-scale aggression of Ukraine February 24th 2022, the president called for the use of armed force in defence of the rights of Russians and Russian speakers in Ukraine, and "to denazify" the country itself.[2] Rather than an anticipated groundswell of support, the Kremlin's military campaign promptly saw the Ukrainian population, regardless of their everyday spoken language, rally around the central government in Kyiv, effectively neutering further efforts by Moscow at manipulating its neighbour's ethnic differences.

On the contrary, in 2022 no region welcomed the invading forces of the Russian Federation. As a full-scale ethnic conflict under the Russian banner failed to materialize, western pundits once again turned to Ukraine, this time seeking to comprehend the strength of its unexpected national resilience. This concise yet wide-ranging volume of articles offers readers a possibility to do exactly this – to look beyond simplistic binaries and demonstrate how Ukraine's differing historical experiences, regional diversity, and compound identities have contributed to an indomitable Ukrainian national character, the shaping of which is happening in front of our eyes.

The essays comprising this volume cover a vast historical period extending from the 16th century to the present, as such they will help the readers navigate the complex history of the Ukrainian lands, divided for centuries between belligerent empires and nationalizing governments. Unsurprisingly, it was these varied historical experiences that determined the disparate character of the regions that now form contemporary Ukraine.[3] Equally, this collection accounts for various ethnic communities who had populated the Ukrainian lands and whose presence is deeply ingrained into the country's cultural landscape. Its contributing authors, however, also seek to move beyond the simple provision of ready-made answers and confront more complicated questions concerning Ukraine's entangled history and identities. Each of the collection's three chronologically organized sections is supplemented by a set of primary sources, as well as conversational pieces with highly esteemed scholars and experts on the history of Ukraine and the region more broadly. In this regard, the aim of this volume is to encourage readers to form their own conclusions about Ukraine, its culture, and its people.

The volume opens with an essential essay by Olesya Khromeychuk, who poses the question of how, historically, a lack of wider international interest in Ukraine has perpetuated numerous myths about the country and its people. Khromeychuk particularly highlights how, prior to 2022, the majority of western academics had continuously omitted, or downplayed, Ukraine as a separate subject in much of their research. As a result, despite having been an independent sovereign state since 1991, Ukraine itself has been missing from Western mental maps or was presented simplistically as part of a wider Russophone cultural sphere, or even as a "lesser Russia". This collection of essays, therefore, takes its cue from Khromeychuk's motion to ensure Ukraine's subjectivity, making the country a fully-fledged subject of historical analysis.

The first section, *Modernity at the Crossroads of Empires*, traces the origins of Ukraine's compound identity between the 17th and 19th centuries. The section opens with three equally important primary sources. The first of these include excerpts from the *Pereiaslav Agreement* of 1654, widely construed by Russian propagandists as a formal unification agreement between Russia and the Ukrainian lands. Its inclusion looks to establish how this treaty was in fact a pact of military alliance between two equal parties – Cossack Ukraine and Muscovy, representing an agreement through which the Muscovite Tsar had offered military assistance to Ukraine in the latter's on-going war of liberation against the Polish-Lithuanian Commonwealth. This is followed with an *Epistle* by "the father of Ukrainian literature", Taras Shevchenko. The poem, written in 1845, is directed "to my fellow-countrymen, in Ukraine and not in Ukraine, living, dead and as yet unborn" and attempts to rally the territory's inhabitants against Russian authoritarianism, its dominance over Ukraine, and highlight the need for national unity and fraternity to overcome ordeals which are yet to come. The final source is a painting by the artist Mykola Ivasiuk, entitled *The Entry of Bohdan Khmelnytsky to Kyiv in 1649*, depicting the renowned Cossack hetman's triumphant entry into Kyiv, where he was celebrated as a national hero by the Patriarch Paisius of Jerusalem and Kyiv metropolitan Sylvester Kosiv, along with a crowd of several thousand residents.

These primary sources are followed by two expert interviews that focus on Russia's imperial legacy. Professor Ewa Thompson at Rice University discusses the origins of the Russian imperialist project. Despite its explicit expansionist nature, Thompson maintains that most western scholars continue to shy off those complex topics, ignoring Russian imperialism's detrimental impact on Ukraine and non-Germanic Central and Eastern Europe more generally. The second expert interview is with Professor Tamara Hundorova at the National Academy of Sciences of Ukraine, who presents the history of Ukrainian literature in the *long durée*, with a particular emphasis on the development of Ukrainian modernism. Hundorova underlines the unique role of literature in dealing with multiple traumas, including the legacies of colonialism or the memory of inter-ethnic violence committed in the Ukrainian lands.

The next four essays tackle different aspects of Ukraine's imperial past. Oleksii Sokyrko starts by examining socio-economic and political changes in the region following the disintegration of the Kyivan Rus, when parts of today's Ukraine were incorporated into the Polish-Lithuanian Commonwealth, and later the Russian Empire. In particular, his essay provides an overview of the history of the Cossack Hetmanate, an early iteration of the Ukrainian state encompassing the provinces of today's Central Ukraine between 1648 and 1764. Fabian Baumann follows up with an exploration of the 19th century, when the Ukrainian lands were split between the Habsburg Monarchy and Romanov Empire. Special attention is devoted to the emergence of the Ukrainian national movement and choices for self-identification available to 19th-century intellectuals. Vladyslava Moskalets offers an intimate account of Jewish life in Eastern Galicia during this same period. Following the partitions of the Polish-Lithuanian Commonwealth, the province was incorporated into Habsburg Austria while remaining home to one of Eastern Europe's largest

Jewish communities. Lastly, Boris Belge evaluates the economic role that the Ukrainian lands came to play as part of the Russian Tsardom and how this economic potential shaped the territory's political status within a unitary and highly centralised empire.

The second section, *Ukrainian Selfhood in the Soviet Era*, problematizes the role of Ukraine as part of the Soviet Union, with particular attention given to the USSR's formative early decades. The documentary block includes the *Fourth Universal of the Ukrainian Central Rada* (Council), which proclaimed full state independence for the Ukrainian People's Republic on January 22nd, 1918, only for it to be crushed by the Bolsheviks later that year. The second source is a letter from a collective farmer to Joseph Stalin depicting the horrors of the man-made famine the devastated Soviet Ukraine from 1932 to 1933. Lastly, the visual source is a triptych by Fedir Krychevsky, entitled *Life* (1925), and is considered to be one of the finest examples of Ukrainian modernism, incorporating elements of the European *art nouveau* and traditional Ukrainian religious painting. These primary sources are followed by an expert interview with Professor Olena Palko at the University of Basel, who discusses the relationship between Russia and Ukraine in a historical perspective. Highlighting examples of how such experiences had been widely abused within Russian propaganda, Palko argues that this distorted historical legacy has led to widespread misconceptions of Ukraine's past and present, especially during the Soviet period.

The seven essays that form the rest of the second section collectively undertake the important task of shifting the readers' perspective away from Moscow and invite them to learn more about its so-called peripheries. These diverse contributions show how important decisions were often influenced by developments and conditions on the ground. The section opens with an essay by Hanna Perekhoda, which analyses political debates regarding a future soviet Ukraine during the Russian Civil War, and the various forms of statehood which were proposed or established on Ukraine's territory during the early years of Soviet rule. Stephan Rindlisbacher reconstructs the chronological process of modern Ukraine's territorial delineation, starting with 1919, the year when the Ukrainian Soviet Socialist Republic was established. Particular attention is devoted to the formation of Russo-Ukrainian border, including the transfer of Crimea in 1954. Olena Palko and Roman Korshuk follow on by examining the challenges Ukraine's linguistic and ethnic heterogeneity posed for the early Soviet authorities, outlining key strategies for managing ethnic diversity employed at the official level.

Matthew Pauly's discussion of early Soviet efforts to sovietise street children in the southern city of Odesa sheds light on Soviet experimentalist practices in early education, and the state's attempts to mould children into model citizens. Soviet social interventionism is also the focus of Oksana Klymenko and Roman Liubavskyi's chapter that evaluates Soviet approaches to create a "New Soviet man" as a prerequisite of the future construction of socialism. Discussion of the interwar Soviet period continues with Daria Mattingly's important essay on the Holodomor, the manmade famine of 1932–33, when some 4 million people died as a consequence of excessive grain requisitioning to aid Stalin's accelerated industrialization drive. Martin-Oleksandr Kisly turns our attention to Crimean Tatars, the indigenous people of Crimea, who's community were subjected to mass deportations from the peninsula in 1944, and the challenges they would subsequently face when seeking to return to their homeland. Lastly, Iuliia Buyskykh explores the evolution of religious identities across the Polish-Ukrainian border, discussing aspects of belonging and self-determination among the Ukrainian Greek Catholic community, which was declared illegal under Soviet rule. Taken together, these essays contribute to the epistemological need to decentre Soviet studies, and allow Ukraine, as well as other former Soviet republics, to reclaim the Soviet past, moving out of the shadows of Russian nationalist ideology and propaganda.

The third section, *Sovereignty Regained: Ukraine in the Post-Soviet Age*, considers the main challenges Ukraine has faced since 1991, paying particular attention to the war which the Russian Federation has been waging since 2014. The section opens with the *Declaration of State Sovereignty of Ukraine* from July 16th, 1990, which determined the supremacy, independence, integrity, and indivisibility of Ukraine's authority within the boundaries of its territory, and its independence and equality in foreign relations. This is followed with a 2014 poem by the author Kateryna Kalytko that intimates the feeling of those displaced by war and sporadic memories which are often used to reclaim the lost home. Finally, our collection features a painting from Kyiv-based Matvey Vaisberg's *The Wall* (2014) cycle, in which the artist, himself an eyewitness, reflected on the tragic events that transpired during the Maidan Uprising, which centred on a series of violent clashes in Kyiv's Independence Square in early 2014.

The conversational block includes two expert interviews on historical and political developments in Ukraine since 1991. Professor David Marples at the University of Alberta exposes the links between historical memory and identity building. Marples considers the contemporary history of Ukraine and how the tragic events post-2014 have changed the face of the country and its people. The subsequent conversation with Professor Maria Popova at McGill University touches upon questions concerning the rule of law, political corruption, and the legal repression of dissent in post-Communist Eastern Europe and Ukraine in particular. Popova evaluates the actions taken by the Ukrainian government in anticorruption and law-enforcement efforts and suggests that the popular mobilization against corruption and electoral fraud witnessed in Ukraine post-2014 has created an important precedent in which political elites have come to accept that they cannot simply resort to autocratic measures in order to maintain power.

The analytical section comprises six essays illustrating the many challenges faced by independent Ukraine. Anna Chebotarova's analysis of the changes that followed the Maidan protests, and the subsequent annexation of Crimea and war in Donbas, detail the impact of a protracted and acute Russian military aggression against Ukrainian society. Volodymyr Kulyk traces the evolution in self-identifications among Russian-speaking Ukrainian citizens, showing how the experience of war contributed to a gradual shift in their sense of allegiance with the Ukrainian government in Kyiv, and identification with the Ukrainians as the country's dominant ethnic group. Oleksandr Zabirko focuses on Ukraine's most eastern industrial region known as Donbas, suggesting how international and domestic perceptions have been heavily influenced by the so-called "Donbas myth", constructed through local politics and literary works, and evaluates the role this region came to play within Ukrainian national politics and the country's future. Tamara Martsenyuk turns our attention to issues of gender equality in Ukraine, examining the origins and evolution of the feminist organisations and their role in ensuring visibility for Ukrainian women in the contemporary era, especially given the large number of female personnel serving in the Armed Forces of Ukraine during the Russian invasion. Finally, Kateryna Botanova challenges the commonly held perspective that reconciliation represents the ultimate purpose of creative culture, unravelling the difficult position many Ukrainian artists and cultural managers found themselves during the 2022 aggression amidst growing pressure from Western observes for expressions of solidarity with their Russian counterparts.

The volume concludes with a historiographical essay by John Vsetecka, listing key works on Ukraine and by Ukrainian scholars which can help overcome the challenges underscored by Khromeychuk's opening discussion. Although his original essay's primary objective was to suggest ways for educators and teachers to make Ukraine more visible in their classrooms, these reading suggestions could help anyone wishing to better understand Ukraine and its entangled history. We agree with Vsetecka that studying Ukraine is more important than ever. While the country's history remains hostage to Russia's ideologically-loaded official narratives, this volume privileges Ukrainian authors so they may be better heard and allowed to speak with their own voice.

Notes

1 For instance, Al-Jazeera, in its report from February 22nd 2014, showed a map of Ukraine divided between a largely Ukrainian-speaking west and a predominantly Russian-speaking east. URL: https://youtu.be/_oRNrZ Ox5Wc . Accessed on 02 December 2022. A similar image of "nationalist west" vs. "pro-Russian east" featured in the Guardian on 21 February 2014: https://www.theguardian.com/world/2014/feb/21/ukraine-western-pro-european-cities-lviv
2 For the transcript of Putin's address from February 21st 2022, see: http://en.kremlin.ru/events/president/transcripts/67828. Accessed on December 2nd 2022.
3 Olena Palko and Constantin Ardeleanu (eds.) *Making Ukraine: Negotiating, Contesting, and Drawing the Borders in the Twentieth Century* (Montreal: McGill-Queen's University Press, 2022).

I. Modernity at the Crossroads of Empires

Primary Sources

Ukrainian Draft Treaty of 1654
A Byelorussian Copy of the Articles sent by the Cossack Envoys Samoylo Bohdanov and Pavlo Teterya on the 14th day of May, 7162 (A.D. 1654)

To Alexei Mikhailovich, by the grace of God Great Sovereign and Grand Duke, Autocrat of all Great and Little Russia, and the Sovereign and Ruler of many states:

We, Bohdan Khmelnytsky, Hetman of the Cossack Army, the whole Cossack Army and the whole Christian Russian world humbly petition Your Tsarist Majesty.

We have been greatly pleased with the great reward and countless favors which Your Tsarist Majesty deigned to bestow upon us. We greet most humbly you, our Sovereign, and will serve forever Your Tsarist Majesty in all matters according to your orders. We only beg most earnestly, as we did in our letter, that Your Tsarist Majesty deign to grant us and show us His Sovereign favor in everything what our envoys will petition.

1. At the beginning deign, Your Tsarist Majesty, to confirm the rights and liberties which have been enjoyed from ancient times by the Cossack Army, including trial according to their own laws and privileges so that no voevoda, boyar or steward should interfere with their army courts and that they should be tried by their elders: where there are three Cossacks, two of them shall try the third one.
2. That the number of the Cossack Army should be fixed at 60,000, to be always at full strength.
3. That those of the gentry in Russia who have taken the oath of allegiance to you, our Great Sovereign, to Your Tsarist Majesty, according to Christ's immaculate commandment, retain their liberties and elect their elders to

serve as officials with the courts and enjoy their properties and privileges, as they did under the Kings of Poland, so that other (peoples), seeing such favors of Your Tsarist Majesty, may also submit under the rule and under the exalted and mighty arm of Your Tsarist Majesty, together with the whole Christian world. Rural and town courts should be directed by officials chosen voluntarily by themselves, as before. Also those of the gentry who invested their money in leased property, should either have their money returned or be allowed to use the properties till the lease expires.

4. That in towns the officials be chosen among our people who are worthy of it and who shall direct and rule the subjects of Your Tsarist Majesty and collect due revenue for the treasury of Your Tsarist Majesty honestly.

5. That the district of Chyhyryn, which was assigned to the Hetman's mace with everything that belongs to it, should now remain under its authority.

6. In case the Hetman should die (which God forbid) – for all men are mortal and this is inevitable – that the Cossack Army be allowed to elect (a new) Hetman among themselves and by themselves and notify His Tsarist Majesty and that he takes no offence since this is an ancient custom with the Army.

7. That the properties of the Cossacks be not taken away from them and that those who own the land and its produce receive titles to these properties. That the children of the widows left by the Cossacks keep the liberties of their ancestors and fathers.

8. That the Secretary of the Army be assigned through the kindness of His Tsarist Majesty 1,000 Zloty (gold coins) for his clerks and a mill for their sustenance, since he has great expenditures.

9. That a mill be assigned for each colonel since they have great expenditures and, if such be the kindness of Your Tsarist Majesty, even more than that, according to the discretion of Your Tsarist Majesty.

10. That the justices of the Army should also be assigned 300 Zloty and a mill and the secretary of the court, 100 Zloty.

11. We also beg Your Tsarist Majesty that the essauls of the Army and those of each regiment, who are always busy in the service of the Army and cannot till land, be assigned a mill each.

12. Concerning the artillery of the Army, we beg Your Tsarist Majesty graciously to provide for the winter quarters and food of the cannoneers and all the artillery workers; also 400 Zloty for the quartermaster (of the artillery).

13. That the ancient rights granted to both clergy and laymen by dukes and kings be not violated in any respect.
14. That the Hetman and the Cossack Army be free to receive the envoys who come to the Cossack Army from foreign countries with good intentions and that His Tsarist Majesty take no offence because of this; and in case there should be something adverse to His Tsarist Majesty, we should notify His Tsarist Majesty.
15. We should prefer that, as it is done with regard to tribute in other countries, a specified amount be paid by those who belong to Your Tsarist Majesty; if, however, it cannot be done otherwise, then no voyevoda should be allowed to deal with these matters. (We suggest) that a voyevoda should be chosen among natives, a worthy man, who would deliver all that revenue honestly to His Tsarist Majesty.
16. Our envoys have been instructed to talk over this matter, because if a voyevoda should come and violate their rights and introduce (new) customs, it would be a great annoyance to them since they cannot soon grow accustomed to a different law and bear such burdens; and if officeholders should be natives, they will rule in accordance with local laws and customs.
17. Formerly the Polish Kings did not persecute our faith and oppress our liberties and all of us always enjoyed our liberties and therefore served (the King) faithfully; now, however, because of the violation of our liberties we have been forced to submit under the mighty and exalted arm of His Tsarist Majesty and our envoys have been instructed to beg earnestly that His Tsarist Majesty give us privileges written on parchment, with suspending seals, one (charter) for the liberties of the Cossacks and another one for those of the gentry, so that they remain inviolable forever. Having received these (charters), we shall ourselves check (the register) and whoever is a Cossack will enjoy Cossack privileges, while peasants shall fulfil their duties with respect to His Tsarist Majesty as before. Also (it should be stated) concerning all those who are subjects of His Tsarist Majesty what their rights and privileges should be.
18. They have to mention during the negotiations the Metropolitan (of Kiev) and our envoys received oral instructions concerning this matter.
19. Our envoys have also to entreat His Tsarist Majesty that His Tsarist Majesty deign to send his army to Smolensk at once without any delay in order that the enemy should not prepare themselves and be joined by others because the troops are now ill-prepared. They should not believe any (enemy) blandishment if (the Poles) make recourse to such.

20. It is also necessary that soldiers be hired, about 3,000 or even more, at His Tsarist Majesty's will, to protect the Polish frontier.
21. The custom exists for the Cossack Army always to receive a salary; and now they beg His Tsarist Majesty that he should appropriate to the colonels 100 thalers each, to the regimental essauls, 200 Zloty, to the army essauls, 400 Zloty, to the captains, 100 Zloty, to the Cossacks, 30 Zloty.
22. In case the horde should invade (Ukraine), it would be necessary to attack these from Astrakhan and Kazan; likewise the Don Cossacks should be ready, however, the peace with them should not yet be discontinued and they should not be provoked.
23. That His Tsarist Majesty would now graciously supply food and powder for the guns at Kodak, a town built on the Crimean frontier, where the Hetman permanently keeps a garrison of 400 men, providing them with everything. That likewise, His Tsarist Majesty would graciously provide for those who guard the Cossack's Headquarters (Kish) beyond the cataracts, since it could not be left without a garrison.

The Author's Note:
The "23 Articles" are the Ukrainian draft of the treaty with the Tsar of Muscovy; therefore they are reproduced here without the resolutions of the Boyarskaya Duma which are included in the Muscovite copy of the document. Also omitted is the final note of the Boyars concerning the return of Muscovite refugees.

Acts pertaining to the History of Southern and Western Russia. Vol. X, Document XI, pp. 446-452.

First published in Alexander Ohloblyn, Treaty of Pereyaslav 1654 (Toronto and New York: Canadian League for Ukraine's Liberation; Organization for Defense of Four Freedoms for Ukraine, 1954). The text is in public domain. https://penelope.uchicago.edu/Thayer/E/Gazetteer/Places/Europe/Ukraine/_Topics/history/_Texts/OHLPER/Appendices/1*.html#ref1. *Accessed on 17 April 2023.*

To My Fellow-Countrymen, In Ukraine and Not in Ukraine, Living, Dead and as Yet Unborn
My Friendly Epistle

Taras Shevchenko

> If a man say, I love God, and hateth his brother, he is a liar.
> I John iv, 20.

Dusk is falling, dawn is breaking,
And God's day is ending,
Once again a weary people
And all things are resting.
Only I, like one accursed,
Night and day stand weeping
At the many-peopled cross-roads,
And yet no one sees me.
No one sees me, no one knows,
Deaf, they do not hearken,
They are trading with their fetters,
Using truth to bargain,
And they all neglect the Lord, –
In heavy yokes they harness
People; thus they plough disaster,
And they sow disaster...
But what shoots spring up? You'll see
What the harvest yields them!
Shake your wits awake, you brutes,
You demented children!
Look upon your native country,
On this peaceful eden;
Love with overflowing heart
This expanse of ruin!
Break your chains, and live
as brothers!
Do not try to seek,
Do not ask in foreign lands
For what can never be
Even in heaven, let alone
In a foreign region...
In one's own house, –
one's own truth,
One's own might and freedom.
There is no other Ukraina,
No second Dnipro in the world,
Yet you strike out for foreign regions,
To seek, indeed, the blessed good,

The holy good, and freedom,
freedom,
Fraternal brotherhood. ... You found
And carried from that foreign region,
And to Ukraine brought, homeward-
bound,
The mighty power of mighty words,
And nothing more than that. ... You
scream, too,
That God, creating you, did not mean
you
To worship untruth, then, once more,
You bow down as you bowed before,
And once again the very skin you
Tear from your sightless, peasant
brothers,
Then, to regard the sun of truth
In places not unknown, you shove off
To German lands. If only you'd
Take all your miserable possessions,
The goods your ancestors have stolen,
Then with its holy heights, the Dnipro
Would remain bereft, an orphan.

Ah, if it could be that you would not
return,
That you'd give up the ghost in the
place you were reared,
The children would weep not, nor
mother's tears burn,
And God would not hear your blas-
pheming and sneers,
The sun pour no warmth out upon the
foul dunghill,
Over a land that is free, broad and
true,
Then folk would not realize what kind
of eagles

You are, and would not shake
their heads over you.

Find your wits! Be human beings,
For evil is impending,
Very soon the shackled people
Will their chains be rending;
Judgment will come, and then
shall speak
The mountains and the Dnipro,
And in a hundred rivers, blood
Will flow to the blue ocean,
Your children's blood… and there
will be
No one to help you… Brother
Will by his brother be renounced,
The child by its own mother.
And like a cloud, dark smoke
will cover
The bright sun before you,
For endless ages your own sons
Will curse you and abhor you.
Wash your faces! God's fair image
Do not foul with filth!
Do not deceive your children that
They live upon this earth
Simply that they should rule
as lords –
For an unlearned eye
Will deeply search their very souls,
Deeply, thoroughly…
For whose skin you're wearing,
helpless
Mites will realize,
They will judge you, – and
the unlearned
Will deceive the wise.

****

Had you but learned the way
you ought,
Then wisdom also would be yours;
But thus to heaven you would climb:
"We are not we, I am not I!
I have seen all, all things I know:
There is no hell, there is no heaven,
Not even God, but only I and The
stocky
German, clever-clever,
And no one else beside…"
"Good, brother
But who, then, are you?"
"We don't know –
Let the German speak!"

That's the way you learn in your
Foreign land, indeed!
The German would say: "You are
Mongols".
"Mongols, that is plain!"
Yes, the naked grandchildren
Of golden Tamburlaine!
The German would say:
"You are Slavs".
"Slavs, yes, Slavs indeed!"
Of great and glorious ancestors
The unworthy seed!
And so you read Kollar, too,
With all your might and main,
Safarik as well, and Hanka,
Full-tilt you push away
Into the Slavophils, all tongues
Of the Slavonic race
You know full well, but of your own
Nothing! "There'll come a day

When we can parley in our own
When the German teaches,
And, what is more, our history
Explains to us and preaches,
Then we will set about it all!"

You've made a good beginning,
Following the German precepts
You have started speaking
So that the German cannot grasp
The sense, the mighty teacher,
Not to mention simple people.
And uproar! And the screeching:
"Harmony and power too,
Nothing less than music!
As for history! Of a free
Nation 'tis the epic...
Can't compare with those
poor Romans!
Their Bruti – good-for-nothings!
But oh, our Cocleses and Bruti –
Glorious, unforgotten!
Freedom herself grew up with us,
And in the Dnipro bathed,
She had mountains for her pillow,
And for her quilt – the plains!"
It was in blood she bathed herself,
She took her sleep on piles
Of the corpses of free Cossacks,
Corpses all despoiled.

Only look well, only read
That glory through once more,
From the first word to the last,
Read; do not ignore
Even the least apostrophe,
Not one comma even,
Search out the meaning of it all,

Then ask yourself the question:
"Who are we? Whose sons? Of what
sires?
By whom and why enchained?"
And then, indeed, you'll see for what
Are your Bruti famed:

Toadies, slaves, the filth of Moscow,
Warsaw's garbage – are your lords,
Illustrious hetmans! Why so proud
And swaggering, then do you boast,
you
Sons of Ukraine and her misfortune?
That well you know to wear the yoke,
More than your fathers did of yore?
They are flaying you, cease your
boasts –
From them, at times, the fat they'd
thaw.

You boast, perhaps, the Brotherhood
Defended the faith of old?
Because they boiled their dumplings
in
Sinope, Trebizond?
It is true, they ate their fill,
But now your stomach's dainty,
And in the Sich, the clever German
Plants his beds of 'taties;
And you buy, and with good relish
Eat what he has grown,
And you praise the Zaporozhya.
But whose blood was it flowed
Into that soil and soaked it through
So that potatoes flourish?
While it's good for kitchen-gardens
You're the last to worry!
And you boast because we once

Brought Poland to destruction...
It is true, yes, Poland fell,
But in her fall she crushed you.
Thus, then, your fathers spilled
their blood
For Moscow and for Warsaw,
And to you, their sons, they have
Bequeathed their chains, their glory.

****

Ukraina struggled on,
Fighting to the limit:
She is crucified by those
Worse-than-Poles, her children.
In place of beer, they draw
the righteous
Blood from out her sides,
Wishing, so they say, to enlighten
The maternal eyes
With contemporary lights,
To lead her as the times
Demand it, in the Germans' wake
(She crippled, speechless, blind).
Good, so be it! Lead, explain!
Let the poor old mother
Learn how children such as these
New ones she must care for.
Show her, then, and do not haggle
Your instruction's price.
A mother's good reward will come:
From your greedy eyes
The scales will fall away, and you
Will then behold the glory,
The living glory of your grandsires,
And fathers skilled in knavery.
Do not fool yourselves, my brothers,
Study, read and learn

Thoroughly the foreign things –
But do not shun your own :
For he who forgets his mother,
He by God is smitten,
His children shun him,
in their homes
They will not permit him.
Strangers drive him from their doors;
For this evil one
Nowhere in the boundless earth
Is a joyful home.

I weep salt tears when I recall
Those unforgotten actions
Of our forefathers, those grave deeds!
If I could but forget them,
Half my course of joyful years
I'd surrender gladly...
Such indeed, then, is our glory,
Ukraina's glory!...
Thus too, you should read it through
That you'd do more than dream,
While slumbering, of injustices,
So that you would see

High gravemounds open up before
Your eyes, that then you might
Ask the martyrs when and why
And who was crucified.
Come, my brothers, and embrace
Each your humblest brother,
Make our mother smile again,
Our poor, tear-stained mother!
With hands that are firm and strong
She will bless her children,
Embrace her helpless little ones,
And with free lips, she'll kiss them.
And those bygone times will be

Forgotten with their shame,
And that glory will revive,
The glory of Ukraine,
And a clear light, not a twilight,
Will shine forth anew...
Brothers, then, embrace each other,
I entreat and pray you!
    1845, Vyunishche

Source of English translation of the poem: Taras Shevchenko. "Song out of Darkness". Selected poems translated from the Ukrainian by Vera Rich. London, 1961, p. 74–80.

Reproduced with permission from the Shevchenko Museum, Toronto, Canada.

Bohdan Khmelnytsky's Entry to Kyiv in 1649 (1912)

Mykola Ivasiuk

Mykola Ivasiuk, *The Entry of Bohdan Khmelnytsky to Kyiv in 1649 (finished in 1912) 4x5,78 m. National Art Museum of Ukraine, Kyiv. Public Domain.*

Conversation Pieces

Revealing Pan-Slavic Russian Imperialism

Ewa Thompson, in conversation with Manuel Férez Gil

Ewa Thompson is Professor of Slavic Studies Emerita and former chairperson of the Department of German and Slavic Studies at Rice University. Before she came to Rice, she taught at Indiana, Vanderbilt, and the University of Virginia, and lectured at Princeton, Witwatersrand (South Africa), Toronto (Canada), and Bremen (Germany) She received her undergraduate degree from the University of Warsaw and her doctorate from Vanderbilt University. She is the author of five books, several dozen scholarly articles, and hundreds of other articles and reviews. Her books and articles have been translated into Polish, Ukrainian, Belarusian, Russian, Croatian, Czech, Hungarian, and Chinese. She has published scholarly articles in *Slavic Review*, *Slavic and East European Journal*, *Modern Age*, and other periodicals and has done consulting work for U.S. government and private institutions and foundations. She is the Founder and former Editor (1981–2017) of *Sarmatian Review*, an academic quarterly on non-Germanic Central Europe.

Manuel Ferez: *You specialize in Slavic studies, Russia and Poland. To start with could you explain the meaning of the term "Slavic", and why this ostensibly neutral term has caused so much controversy within Russian historical revisionist paradigm, led by Vladimir Putin and supported by state-sponsored historians in Russia, especially when we speak of Ukraine and its identity?*

Ewa Thompson: The word "Slavic" refers to linguistic and anthropologic similarities rather than to cultural proximity. Slavic languages include Russian, Polish, Ukrainian, Belarusian, Czech, Slovak, Serbian, Croatian, Slovene. However, the people who speak these languages belong to very different and sometimes antagonistic cultures.

Within this linguistic family two different alphabets have been used: Latin, used by Czechs, Slovaks, Poles, Croats, and Slovene – and Cyrillic, used by Russians, Ukrainians, Belarusians, and Serbs. Unlike the linguistic family of Romance languages that includes Spanish, Portuguese, Italian, Romanian and French, the Slavic group is so culturally diverse that it does not even share an alphabet. Some Slavs belong to Western European culture, while others stress their Byzantine connection. Russians in particular are also connected to the legacy of the Mongols, who ruled Moscow for two and a half centuries (something Russians do not like to remember). In contrast, the territories that are now Ukraine and Belarus were wrenched away from the Mongols by Lithuanians, and then because of dynastic arrangements (a Lithuanian prince married a Polish heiress to the throne, became the King of Poland and joined his lands to Polish territory, creating the Polish-Lithuanian Commonwealth, a country that survived from 1386 to 1795) became associated with Western European culture. Therefore, Belarus and Ukraine, even though they share the alphabet and Orthodox Christianity with Russia, developed Western notion of state organization and individual freedom. They reject Moscow control and want to be ruled by their own leaders. Eastern Ukraine fell into Russian hands in the second part of the seventeenth century, while parts of western Ukraine did not know Russian rule until the Second World War.

Such is an abbreviated history of Russia, Ukraine, and Belarus. They differ from one another because their histories are different.

In the United States and in other English-speaking countries, the word "Slavic" is commonly used to designate departments where languages and literatures of non-Germanic Central and Eastern Europeans are taught. This includes also Baltic and Hungarian language and literature, neither of which is Slavic.

M.F.: *In general terms, Tsarist Russia, the Soviet Union and Putin's Russia can be defined as expansionist projects, as they underwent constant expansion, whereby they colonized and subdued various cultures and nations. What are the similarities and differences between these three projects – Tsarist, Soviet and modern Russia in this aspect?*

E.T.: Indeed, Tsarist Russia, Soviet Russia, and post-Soviet Russia have been expansionist. In my view, Muscovy (the name associated with the Russian lands until the eighteenth century) continued the drive to conquer characteristic of the Mongols who invaded Europe in the twelfth century and got as far west as the city of Legnica in today's Poland. Tsarist Russia cultivated this drive to conquer using military force and diplomatic deceit. Russia claimed that by conquering territories in Asia it was "civilizing" them, much as the

British "civilized" Asia and Africa through their colonial conquests. As I argued in my book *Imperial Knowledge: Russian Literature and Colonialism*, Russia was unable to civilize itself, let alone anyone else. A major reason Russia tried to conquer Siberia (and succeeded in doing so) was economic and military: gold mines in eastern Siberia and numerous other resources of Asian lands enriched Russia, just as Western colonialism enriched Western Europe. The money thus obtained allowed the tsars to build facsimiles of Western cities in European parts of Russia. Polish poet Adam Mickiewicz wrote that the eighteenth-century palaces of St. Petersburg were paid for by wealth stolen from Lithuania and Poland: Russia appropriated the wealth of its Western colonies as well. So far as I know, there have been no comprehensive studies detailing Russia's expansion from the economic standpoint. Russian authors have considered it a matter of fact that the colonies were there to be exploited.

As to the Soviet period, an additional factor has to be taken into account: the communist ideology. Ostensibly, communism did not pay attention to nationality, and this weakened to some extent the pressure and national discrimination of non-Russian nations within the USSR, particularly in the early period of USSR's existence. Members of non-Russian nationalities could advance in the political world just as Russians could. But that did not mean that exploitation of Siberia's and Eastern Europe's natural resources was any less oppressive. In the early days of communism, the slogans about the "nationless" communist world were taken seriously, but as time went on nationless communism transformed itself into Russian chauvinism. The wealth of colonized countries and territories was appropriated by Moscow and its native Russian inhabitants. It paid for the famous Russian ballet and opera, and it underwrote Russian scientific and research facilities.

M.F.: *Why have Russian colonialism and imperialism been ignored, generally speaking, by academia? One usually reads about U.S. imperialism but one does not usually think of Russia as a similar imperialist state.*

E.T.: This is because Soviet Russia helped foment anti-colonial sentiments in the countries of Asia and Africa, and many early students and promoters of anti-colonialism came from these territories. Soviet Russia supplied anti-colonial rebels with money, weapons, and other resources necessary to win condemnation of colonialism in the international arena. Soviet Russia offered generous scholarships to students from oppressed countries. After several years of study in Moscow or Leningrad, these students returned to their respective countries with a deep conviction that communism is the wave of the future and Russia leads the world in introducing it. Under such circumstances, it would have been awkward to raise questions about the Chechens, for instance, whose risings against Russian domination were frequent and bloody. One can also ask why Soviet Russia was a close friend of Nazi Germany during the first two years of the Second World War (1 September 1939 till 22 June 1941, when Nazi Germany broke off the friendship agreement and invaded the USSR without declaring war).

Only after the Soviet Union disintegrated and some of its colonial doings were exposed, the researchers who wanted to deal not only with British or French but also with Russian colonialism gained certain minimal acceptance in the scholarly world. This acceptance is still minimal: by and large, the English-speaking academia is still sympathetic to Russia because the old narrative about Russia helping to liberate the West's colonies lingers on. There are many scholars who ignore Russian colonialism and write books and articles as if it had never existed.

M.F.: *Is it possible that Russia's imperialist, aggressive and expansionist vision will change in the future? I am referring to imagining a future in which Russia manages to establish bilateral and regional relations (Central Asia, Caucasus, Baltic, non-Germanic Central Europe) on a horizontal level.*

E.T.: Everything is possible in history; whether it is likely is another matter. I think it is very unlikely to happen in the foreseeable future. Please remember that Germany changed from Nazi to democratic only because foreign armies defeated German armies and occupied Berlin. Germans were compelled to reject Nazism; had they won the war, they would have continued to worship Hitler who brought them victory. Similarly, if foreign armies occupied Moscow and forced the Russians to reject their expansionist policies, a radical change in the Russian political system would have become possible. But this is very unlikely to happen. As things stand now, there are not enough Russians to fight against the empire. To put it differently, Russians prefer empire to freedom. A candidate whom Putin defeated in an election, one Mr. Navalny, is on record as saying that the Crimea should be Russian. In other words, he supports Putin's attack on sovereign Ukrainian territory. I think that it would be useful to replace Putin as leader, because a change of leadership in Russia usually involves a few years of internal turmoil, hence a few years of peace for Russia's neighbours. But when the new leader establishes himself, he will become another Putin.

M.F.: *In your publications on what you call "non-Germanic Central Europe" you distinguish between "imperialist nationalisms" and "defensive nationalisms". Following this approach, how do you understand Ukrainian nationalism, and how will it develop in the future taking into account Russian aggression, actions undertaken by Ukrainian academic diaspora and media, academic and political attention that Ukraine currently enjoys?*

E.T.: Indeed, I make a distinction between aggressive and defensive nationalism. Throughout history, humanity has divided itself into nations that function as administrative, cultural, and psychological units offering models of productive life to their members. Unfortunately, some of these units "derailed" and adopted the attitude of "the more the better," stealing land and resources from their neighbours. This is what I call aggressive nationalism. In response to this aggression, there developed defensive nationalisms that have been trying to preserve, support, and defend the communities who speak the same language and share the same history. By and large, such are the nations of non-Germanic Central Europe.

The Ukrainian nation is going through a period of great hardship, but it also is gathering the fruits of its remarkable determination and resilience. It has managed to get genuinely reconciled to the neighbouring Poland, and this is a development of great future importance: the two nations had fought each other in centuries past. Their reconciliation creates a new political situation in non-Germanic Central Europe. It makes it easier to respond together to potential Russian attacks in the future. It confirms the agreement concerning borders – neither Poland nor Ukraine have any territorial claims on each other. This is a major European development, and it bodes well for the future of Central Europe.

M.F.: *Finally, I would like to ask you about your medium- and long-term vision of Europe, not only of the European Union but of the European project that includes countries such as Ukraine, Georgia and a post-BREXIT United Kingdom.*

E.T.: The lessons we are learning from the present conflict should have been learned earlier; yet it is not too late to start now. I think that the Russian-Ukrainian war has exposed the mistakes of German policy over the last several decades. As a European leader, Germany has failed its neighbours. Over the last several decades, Germany promoted Russia in every way imaginable. It encouraged Europe to become dependent on Russian gas and oil, and it assured its neighbours that Russia has abandoned its aggressive posture and has become a normal post-World War Two European country. It turned out that this is not the case, that Russia has not abandoned its goal of changing European borders by force. It has been advantageous for Germany to develop its close relationship with Russia, but the results are disastrous for other European countries. The leadership question in the EU has to be rethought and renegotiated. Perhaps the time has come for the peripheries of Europe to assume leadership.

First Published on 24 May 2022. This interview first appeared in Spanish on https://orientemedio.news.

Works Cited

Thompson, Ewa. *Imperial Knowledge: Russian Literature and Colonialism* (Westport, Conn: Greenwood Press, 2000).

Ukrainian History through Literature

Tamara Hundorova, in conversation with Manuel Férez Gil

Professor Tamara Hundorova is a leading scholar at the Institute of Literature of the NAS of Ukraine, Associate Fellow at the Harvard Ukrainian Research Institute, and Dean at the Ukrainian Free University in Munich. She is the author of several books including "The Post-Chornobyl Library. The Ukrainian Postmodernism of the 1990s" (2019), "Tranzytna kultura. Symptomy postkolonial'noï travmy" (2013); "Pisliachornobyl's'ka biblioteka. Ukraïns'kyi literaturnyi postmodernism" (2005, second edition 2013);" Kitsch i literatura. Travestiï" (2008); "Proiavlennia slova. Dyskusiia rannioho ukraïns'koho modernismu" (1997, second edition 2009); "Franko i/ne Kameniar" (2006); "Femina melancholica. Stat' i kul'tura v gendernii utopiï Ol'hy Kobylians'koï" (2002) as well as numerous publications on modernism, postmodernism, feminism, postcolonial studies, and the history of Ukrainian literature.

Manuel Ferez: *Could you start by telling us about the origins of Ukrainian literature, what were its key themes and who were its founding authors?*

Tamara Hundorova: Ukrainian literature has a longstanding tradition, both published and spoken, dating back to between the 11th and 13th centuries, the period of Kyivan Rus. However, it began to develop more actively from the end of the 18th century. Hryhorii Skovoroda (1722–1794), often called the "Ukrainian Socrates", was a recognized writer, philosopher-mystic, and traveler. The main themes of his dialogues, fables and parables were self-knowledge, goodness, the harmony of the macrocosm (the universe), and the microcosm (the human soul). Skovoroda was also known for developing the concept of "congenial work": a natural form of human activity that meets the needs of the soul and brings freedom and happiness.

The writer Ivan Kotliarevsky (1769–1838) marked the beginning of the modern period in Ukrainian literature. He is known primarily as the author of the burlesque *Eneida*, the first parts of which were published in 1798. This is a parody of Virgil's epic poem *The Aeneid*. However, instead of using the Latin language and a high epic style, Kotliarevsky employs vernacular Ukrainian language and burlesque, humorously narrating the adventures of Aeneas. *Eneida* gained great fame and was distributed in handwritten copies. At the same time, the poem also contains a more serious form of historical subtext and allegory. The adventures of Aeneas in the *Eneida*, when translated into the Ukrainian language, were very much reminiscent of the Cossack wars and the Cossack freedmen of early modern Ukraine, with much of it being set against the backdrop of traditional Ukrainian life, particularly that of the small *panstvo* (nobility). Indeed, *Eneida* is often called the "encyclopaedia of Ukrainian lifestyle": Kotliarevsky used much of the text to record the richness of the Ukrainian language and provided whole lists of dishes, drinks, clothes, card games, and other aspects of everyday life which were popular at that time. Although Virgil main themes and ideas remain largely unchanged in the Ukrainian adaptation, with Aeneas still being charged with a mission to found Rome and glorify the Roman Empire, Kotliarevsky's work ultimately serves as a literary vehicle for praising the inherent value and autonomy of Ukrainian history, language, and traditional lifestyles.

Taras Shevchenko (1814 – 1861), who was born into a serf family and only gained his freedom at the age of 22, emerged as the first Ukrainian national poet of the period of Romanticism. His first book, *Kobzar*, was published in St. Petersburg in 1840 and reveals him as a talented artist and poet who relies primarily on folklore and identifies himself with a kobzar, a traditional folk singer and bard. In the center of Shevchenko's artistic world is the Ukrainian world, which he imagines and fantasizes while being abroad, in the capital of the Russian Empire and later in exile as a soldier of the Imperial Russian Army. Despite this, he is nourished by the memories of his native Ukraine, memories of his childhood, and stories of the Cossack past enshrined in traditional folk tales and songs. At the same time, Shevchenko's poetry has a lyrical tone and becomes a symbolic autobiography of the author that reflects a life split between his native Ukraine and the foreign land where he had to live.

Having visited Ukraine, the poet is especially concerned about the suffering and tribulations of his compatriots. He also speaks sardonically of the Russian imperial family and the colonization of Ukraine, which destroys the world of the people by uprooting their heroic sense of history. The popular imagery employed in Shevchenko's work includes the following: the fate of the offended woman and mother, pity for one's native land, scenes of a popular uprising, and the historiosophy of a Ukrainian national history that intersects with those of the Poles and Jews, as depicted in his poem *Haydamaky*. Shevchenko also widely uses biblical plots and imagery in order to create national myth while also addressing the moments of collective memory and identity.

Ukraine in Shevchenko's poetic visions is often identified with a *pokrytka*: a girl who gave birth to a child out of wedlock. The remnants of Ukraine's autonomy have been destroyed, the Ukrainian world is distorted and far from God's heavenly kingdom, the family is devastated, and motherhood is threatened. In Shevchenko's romantic vision, Ukraine is also tragically split in half and dislocated: it seems to be, on the one hand, an ideal community, a paradise, and on the other it is a hell. For rebellious poems and anti-tsarist sentiments, Shevchenko was sent to the army for ten years while also being banned from writing and painting. Yet his personal voice is still associated with that of the entire nation; the cult of Shevchenko, which was formed during his lifetime, has been preserved throughout the ages.

M.F.: *What role did Ukrainian writers and poets play in the development and evolution of modern Ukrainian nationalism?*

T.H.: The national idea has been one of the dominant themes in Ukrainian literature since the time of Shevchenko. The affirmation of the identity of the people, history, language, the right of Ukraine to exist, and its division between two empires – with the western part belonging to Austria-Hungary and the eastern part to the Russian Empire, is at its core. While Shevchenko formulated a romantic image of Ukraine, the writer and poet Ivan Franko recreated a more realistic social and psychological understanding during the second half of the 19th century. Franko carried out an analysis of Ukraine, being influenced by writing of Emil Zola, in particular the region of Eastern Galicia (Halychyna), where he lived, showing real imagery depicting the transformation of the traditional rural society, the formation of national intelligentsia and the lives of different social strata: workers, peasants and the nobility. He also illustrated the various ethno-national groups and environments, notably the Ukrainians, Poles, and Jews and planned to create an epopee of the social life of his time. Franko embodied his national ideal in the poem *Moisey* (Moses), having been nicknamed "Moses" during his lifetime, where he depicted the deep personal drama of a national leader who is not understood and rejected by his people. Franko also endowed the national ideal with an existential and personal character, paying attention to the psychological and moral doubts and bifurcation of the Ukrainian intellectual. An important theme in his work is international relations and conflicts, particular those between Ukrainians, Poles, and Jews. The diversity and multifaceted nature of Franko's work also heavily evokes that of Johann Wolfgang von Goethe, whom he translated, while Franko was known to have written in Ukrainian, Polish, and German.

The idea of nationalism continued to fuel Ukrainian literature throughout the 20th century, occupying a particularly special place in the 1920s during a period known as the "Red Renaissance". The key figure in this movement was Mykola Khvylovy (1893–1933), who proclaimed the slogan "Get away from Moscow! ", calling for Ukrainian authors to move away from simply imitating Russian literature and to focus on what he termed "psychological Europe". Being a follower of Oswald Spengler, he also called for an "Asian renaissance" in Ukraine. A romantic and a communist, Khvylovy's works of the 1920s reflected the clash of socialist ideal with the bourgeoisie, conveying a sense of disappointment in the ideas of the revolution, as well as the utopian nature of the "Blue Commune", which represented the dream of socialism for him. Notable among his achievements was creating a phantasmagoric image of the eastern Ukrainian city of Kharkiv, which appears on the border between reality and hallucination, city and steppe. Committing suicide on his birthday, Khvylovy sought to present his death as a protest against the repressive Stalinist campaign launched against the generation of Ukrainian writers to which he belonged.

M.F.: *Could you identify any similarities and differences between contemporary Ukrainian literature and that of other nations, which became independent after the dissolution of the Soviet Union?*

T.H.: Post-Soviet Ukrainian literature is characterized by its post-colonial and post-totalitarian nature. During the 19th century in the Russian Empire, the Ukrainian language was considered unsuitable for literature. Indeed, it was even illegal to publish serious literary work or perform plays in the theater that were scripted in Ukrainian (*The Ems Ukaz*, 1876). This policy stemmed from the belief that language and culture served as agents of nationalism and separatism. Later, in Soviet times, entire cultural strata, such as the Ukrainian avant-garde, were erased from memory, with the names of its representatives being incorporated into the history of Russian culture while many Ukrainian writers were repressed or killed, especially during the Stalinist era.

All this determines the relevance of post-colonial criticism in post-Soviet Ukrainian literature as a way of restoring the national tradition, renewing the literary canon, and reclaiming the names of previously banned authors and literary works. At the same time, a new literature is being formed starting from the 1990s, devoid of official pathos, didacticism, and socialist ideology. The field of literature is being transformed thanks to rewriting the national tradition and connecting it to the experience and dictionaries of world culture. As a result of the break with the socialist realism and its heroic narratives the tradition of burlesque and avanguardism performances, the experimental character of Ukrainian literature, is being revived. As a whole, it represents different social strata, time periods, psychological and cultural transition coming to embody the development of a new modern nation.

The process of "carnivalization" in the 1990s encompasses all spheres of life and serves as a means of restoring a full-fledged national entity and more positive literary models of self-perception. It also helps to banish the lingering consciousness of a totalitarian person. An important cultural role in this process is played by the group "Bu-Ba-Bu", whose name stands for "burlesque, balagan, and buffonada". Its members Yuri Andrukhovych, Viktor Neborak, and Oleksandr Irvanets use gamified types of communication, creating new types of characters that serve as guides between the past and the present, between physics and metaphysics, one's own and someone else's. The group's stated goal is also about forming a new Ukrainian-speaking readership, which has been achieved during the years of independence.

Alongside this, Andrukhovych's postmodern novels, *Recreations*, *The Moscoviad*, and *Perversion*, in which he traced the adventures of his hero-trickster in times of global changes, also became literary iconic for this period. The author allows him to undergo trials at home in Ukraine, in Moscow – the capital of the already dead Soviet Empire, and in the new Europe of the late 20th century. Andrukhovych proves the polymorphic and protean nature of the character, close to bohemian, and presents his bifurcation and play as an attempt to overcome post-totalitarian trauma. The dialogic structure of the novels, quotability, pastiche, stylistic play – all this ensured the enduring popularity of Andrukhovych's works.

Colonial trauma destroyed generations, affected language, destroyed the intimate space of the family. Consequently, the post-totalitarian period in Ukrainian literature is characterized by a generational conflict. It also creates a sense of homelessness and resentment towards the world of adults who comprise what Serhii Zhadan (born in 1974) called "the last Soviet generation."

In the 2000s, Zhadan becomes the biographer and leader of this generation. In his published works, *Quotations, Depeche Mode, Anarchy in the Ukr*, and *Voroshilovgrad*, he depicts the consciousness of a teenage character who experiences disappointment in the world of his parents, who are associated with the post-Soviet country and its diminished values. The protagonist lives in a fragile house of existence, considers himself a loser, distancing himself from society, and does not want to become an adult; Zhadan's work very much records the evolution of this generation.

The appearance of women's writing and a number of prominent female authors, among whom Oksana Zabuzhko (born in 1960) has been the most prominent, is also a characteristic of post-Soviet Ukrainian literature. In her novels, *Fieldwork in Ukrainian Sex, The Museum of Abandoned Secrets*, as well as numerous essays, Zabuzhko expresses how colonization, including that of the Soviet period, destroys generations, leads to demasculinization, and erases collective historical memory. Her typical heroine is an intellectual who wears different masks, has different guises, maintains a dialogue with past eras and sometimes aggressively fights for her freedom.

M.F.: *What are the most notable stereotypes that contemporary Ukrainian literature had to overcome? Historical prejudice about Poles, Jews, Russians, and other minorities for example, often come to mind.*

T.H.: Modern Ukrainian literature actively works with memory narratives. Moreover, the latter is increasingly associated with the international, multicultural history of Ukraine. At the same time, specific stories from the lives of different ethnic groups acquire a meta-historical character and unfold on different levels – from private to transgenerational, multinational, and postcolonial. Thus, Sofia Andrukhovych's novel *Felix Austria* is addressed to the rather complicated history of Polish-Ukrainian relations through the fate of one household consisting of both Poles and Ukrainians. This is also a story of two girls, Stefa and Adele. Both are around the same age and could almost be considered sisters, although the Ukrainian Stefa plays the role of a servant, while the Polish Adele is her mistress. The novel was written on behalf of Stefa and depicts in detail the atmosphere of a provincial Galician town at the beginning of the 20th century. However, the story is not only about sisterly love and devotion, but also explores issues inequality and hidden jealousy set against the political passions and nationalist conflicts raging across the Austro-Hungarian Empire. Although this is nominally a Galician text that focuses on the province of Halychyna, at the same time it is also describes the reasons for the fall of the Habsburg Monarchy. Small conflicts, innocent at first glance, jealousy manifest as hidden catastrophe, which eventually explodes on the outskirts of Europe and destroys the Habsburg idyll.

Another novel, *Vichnyi kalendar* (*The Eternal Calendar*), by Vasyl Makhno, shows how destinies and events are intertwined and the landscape of memory is transformed over the course of three centuries in one small town in Podillia, an area inhabited by Poles, Ukrainians, Jews, and Turks. Although these communities periodically fight, they also intermarry, convert to one-another's faiths, work together, and raise their children. *Vichnyi kalendar* describes the key events of recorded history, which is often demarcated by wars, but also records individual names, dates, and events on a smaller scale that are otherwise erased from memory and forgotten.

The Jewish theme, which has been silenced for a long time, is actively present in Ukrainian literature. In particular, the development of modern urban prose clearly testifies that Jews are an important part of the urban community and the urban landscapes of both Kyiv and Lviv. Zabuzhko and her contemporaries Larysa Denysenko and Yuriy Vynnychuk, present their stories not only as a clash of one's own and someone else's, but also because of the similarities of the traumas experienced and the shared experience of survival. This common sense of shared Ukrainian-Jewish past appears after decades and almost mystically echoes across generations, as in Zabuzhko's novel saga *The Museum of Abandoned Secrets*, where, as if in a kaleidoscope, patterns of destinies and parallel worlds are formed.

M.F.: *Russian aggression and the invasion of Ukraine will have many effects, what do you think will be its long-term impact on Ukrainian literature in the future?*

T.H.: The war in Donbas, which has been ongoing in Ukraine since 2014, brought another important topic to Ukrainian literature and resulted in many prose and poetic works on the subject of war. A large proportion of them were written by participants in the war in Donbas such as *Tochka nul* (Point Zero) by Artem Chekh and *Svitlyi shliach* (Bright Way) by Stanislav Aseyev. These publications are often autobiographical and documentary, while also being written by both men and women, and include various genres such as non-fiction, poetry, prose, and adventure literature. For example, Olena Herasymyuk, a participant and volunteer, performed a live reading of the collection *Tiuremna Pisnia* (Prison Song), which combines almost folk melodies with harsh military vocabulary in a completely hybrid way. In the poetry collection *Abrykosy Donbasu* (Apricots of Donbas), Liubov Yakymchuk describes the Luhansk oblast in Donbas region, where she grew up, its landscapes and signs, and dedicates her poems to her parents who remain in the occupied territory. Tamara Horikha Zernia in her narrative *Dotsia* (Daughter) describes the story of a female volunteer who dedicates her life to helping soldiers and challenges the traditionally militaristic discourse of war in terms of gender. To date, the most famous novel about the war has been Serhii Zhadan's *Internat* (The Orphanage), where the author depicts, against the background of a story about male initiation, how the "last Soviet generation" grows up and learns to defend its "last" territory.

First published on 10 July 2022. This interview first appeared in Spanish on https://orientemedio.news.

Translated from Ukrainian by Olha Chyzmar.

Works Cited

Andrukhovych, Sophia. *Felix Austria*. Translated by Vitaly Chernetsky. Harvard Library of Ukrainian Literature (Cambridge Mass.: HURI, 2023).
Aseyev, Stanislav. *The Torture Camp on Paradise Street*. Translated by Zenia Tompkins
 and Nina Murray. Harvard Library of Ukrainian Literature (Cambridge Mass.: HURI, 2023).
Chekh, Artem. *Absolute Zero*. Translated by Olena Jennings and Oksana Lutsyshyna (London: Glagoslav Publications, 2020).
Yakymchuk, Liubov. *Apricots of Donbas*. Translated by Oksana Maksymchuk, Max Rosochinsky, and Svetlana Lavochkina (Washington: Lost Horses Press, 2021).
Zabuzhko, Oksana. *The Museum of Abandoned Secrets*. Translated by Nina Shevchuk-Murray (Washington: Amazon Crossing, 2012).
Zabuzhko, Oksana. *Fieldwork in Ukrainian Sex*. Translated by Halyna Hryn (Washington: Amazon Crossing, 2011).
Zhadan, Serhii. *The Orphanage*. Translated by Reilly Costigan-Humes, and Isaac Stackhouse Wheeler. A Margellos World Republic of Letters Book. (New Haven: Yale University Press, 2021).

Zhadan, Serhii. *Voroshilovgrad*. Translated by Serhii Zhadan, Isaac Stackhouse Wheeler, and Reilly Costigan-Humes, *Voroshilovgrad*, First edition (Dallas, Texas: Deep Vellum Publishing, 2016).

Zhadan, Serhii. *Depeche Mode*. Translated by Myroslav Shkandrij (London: Glagoslav Publications, 2013).

Analytical Articles

Between East and West: Understanding Early Modern Ukraine

Oleksii Sokyrko

The face of modern Ukraine was shaped between the 16th to the 18th centuries. As the successor of the Slavic principality of Kyivan Rus, the various state entities that emerged on the Ukrainian lands, or Ukraine-Rus, during this early modern period, absorbed the heritage of Eastern Christian Byzantium while also existing within the cultural and political orbit of Central and Western Europe. During this period, the lands of the medieval Rus were incorporated into a succession of polities beginning with the Grand Duchy of Lithuania during the 14th century. These areas when subsequently absorbed into the Polish-Lithuanian Commonwealth from 1569 before becoming part of the Cossack Hetmanate after 1648.

The early modern period of Ukraine's history was defined by constant exchange and conflict with its convenient geographic location at the intersection of the agricultural and nomadic worlds made it an important transit hub for regional trade. Notable among these was its position along the salt road, better known as the key trade route between the Varangians and the Greeks, and the Silk Road spanning across Eurasia and connecting its eastern and western extremes. New trade arteries, which had emerged between the 11th and 16th centuries, also served to link Eastern and Central Europe to the Baltic States and the Black Sea region, further reinforcing Kyivan Rus and Ukraine's economic importance. However, its status as geopolitical borderland also meant that these economic benefits were accompanied by a series of seemingly never-ending wars.

At that point in history, the most powerful political actors in domestic and foreign trade were the Rus ruling princes, descended from the medieval Rurik and Gediminas dynasties; the boyars and *shlakhta*, who formed a caste of minor nobles and landowners; and Cossack officials (*starshyna*), as well as the local Orthodox clergy. This domination was itself derived from vast landed estates that granted these elites access to vast economic power, reinforced by political influence. The second most influential category included colonies of foreign merchants, from Greeks and Armenians to Turks and Jews, whose business and social status were also dependent on maintaining stable relations with those in power. Nevertheless, the failure of the Ukrainian-Rus elites to reach a consensus for the sake of independence in the 14th and 15th centuries had precipitated the partition of the former principality's territories and their incorporation into Poland, Lithuania and Hungary.

However, those among the old Rus elite who had seen their lands incorporated into Lithuania had retained a significant portion of their social and property rights. Although this did not create any impetus for political autonomy, the idea of establishing a Grand Duchy of Rus did emerge within the political discourses of the mid-15th century. Through various strategic marriages, Rus aristocrats not only became the relatives of Polish Kings and Lithuanian Grand Dukes, but also came to occupy important state positions as well as appearing as proponents of new models of governance based on the idea of a socio-political contract between monarchs and political elites that challenged the earlier systems of feudal power. This was best exemplified in the 1569 Union of Lublin, which united the Grand Duchy of Lithuania and the Kingdom of Poland into a single state: the Polish-Lithuanian Commonwealth. At the time, this new polity included most of the lands that had previously formed Kyivan Rus.

In the first half of the 17th century, on the Rus territories which the frontier between the Polish-Lithuanian Commonwealth and the "Wild Fields" (*Dyke Pole*, Lat. *Loca Deserta*), forming the Pontic steppe which is now located in the territory of present-day eastern and southern Ukraine and southern Russia, north of the Black and Azov seas, two new social strata were established: the Ukrainian *shlakhta* and the Zaporizhian Cossacks. Within this comparatively brief timeframe, the Cossacks turned from serving as mercenaries in the Polish army into an organized elite capable of taking power within the vast territories on either side of the Dnieper River. In 1648 a major uprising broke out across the region, which quickly escalated into outright political revolution. What subsequently came to be now as the Cossack Revolution or Khmelnytsky Uprising, having been led by the Cossack Hetman Bohdan Khmelnytsky (1596–1657), resulted in the creation of a newly autonomous polity that included some 30 per cent of the Commonwealth's territory with the Cossacks successfully wresting political power from the old Rus aristocracy. This new self-governing entity came to be known as the Zaporizhian Host, or Cossack Hetmanate; all state institutions were directly modelled on the Cossack military with its commander (*hetman*) serving as head of state. Despite these political reforms, however, the Hetmanate retained much of previous cultural and social traditions that had developed under the direct rule of the Polish-Lithuanian Commonwealth.

Having successfully acquired autonomy, the Hetmanate immediately launched a war for full sovereign independence, concluding alliances with the Crimean Khanate, the Ottoman Empire, the Kingdom of Sweden, and various other Eastern European states. These wars and alliances radically changed the international balance in the region. Of these, the most decisive was the union with the Tsardom of Muscovy, known interchangeably as Russia since the accession of Tsar Ivan IV in 1547, established under the Treaty of Pereiaslav of 1654. Although the then Tsar Alexis represented the weakest link in a series of potential allies-cum-neighbours, he extended recognition to the Cossack Hetmanate only under pressure from Khmelnytsky who had presented him with the unappealing alternative of the Host becoming an Ottoman protectorate. The Cossack elite was therefore able to establish relations with Moscow on a negotiated contractual basis, placing them within a legal framework previous unknown to the Muscovite tradition. Thus, the Treaty of Pereiaslav became the biggest obstacle to the Tsardom's assimilation efforts as it compelled the Russians to continually refer back to its original clauses in order to give their actions an air of legitimacy. Moreover, even after the fall of the Hetmanate, the Ukrainian Cossack elite still thought in terms of contracts as the basis of a Ukraine-Russian union, requiring the tsar to maintain his legal commitments. Consequentially, the latter's nominal supremacy was never considered permanent or without an alternative.

The new Ukrainian elite declared the Cossack Hetmanate as a successor to Kyivan Rus, delineating the borders of the restored state based on those territories populated by ethnic Ukrainians. The concept of turning the Hetmanate into a Grand Principality of Rus, an idea long-cherished by the territory's leaders since the time of Hetman Ivan Vyhovsky (?-1664), was, above all, a reflection of ongoing attempts at reconciling the majority with the that of the nobility as the region's traditional elite. Such a "momentous blend" not only had to take place between the ruling echelons of Ukraine and the Polish-Lithuanian Commonwealth, but also, and even more so, within wider Ukrainian society itself, a situation that saw growing unrest and a series of local Cossack revolts. Despite official attempts at reconciliation, best illustrated by the 1658 Treaty of Hadiach, signed between the Cossack and Polish-Lithuanian diplomats, however these efforts ultimately proved unsuccessfully in restoring socio-political cohesion.

The failure of Hadiach also served in triggering the gradual erosion of Ukrainian statehood, which later provided grounds for a pessimistic retrospective evaluation of the ability of the then Ukrainian elite to adequately represent society. Indeed, the inability of the Cossack *starshyna* to find any workable solutions resulted in political division and fragmentation along the Dnieper River, culminating in the loss of Right-bank Ukraine and the Hetmanate's gradual curtailing of the Hetmanate's sovereignty in the Left-bank by the Russian Tsardom that continued for over a century. However, successive hetmans never abandoned the notion of its statehood at the intellectual level, being in no doubt that the gathering of all ethnic Ukrainian lands within a single state had to remain a key priority. However, while those such as Petro Doroshenko (1627–1698) and Ivan Mazepa (1639–1709) approached this issue at the level of strategic state policy, those less adept were often undermined their own position through tactical retreats, further narrowing the window of opportunity through which full Ukrainian statehood might have been achieved during the early modern period.

Despite resistance to unification, the Cossack *starshyna* was invariably committed to ideas that they represented a distinct political and social elite for whom the establishment of the Cossack Hetmanate as a sovereign entity would remain a goal from the of Mazepa, through the mid-18th century and even after its political dissolution. Indeed, the concept of the Zaporizhian Host as a polity with historical roots that went deeper than simply the era of Kyivan Rus, being linked to Russia only though the figure tsar, remained at the heart of this elite's guiding convictions. Thus, under Hetman Kyrylo Rozumovsky (1728–1803), the *starshyna* were able to articulate a programme of reform designed to restore not only the internal self-sufficiency of the Hetmanate but also its independent standing in the international arena.

The Ukrainian national myth that had begun to emerge in the 18th century was well-tuned to the challenges of the early modern period. It legitimized the establishment of the Cossack Hetmanate in line with the requirements of the times, while at the same time rejecting Muscovy's territorial claims to the Ukrainian lands. Over time, Ukrainians were able to enlist the help of Orthodox intellectuals, who began emphasizing the historical links between the Cossack Hetmanate and earlier traditions of political independence. Under Mazepa, new ideological conceptions were constructed to highlight the Zaporizhian Host's perceived historic mission as a successor of Kyivan Rus.

Despite Russia's expanding political and cultural influence, the intellectual heritage of the Ukrainian Cossack elite was not lost: beginning in the 19th century, some among their descendants were once again seeking to build a new Ukraine. Most importantly, the historical and legal work produced by this earlier movement would serve as a blueprint for the intellectual birth of modern Ukrainian national identity. This closely mirrored what had happened in earlier centuries when a portion of the nobility had been integrated into Cossacks society; these new incomers proved vital in enriching the territory's intellectual culture and providing the latent precedent for the restoration of the Ukrainian state. In this way, a sense of continuity was preserved among the remnants of the Ukrainian elite, preventing its complete absorption into those of the wider Russian Empire. Responding to the new challenges of the time, those who had established early-modern Ukrainian statehood were also able to lay the ideological foundations necessary for the creation of a fully independent state. Such foundation proved to be strong enough to both outlive the Cossack Hetmanate and fuel the rise of the modern Ukrainian national idea during the 19th century.

The *Lithuanian Statutes* were especially significant within the European legal and political culture of the Ukrainian elite, representing the first official codes that regulated the basic principles of government as well as civil, criminal, and property law. The Statutes also synthesized the legal traditions of the various regions that had comprise the former Grand Duchy of Lithuania – specifically the Belarusian, Lithuanian, and Ukrainian lands – and based on customary law and "Rus Truth" (*Pravda Rus'kaia*). Following in the Renaissance fashion that centred on the structures of Roman law, the codes also incorporated the norms of the Polish, Czech, and German traditions. Indeed, from a contemporary perspective these statutory norms would appear quite modern for the time with the inclusion of elements such as equality before the law, the full right to a fair trial, and the right to representation for different minorities and ethnic communities. The depth with which the Statutes had influenced legal norms guaranteed their persistence within the territory's judicial framework and continued use within the Ukrainian lands that formed part of the Polish-Lithuanian Commonwealth after 1569. Under the Hetmanate, the norms of the Statutes also subsequently became the basis of the first "Cossack Code", delineating the "Rights under which the people of Little Russia are judged" (1743). Even in the imperial era of Ukrainian history, Lithuanian-Rus law remained in force, being revived either in the form of the new Russian imperial rights, that existed between 1807 and 1835, or in the practices of the Kyiv Magdeburg, which was only abolished in 1834.

Ukraine's social institutes also had much more in common with those of Central and Western Europe, particularly the Magdeburg Rights (Lat. *Jus Municipale Magdeburgense*) and craftsmen unions. Municipal self-governance was introduced at the same time as its cities revived from the Tatar-Mongol invasion of the 13th century, leading to a subsequent increase in their economic role. Self-governance itself traditionally overseen by magistrates: community governments comprised of two elected collegiums. Moreover, most of these municipal governments, including local mayors, were elected, effectively creating virtual city-states with their own governance, laws, taxes, police, even systems of measurement.

The village community was another element of what was still largely an agrarian-based economic and social system, guaranteeing that skilled peasants – in partial or total serfdom – continued to remain in service to their landlords or the state. American historian Steven Hawk even describes these communities as having primarily been a mechanism of mutual social control within rural Russian society. Such systems were based on the levelling principle and developed a specific labor ethic whereby those outside the privileged class of elders and estate managers were expected to remain obedient and working as much as was necessary to meet their economic needs. Consequently, Russian peasants were generally no poorer or richer than their counterparts further west. However, their attitude to work was entirely different, dominated by stifled initiative, fear of punishment, envy, and hostility towards their neighbours.

The Cossack Hetmanate's foreign trade that generated much of the revenues needed to maintain the central budget went in two major directions: west, by way of the Commonwealth and Habsburg Monarchy, and south-east where the Ottoman Empire and Crimea were the major trading partners. The westward trade corridor, through which cattle, grain, *horilka*, and other agricultural products were shipped to other European countries dated back to the 16th century and connected Ukrainian merchants from Poltava and Starodub with Gdansk, Breslau, Stettin, Marburg, Riga and other early modern trade centres. Nevertheless, the success and productivity of this vital economic artery was ultimately dependent on protection of the state government. The south-eastern route was no less lucrative with trade between Cossack Ukraine and Crimea being worth half a million ducats by the end of the 18th century, an enormous sum at that time. However, merchants still required secure routes for moving the luxury goods they acquired, leading most to favour a more indirect journey through Right-bank Ukraine, under the rule of the Polish-Lithuanian Commonwealth, that allowed them to avoid attacks by bands of armed Tatars and the Zaporizhian Cossacks, as well as the threat of epidemic diseases. It was from there that wines, sugar, cereals, dried and smoked food, Turkish delight, silk, weapons, and Ottoman-crafted jewellery flowed into the Hetmanate and a number of provinces in southern Russia, while the steppe routes were mostly used for cattle, salt, and fish. This segment of commerce was entirely controlled by the Ottoman Turk, the Cossacks and *chumaky*, Ukrainian merchants who traded salt extracted on the Crimean Black Sea coast and who were better adapted to the extreme conditions of life on the steppe.

Just as in other European countries, commercial life in Ukraine was centred around two key spheres, with the main one being agriculture followed by urban craftsmanship and trade. These served as the basis for property rights and economic self-organization expressed through the territory's network of craft workshops and commerce. Having remained open and relatively unpopulated until the 18th century, Ukraine's steppe regions offered plenty of opportunities for commercial colonization. This led to the development of a special social type of entrepreneurial landowner who constantly competed with nature and nomads while relying only on their own resources. This made it somewhat comparable to Europe's other "buffer zones" that boasted similar agricultural-based economies such as the Balkans or the Pyrenees during the period of Muslim rule over the medieval Iberian Peninsula.

Prior to the start of the 18th century, the Russian economic model had had little contact with external influences. This started to change, however, with the launch of Tsar Peter I's, more commonly known as Peter the Great's, Westernisation reforms that sought to turn the Romanov Empire into a major European power and player on the international stage. It's historical predecessor the Grand Duchy of Muscovy, had also sought to introduce Western innovations and organization practices as means of releasing its already vast territory's economic potential, while retaining traditional methods mostly based on domination by the state, centralised administration, distribution of assets, and the marginalization of private initiatives. For Ukraine, the lands of which were progressively drawn into the Russian orbit throughout the 17th and 18th centuries, this entailed the crushing and transformation of the economic and social structures established in the late Middle Ages and their reconstruction along completely different principles. The Ukrainian state and its institutions, whether under Polish-Lithuanian rule or during the Hetmanate, had never had total influence and control over the economy, allowing it to develop freely in response to external markets and domestic demand.

The situation changed when Russia began to pursue its political and economic interests in the early 18th century. Through its victory over the rival Swedish Empire in the Great Northern War (1700–1721), the Russians were granted a hand in being able to redistribute political influence in Central-Eastern Europe while perpetuating the spread of their own preferred economic model and business practices. By 1714, St. Petersburg had monopolized trade in most of the region's strategic goods including Ukrainian potassium, flax, goat fat, and timber for shipbuilding. Moreover, Ukrainian merchants were now ordered to direct their goods to northern ports in Riga and Arkhangelsk instead of the common routes to Krakow, Gdansk, and Breslau.

Surprisingly, even in times of conflict the southern trade routes continued to yield high profits; during the 18th century there were as many as four major wars between the Russian and Ottoman empires. During this period, St. Petersburg had eagerly commissioned Ukrainian merchants to aid in provisioning the Imperial Russian Army owing to the comparative cheapness of their goods and detailed knowledge of the southern steppes and major river crossings. The situation changed dramatically after the Sixth Russo-Turkish War (1768–1774), which severely disrupted trade with Crimea while creating new prospects for transporting goods via the Black Sea ports and bases of which Kherson was initially the largest.

However, Ukrainian merchants once again found themselves out of favour as the Russian Empire sought to first colonize its newly annexed western territories before undertaking economic development measures. Successive governors-general, alongside high-ranking court figures, Russian merchants, and foreign investors, were instead charged with organizing the wholesale trade of agricultural products intended for export. Left without government support, Ukrainian merchants were consequently forced to switch to domestic wholesale and retail trade. Historians have observed that in the second half of the 18th century, trade fairs boomed but were not accompanied by an increase in the number of merchants, implying that both the urban and rural populace, including the Cossacks, were now involved in trade. This was also facilitated by the Cossack *starshyna* and monasteries, which were very active in the domestic market and had enjoyed significant privileges granted under the hetmans' rule. However, from the 1780s, the Russian government began to prohibit both from engaging in trade in order to protect the economic interests of the expanding cities.

These measures were followed by the increasing regulation of the legal status of the territory's merchant and entrepreneurial class with any economic activity being exclusively limited to those registered as Russian subjects. The problem was only exacerbated by the Ukrainian market being re-oriented towards the export of raw materials while stifling domestic industries through the import of finished Russian products. This process also involved the Russification of the cities, where Russian-speakers emerged as the most economically powerful group. The events of the late 18th century thus represented the end of the early modern period of Ukrainian history, in which the territory had existed as part of both the Western and Eastern cultural traditions. The 19th century would mark the beginning of a new phase in the Ukrainian history – the Imperial Period.

Selected Bibliography

Frost, Robert. *The Oxford History of Poland-Lithuania. Volume 1: The Making of the Polish-Lithuanian Union, 1385–1569* (Oxford: Oxford University Press, 2015).

Historical Dictionary of Ukraine ed. Zenon Kohut, Bohdan Y. Nebesio and Myroslav Yurkevich (London: Lanham, 2005).

Isaievych, Iaroslav. *Voluntary Brotherhood: Confraternities of Laymen in Early Modern Ukraine* (Edmonton and Toronto: Canadian Institute of Ukrainian Studies Press, 2006).

Kohut, Zenon. *Making Ukraine. Studies on Political Culture, Historical Narrative, and Identity* (Edmonton and Toronto: Canadian Institute of Ukrainian Studies Press, 2011).

Kohut, Zenon. *Russian Centralism and Ukrainian Autonomy. Imperial Absorption of the Hetmanate, 1760s–1830s* (Cambridge, Mass.: Harvard University Press, 1989).

Plokhy, Serhii. *The Origins of the Slavic Nations: Premodern Identities in Russia, Ukraine and Belarus* (Cambridge: Cambridge University Press, 2006).

Plokhy, Serhii. *The Gates of Europe: A History of Ukraine* (New York: Basic Books, 2015).

Rudnytsky, Ivan L. and Himka John-Paul (eds.) *Rethinking Ukrainian History* (Edmonton: The Canadian Institute of Ukrainian Ivan L. Rudnytsky Studies, The University of Alberta, 1981).

Ševčenko, Ihor. *Ukraine between East and West: Essays on Cultural History to the Early Eighteenth Century,* second, revised edition (Toronto: University of Alberta Press, 2022).

Between Empires:
Ukraine in the Nineteenth Century

Fabian Baumann

The 19th century was a time of empires in the history of Eastern Europe; there was neither a Ukrainian state nor a territory defined as Ukrainian within a state. Instead, the territory of modern-day Ukraine was governed by two imperial states, with their border going back to the partitions of Poland in the 18th century. To the west, Austria ruled over the crownlands of Galicia and Bukovina, while the region of Transcarpathia was a rural backwater on the edge of the Kingdom of Hungary, the other half of the Habsburg Monarchy. On the border's eastern side, nine provinces of Russia had a predominantly Ukrainian-speaking population. Three of these were situated on the right bank of the Dnieper River: the provinces of Kiev, Volhynia, and Podolia. Another three were located further east on the river's left bank: Poltava, Chernigov, and Kharkov. The remaining three were sprawled out over the southern steppes down to the Black Sea: Ekaterinoslav, Kherson, and the Tauride (including Crimea) – these provinces were at the time also known as New Russia. The Russian part of Ukraine was much larger in terms of its population, boasting 25 million inhabitants to Galicia's four million.

Over the course of the 19th century, both empires underwent significant modernization, albeit in different ways. The Austrian half of the Habsburg Monarchy developed into a relatively democratic constitutional state that offered its multilingual and multiconfessional population wide-ranging cultural autonomy. Starting in the 1860s, Vienna instituted an all-imperial parliament and regional assemblies. They were elected on an ever-broadening franchise until universal male suffrage was introduced in 1906. Meanwhile, the Russian Empire remained a bureaucratically governed autocracy. Only after 1905 did it cautiously begin to introduce constitutional structures. Saint Petersburg attempted to preserve the supremacy of the Russian language and the Orthodox religion in the empire, especially in Ukraine. In both cases, the most important watershed in terms of social history was the abolition of serfdom, which legally freed the peasant majority from their noble landlords. Serfdom was abolished in Habsburg Galicia in 1848, while the Russian Empire's peasants had to wait until 1861.

Like many East European regions, 19th-century Ukraine had a diverse population in terms of language and religion. What was typical for Ukraine, especially its western regions, was that linguistic and religious categories often corresponded to socio-economic status. This was especially applicable to the territory's three major groups: Orthodox speakers of Ukrainian, Catholic Polish-speakers, and Yiddish-speaking Jews. Each of these categories had a tendency to belong to certain professions and occupy specific social positions. As the historian Andreas Kappeler noted, Ukrainian society was characterized by an "interethnic division of labor" – a clear socio-ethnic ordering of the population.

Orthodox speakers of Ukrainian dialects formed a majority in most regions of what is today Ukraine. Many of them were illiterate and spoke local dialects rather than modern standard Ukrainian. From a socio-economic perspective, most Ukrainian speakers were peasants working in agriculture. During the 19th century, many migrated to the cities and towns, where they found employment as artisans or factory workers. In the process of urbanization and social mobility, they tended to assimilate by adopting the Russian or Polish language. Ukrainian dialects were thus spoken mostly in the countryside and in smaller towns by those with little or no formal education. A rare but important exception were rural priests, from whose ranks many of the earliest Ukrainian-speaking intellectuals emerged. There were also some Orthodox elites in the cities of Russian Ukraine, such as bureaucrats, soldiers, priests, academics, or medics. These elites consisted of assimilated Ukrainians and Russian immigrants from the empire's central provinces.

Ukraine's Polish-speaking population mostly descended from the *szlachta*, the Polish nobility. Usually Catholics, Polish-speakers were concentrated in the west of Ukraine, where they formed an upper class living in cities or on country estates. The *szlachta* were very diverse in terms of wealth, ranging from impoverished, peasant-like nobles to magnates who owned thousands of serfs and influenced high politics in both Russia and Austria-Hungary. Some magnates even owned entire, largely Jewish, towns such as the *shtetl* of Berdychiv, which belonged to the Radziwiłł family. In Galicia, the Austrian state reached an agreement with these Polish elites in 1867, handing them control over the provincial administration. Subsequently, all Galician governors were Poles, and the crownland increasingly fell under Polish cultural dominance.

The Jewish population was mostly settled in large villages and small towns, called *shtetlekh* in Yiddish, and often occupied mediating positions between the nobles and the peasants. Jews worked as innkeepers, grain merchants, or stewards on rural estates. This economic role fueled antisemitic resentment among the Slavic Orthodox majority: if a peasant encountered state power, it was usually embodied not by a bureaucrat or nobleman but by a Jewish steward collecting taxes or an innkeeper lending money with interest. This situation gave rise to the antisemitic stereotype of supposedly parasitic Jews oppressing the Christian peasants through usury and alcohol, a caricature later adopted by Russian, Polish, and Ukrainian nationalists alike.

Thus, Orthodox Ukrainian peasants formed a majority in the countryside, while towns and cities were Jewish, Polish, or imperial Russian enclaves. This socio-ethnic order was most pronounced in Western Ukraine. The southern provinces of so-called "New Russia" had a different demographic structure, having been conquered and colonized considerably later by the Russian Empire. Here, Slavic peasants mixed with Tatar Muslims and immigrants from all over Europe, including German settlers and Greek merchants. Serfdom was less rooted and ethnic categories less rigid than in the rest of Ukraine. In left-bank (Eastern) Ukraine, by contrast, the population was more linguistically and confessionally homogeneous, with fewer Jews and almost no Catholics. Eastern Ukraine's nobility was Orthodox and comprised largely of former free Cossack officers who had been co-opted into the Russian nobility during the 18th century. Most left-bank nobles were loyal to the imperial state, and some of them reached high positions in the government service. Thus, the state offered opportunities to those Ukrainians who chose to assimilate. Still, some Cossack nobles glorified the earlier period of Cossack freedom and a few of them became the first inspirers of modern Ukrainian nationalism.

The ideological basis of the later Ukrainian nation state was established in the 19th century: the idea that the territory had a common culture, that its (East Slavic Orthodox) inhabitants formed their own nation, and that they ultimately had a right to self-determination. During the early 1800s, scholars began to collect popular songs and Cossack chronicles; writers used the Ukrainian language in ballads and stories, often for comical effect. These developments were in line with European Romanticism, as intellectuals across the continent grew interested in the lives of common people. However, they often viewed Ukrainian culture from an antiquarian perspective, as a relic that would eventually die out.

The politicization of Ukrainian national romanticism began in the 1840s, as intellectuals connected their interest in popular culture with a critique of social injustice and political oppression under Tsarism. Since most Ukrainian speakers were peasants, these intellectuals conceived of Ukrainians as a particularly democratic or "plebeian" nation. The most prominent figure of this period was the writer Taras Shevchenko, today venerated as Ukraine's national poet. Born a serf, Shevchenko revolutionized the Ukrainian literary language and wrote highly political poems that propagated the myth of Ukrainian Cossack and sometimes included anti-Polish, anti-Jewish, as well as anti-Russian invective. The connection between Ukrainian patriotism and the idea of peasant revolution would remain characteristic for most Ukrainian nationalists of the century. Complete independence was rarely their declared goal; most of them envisioned the transformation of the Russian Empire, or even all Slavic lands, into a federation of national territories. In Austrian Galicia, nationalists also began to write in Ukrainian and attempted to reach out to the peasants.

The Russian authorities soon cracked down on Ukrainian high culture and demands for autonomy. Shevchenko and his peers were exiled from Ukraine in the late 1840s. Consequently, whenever these so-called "Ukrainophiles" sought to re-politicize their cultural circles, the imperial state would intervene. In 1863, a Circular issued by the Russian Interior Minister, Petr Valuev, prohibited most publications in Ukrainian, infamously declaring that "[...] there was not, is not, and cannot be any special Little Russian language, and that their dialect, as used by uneducated folk, is the same Russian language, only corrupted by Polish influence." In 1876, Tsar Alexander II signed the Ems Ukaz, tightening the earlier law and even prohibiting Ukrainian theater performances.

Imperial propagandists and Russian nationalists repeatedly sought to denigrate the Ukrainian literary language as artificial, claimed that the national movement was in fact a Polish intrigue, and insinuated that its goal was to sow division among the Russian population. For them, Ukraine's peasants were Little Russians, a peculiar yet integral branch of the Russian nation that formed the ethnic core of the empire. They hoped to assimilate these Little Russians completely into imperial Russian culture as they became literate, creating a bulwark of a loyal Russian population on the Western border. Conversely, Ukrainian nationalists wanted to educate these peasants without assimilation, or, put the other way round, to strengthen the peasantry's social position by turning Ukrainian from a peasant dialect into a literary language suitable for all spheres of society. It is difficult to say how the broad population of Ukraine identified in national terms, however. While some may have viewed themselves as Ukrainians in the national sense, others defined themselves regionally as Little Russians or as Russians writ large. Many were probably indifferent and saw themselves above all as peasants or Christians, defying the claims of the competing national movements.

Besides Ukrainian and Russian nationalists, Polish nationalists also claimed at least Western Ukraine as part of their national territory. In 1830 to 1831 and 1863, Polish nobles staged uprisings against Russian rule. The Russian state repressed these revolts with force, confiscated nobles' estates, and removed thousands of Polish administrators from their posts. Meanwhile, the Polish nobility was de facto able to govern Austrian Galicia thanks to Vienna's classic "Divide and rule" policy. This policy also meant that Vienna saw the Ukrainian movement as a welcome counterweight to the powerful Polish nobility and treated it relatively well. During the closing decades of the 19th century, the first Ukrainian political parties were formed in Galicia, including both social-democratic and national-liberal groups. Galicia's Ukrainian-language press flourished, schools were permitted to teach in Ukrainian, and the provincial capital of Lemberg introduced Ukrainian-language chairs at its university. By the outbreak of the First World War, the Ukrainian educational society *Prosvita* had over 36.000 members in Galicia and reached 200.000 people through its libraries and reading clubs.

Who were the people who gave rise to the Ukrainian national movement during the 19th century? A distinguishing feature was that most of them had received a good education at universities or religious seminaries. Just as importantly, most Ukrainian nationalists made a conscious decision to see themselves as Ukrainians. A notable case in point is the biography of the Ukrainian historian Volodymyr Antonovych. Born Włodzimierz Antonowicz in a village west of Kyiv in 1834, he was the son of an impoverished Polish gentry family. His autobiography describes his youth on a noble estate where his mother worked as a governess. Young Antonovych became increasingly disgusted with the arrogance of the Polish nobility, who believed the peasants to be drunk and primitive good-for-nothings and did not see any need to educate them.

As a student, Antonovych's reading of French Enlightenment philosophy led him to identify the peasants as a democratic element within Ukraine's society. On several hikes across rural Ukraine, he stayed with local peasants and tried to learn about their lifestyle. In the late 1850s, he co-founded a secret school in Kiev to educate peasant children in a democratic and Ukrainian-national spirit. Unsurprisingly, the Polish intelligentsia was not amused, insulting Antonovych as a *khlopoman* (peasant lover) and turncoat. In 1862, he published an article entitled "My Confession," where he proudly embraced this epithet, declaring that a conscientious Polish nobleman in Ukraine had the moral duty to "to love the people in whose midst he lived, to become imbued with its interests, to return to the nationality his ancestors once had abandoned, and, as far as possible, by unremitting labor and love to compensate the people for the evil done to it."

Thus, Antonovych consciously chose the Ukrainian nationality for himself for political reasons and encouraged others to do the same. Feeling guilty before the exploited peasantry, he tried to repay his debt by working towards their socio-economic and national liberation. Antonovych almost experienced his self-Ukrainianization as a religious conversion, and indeed he did convert from Catholicism to Orthodoxy. Having grown up in Polish-speaking surroundings, he made the effort to learn Ukrainian as an adult (his fifth language after Polish, Latin, Russian, and French). Despite his subversive views, Antonovych became a history professor at Saint Vladimir Imperial University of Kiev, where he founded a social historical school that focused on the life of the common people. He wrote his works in Russian, since Ukrainian was restricted, and while he openly denounced the historical role of the Polish nobility, his criticism of the Russian state remained subtle and restrained.

Individuals like Antonovych had various options for national identification, each of which was linked to a political project and broader worldview. Antonovych's family background would have enabled him to be a Catholic Pole and a member of the Polish rural gentry, which would likely have gone along with the political project of Polish autonomy or even the re-establishment of an independent Polish state. His education at Russian universities enabled him to become a professor and he could easily have assimilated fully into Russian culture. This would have been a political decision for the imperial state, with the possibility of a successful career in the administration. Instead, Antonovych chose the third option of learning the language of the peasantry, working towards the advancement of Ukrainian high culture, and becoming a member of a peasant nation. His decision to identify as Ukrainian resulted from his political loyalty to the project of nationally based Ukrainian socialism. Like Antonovych, many 19th-century Ukrainian nationalists were not native speakers of Ukrainian. Among them were Russian- and Polish-speaking nobles as well as Jewish intellectuals and even individuals with French or Swiss ancestors. The Ukrainophiles were not connected by their ethnicity or native tongue but by their political dedication to the peasants' cultural and societal improvement.

For much of the 19th century, Ukrainian nationalism remained the project of a small intellectual elite. In the Habsburg Monarchy, various clubs and economic co-operations took advantage of the relatively liberal legal regime to turn it into a true mass movement by the early 20th century. Consequently, the earliest demands for an independent Ukrainian state were voiced in Galicia around the turn of the century. Meanwhile, in Russia, the number of self-declared national Ukrainians slowly rose among the educated population, especially university students and teachers, but a mixture of repression and popular indifference delayed the formation of mass organizations. Only during the 1917 revolutions would Ukrainian nationalism become a truly relevant political force in Kiev, as the Ukrainian movement profited from the post-imperial power vacuum and briefly managed to establish a nation-state. However, as the subsequent civil war showed, the idea of Ukrainian nationhood was not yet sufficiently anchored in the population to guarantee Ukraine's independence in the face of several competing political forces. A combination of state policies, bottom-up mobilization, and extreme violence would change this over the course of the twentieth century, ultimately leading towards the establishment of a more sustainable independent Ukrainian state in 1991.

Selected Bibliography

Bilenky, Serhiy (ed.) *Fashioning Modern Ukraine: Selected Writings of Mykola Kostomarov, Volodymyr Antonovych and Mykhailo Drahomanov* (Toronto: Canadian Institute of Ukrainian Studies Press, 2013).

Bilenky, Serhiy. *Romantic Nationalism in Eastern Europe: Russian, Polish, and Ukrainian Political Imaginations* (Stanford, CA: Stanford University Press, 2012).

Hillis, Faith. *Children of Rus': Right-Bank Ukraine and the Invention of a Russian Nation* (Ithaca, NY: Cornell University Press, 2013).

Kappeler, Andreas. *Kleine Geschichte der Ukraine*. 7th ed. (Munich: C.H. Beck, 2022).

Kohut, Zenon E. *Russian Centralism and Ukrainian Autonomy: Imperial Absorption of the Hetmanate 1760s–1830s* (Cambridge, Mass.: Harvard Ukrainian Research Institute, 1988).

Magocsi, Paul R. *A History of Ukraine: The Land and Its Peoples*. 2nd ed. (Toronto: University of Toronto Press, 2010).

Miller, Alexei. *The Ukrainian Question: The Russian Empire and Nationalism in the Nineteenth Century* (Budapest: Central European University Press, 2003).

Remy, Johannes. *Brothers or Enemies: The Ukrainian National Movement and Russia, from the 1840s to the 1870s* (Toronto: University of Toronto Press, 2016).

Jews in Habsburg Galicia: Challenges of Modernity

Vladyslava Moskalets

The 19th century was a period of crucial transformations for Polish Jews. During this century, these communities entered an era of secularization, encountered economic modernization, and appropriated modern ideologies, such as nationalism and socialism. At the end of the 18th century, the Jews of the former Polish-Lithuanian Commonwealth were divided between the Russian and Austro-Hungarian empires, following the partitions of Poland, with the majority living in the Ukrainian provinces of the Russian Empire. In 1772, following the first partition, the Habsburg Monarchy established a new province on its north-eastern border and named it the Kingdom of Galicia and Lodomeria, alluding to the medieval Ruthenian state which had previously existed on those territories. Three main ethnic groupings dominated the population of Galicia: Ukrainians, Poles, and Jews, who also constituted the three main religious groups, namely, Greek Catholics, Roman Catholics, and those adherents of the Judaism. The territory also included various smaller minority communities, such as Germans, Armenians, Hungarians, and Romani. According to some estimates the Jewish population in 1772 was between 150.000 and 200.000, constituting 6–7% of the general population. Despite representing the smallest of the main groups, the number of Jews residing in this area of the Habsburg Monarchy was already unprecedented, and continued to grow during the next century. In 1849, the Jewish population of Galicia had more than doubled, rising to approximately 328.000, or 6.7 per cent of the populace. Later in the century, this had reached 11.7 per cent. In both empires, Jews mainly lived in the cities, though there were attempts to promote Jewish agricultural settlements, while smaller Jewish communities continued to perform some essential intermediary functions in the villages.

Differences between these two empires made Jewish experiences in each unique. Political participation, opportunities for integration, censorship, and exposure to state and localized violence manifested in different ways. Economically, however, Jews on both sides of the border lived very similar sorts of lives. Despite the differences, there were a lot of cross-border interaction between both empires, such as the *Hasidism* or *Haskalah* movements. Moreover, the emancipation of the Jews in the Habsburg lands was the outcome of a series of different legal reforms, only being finalized in 1867 when Emperor Franz Joseph II granted them full equal rights.

This chapter will provide an overview of the most important processes that took place within the Jewish communities of Galicia, in the context of their living within a multinational environment. The shifting political, economic, and religious contexts of the 19th century are therefore crucial for understanding Ukrainian-Jewish relations.

Economic Life and Opportunities

Galicia was one of the poorest provinces of what came to be known as the Austro-Hungarian Empire after 1867, with much of its economy revolving around agriculture. Besides a few exceptions, there were no major modern industry, and even big cities like Lviv (Lemberg/Lwów), were mostly centres of trade and services. The economic decline of the smaller towns made Jews migrate to a few big cities, or emigrate abroad, with the number living in Lviv rising from a third to the majority of the city's population. Jews in Galicia were engaged primarily in trade with 51 per cent of those actively working as merchants or retailers being Jewish. In general, the occupational structure of Jews in Galicia differed from the western provinces of Austria-Hungary with a higher percentage engaged in industry than in more industrialized areas like Bohemia. Moreover, a high rate of Jews in Galicia were not professionally active.

Since the presence of the Polish nobility continued to dominate the territory's politics and administration, they continued to hire Jewish managers to work on rural estates as intermediaries between the ruling elites and the largely Ukrainian peasantry. A group of wealthy Jewish landowners were also present, living mainly in the area around the city of Ternopil, and were similar to their Polish counterparts.

Despite its largely agrarian character, industries did exist in a few places. The county of Boryslav in eastern Galicia and Krosno in the west, for instance, developed into centres for the Austro-Hungarian oil industry, which employed a lot of Jews as entrepreneurs, workers, or overseers and played a crucial role in the growth of the Jewish industrial proletariat. Similarly, the city of Kolomyia was home to the "Big Tales" prayer shawl factory, which mainly employed Jews. The presence of Jewish workers was significant for philanthropists and international observers since working in manufacturing or extraction industries was considered more "productive" and ethically more appropriate than trading.

At the other end of the social spectrum, a new generation of acculturated Jewish elites were more integrated into the so-called free professions, becoming doctors or lawyers. This transition was especially prevalent among banking and trader families who could provide their children with a university education in Lviv or Vienna.

The area around the city of Stanislav (today's Ivano-Frankivsk Oblast), also included a number of villages with a relatively significant Jewish population, some of whom continued to serve as local middlemen as well as shop-keepers, millers, or wandering traders. The mid-19th century had also seen an influx of Jews into villages after they had obtained the rights to land holdings. However, many also engaged in agriculture and lived similarly to non-Jewish peasants. Being more isolated from their mostly urban-based religious institutions, these rural Jews tended to interact more often with the Christian Ukrainian peasants rather than with their coreligionists.

During this period, both the Polish and Ukrainian national movements were increasingly preoccupied with local economic problems and differences in Galicia's occupational structure. Since Jews were overrepresented in commerce and trade, Ukrainian and Polish intellectuals often blamed them for exploiting the peasantry. The end of the 19th century also saw a rise in cooperation between Polish and Ukrainian national cooperative networks, which pushed and increasing number of Jewish traders out of the villages and into the urban centres. In response to this, Jewish activists, tried to encourage Jewish youths to pursue more vocational forms of education and qualify as craftsmen. During the interwar period appeared, this would manifest in the form of a Jewish cooperative movement, which traded kosher meat and milk.

Mass Migration

Although the wave of anti-Jewish pogroms that took place in the Russian Empire from 1881 to 1882 served as one of the key triggers for much of the migration of the 19th century, this process was as much the outcome of a range of long-term socio-economic changes. The decay of the *shtetls* (towns, where Jews had previously constituted most of the population) meant that numerous artisans, merchants, and peddlers did not have the means for survival. Moreover, urbanization was unable to solve the problem since the major cities lay outside the Pale of Settlement were the majority of Russian Jews were forced to live.

Migration rates intensified more towards the end of the 19th century, when Jews had already established effective international support networks and the accepting countries, such as Canada, the United States, and Argentina, required a larger workforce for their burgeoning textile industries. Large number of Ukrainians and Poles also migrated during this period, however, their movement patterns differed to those of their Jewish counterparts. Ukrainian migrants, in particular, were mainly peasants who sought out seasonal agricultural work in the USA, Canada, and Brazil. Additionally, unlike these Ukrainian peasants, who often returned from overseas once their contracts came to an end, Jewish migrants usually took their families with them settled abroad permanently. Those Jewish who emigrated from Russia usually travelled illegally via the border crossing in Brody on the Austro-Hungarian border. One of the most famous Yiddish writers, Sholem-Aleichem, described an illegal border crossing by a Jewish family in his novel *Motl, the Cantor's Son*. Differences between Jews from the Russian Empire and those from Habsburg Galicia became especially apparent among the emerging diaspora communities in the USA, where the latter received the somewhat derogatory name of *Galitzianers* and were stereotypically portrayed as backward and orthodox.

Another major problem was the slave trade, notably the coercion of women into prostitution. Those who often operated networks of slave traders were Jewish, which influenced the prevalence of antisemitic discourses in the press, even though Jewish women were as likely to fall victim as their Polish or Ukrainian counterparts. Pauperization, lack of education, and prostitution caused concern among international philanthropic networks, such as the Baron Hirsch Foundation, the French Alliance of Israelites (*Alliance Israelite Universelle*), and those operated by the Rothschild family in the United Kingdom. These Jewish charitable organizations often tried to help integrate Jews into more productive occupations or provide them with vocational training which would allow the latter to find stable employment. The Austrian-Jewish social activist Berta Pappenheim (1859–1936), in particular, was noted for her investigations into the trafficking of Jewish girls in Galicia and attempting to fight against prostitution.

The Social Transformation of Judaism in Galicia

During the 18th and 19th centuries, European Jewish communities underwent major internal transformations, among which the most significant were Hasidism and Haskalah. The former was a charismatic religious movement inspired by the Jewish mystic Baal-Shem Tov (1698–1760), which emerged in Galicia's eastern Podolia region. One of the key tenants of Hasidism was the possibility of connecting with God transcendentally through emotional experiences rather than just through learning the *Talmud*. The popularity of the Hasidism movement transformed the traditional *kahal* system and undermined the established Jewish authorities, being organized around charismatic leaders known as *tzaddiks*, who lived in the small cities and held courts where their adherents could visit them. Among the most famous of these was the Chornobyl court established by Mordekhai Twersky.

Although Habsburg and Russian officials tended to regard the movement with suspicion, the former tended to be less repressive, prompting some of the tzaddiks from Russia to emigrate. A famous example was tsaddik Yisroel Friedman from Ruzhin, who fled to the then Austrian Empire after being accused of murder and persecuted by the Russian authorities. He subsequently established his court in Sadagora, near Chernivtsi in eastern Galicia, which attracted numerous adherents from both sides of the border. The Hasidic lifestyle itself, encompassed different elements borrowed from both Polish and Ukrainian culture. Tsaddiks usually organized their courts in a manner similar to the Polish nobilities' country estates, while the movement's songs and melodics often took inspiration from Ukrainian peasant folk traditions.

Besides the state authorities, Hasidism's popularity also drew suspicion from the adherents of the Jewish Enlightenment movement, the Haskalah. This movement appeared at the end of the 18th century among Jewish intellectuals in Berlin who wished to promote moderate Jewish integration within their respective societies. The incorporation of Galicia into the Habsburg Empire led to many new changes and cultural influences brought German-speaking acculturated Jews from Moravia and the German lands brought recent changes, including the Haskalah. Brody – the main border city between the Habsburg and Romanov empires- became one of the movement's centres and a n conduit for spreading its ideas to Russia. In Galicia itself, however, the movement's priorities quickly shifted away from social integration and towards criticizing of Hasidim. It's leading activists, the *Maskilim*, argued that the tzaddiks deliberately fooled the uneducated and impoverished Jewish masses in order to financially exploit them. Some famous maskils, such as Yosef Perl (1773–1889) from Ternopil, even employed more novel methods, such as parody, in order to undermine Hasidism's influence.

Prior to the mid-19th century, however, the Haskalah's influence was somewhat restricted to a small circle of elites. However, it would subsequently come to influence more popular movements, such as Reformed Judaism. In the 1840s, a Reformed synagogue, *Tempel*, and a Hasidic counterpart, *Jakub Glanzer Shul*, were built almost simultaneously in Lviv's Kraków suburb. Supporters of Reformism financed the former's construction and invited a prominent pro-Reform rabbi from Moravia, Abraham Kohn, to Lviv in order to promote the movement. Kohn's stay in the city was brief and prompted resistance from part of the community, who objected to his appointment as Chief Rabbi of Lviv. In 1848, an Orthodox Jew poisoned him in retaliation, with the community because by the new of one of its first ideologically motivated murders. Nevertheless, the Reformed community in Lviv continued to grow in size and influence, that saw Kohn being elevated to status of a spiritual founder with a Jewish school being named in his honour.

Jews in the Galician Political Context

During the 19th century, the Jews of Galicia increasingly found themselves at the crossroads of a major cultural shift. While the older generation had tended to embrace the German cultural milieu, publishing their writings in German, the latter half of the 19th century witnessed a growing trend towards Polish acculturation. Marsha Rosenblit describes Jews in the Habsburg Monarchy as holding as sense of triple identity: political loyal to the empire, cultural loyalty towards a Polish or German-speaking milieu, and an inherent ethno-religious loyalty towards Judaism itself. The political climate of the Austro-Hungarian Empire also contributed to the creation of various organizations that were a place of socialization and a way of influencing politics. Moreover, the increasing diversity of these organizations after 1850 came to reflect the growing cultural and political divisions within the Jewish community.

The *Shomer Israel* organization represented the most notable expression of German-Jewish acculturation, having been founded in 1868 and publishing its own German-language newspaper *Der Israelite*. In 1876, at the initiative of Shomer Israel, the Lviv Kahal adopted a new charter that favoured community members who had received a secular education. In response, the rival Orthodox organization *Mahzikei HaDat* was formed in order to counter the perceived effort to forcibly secularize he community, publishing its own newspaper of the same name. By 1883, *Mahzikei HaDat* boasted around 40.000 members.

In the political context of late-19th century Galicia, Jewish leaders and organizations also had to interact with newly emerging Polish and Ukrainian political forces. Following the 1867 Constitution, in particular, Polish politicians had come to dominate the Galician provincial government. Indeed, the Monarchy's Orthodox subjects even attempted to maintain a degree of influence over imperial politics by siding with the powerful Polish bloc that emerged in the Austrian parliament. Between 1882 and 1892, a pro-Polish political organization, *Agudas Achim*, also proved highly influential, using its own printed publication, *Ojczyzna*, as a mouthpiece for promoting the interests of Poles.

Galicia's other groupings subsequently attempted to cooperate in response such as during the 1873 elections that saw the emergence of a Ukrainian-Jewish political alliances when the pro-Ukrainian Ruthenian Council and Shomer Israel agreed to work together in order to limit Polish domination in Galicia. As part of their strategy, the Council sent letters to the Central Election Committee of the Jews of Galicia (*Central-Wahl-comité der Juden in Galizien*), which Shomer Israel supported with a proposal for backing Jewish candidates in the cities on the condition that Jewish voters living in the villages supported Ukrainian ones. Although the alliance worked mostly in the Ukrainians' favour, the Jewish press spoke positively about the political mobilization of Jews and the overcoming of mutual Ukrainian-Jewish prejudices in the villages.

By the end of the 19th century, however, Zionism had emerged as a stronger ideological alternative. Early Zionism in Galicia took the form of a so-called "diaspora nationalism" as it did not presume that the region's Jews would immediately emigrate to Palestine. While this remained an important symbol for the movement, Zionist leaders continued to imagine remaining in Galicia as their more likely future, becoming increasingly focused on the local political climate as a result. Consequently, Ukrainian and Jewish nationalism developed simultaneously and faced similar challenges within the Habsburg Monarchy. Jews were not even considered to be one of the Monarchy's constituent nations; a nation was broadly defined as being based on a distinct language, of which Yiddish was not recognized. The first proposal for granting national recognition to the Habsburg Jews was not put forward until 1905, when the Ukrainian politician Iulian Romanchuk suggested it to the Austrian parliament. This support was itself the result of decades of cooperation between Ukrainian and Jewish national movements, which achieved its climax during the 1907 parliamentary elections, the first to permit universal male suffrage. The idea behind this cooperation was to encourage Ukrainian peasants to vote for Jewish candidates while urban Jews backed Ukrainians in order to counter the threat of Polish domination. Numerous political rallies during the electoral campaign demonstrated the popularity of this decision as well as reflecting the general politicization of the Galician populace. As a result, four candidates from the Jewish party and 27 Ukrainian deputies were elected to Parliament, demonstrating the strategy's success.

The Development of Modern Jewish Culture

Of the developments that came to represent the rise of modern Jewish culture in Galicia, Yiddish theatre was one of the modern notable, growing out of the *Purim-shpiel* plays dedicated to the Jewish holiday of *Purim*. Some of the first performances staged in Galicia were organized by the Broder singers, independent performers originally from Brody who sang and entertained the public in taverns and restaurants. Their performances were inspired by traditional *badkhonim* (wedding entertainers) and cantorial music. A more permanent Yiddish theatre in Lviv appeared in 1889, moving from place to place. Its founder, Yaakov Ber Gimpel, had been a former singer in the Polish theatre, with its most popular performances being operettas written and directed by the famous playwright Abraham Goldfaden. Yiddish theatre was also a very egalitarian form of entertainment that brought together people from different social spheres.

A number of influential Jewish artists were also born in Galicia, including Maurycy Gottlieb (1856–1879) who hailed from the western city of Drohobych and later received an artistic education in Kraków at the workshop of the famous Polish artists Jan Mateiko. Gottlieb's own works were remarkable for his usage of personages and stories from Jewish and world history and literature, such as *Shylock and Jessica* (1876), based on William Shakespeare's *Merchant of Venice*. Another Drohobych-born artist, Ephraim Moshe Lilien (1874–1925), became famous for his woodcuts dedicated to the Zionist movement, especially a portrait of the modern movement's founder Theodore Herzl.

Modern Jewish literature had started to develop with the rise of the Haskalah movement. As Galicia was one of its main centres, a few prominent authors also resided there, developing their own literary approaches through constant dialogue with the movement's Vienna and Berlin branches. A remarkable feature of modern Jewish literature was its multilingualism with authors employing a mix of Hebrew, German, and Yiddish. The first of these writers were *maskils*, usually from wealthy families, who had been fortunate to receive private education and wrote in their free time being mostly based in Lviv, Brody, Zhovkva, and Ternopil. Yitshak Erter (1791–1851), for example, was famous for his satirical fiction, which was highly critical of Hasidim. The most famous work of this kind was *The Revealer of Secrets* (1819) by Yosef Perl. The book consisted of letters allegedly written by Hasidim revealing terrible things about the religion. Paradoxically, the text became popular among Hasidim, who's adherents often failed to recognize the satirical form.

Menahem Mendel Levin (1749–1826) also wrote satirical works condemning Hasidic ideas, notably the novel *Moral Accounting* (1808). The most famous of these authors, however, was the philosopher Nahman Krochmal of Zhovkva (1785–1840), for whom Haskalah was viewed as a possibility to discuss religious problems within a modern philosophical context. His student, Meir Letters (1800?–1871), later became pioneer of Hebrew romantic poetry, though he also wrote in German.

The other significant development of Jewish literature was the appearance of Yiddish neoromanticism at the turn of the 20th century. Among the most famous poets were Shmuel Yankev Imber, Melech Ravitch, Dovid Kenigsberg, and Uri Tsvi Grinberg. Their decision to write in Yiddish, was itself a consciously artistic choice. The Yiddish literature movement in Galicia was itself precipitated by the opening of the newspaper *Lemberger Togblat* in Lviv in 1904 by Gershom Bader (1868–1953), which gave young authors an opportunity to publish their prose and poetry. The period preceding the First World War subsequently witnessed a flourishing of Yiddish literature in Lviv, however, most of this movement's leading figures subsequently moved to Vienna after 1914.

The End of Galicia

Jewish Galicia would ironically, outlive the Kingdom of Galicia and Lodomeira, which ceased to exist with the dissolution of Austria-Hungary at the end of the First World War. As some of the Habsburg's most loyal subjects, the fall of the Dual Monarchy represented a major identity crisis for the territory's Jewish inhabitants. Many were subjected to antisemitic violence during and after the war, such as the Lviv Pogrom of 1918. During the interwar period, Galician Jews were obliged to integrate into the post-war Second Polish Republic, where they also faced new problems such as political radicalism and social insecurity, as well as new opportunities including the possibility of emigrating to Palestine. The Galician past was also as problematic by some Jewish intellectuals, who considered the experience of life under the Monarchy as one of cultural Germanization. During the 20th century, however, Galicia would become mythologized within literature, such as the writings of the Galician-born author Joseph Roth as well as numerous memoirs.

Selected Bibliography

Bartal, Israel. *The Jews of Eastern Europe, 1772–1881* (Philadelphia: University of Pennsylvania Press, 2011).
Gąsowski Tomasz. *Między gettem a światem. Dylematy ideowe Żydów galicyjskich na przełomie XIX i XX wieku. Rozprawa habilitacyjna* (Kraków: Księgarnia Akademicka, Instytut Historii Uniwersytetu Jagiellońskiego, 1996).
Liptzin, Solomon. *A History of Yiddish Literature* (New York: Jonathan David Publ., 1988).
Manekin Rachel. "Galicia" https://yivoencyclopedia.org/article.aspx/galicia#i doara.
Manekin, Rachel. "Galitsianer" https://yivoencyclopedia.org/article.aspx/Galitsianer.
Manekin, Rachel. "Politics, Religion, and National Identity: The Galician Jewish Vote in the 1873 Parliamentary Elections," *Polin: Studies in Polish Jewry* 12 (1999): 100–119.
Mendelsohn, Ezra. *Painting a People: Maurycy Gottlieb and Jewish Art* (Hanover: University Press of New England, 2002).
Shanes, Joshua. *Diaspora Nationalism and Jewish Identity in Habsburg Galicia* (Cambridge: Cambridge University Press, 2019).
Sholom Aleichem. *The Adventures of Mottel, the Cantor's Son*, trans. Tamara Kahana (Sholom Aleichem Family, 1999).
Sikorska, Oksana. "Gimpel's Theatre in Lviv: Its Role in The Jewish Community's Life and Its Place In The City's Cultural Space" https://lia.lvivcenter.org/en/themes/?ci_themeid=86.
Tenenbaum Józef. *Żydowskie problemy gospodarcze w Galicyi* (Wieden, 1918).
Wolff, Larry. *The Idea of Galicia History and Fantasy in Habsburg Political Culture* (Palo Alto: Stanford University Press, 2012).

Grain, Coal, and Gas.
Ukraine's Economy since the Eighteenth Century

Boris Belge

The port of Odesa is undoubtedly one of the flashpoints for Russia's war of aggression against Ukraine. Already after the annexation of Crimea and the establishing of Russian control over the Kerch Strait, commercial shipping became virtually impossible for Ukrainian merchant enterprises. Nevertheless, after entering a full-scale war, Russia effectively blockaded the port and cut it off its sea routes in the spring and summer of 2022.

In contrast to the 19th century, grain exports from Odesa are less important for Europe and predominantly feed many African and Asian countries such as China, Egypt, Turkey, Iran, Pakistan, and Bangladesh. Perhaps these new routes, distant from more Western countries, have made the importance of Odesa's grain exports to the world economy less visible in the present.[1] It was not until the Russian war of aggression against Ukraine that the significance of Odesa and its port in global food distribution became abundantly clear – a place that Odesa had won due to far-sighted decisions and the development of transnational links in the early 1800s and regained with considerable determination after Ukrainian independence.[2]

What applies to the port of Odesa also applies to the wider economy of Ukraine – it has a troubling imperial and Soviet past and a contested present. The history of Ukraine's economy examines its evolution, including structures, institutions, and processes, and the relationships between economic and non-economic factors such as politics, culture, and demography. This chapter will illuminate some key areas of Ukraine's economic history from the 18th century up to the 2022 Russian military invasion from a birds-eye perspective.

I will give an insight into Ukraine's multifaceted history by concentrating on three commodities, or resources, that encapsulate much of Ukraine's economy: wheat, coal, and natural gas primarily used for burning. As a country incredibly rich in raw materials and fertile soil, Ukraine's economy has been oriented around food and energy for centuries. It is no exaggeration to say that Ukraine fueled the Russian Empire, the Soviet Union, and several parts of the modern world.

The story of wheat, coal, and gas also helps answer the following questions: who sets the course of the Ukrainian economy – local, regional, national, imperial, or global actors? When did Ukraine experience economic autonomy, and how high was its interdependence within imperial or global economic geographies? Which financial goals were followed and what were the models? In this contribution, I intend to use economic history as a lens into the political, social, and cultural phenomena of Ukraine's history in the 19th and 20th centuries. A better understanding of Ukraine's economy helps to gauge the imperial and Soviet legacies within present-day Ukraine, both as a burden and an opportunity.

Ukrainian history is largely the history of a region that did not merge into a legal national entity. The question of when exactly, and how, Ukrainian history began is widely disputed.[3] From the perspective of economics, a nation-state is needed as a container to facilitate a national economy, and things tend to get messy in the Ukrainian case. Although Ukraine lacked legal sovereignty, in many respects, it was still a distinct economic region separated from the so-called Russian "Motherland". In the following chapter, I will use the established approach for circumventing this problem by focusing on the area that is today's territory of Ukraine – Left and Right Bank Ukraine, Southern Ukraine, and Crimea – territories that had previously been divided between the Habsburg, Ottoman, and Russian Empires.

Imperialism and Economy

The following map (Fig. 1–1) shows the main industrial products for every region of Ukraine in 2006. While the numbers might have changed, it is still helpful for providing a general overview of Ukraine's key industrial centers. What immediately catches the eye is the fact that most mining and metallurgical production is concentrated in the country's south-east. The center of all this is the Donets Coal basin (better known as Donbas), a mining area comparable to the German *Ruhrgebiet*, which also fueled the country's industrialization (and militarization).

Boris Belge: Grain, Coal, and Gas. Ukraine's Economy since the Eighteenth Century 103

Fig. 1–1: Ukrainian Economy, 2006. Wikipedia Commons.

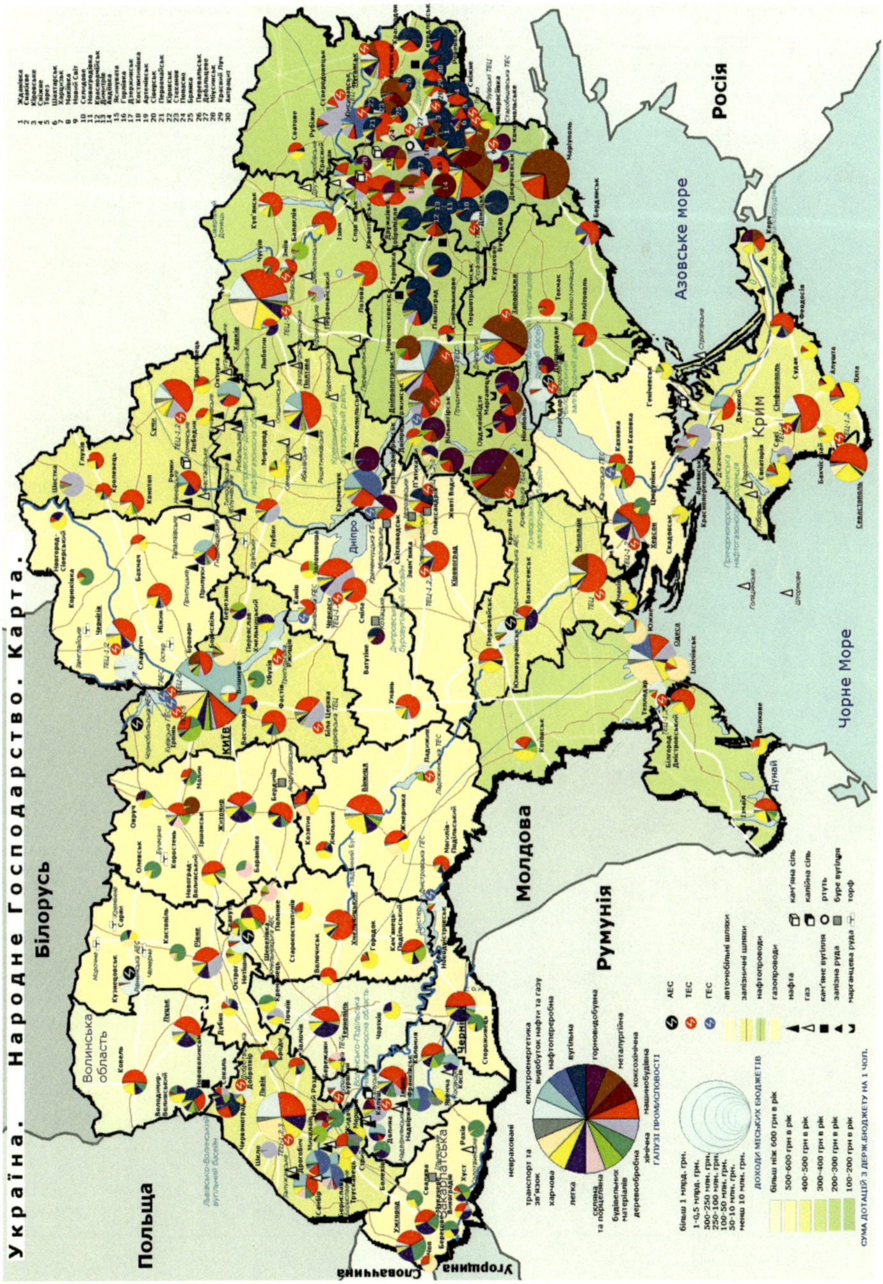

Fig. 1–2: Soil Map of Ukraine. Source: General Directorate of Surveying and Cartography of the Soviet Ministry, GUGK, SSSR, 1977. Downloaded from the European Soil Data Centre (ESDAC).

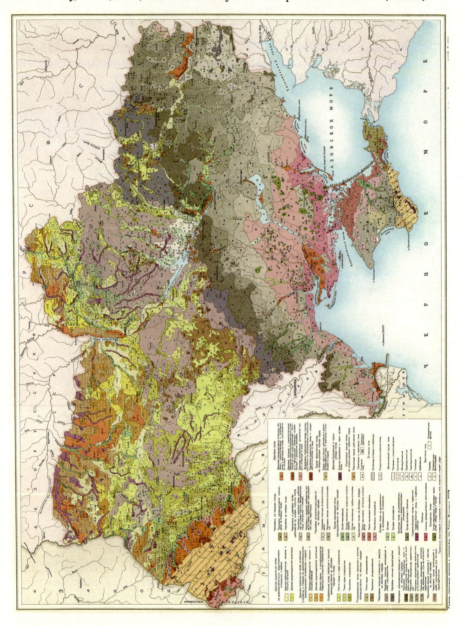

The second map (Fig. 1-2) gives an impression of the different types of Ukrainian soil. Attention needs to be drawn to the grey and pink areas where the so-called "chernozem" (black soil) and "castanozem" (brown earth) are located. Chernozem is fertile soil rich in humus and, therefore, most appropriate for cultivating grain. As a consequence, Ukraine was, and remains, one of the biggest international producers of wheat and rye.[4]

Both maps highlight Ukraine's extraordinary wealth of resources. This alone is not enough for an economy to flourish, however. Resources must be developed, mined, cultivated, and introduced into economic cycles. The fundamental question about this process is not only *how* these processes took place but also for *whose profit*. The answer to the latter question reveals the nature of the area's historical power structures, of which this chapter explores one, in particular. Scholars have previously considered whether Ukraine could be described as Russia's colony, a topic that has caused heated debates.[5] This uneasiness is mainly rooted in understanding colonialism as a cultural operation, forcing hegemonic representations of a ruling elite onto local populations.[6] A point of concern is, for example, the applicability of cultural terms such as "racism" within the Russian context. However, it is important to note that colonialism emergence as an analytical concept was initially defined in economic terms, being understood as "the process of control of supplies of raw materials, mineral resources and markets in underdeveloped and pre-capitalist regions."[7] Much of the literature since being published has also tended to distinguish between different types of colonialism. When taking a closer look at Ukraine's history, three forms of colonialism are especially applicable: exploitation colonialism, settler colonialism, and internal colonialism. These three types are not mutually exclusive but instead provide different perspectives on the complex process of colonization.

Exploitation colonialism is focused on the extraction (and exploitation) of resources or labor force for the benefit of the imperial metropole. The dominant form of colonial presence in the colonized territories is thus the trading post and colonial centers in which a small group of colonists constitute the political, economic and administrative elite. The early colonization of Northern America and Africa are a paradigmatic example for this type of colonization. It is also applicable to the colonization of Siberia in the 17th and 18th centuries.

Settler colonialism is "a distinct type of colonialism that functions through the replacement of indigenous populations with an invasive settler society that, over time, develops a distinctive identity and sovereignty".[8] This large-scale immigration of settlers is often driven by religious, political, or economic motives. However, it also differs from other forms of colonialism in that settlers frequently become a permanent social presence, perpetuating forms of living, domination, and economies that endure beyond the end of formal colonial rule.[9] In Ukraine, this process can be observed beyond the second half of the 19th century, when the settlement of Southern Ukraine ended and the territories of "Little Russia" and "New Russia" were incorporated into the Russian Imperial framework.

Finally, *internal colonialism* is a widely used term that differentiates Russia's colonial experience from the British (or French, or Portuguese) example. Legally, the colonized territories are already part of the state and not discriminated against by the center. Still, the structural power between these areas of the state is unevenly distributed, especially when it comes to the exploitation of resources.

As I will demonstrate in this chapter, Ukraine witnessed all three types of colonialism. Moreover, over the past decades, scholarly understanding of colonialism has also widened considerably, bringing social, political, and cultural factors into the equation. Culturally inspired historiography, however, has increasingly turned a blind eye to economics, focusing on people and cultural signs. In this context, the exploitation model of colonization differs from these approaches in that it places resources at the center of attention. Bringing these material factors back into the analysis and returning to an economic narrative of Ukraine's history inside the imperial framework of the Russian Empire, the Soviet Union, and even the 1990s can therefore offer new insights. I will do so by elaborating upon three different arguments. First, I will assess the history of the grain trade in Ukraine and what this tells us about Ukraine as a cornerstone in Russia's imperial framework. I will then consider how the Donbas served as the coal mine of the Russian Empire and the steel plant of the Soviet Union, but St. Petersburg and Moscow's rule over Ukraine did not mean colonial exploitation of the latter entirely. Instead, Ukraine's East became an industrial center by itself. Finally, I will discuss how the construction of the main Russian gas pipeline through Ukraine undisputedly tied Ukraine's economy to Russia's, a problem that became virulent in the 1990s and 2000s when both states acquired independence and began to drift apart politically.

Grain

The cultivation of grain and Ukrainian national identity are inextricably linked. In fact, the country's flag is said to present a blue sky over a golden wheat field. In the history of Ukraine, grain served three functions: it was a foreign trade commodity, a geopolitical weapon, and the main source of food. I will explore these different functions in turn.

The territories of Ukraine have always been used to cultivate grain. In Ukraine, peasants grew rye in the north and wheat in the south (with some small portions of oat and hops). Today, sunflowers have also come to share a large proportion of Ukraine's agricultural fields. Russia claimed Ukraine's wheat early on. In the time of Tsar Peter I, Left-Bank Ukrainian merchants were forbidden from dealing directly with their Western counterparts since the state tried to monopolize trade. In the middle of the 18th century, Left-Bank Ukraine was itself integrated into the Russian market.[10]

Catherine II's conquest campaigns from the 1770s to the 1790s were also driven by the desire to get better access to the Black Sea and provide Russia with the ability to ship larger quantities of grain.[11] In 1794, the Tsarina's troops conquered the Turkish city of Khadzhibey, leading her to announce the founding of a new imperial Russia city at this century-old place of settlement. Odesa would soon become Russia's biggest port for grain export.[12] Short transportation routes to export corridors quickly fueled the rapid expansion of Ukraine's agriculture with the hinterland of these Russian-ruled Black Sea ports, then called "New Russia" or *Novorossiya*, developing into the breadbasket of Europe.

In the 19th century, as the population of Ukraine and the wider Russian Empire continued to grow and European-led globalization started to accelerate, capitalist logic began to influence grain cultivation. To Russia's economic planners it was evident that they had to exploit Ukraine's soils as much as possible since grain promised an export surplus that the Empire could then leverage in order to join the international gold standard. This was a monetary system in which the standard economic unit of account was based on a fixed quantity of gold – making money convertible, serving as basis for the international monetary system from the 1870s to the early 1920s, and effectively until the 1970s. Membership in the club of gold standard states also increased its attractiveness to foreign debtors.[13] The plan to join was concocted by the Imperial Finance Minister Sergei Ju. Witte. This plan worked: Russia's trade balance profited from exporting ever more grain up until the 1900s (Fig. 1–3).

*Fig. 1–3: "Wheat Exports of the Russian Empire (including Ukraine), 1861–1913",
Source: Falkus, M.E., Russia and the International Wheat Trade, 1861–1814,
New Series, Vol. 33, No. 132 (Nov., 1966), p. 417.*

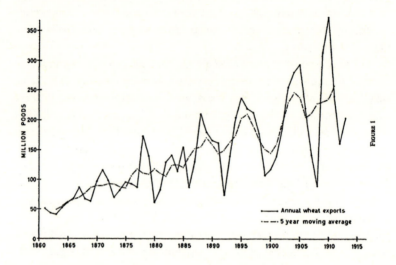

Grain was not only a commodity, however. During the Soviet period, it also came to be regarded as a weapon for social engineering; in the 1930s, Joseph Stalin and his entourage had grain firmly in their sights when ordering the forced collectivization of farmland. Ukraine, one of the agricultural hotspots of the Soviet Union, was hit to a catastrophic extent by this assault on local peasants, ushering in what came to be known as the "Holodomor", highlighting the genocidal consequences behind Stalin's intent to break the Ukrainian peasantry through brute force.[14] While the US Congress and the German Bundestag (among other parliamentary bodies) later acknowledged the Holodomor as a genocidal crime, scholars still discuss to what extent Stalin had waged war against the peasantry in general, or specifically against Ukrainians. Without question, economic rationale had played a role: the Holodomor could not have happened without Stalin's plan to boost the heavy industrialization of the country and the inevitable demands this created for workers and food, and the simultaneously forced collectivization of the countryside.

This relates to the third point: grain is, first and foremost, a food stuff. Large armies need food as much as weapons – the present war is no exception and supplying food is an essential task for the state. There were mainly two reasons for the lack of grain in the 19th and 20th centuries: famines and wars. While bad harvests stemmed from natural causes, such as drought, sandstorms, or heavy rain, the resulting famines were often the cause of political decisions.[15] In principle, Russia rarely suffered from harvesting too little grain and would have been able to provide for its population through improved redistributing across the empire and access to grain stores. This, however, seldom happened. Conflict also tended to exacerbate the scarcity of food, with the grain fields of Ukraine serving as a battleground in both world wars. The main reasons for the first Russian Revolution in 1905 and the February Revolution of 1917 (for which Ukraine was a major theater) were not cultural or political in nature, but stemmed from economic conditions, specifically high bread prices and widespread starvation under the impression of two wars (the Russo-Japanese War of 1905 and World War I).

Throughout the first half of the 20th century, Stalinism and the Second World War deprived Soviet Ukraine's recovery as a producer of grain. During the Cold War era, Stalin's successor Nikita Khrushchev implemented some concessions that allowed local peasants to conduct independent small-scale agriculture. As a result, the peasantry was incorporated into the Soviet welfare state. However, the deficiencies of collectivized agriculture soon became apparent, and by the 1970s, the Soviet Union had become a net importer of grain.[16] The heavy legacy of the Soviet era continued to affect Ukraine's agricultural sector, with the *kolkhoz* (collective farming) system remaining in place until 2000. By the end of the 1990s, agricultural production had dropped to just 50 per cent of its 1989 level. Since 2000, there has been a slow recovery in the agricultural sector. In 2008 and 2009, the country once again ranked as the sixth largest grain producer in the world.[17] However, the lingering effects of the Soviet era are still felt today, as Ukraine continues to grapple with the challenges of transitioning from a collectivized agricultural system to a more modern, market-based approach.

The story of grain is as much about internal politics as it is about Ukraine's entanglements with Russia, Europe, and the wider world. Still, Russia's hunger for grain – both rye for domestic use and wheat as a trade commodity – turned Ukraine effectively into a grain-supplying "colony", dominated by the imperial center. This led to another problem: asymmetrical trade relations and resulting dependencies. Since Ukraine's economy was set to achieve Russia's agricultural surplus, Ukrainians could not always choose between several development opportunities freely.

Coal

While the story of grain could easily fit into a colonial narrative for Ukrainian history, the story of coal, being in some ways, like grain, a fuel supply, is much more complicated. In fact, the beginning of coal mining in the South-Eastern Ukrainian region of Donbas in the 1870s marked a fundamental shift in its economy. Ukraine now started to develop into a major European industrial region rather than being "only" an agricultural supplier of grain for the Russian and wider European economy. Prior to the rise of oil, coal was the dominant energy source, with the Donbas providing about 70 per cent of that consumed in the Russian Empire.[18]

After the Russian Civil War, industrial production in the Soviet Union had fallen to one-tenth compared to the pre-war level. It was Ukraine's coal that would fuel the recovery of the Soviet economy. Already in 1926, the Ukrainian coal industry had returned to 95 per cent of the pre-war level. With Stalin's decision to force the country's industrialization, Ukraine became even more important to the Soviet economy of the 1920s and 1930s. Without Ukraine's coal and iron, the Union would not have been able to produce the amount of steel projected for the first five-year plan. Indeed, from 1932 to 1933, the industrial region of Donbas-Dnipropetrovs'k-Kryvyi Rih produced 70 per cent of hard coal and 70 per cent of iron for the entire Soviet Union. From a global perspective, the numbers are equally impressive. In 1937, Soviet Ukraine was the third-biggest producer of iron and fourth biggest for coal in the world. In the first two decades of Soviet rule, southern Ukraine became an industrial region, and the number of workers quadrupled in only a few years. During this time, urbanization in South-Eastern Ukraine also increased, leading to significant population growth in cities like Stalino (Donetsk) and Zaporizhzhia. Between 1926 and 1939, the populations of these cities grew from around 105.000 to 462.000 in Stalino and from 56.000 to 289.000 in Zaporizhzhia.[19]

In Marxist (and thus Bolshevik) ideology, industrial workers represented the core of revolutionary movements. In the early 1900s, strikes by mineworkers in Southern Ukraine challenged the authorities and led to revolts during the 1905 Revolution. The history of coal challenges the narrative of Ukraine being a colony of Russia. While being politically ruled by Moscow, Southern Ukraine was portrayed as the beating heart of Russian industrialization, as a famous poster from 1921 showcased (Fig. 1–4).

Fig. 1–4: "Donbass serdtse Rossii." The New York Public Library Digital Collections. 1921.

Donbas was not an exploited periphery but developed into a full-fledged economic center for the rest of the Empire. This gave the region and its people some leverage, influence, and attention. Southern Ukraine became *the* place "where the steel was tempered", to paraphrase Alexander Ostrovsky's famous novel, in the late Russian Empire and the first decades of the Soviet Union. This was made possible by large investments from foreign investors and protectionist policies that ensured Ukrainian coal stayed in the country. The Donbas' development into a center of heavy industry also transformed the wider region with workers from all over the Russian Empire and Soviet Union migrating to south-eastern Ukraine.[20] What emerged was not the "russification" of the region but, instead, the development of a specific regional identity, filled with pride as being the "heart of Russia" (*Rossiia*), and fueling the economy of the Soviet Union.

This central economic position of Donbas was challenged in the early 1930s when Stalin's prized megaproject, the new city of Magnitogorsk, shifted the Soviet Union's economic geography towards, and beyond, the Ural Mountains. However, Donbas (and with it, Ukraine) remained an industrial center of the Soviet Union – continuing to exert a socio-economic gravitational force over those Russians who came to work and live there. In the last Soviet Census of 1989, 45 per cent of the population of Donbas reported their ethnicity as Russian.[21] This high percentage distinguished this region from other parts of independent Ukraine, with the Donbas emerging as a regional bastion of the pro-Russian former Ukrainian president Viktor Yanukovych and the oligarch Rinat Akhmetov, the wealthiest man in Ukraine and known as financier and unofficial leader of the Party of the Regions.

Natural Gas

Long before the annexation of Crimea and the start of its war of aggression against Ukraine, Russia had already waged a certain type of war throughout the 2000s that saw a series of "gas wars" between both countries.[22] During this decade, Russia weaponized its gas pipelines running to and through Ukraine to exert influence over the country's political landscape, setting the price of gas in conflict with the transit fees being demanded by Ukraine. As part of the post-Soviet economic space, Ukraine had benefitted from reductions in gas prices and fees paid by the Russian Federation for flow rights. This advantage turned into a big disadvantage when the Ukrainian leadership lost favor with Russia, and the Kremlin started to use gas pricing and delivery for blackmailing. The contemporary picture of Ukraine as a transit country for natural gas overshadows the fact that it had previously possessed its own natural deposits. After the Second World War, Soviet Ukraine was one of the main gas producers within Comecon, the Eastern counterpart to the then European Economic Community. Most of the gas consumed in Poland, for example, came from Ukraine. Indeed, during the 1950s, the Ukrainian gas fields amounted to almost half of total Soviet gas production. Two decades later, the yield from Shebelinka,

Ukraine's biggest gas field in Kharkiv oblast, peaked at 68.7 million rubles in 1975. This was 23.8 per cent of the Soviet production volume.

In the late 1960s, West Germany reached out to the Soviet Union to satisfy its own economic hunger for natural gas, exacerbated by multiple crises in the oil market. Given the growing demand for gas, the Soviet Union could only meet these requests if it could develop the vast gas fields of western Siberia. However, under Leonid Brezhnev, the country lacked the necessary funds, prompting it to reach out to potential partners on the other side of the Iron Curtain. While the United States and Japan refused to respond to Brezhnev's appeal, the Soviet Union and West Germany instead embarked on a new path of collaboration: the "gas for pipes" deal. This provided the Soviet Union with loans and necessary materials (around 1.2 million tons) for building the new pipelines – under the condition that it would deliver 3 billion cubic meters in natural gas to Germany on an annual basis.[23]

Representing the biggest deal between the Soviet Union and Germany since the Third Reich's invasion, the agreement itself was celebrated as a significant cornerstone of German *Entspannungspolitik*, easing tensions across the blocs and (in an admittedly rather teleological perspective) leading to the fall of the Berlin Wall and the end of the Cold War. This specific deal is also at the root of later economic entanglements between Germany, the Soviet Union, and its legal successor state, the Russian Federation. The *idée fixe* of making peace by making business was as strong as it proved to be ultimately flawed. One of these deficiencies was that it overlooked the tremendous costs forced upon Ukraine. As early as the Winter of 1973–74, the Soviet Union experienced its own shortage in gas supply, but still insisted on meeting its delivery obligations with Western partners. To fulfill these obligations, Moscow simply rechanneled natural gas initially designated for Soviet Ukraine to West Germany, causing a major disruption to the former's gas supply. Factories were closed, and households could not be heated. Jeronim Perović pointedly observes that "in the Soviet Union, the country with the world's largest proven fossil natural gas reserves, its own citizens were freezing."[24]

This early example shows that depriving Ukraine of its gas supply is not a post-Soviet phenomenon, but a development deeply rooted in the German-Russian gas business. However, the tension between Russia and Ukraine intensified after 1990. Overnight, Ukraine became a transit country and a large importer. Utilizing the country's economic dependence and debt to Russia, exerting pressure on this newly independent nation providing a means of consolidating regional control. When Russia reduced its gas delivery (again) in 1993 and 1994, a major energy crisis broke out. Consequently, the early 2000s were marked by ongoing negotiations between Russian and Ukrainian officials over the latter's debt towards *Gazprom*, with the matter only being resolved shortly before the outbreak of the Orange Revolution of 2004.

During the late 2000s, Russia and Ukraine engaged in ongoing discussions regarding the gas pipelines that linked their economies. However, it is notable that from 2005 onwards, there was a significant decrease in the import of gas from Russia to Ukraine, with the European Union beginning to play an increasingly larger role in the energy relationship between the two countries. This shift in the energy dynamic between Russia and Ukraine highlights the complex nature of the issue, but it is also important to consider the deteriorating relationship between the two countries. Russia, specifically, has attempted to bypass Ukraine with the building of the North Stream pipelines, which were designed to transport gas directly to Germany, effectively cutting out Ukraine and depriving it of transit fees. Thus, the colonial situation in the case of gas represented a sequence of resource exploitation, followed by control and dominance over energy supply: the Soviet Union drained the Ukrainian gas fields in the 1960s and 1970s, advertently or inadvertently forcing Ukraine to become dependent on Russia for gas imports.

Conclusion and Afterthoughts

Russia was a unique type of imperial state. Deprived of access to overseas territories, Russian imperialism took a different shape to that of the British or French. Andreas Kappeler was among the first to point to the peculiarities of the widely asymmetrical and complex political, social, cultural, and economic fabric of the Russian Empire.[25] The blurriness between the "center" and the periphery stands out as one of the key features. The case of Ukraine, as well as that of the other Western "provinces" of the Empire, underlines this argument. This should, however, not distract us from the clear and direct power relations that benefited some while harming many.

In conclusion, examining Ukraine's economic history helps us to understand the flow of goods within and outside of this important economic space. It allows us to draw borders between regions and take a closer look at the spatial ordering of Ukraine and its relations with other countries and regions. Moreover, it is also important to consider the role of resources, soil, economics, politics, and culture in shaping these borders. Ukraine was both a colony *and* a core part of an empire, and this Janus-faced integration had a significant impact on its socioeconomic development. Willard Sunderland pointed out that "Russia's 'internal expansion' (the intensification of settlement and the reorganization of society) and 'external expansion' (colonial conquest and immigration) proceeded together"[26] leading to its ambivalent relationship with other European economies and its disentanglement from Russian dominance. This shared past with Russia continues to influence Ukraine's economy today.

Notes

1   Boris Belge, "Odessa und das Getreide," *Geschichte der Gegenwart*, 20.07.2022. https://geschichtedergegenwart.ch/odessa-und-das-getreide/, Accessed on 10 January 2023.
2   Patricia Herlihy, *Odessa: A History, 1794–1914* (Cambridge, Mass.: Harvard University Press, 1986); Evrydiki Sifneos, *Imperial Odessa: People, Spaces, Identities* (Leiden, Boston: Brill, 2018).
3   Andreas Kappeler, *Kleine Geschichte der Ukraine* (München: C.H. Beck, 2014), pp. 7–10.
4   Darra Goldstein, *The Kingdom of Rye: A Brief History of Russian Food* (Oakland: University of California Press, 2022); Robert E. Jones, *Bread Upon the Waters: The St. Petersburg Grain Trade and the Russian Economy, 1703–1811* (Pittsburgh, Pa: University of Pittsburgh Press, 2013); Scott Reynolds Nelson, *Oceans of Grain: How American Wheat Remade the World* (New York: Basic Books, 2022); John LeDonne, "Geopolitics, Logistics, and Grain. Russia's Ambitions in the Black Sea Basin, 1737–1834," *International History Review* 28 (2006): 1–41.
5   Oleksii Sokyrko, "From Private Property to Feudalism," *The Ukrainian Week* 22 August 2013 (https://ukrainianweek.com/History/87585); Stephen Velychenko, "The Issue of Russian Colonialism in Ukrainian Thought: Dependency Identity and Development," *Ab Imperio* 1 (2002): 323–67; Aleksandr Ėtkind, *Internal Colonization. Russia's Imperial Experience* (Cambridge: Polity, 2011).
6   Margaret Kohn, and Kavita Reddy. "Colonialism," in Edward N. Zalta (ed.) *The Stanford Encyclopedia of Philosophy* (Stanford: Stanford University Press, 2022). https://plato.stanford.edu/archives/sum2022/entries/colonialism/; Jürgen Osterhammel, *Colonialism: A Theoretical Overview* (Princeton: Markus Wiener Publishers, 2005).

7   M. Abdel-Fadil, "Colonialism," in Matias Vernengo, Esteban Perez Caldentey, Barkley J. Rosser Jr. (eds.) *The New Palgrave Dictionary of Economics* (London: Palgrave Macmillan UK, 1987), p. 2.
8   Adam Barker, and Emma Battell Lowman, "Settler Colonialism," in *Global Social Theory*. https://globalsocialtheory.org/concepts/settler-colonialism/. Accessed on 26 April 2023.
9   Ibid; Olivia Irena Durand, "'New Russia' and the Legacies of Settler Colonialism in Southern Ukraine," *Journal of Applied History* 4:1–2 (2022): 58–75.
10 Kappeler, *Kleine Geschichte der Ukraine*, p. 99.
11 Kelly O'Neill, *Claiming Crimea: A History of Catherine the Great's Southern Empire* (New Haven, London: Yale University Press, 2017); Patricia Herlihy, *Russian Grain and Mediterranean Markets, 1774–1861* (Philadelphia: University of Pennsylvania, 1963); Barry Goodwin, and Thomas Grennes. "Tsarist Russia and the World Wheat Market," *Explorations in Economic History* 35:1 (1998): 405–30; David Moon, "In the Russians' Steppes: The Introduction of Russian Wheat on the Great Plains of the United States of America," *Journal of Global History* 3:2 (2008): 203–25; Martin Bühler, *Von Netzwerken zu Märkten: Die Entstehung eines globalen Getreidemarktes* (Frankfurt: Campus, 2018).
12 Lewis Siegelbaum, "The Odessa Grain Trade: A Case Study in Urban Growth and Development in Tsarist Russia," *Journal of European Economic History* 9:1 (1980): 113–51; Patricia Herlihy, *Odessa Recollected: The Port and the People* (Boston, MA: Academic Studies Press, 2019).
13 Gregory, Paul R. *Before Command: An Economic History of Russia from Emancipation to the First Five-Year* (Princeton: Princeton University Press, 2014), pp. 55–81.
14 Anne Applebaum, *Red Famine: Stalin's War on Ukraine* (New York: Doubleday, 2017); Andrea Graziosi, "The Soviet 1931–1933 Famines and the Ukrainian Holodomor: Is a New Interpretation Possible, and What Would Its Consequences Be?" *Harvard Ukrainian Studies* 27:1/4 (2004): 97–115; Guido Hausmann, and Tanja Penter. "Instrumentalisiert, verdrängt, ignoriert: Der Holodomor im Bewusstsein der Deutschen," *Osteuropa* 70:3–4 (2020): 193–214.
15 Nikolai M. Dronin, *Climate Dependence and Food Problems in Russia, 1900–1990: The Interaction of Climate and Agricultural Policy and Their Effect on Food Problems* (Budapest: Central European University Press, 2008); Alfred Eisfeld, Guido Hausmann, and Dietmar Neutatz (eds.) *Hungers-*

nöte in Russland und in der Sowjetunion 1891–1947: Regionale, ethnische und konfessionelle Aspekte (Essen: Klartext, 2017).
16 Manfred Hildermeier. Die Sowjetunion: 1917–1991 (Berlin; Oldenbourg Wissenschaftsverlag, 2014); Manfred Hildermeier. Die rückständige Großmacht: Russland und der Westen (München: C.H. Beck, 2022).
17 Kappeler, Kleine Geschichte der Ukraine, p. 316.
18 Ibid. p. 127.
19 Ibid. p. 198.
20 Hiroaki Kuromiya, Freedom and Terror in the Donbas: A Ukrainian-Russian Borderland, 1870s-1990s (Cambridge, Mass.: Cambridge University Press, 2003); Theodore H. Friedgut, Iuzovka and Revolution (Princeton: Princeton University Press, 1989).
21 Don Harrison Doyle (ed.). Secession as an International Phenomenon: From America's Civil War to Contemporary Separatist Movements (Athens: University of Georgia Press, 2010), pp. 286–287.
22 Thane Gustafson, The Bridge. Natural Gas in a Redivided Europe (Cambridge, Mass.: Harvard University Press, 2020).
23 Simon Pirani, and Anne Emmert. "Am Tropf: Die Ukraine, Russland und das Erdgas," Osteuropa 60:2/4 (2010): 237–55.
24 Jeronim Perović. Rohstoffmacht Russland: Eine globale Energiegeschichte (Wien Köln: Böhlau Verlag, 2022).
25 Andreas Kappeler, Ungleiche Brüder: Russen und Ukrainer vom Mittelalter bis zur Gegenwart (München: C.H. Beck, 2017); Andreas Kappeler, Zenon E. Kohut, Frank E. Sysyn, and Mark von Hagen (eds.) Culture, Nation and Identity: The Ukrainian-Russian Encounter (1600–1945) (Toronto: Canadian Institute of Ukrainian Studies Press, 2003); Andreas Kappeler, The Russian Empire: A Multiethnic History. Translated by Alfred Clayton (Abingdon: Routledge, 2013).
26 Willard Sunderland, Taming the Wild Field: Colonization and Empire on the Russian Steppe (Ithaca: Cornell University Press, 2004), p. 5.

Selected Bibliography

Balabushevych, T. A., Baran, V. D., Baran, V. K. (eds.) Ekonomichna istoriia Ukraïny. Istorychno-ekonomichne doslidzhennia, u 2 t. (Kyiv: Nika-Tsentr, 2011).

Dean, James. "Ukraine: Europe's Forgotten Economy," *Challenge* 43:6 (2000): 93–108.

Ėtkind, Aleksandr. *Internal Colonization. Russia's Imperial Experience* (Cambridge: Polity, 2011).

Goldstein, Darra. *The Kingdom of Rye: A Brief History of Russian Food* (Oakland: University of California Press, 2022).

Havrylyshyn Oleh (ed.) *The Political Economy of Independent Ukraine: Slow Starts, False Starts, and a Last Chance?* (London: Palgrave Macmillan, 2017).

Herlihy, Patricia. *Odessa Recollected: The Port and the People* (Boston, Mass.: Academic Studies Press, 2019).

Koropeckyj, I. S. *Ukrainian Economic History: Interpretive Essays* (Cambridge, Mass.: Harvard University Press, 1994).

Kuromiya, Hiroaki. *Freedom and Terror in the Donbas: A Ukrainian-Russian Borderland, 1870s-1990s* (Cambridge: Cambridge University Press, 2003).

O'Neill, Kelly. *Claiming Crimea: A History of Catherine the Great's Southern Empire* (New Haven: Yale University Press, 2017).

Siegelbaum, Lewis. "The Odessa Grain Trade: A Case Study in Urban Growth and Development in Tsarist Russia," *Journal of European Economic History* 9:1 (1980): 113–51.

II. Ukrainian Selfhood in the Soviet Era

Primary Sources

Ukrainian Declaration of Independence (1918)
January 9th, 1918

People of Ukraine!

Through your efforts, your will, and your word, a Free Ukrainian People's Republic has been created on Ukrainian soil. The ancient dreams of your warrior ancestors for the freedom and rights of the working people have finally been achieved. But Ukraine's freedom has come at a difficult time. Four years of brutal war have weakened our country and its people, factories no longer produce goods, industry has stalled, the railroads are in chaos, and the currency continues to plummet in value; there is less bread and famine now looms. Mobs of bandits and thieves have spread across the countryside, especially during those times when soldiers deserted from the front, brining death, disorder and ruin in their wake. Due to all this, elections to the Ukrainian Constituent Assembly could not be held on the date set by our previous Universal, and this assembly, which had been scheduled to convene today, could not meet to finalize the new temporary, supreme revolutionary authority in Ukraine that might institute order in our People's Republic and form a new independent government. Meanwhile, the Petrograd Government of the People's Commissars, in an attempt to bring the Free Ukrainian Republic back under its rule, has declared war against Ukraine and is sending its armies of Red Guards and Bolsheviks, who steal the bread from our peasants, without even sparing the grain set aside for seed, carrying it off to Russia and offering nothing in the way of compensation; they kill innocent people while spreading lawless, looting and disillusion wherever they go.

We, the Ukrainian Central Rada, have done everything possible to prevent the outbreak of this fratricidal war between neighbouring peoples, but the Petrograd Government has refused to match our efforts, and instead continues to wage a bloody struggle against the Ukrainian people and the Republic; moreover, this same Petrograd Government of People's Commissars has even sought to delay the peace efforts and is now calling for a new war, which it characterizes as a secular holy war. Again, blood will flow, again the ill-fated working people will be forced to lay down their lives.

We, the Ukrainian Central Rada, elected by the congresses of peasants, workers, and soldiers of Ukraine, cannot agree to this and refuse to support further war, for the Ukrainian people want peace; and a democratic peace must come about promptly. Moreover, in order to ensure that neither the Russian nor any other government shall obstruct Ukraine's efforts at instituting this desired peace, to be able to bring order to our country, to create work, and to the strength the revolution and our freedom, we, the Ukrainian Central Rada, proclaim to all citizens of Ukraine:

From this day forth, the Ukrainian People's Republic stands as an independent, free and sovereign state of the Ukrainian People, subject to no one else.

We wish to live in harmony and friendship will our neighbouring countries: Russia, Poland, Austria, Rumania, Turkey, and others, but none of these may interfere in the life of the independent Ukrainian Republic, where power shall belong only to the people of Ukraine, in whose name, we, the Ukrainian Central Rada, representatives of the toiling peasants, workers, and soldiers and our executive arm, henceforth known as "the Council of People's Ministers", shall govern until the convocation of a new Ukrainian Constituent Assembly.

Firstly, we direct the government of our Republic, the Council of People's Ministers, to continue, on an independent basis, to pursue the peace negotiations that have already been initiated with the Central Powers, and to carry them through to conclusion – without regard for the interference by any other part of the former Russian Empire – and to establish peace, so that our country may begin its economic life in tranquillity and harmony.

As to the so-called Bolsheviks, and all other aggressors who would seek to destroy and bring ruin to our country, we direct the government of the Ukrainian People's Republic to take a firm and determined stand against them, and we call upon all citizens of our Republic to defend their welfare and liberty while not sacrificing their own lives. Our Ukrainian People's state must be cleared of the violent intruders sent by Petrograd, who trample upon the rights of the Ukrainian Republic.

This long and arduous war, launched by the bourgeois government, has left our people weary, destroyed our country, and ruined the economy. It must now be brought to an end. While the army is being demobilized, we order that some be released from military service; after the ratification of the peace, the army is to be disbanded completely.

In the future, rather than maintaining a standing army, a people's militia will be established, so that our fighting forces may serve as defenders of the working people, and not as tools of the ruling elite.

Those districts destroyed by war and the chaotic process of demobilization are to be rebuilt with state aid and through the initiative of our national treasury. When our soldiers return home, new elections to the people's councils, district, county and city dumas will be called at a time yet to be announced, so that our soldiers may be granted a political voice. In the meantime, local administrations will be established and trusted to uphold the revolutionary and democratic principles of the people. The government should encourage cooperation between the various councils of peasants', workers', and soldiers' deputies, all of whom will be elected from among the local population.

On the matter of land, the commission elected at our last session has already devised new legislation concerning the transfer of land holdings, without compensation, to the working people, taking, as its base, our resolution on the abolition of property and the socialization of the land which was passed at the eighth session. In a few days the Central Rada will convene to scrutinize this legislation.

The Council of People's Ministers will use all means to ensure that the transfer of land from the land committees to the working people takes place before the beginning of spring tilling, without fail.

Forests, bodies of water, and all mineral resources – representing the wealth of the Ukrainian working people – are hereby placed under the jurisdiction of the Ukrainian People's Republic.

The war has also depleted our country's national manpower. Most of the factories, enterprises, and shops have been producing only that which was necessary for the war effort, and the nation has been left entirely without goods. Now that the war has come to an end, we direct the Council of People's Ministers to begin, without delay, the process of transferring all factories and manufacturing enterprises back to the peace-time production of goods most needed first and foremost by the toiling masses.

This same war has also seen a proliferation of hundreds of thousands of unemployed workers and invalided veterans. In the independent People's Republic of Ukraine, no working man should suffer. The government will therefore work to increase the industrial output of the state, seek to develop all areas of the economy in which the unemployed may find work and to which they may apply their strengths, and use all means at its disposal to ensure that those left maimed and of those who continue to suffer the effects of the war are provided for.

Under the old order, merchants and all sorts of middlemen gained vast wealth through their exploitation of the poor oppressed classes. Henceforth, the Ukrainian People's Republic takes into its hands the most important branches of national commerce, and all profits derived from these industries shall be used for the benefit of the people. Our state itself will supervise the management of both imported and exported goods to prevent the high prices, set by speculators, which bring only hardship to the poorest classes. To achieve this aim, we direct the government of the Republic to prepare, and present for approval, new legislation concerning the establishment of state monopolies in iron, leather, tobacco, and other products and merchandise on which the greatest profit has been drawn from the working classes for the benefit of the non-toilers.

Likewise, we order the institution of state control over all banks whose credits and loans to the non-working masses aided in the exploitation of the toiling classes. Henceforth, bank loans are to be granted primarily to support the working population and the economic development of the Ukrainian People's Republic, and not for use in speculation and various forms of exploitation previously practiced by the banks, or for profiteering.

Due to the ongoing political anarchy, widespread social anxiety, and a shortage of goods, discontent is growing among a certain segment of the population. Various dark forces are using this unrest and trying to lure unenlightened people back to the old system. These dark forces seek to roll back the people's newly won freedom under the restored yoke of Tsarist Russia. The Council of People's Ministers should therefore stand firmly against all counter-revolutionary forces. Anyone who calls for an uprising against the independent Ukrainian Republic, and a return to the old order, must be punished for treason against the state.

All democratic freedoms proclaimed by the Third Universal are reaffirmed by the Ukrainian People's Republic, with particular emphasis on the following: in the independent Ukrainian People's Republic all nations enjoy the right of national-personal autonomy, granted to them by the Law of January 9th.

Whatever matters enumerated in this Universal which we, the Central Rada, will not have time to accomplish, should be completed, rectified, and approved by the Ukrainian Constituent Assembly. We therefore call upon all citizens to fulfil their duty in the forthcoming elections with due diligence, using all means to ensure the fastest tabulation of votes possible, in order that our Constituent Assembly – the highest governing authority in our land – may convene within a few weeks, to constitutionally enshrine freedom, harmony, and welfare as the founding principles of the independent Ukrainian People's Republic, for the benefit of the whole toiling people, now and in the future.

This, as our highest representative body, will determine the nature of our federative ties with the people's republics of the former Russian state.

Until that time, we call upon all citizens of the independent Ukrainian People's Republic to stand in vigilant defence of the freedom and rights won by our people and to protect their fate with all their might from all enemies of the peasants' and workers' independent Ukrainian Republic.

Original Source: Universal Ukraïns'koï Tsentral'noï Rady (IV), adopted on 9 January 1918. Verkhovna Rada Ukraïny. https://zakon.rada.gov.ua/laws/show/n0001300-18#Text *(Accessed on 05 February 2023).*

Translated by Olena Palko and Samuel Foster.

Letter from the Collective Farmer Mykola Reva to Joseph Stalin about the Famine of 1933 in Ukraine

1 May 1940

Dear Joseph Vissarionovich,

You are, it would seem, our friend, teacher, and father, so the bold idea occurred to me of writing to you with the whole truth....
 The dark reaction of the hungry year of 1933, when people ate tree bark, grass, and even their own children, when hundreds of thousands of people died of starvation, and all this before the eyes of the communists, who drove their cars across our bodies and impudently praised life....
 ...[T]he people were dying of hunger not because there was a poor harvest but because the state took their grain, and that grain lay in the Zahotzerno [Grain Procurement] warehouses in elevators and was being distilled into alcohol for intoxication, while people were dying of hunger.... [I]n 1933, when hungry people gathered grains of corn by the Zahotzerno warehouse at the Khorol station, they were shot like dogs; a detachment of mounted police was dispatched from the town of Khorol, and like lions, with sabers drawn, they pursued us hungry ones, and there was grain in the warehouses, there was flour, but people were dying of hunger, which means that all this was carried out deliberately by the state, and the state knew about this....
 The village council does not issue death certificates for 1933 because mortality in that year was so great that in more than fifty years so many people did not die as in that year. Whoever was left alive, having endured such difficulties – that person is already ruined because, as I know from my own experience, we collective farmers were swollen from hunger, we fell on our feet, we lost our ability to think, we lost a certain percentage of our eyesight, there is no health, no strength, a general weakness of the bodily organism, and a great incidence

of hospital visits and many sick people in those areas where the year 1933 made itself felt. All this took place before the eyes of the communists – how can they not be sorrowful and ashamed that they could not besiege the higher authorities and sound the alarm about this misfortune, so that it would not exist....

[T]he communists cared more for their own skins, for if anyone endeavored to stand up for the people with a mere word, his fate would be settled along with ours. That is how we are valued, Joseph Vissarionovich....

N. Reva

Originally Published in Rozsekrechena pam'iat' (2007). Excerpts, pp. 573–75, 576. Translated by Bohdan Klid.

Reprinted from Bohdan Klid and Alexander J. Motyl (eds.) Holodomor Reader: A Sourcebook on the Famine of 1932–1933 in Ukraine (Toronto: CIUS Press, 2012). Reproduced with permission from the Canadian Institute of Ukrainian Studies.

Fedir Krychevsky, Life Triptych (1925)

Fedir Krychevsky, Life: Triptych (Love, Family, and Return) (1925–7). National Art Museum of Ukraine, Kyiv. Public Domain.

Conversation Pieces

Ukraine: Between Empires and National Self-Determination

Olena Palko, in conversation with Manuel Férez Gil

Olena Palko is Assistant Professor at the University of Basel. She was awarded her Ph.D. from the University of East Anglia in 2017 and previously held a position of the Leverhulme Early Career Fellow at Birkbeck College, University of London. Her first book, Making Ukraine Soviet. Literature and Cultural Politics under Lenin and Stalin (Bloomsbury Academic, 2020) was awarded the Prize for the Best Book in the field of Ukrainian history, politics, language, literature and culture (2019–20) from the American Association for Ukrainian Studies. She is also a co-editor of an edited collection, Making Ukraine: Negotiating, Contesting, and Drawing Borders in Twentieth Century (McGill Queens University Press, 2022). Her research interests lie in the field of early Soviet cultural history and the interwar history of Eastern Europe.

Manuel Ferez: *Thank you so much for talking to us. Please tell us a little about yourself and your academic and professional career.*

Olena Palko: I was born in Ukraine, in the small town of Shepetivka, which up until 1939 was situated right on the Polish-Soviet border. I studied philosophy and political sciences at the Kyiv National Taras Shevchenko University, before embarking on a PhD programme in history at the University of East Anglia in Norwich. In 2018, I started my post-doctoral research at the Department of History, Classis and Archaeology at Birkbeck College, University of London, and a junior research fellow at the Polish Institute of Advanced Studies in Warsaw. My research was a comparative study of the Polish minority in Ukraine and the Ukrainian minority in Poland during the interwar period. Aside from this, I have been working on several projects examining Soviet Ukrainian culture, the formation of modern Ukraine's territorial borders, and the modernisation of Soviet Union. Most of my studies, to date, have focused on these developments during the 1920s and 1930s.

M.F.: *Much has been said in recent weeks about Ukraine, its history and national identity. Beyond the political and ideological narratives, could you suggest a more scholarly reference from which to think about Ukraine and Ukrainian identity?*

O.P.: Much of what is being said about Ukraine is informed by current affairs. Observers try to understand the events of 2014, when Ukrainians took to the streets protesting the reversal of the country's foreign policy trajectory under the then President Viktor Yanukovych. Those protests, known as Euromaidan, forced Yanukovych to flee the country and a new pro-Ukrainian government was formed. Unfortunately, such developments did not satisfy Russia, since its government feared Kyiv would slip out of Moscow's sphere of influence. Russia used the momentum of the disruption in Kyiv and other Ukrainian cities to seize Crimea and occupy the eastern parts of Donetsk and Luhansk regions. To understand these events, many foreign observers fell back on easy explanations of their actually being 'two Ukraines', based on a linguistic and regional divide, arguing that Russian-speakers in Ukraine's east and south are uniformly pro-Russia, while Ukrainian-speakers in Ukraine's west are uniformly pro-European.

Nonetheless, the subsequent political crisis and the on-going Russo-Ukrainian War have shown only too well that this simplistic binary of east verses west does not help us understand contemporary events, or Ukraine's history more generally. Despite its ethnic and cultural heterogeneity, Ukraine is united. As I write, the territories around Kyiv, Kharkiv, Sumy, Chernihiv, and the cities on the Black Sea coast are being bombed by Russian planes, even though these areas are predominantly Russian speaking. The intensity of resistance to the Russian invasion proves that the Ukrainian people, regardless of everyday language, are united in their desire for a strong, free, and democratic Ukraine. The Russian invasion will help solidify the Ukrainian nation even further leading to a new and inclusive understanding of national identity.

I would also like to mention that the Ukrainian lands have always been a meeting point of different cultures, traditions and religions. It is this ethnic, and religious heterogeneity which, I would claim, has served as the true foundation of the country's national identity. While ethnic Ukrainians constitute a majority of the population, numerous other communities, including Russians, Crimean Tatars, Jews, Poles, Hungarians, and Greeks, also call Ukraine their home. The Ukrainian lands also had a long history of division between three major continental empires – Imperial Russia, Austria-Hungary, and the Ottoman Empire, each of which left its own legacy on Ukraine and its people. Many prominent and world-renown cultural figures were also born on the territories which now form modern Ukraine such as the writer Joseph Roth, the poet Paul Celane, and the painter Bruno Schulz. These names became part of the world cultural heritage, and Ukraine faces an equally important task of incorporating them into its national narrative too. That said, to understand Ukraine and its national identity, one ultimately has to refrain from the language of essentialist nationalism, which has informed and conditioned Ukrainian studies worldwide for decades.

M.F.: *Some essentialist narratives claim that, in reality, Ukrainians, Russians and Belarusians belong to the same people. What are these narratives corresponding to and how have they affected and conditioned the historical evolution of the Ukrainian state?*

O.P.: I am not sure what you mean by "essentialist narratives". The idea of a Great-Russian nation, to which Ukrainians, Russians, and Belarusians belong is a modern construct of Russian ideologists. It was first introduced by the official Russian historian Nikolai Karamzin. In his twelve-volume *History of the Russian State*, published between 1781 and 1826, Karamzin developed an argument according to which the history of Russia and Ukraine was that of one "slavic-Russian" people. This understanding of the Great-Russian nation as comprising three different peoples laid the foundation for Russia's unjustified claim over the Ukrainian past, its language and culture, and most recently, its future.

Ever since, Russian propaganda has insisted on this idea of "the same nation". The language argument is used to substantiate those claims. Under the Russian Empire, the Ukrainian language was defined as "a Little Russian vernacular". But even in such a diminished state, the tsarist authorities did everything they could to further limit the use of Ukrainian in the public sphere. For instance, the *Valuev Circular* of 1863 placed limits on Ukrainian-language publications, stating that "no separate Little Russian language ever existed, does not exist, and could not exist." The circular also banned the publication of all literature directed at the common people, while restricting its usage to fiction primarily. More restrictions were introduced under the 1876 *Ems Circular*, which reduced the use of the Ukrainian language to the private setting only. This decree remained in force until the first Russian Revolution of 1905. However, even with the consolidation of Soviet rule in Ukraine, this state desire to assimilate and Russify the Ukrainian peoples remained. Apart from a short period in the 1920s, known as *korenizatsiia* (or indigenization), which is the focus of my 2021 book *Making Ukraine Soviet. Literature and Cultural Policies under Lenin and Stalin*, the tendency of the Soviet government was to enforce the dominance of the Russian language while seeking to diminish the status of Ukrainian. So, when the Russian president Vladimir Putin in 2022 says that no Ukrainian nation exists, he is simply reviving this earlier assimilationist imperial rhetoric.

M.F.: *The extent of a nation and the territory it claims as its homeland sometimes do not coincide. This often gives rise to debates about the limits of both nation and homeland. In the Ukrainian case, what would be its "borders"? Where do they connect and disconnect "the Ukrainian" with "the Russian"?*

O.P.: The process of constructing the Ukrainian nation and defining the geographical extend of its territory started in the mid-19th century, when ethnographers, historians, as well as statisticians and demographers began searching for specific characteristics to define "the Ukrainian nation" that they believed had been split between the two, or even three regional empires. That said, the first "Ethnographic map of Little Russia," dating back to 1862, demarcated a continuous territory populated by "Little Russians", which extended across the Habsburg, Romanov, and Ottoman empires. The ethnographic principle, which emphasizes commonality of language and its use in everyday life, allowed Ukrainian ethnographers and political geographers to lay claims for the vast territories often populated by ethnically ambiguous communities located in these border regions, who could not clearly define their ethnic belonging.

Let me give you an example. In 1871, the linguist Kostiantyn Mykhalchuk prepared a map outlining "the South-Russian dialects and vernaculars", which is widely regarded as the first ethnographic map to provide a scientific basis for the Ukrainian national space. At around the same time, in 1903, a linguist from Saint Petersburg Imperial University called Yefim Karskiy, created the *Ethnographic Map of the Belarusian People*, illustrating the area where the Belarusian language was spoken. If we compare these two ethnographic maps, we will see a significant overlap in the region of Polissia. In such a situation where identities were fluid, and no codified languages existed, it was up to these linguists and ethnographers to establish categories and define the ethnic belonging of heterogeneous and mixed local communities. With the demise of the

Russian Empire and the rise of national movements across its former western provinces, these two maps respectively laid the foundations for the future territorial claims of the Ukrainian and Belarusian People's Republics. The resultant Ukrainian-Belarusian border was officially agreed upon in 1919 by representatives of these two republics. As with most borderlines either in Eastern or Western Europe, this was always based on compromise.

If we turn our attention to the process of defining the Russo-Ukrainian border, a similar conflict of interest can be observed. The Ukrainian national government formed in March 1917 laid claim to the territories of Soviet Russia historically populated by Ukrainians, such as the Kuban, Voronezh, and Kursk provinces. If you consult the above-mentioned ethnographic maps of Ukraine, those areas were presented as part of the Ukrainian nation. It should also be noted that the Soviet Ukrainian government in Kharkiv, formed in 1919, made use of the same ethnographic considerations in order to appeal for these areas to be incorporated into Soviet Ukraine. While Soviet propaganda equally endorsed ethnographic knowledge and used it as a principle for its administrative reforms, the central Soviet government in Moscow was driven first by economic concerns, and the desire to maximise access to natural resources. The border negotiations between the Ukrainian and Russian governments lasted until 1929 with only minor alterations on both sides agreed.

As for the contemporary Russo-Ukrainian border, the demarcation line is based on the agreement on the Ukrainian-Russian state border, signed between Ukraine and the Russian Federation on January 28, 2003. It should be noted, however, that up until 2014, Ukraine's northern and eastern boundaries only existed on paper, hence the relative ease with which Russia could penetrate and annex parts of the country in 2014.

M.F.: *Along with Constantin Ardeleanu, you have also co-edited a volume of essay entitled "Making Ukraine. Negotiating, Contesting, and Drawing the Borders in the Twentieth Century". In the book, the various contributing authors re-examine Ukraine's territorial definitions and physical borders. Tell more about this project and how it helps us better understand the current crisis.*

O.P.: Ukraine has land border with seven countries, four of which (Poland, Slovakia, Hungary, and Romania) are members of the European Union. While Ukraine's border with three former Soviet republics (Russia, Belarus and Moldova) was a result of internal party negotiations during the 1920s, its western border came into existence in the aftermath of the Second World War as a result of various diplomatic agreements among the then Great Powers. Since 1991, however, the borders of independent Ukraine have been confirmed by interstate agreements signed by Ukraine with each of its neighbours.

However, the illegal annexation of the Crimean Peninsula in 2014 and Russia's support for separatist groups in Donetsk and Luhansk has raised questions regarding the presumed longevity of these political borders. Such events showed that, like with the late-1930s, state boundaries are by no means primordial or fixed. It also led to the realization that even in a globalized age, where freedom of movement and mobility have become almost the norm, the unguardedness of state borders could become detrimental to a country's territorial integrity and national security.

Since 2014, Ukraine has fallen under the spotlight of Western media and scholarship. However, no comprehensive account of the processes of Ukrainian border-making across time and space existed up to that point. That was why Constantin and I invited various internationally renowned scholars from eleven countries, representing different academic traditions and disciplines, to provide specialized accounts on the history of Ukraine's border formation and offer detailed analysis on the processes of negotiation, delineation, and contestation that shaped the country's political boundaries during the past century.

The essays featured in this volume consider how, when, and under what conditions the borders that historically define the country of Ukraine were agreed upon. They cover a diverse set of (trans)national contexts, focusing mostly on, but not limited to, the critical period of 1917 to 1954 and are organized around three main themes. Section one comprises four essays investigating the impact of various peace treaties that resulted in the re-drafting of Ukraine's borders: the Brest-Litovsk Peace Treaty of 1918, signed between the Ukrainian People's Republic and the Central Powers; the Paris Peace Conference of 1919, where the Ukrainian delegation presented their case for international recognition; the Polish-Soviet agreements of the Riga Peace Treaty of 1921; and the "Big Three Agreements", which were mostly reached towards the end of the Second World War. Section two examines the processes of border delineation between the western Soviet republics of Belarus, Russia, and Moldova, and has particular relevance to the situation currently facing present-day Ukraine. This includes the contentious issue of Crimea, as well as the various 'frozen' post-Soviet territorial disputes, particularly in the case of Moldova. Finally, section three investigates the inter-state contestations behind the formation of the western Ukrainian border, discussing the demarcation of Ukraine's boundaries with Poland and Romania, alongside the territorial delineation of the Transcarpathian region in the south-west. While this volume provides invaluable insight into the process of border formation, it also suggests that conflict with Russia should not be seen as inevitable. In fact, the formation of each and every aspect of Ukraine's border occurred in a very similar context in which those tasked with demarcation had to contend with areas populated by ethnically and linguistically mixed communities. Hence, in order to understand the current war, we need to look more closely at Russia, rather than Ukraine. Russia's invasion reflects deeply rooted imperialistic tendencies within the Russia society which can affect every state and people that happened to be part of the Russian Empire or the Soviet Union.

M.F.: *The Soviet era and the transition to independence during the 1990s left dangerous legacies and resulted in debates about the territorial limits of some nations. How was Ukraine actually established during early Soviet times, including the incorporation of Crimea, Donbass, and Luhansk, and what sorts of obstacles has it had to face when trying to integrate these often culturally disparate and politically disputed regions as an independent country?*

O.P.: The Ukrainian Soviet Socialist Republic was established in 1919 and was a founding member of the Soviet Union in 1922. The decision to form a separate soviet republic was, however, a necessary compromise on the Bolshevik's part. If we look at Bolshevik propaganda during the Russian Civil War of 1917 to 1923, there is clear evidence to suggest that the Bolshevik wished to control all the territories of the former Russian Empire. Nevertheless, in the context of the civil war in Ukraine that lasted incessantly from 1917 and 1921, the Bolsheviks in Russia needed to incorporate a prevalent national discourse into their agenda and offer a viable alternative to the Ukrainian People's Republic, which proclaimed itself an independent state in November 1918.

There were also various foreign policy considerations for forming a separate Soviet Ukraine. Since late 1917, the weakened Russian government had been seeking separate peace negotiations with Imperial Germany and the other Central Powers in order to extrapolate Russia from its ongoing participation in the First World War. This was achieved in early March 1918 when the Bolshevik government signed a separate peace treaty in Brest-Litovsk. Within this agreement, Russia had pledged to respect the Ukrainian People's Republic, which in turn had already been recognized as an independent state by the Central Powers. However, a puppet Soviet government in Ukraine could still engage in open war with the People's Republic without breaking any international agreements.

Although declared as an independent Soviet republic, the status of Soviet Ukraine was significantly undermined by the fact that the Communist Party of Ukraine's executive had acknowledged the authority of Moscow's leadership. In addition, the authority of the Ukrainian Soviet government was significantly limited. Indeed for "defence purposes", the most important ministries, or commissariats, in Soviet Ukraine, Belarus, as well Russia were unified and jointly controlled from Moscow. These included the ministries of war, national economy, railways, finance, and labor.

The regions of Luhansk and Donetsk were (and are) an integral part of Soviet Ukraine. Crimea, by contrast, was only transferred to Soviet Ukraine in 1954. Luhansk and Donetsk are also predominantly Russian speaking, while Crimea has, in addition, a mostly ethnic Russian population. The Russian character of these regions is itself an imperial legacy. Since the time of the tsars, Russian was the *lingua franca* of the cities, while the surrounding countryside was mostly Ukrainian speaking. This state of affairs was reinforced during Soviet times, when the regime encouraged migration between the different republics in order to limit the potential growth of Ukrainian nationalism with many Russians coming to live in Ukraine, and vice versa.

Let me give you an example of how this migration affected Crimea. Before the Second World War, 25 per cent of its population were Crimean Tatars, 10 per cent were Ukrainians, and 40 per cent were Russians. In 1944, almost 200,000 Crimean Tatars were deported from the peninsula, having been accused of collaboration with Nazi Germany during the Axis invasion of the Soviet Union. Instead, the Moscow authorities initiated the forced relocation of entire collective farms to Crimea from other regions of Soviet Ukraine and Russia. As a result, the ethnic composition of Crimea's population changed drastically. By 1959, the proportion of Russians accounted for 71 per cent of the population, with Ukrainians now comprising 22 per cent.

With the dissolution of the Soviet Union in 1991, people in all regions, regardless of their everyday language, overwhelmingly supported the independence of Ukraine. In Luhansk and Donetsk some 84 per cent of voters were recorded as having answered 'yes' to the question of whether they backed independence. Even in Crimea, where opposition was notably higher than the national average, support still stood at 54 per cent.

The reasons for the relative ease with which Russia was able to annexe Crimea can be found in the dominant role Russians have continued to play on the peninsula since 1991. Even after independence, there were still hardly any Ukrainian-language schools, while Ukrainian and expression of Ukrainian culture were almost completely absent from the public sphere. It is, therefore, unsurprising that the majority of people living on the peninsula have never felt part of Ukraine, did not feel engaged in Ukrainian national politics, and saw themselves as being ignored or viewed with contempt by successive Kyiv governments. Indeed, the most resolute support for Kyiv was observed among the Crimean Tatars, who had started to return after 1989. One must also look for economic and social reasons to explain the events in Ukraine's east. Much of the support for separatist militia groups came from people hoping that the areas in which they lived would also eventually become part of Russia, where pensions and other social benefits were believed to be higher than in Ukraine.

M.F.: *The Caucasus have also experienced Russian-led conflicts in Georgia's Abkhazia, Ossetia, and Adzharia provinces, as well as Moscow's ongoing involvement in Armenia and Azerbaijan's ongoing dispute over Nagorno-Karabakh. Additionally, besides Ukraine, several countries in Central Asia, most recently Kazakhstan, have been targeted by Vladimir Putin's foreign (and to some extent, domestic) policy. Tell us about these processes and conflicts and how you see them progressing in the future.*

O.P.: There are three equally important processes that inform Russia's regional foreign policy. The first one I would define as "war scare". Russia's propaganda machine hinges on the dichotomy of Russia versus the West (read, the United States). In this view, the US (and by extension NATO) poses a direct threat to Russia's sovereignty and integrity. To withstand this perceived challenge, Russia needs to continuously increase its military capacity. At the same time, most of the former Soviet republics cannot be permitted to join NATO since it would put Russia's security at immediate risk. Russia had little to say when the Baltic states, Estonia, Lithuania, and Latvia, became members of NATO and the European Union. Nonetheless, there could be no doubt that Moscow would have remained silent had any other post-Soviet republics initiate conversations with Western partners.

Russia's disagreements with Ukraine's foreign policy always evolved around the latter's potential membership of NATO. For instance, Ukraine was promised an opportunity to join the organization back in 2008, but any such plans were shelved following the 2010 presidential elections, in which the pro-Russian Viktor Yanukovych became president. Since 2014, Ukraine has restated its desire to join both NATO and the EU and even added these aspirations as clauses to its amended constitution. In Moscow's eyes, even the mere intention of the Ukrainian government seeking to join NATO in the distant future is deemed unacceptable since it would likely lead to the establishment of Alliance military bases on Russia's borders, as well as the loss of its former satellite. Hence, one of Putin's demands for bringing the current war to and end is a rewriting of the Ukrainian constitution and for Ukraine to declare itself fully neutral.

This scenario would be very similar to one enacted in Georgia in 2008, following Russia's military invasion, that resulted in the proclamation of the breakaway republics of South Ossetia and Abkhazia. By creating such destabilising enclaves, either in Georgia or Ukraine, Russia makes it impossible for these governments to even begin the procedure for NATO accession.

The second process underpinning Russia's foreign policy I would define as the "gendarme complex". This articulates Russia's desire to remain a regional leader and guarantor of security for the entire post-Soviet space. Such a consideration becomes most obvious when we speak of the conflict between Armenia and Azerbaijan around Nagorno-Karabakh. Even in light of the current war in Ukraine, Armenia did not defy its long-standing Russian ally since it continues to provide military support to the Armenian government against Azerbaijan. In exchange for these security guarantees, Armenia must continue to allow for an extended Russian military presence within its own borders.

The third premise can be described as the "Crimea effect". The origins of Putin's regime can be found in the successful reinvasion of Chechnya in 1999, launched when he only recently become prime minister and was still a relatively unknown figure in Russian politics. Since then, there has existed a clear corelation between successful military interventions and the rise of public support for the Russian president. Popular support for Putin in Russia after the 2014 invasion and annexation of Crimea, for example, increased from 60 per cent to 80 per cent. One can assume that Putin expected the same to happen after he signed off on the invasion of Ukraine in February 2022. While the occupation of Crimea happened "with no blood spilled", the latest fully-fledged invasion has already cost Russia some 12.000 casualties. All efforts are made to hide those numbers from the Russian population, including a nationwide ban on Facebook, Twitter, and other foreign-owned social media channels. Regardless of the number of casualties, it is telling that, according to official pollsters, about 70 per cent of Russians still approve of the so-called "special military operation" in Ukraine, at the time of recording.

As for the future, everything of course depends on the outcome of the war in Ukraine. Already now we see a split among the former Soviet republic, with some providing Russia with open or tacit support, like Belarus and Armenia, while others, such as Kazakhstan, are attempting to mediate in order to end the war. The weaker Russia becomes as a result of this conflict, the more sovereignty each and every post-Soviet republic will enjoy in defining its foreign and internal affairs. Russia losing the war with Ukraine will ultimately represent the final nail in the coffin of its ambitions to recreate the Soviet Union, or even the Russian Empire. This collapse of its imperialist policies will provide unique opportunities for its neighbours to develop new political, economic, and military alliances, ensuring a greater security in the region by allowing each country an equal footing.

M.F.: *Finally, how far can Ukrainian nationalism be elastic and integrative? Ukraine is a country with significant ethnic diversity but also with strong Slavic (and even racist) tendencies. Is a more inclusive Ukrainian nationalism possible or are we heading towards a more essentialist and marginalizing one of differences?*

O.P.: Western views on Ukrainian nationalism originate in Russian propaganda. Of course, there is a radical far-right element, but this also exists in Spain, Germany, or indeed in Russia. Their influence on the political processes in Ukraine is marginal, however. Since 2014, no ultranationalist political party has achieved representation in the Ukrainian parliament. Moreover, Ukraine is a country where almost half of the population speaks Ukrainian, while the other half speaks Russian. Yet, in 2018, 73 per cent of Ukraine's population elected Volodymyr Zelensky, a Russian speaker of Jewish origin, as their president. How much more elastic and integrative can Ukrainian nationalism be?

It has become something of a norm to equate Ukrainians with nationalists, either in political or even in academic discourse with scholars who study and publish on Ukraine having to declare their orientation in order to not to be branded as apologists for "nationalism" and so on. Hardly any other scholarly community faces such a burden. Every time one poses a question on the prevalence of nationalistic discourse they play into Russia's hands.

It is in Russia's interest to call Ukraine "a fascist" state (their post 2014 rhetoric) or declare their aim being to "de-Nazify" the country (a new term introduced in 2022). This is what feeds Russian propaganda. Instead, the post-Maidan political crisis and the on-going war with the Russian Federation has resulted in unifying Ukrainians regardless of language or ethnic origin. In fact, Ukraine is now witnessing the formation of a strong civic (rather than ethnic) identity, whereby loyalty to the state and its Western orientation brings more and more people together. So, it is high time to start seeing beyond the post-Cold War cliches and create a new narrative for Ukraine, its history, and its people.

First published on 9 March 2022. This interview first appeared in Spanish on https://orientemedio.news.

Works Cited

Palko, Olena. *Making Ukraine Soviet: Literature and Cultural Politics under Lenin and Stalin*, Library of Modern Russia (London; New York: Bloomsbury Academic, 2021).

Palko, Olena and Constantin Ardeleanu (eds.) *Making Ukraine: Negotiating, Contesting, and Drawing the Borders in the Twentieth Century* (Montreal; Kingston: McGill-Queen's University Press, 2022).

Analytical Articles

The Ukrainian Revolution, the Bolsheviks, and the Inertia of Empire

Hanna Perekhoda

On February 21, 2022, Vladimir Putin gave a long speech justifying the Russian Federation's formal invasion of Ukraine, announced three days later. In it, Putin asserted what he considered to be irrefutable truths: Ukrainians and Russians are "one and the same people", while the distinct national identity of Ukrainians is a pure invention, a result of a conspiracy plotted by those who wished to divide Russia.[1] These ideas are not new or marginal, having actually formed part of the Russian national narrative at its inception during the 19th century. During this period the Tsarist elites believed that rival powers were fueling Ukrainian national sentiment in order to weaken the Russian Empire as an international player. Two centuries later, Putin expressed the same obsessions, which shaped both his rhetoric and political actions. Conversely, his historical agenda did not give much room for intellectual substantiation because, according to the Russian president, these facts have always been "common knowledge". Putin instead preferred to build his understanding of history around a specific episode that should, according to him, shed light on "the motives behind Russia's actions" and explain "what we [the Russian authorities] aim to achieve":

> I will start with the fact that modern Ukraine was entirely created by Russia or, to be more precise, by Bolshevik, Communist Russia. This process started practically right after the 1917 revolution, and Lenin and his associates did it in a way that was extremely harsh on Russia – by separating, severing what is historically Russian land.

The war that Russia launched against Ukraine and its people from February 2022 was therefore justified, according to Putin, by the need to correct the errors of 1917 committed by Vladimir Lenin and his followers. The Russian president insisted in particular that the broader region of eastern Ukraine, "the

Donbass"[2], was "stolen" from Russian by the Bolsheviks and then "given" to Ukraine.

"Isn't it a fact that the Donbas is a region that is historically more Russian rather than Ukrainian?" This is a question that researchers often heard in 2014, when Russia was already orchestrating a "civil" war in eastern Ukraine. When atrocities committed by the Russian army in Ukraine in 2022 come to light, however, few observers dared to openly question the historical legitimacy of Ukrainian independence as they could afford to do it 2014. Nevertheless, a similar idea predicated on much the same lines as President Putin's notion of history on the eve of the invasion continues to circulate: that "the Donbas" is a region with an ambiguous sense of historical belonging, where the population's state affiliation could thus be subject to revision.

At the time of writing, Ukraine is still undergoing the violation of its territorial integrity by Russia. In this specific context, the process of defining its boundaries, and especially its border with Russia, inevitably becomes a politically charged issue. Russian historians openly put forward the irredentist and neo-imperial view of Russian history and, when talking about eastern and southern Ukraine, insist on the allegedly unbreakable historic link between these lands and Russia. Ukrainian historians, on the other hand, have sought to legitimize the internationally recognized borders of their country by arguing that the ancestors of the modern Ukrainian people have inhabited this territory since time immemorial. It is important, however, not to give in to the temptation to adopt a teleological and anachronistic approach typical of national historiographies. In reality, the territorial future of Ukraine, just like that of all other countries that emerged from the disintegration of the Russian Empire, including the Russian Federation itself, was anything but predetermined. The revolutionary period of 1917 to 1922 is, in fact, decisive for understanding the way in which Ukraine's present geographical form was established on the political map.

Historians have produced a large number of works on the issue of state-building and nation-building strategies that the Soviet authorities began to develop as soon as they came to power in order to bring and maintain the lands and populations of the former Romanov Empire under their control.[3] However, the controversies surrounding the territorial delimitation between Ukraine and Russia, and more specifically the question of "where the Donbas belongs", have never been explicitly addressed. Even in works written by specialists in the regional history of the Donbas[4] this question appears only as a point of cursory interest, never problematized as an object of research. A recent collection of essays edited by Olena Palko and Constantin Ardeleanu[5], being the first comprehensive account on the making of Ukraine's modern borders, represents a significant contribution to the field. Its chapter on the Russo-Ukrainian border by Stephan Rindlisbacher in particular, provides a more considered understanding of the logic and mechanisms behind the formal delimitation of the boundaries between the two Soviet republics in the early 1920s.[6] A few articles by Ukrainian historians are also worth mentioning as they introduce interesting historical sources.[7] However, before reconstructing the process by which these modern state borders were actually established, it seems necessary to first understand when and how the spatial representation of Ukraine as we know it today became a self-evident idea for the Bolsheviks; for although they did not "invent" Ukraine, they were in fact the ones who had to resolve the problem of what ultimately constituted this country's territory and, more specifically, where its borders were supposed to lie. However, drawing the boundaries of a new country within a previously centralized, transcontinental empire was not a trivial matter. Why did the provinces of Kharkiv and Katerynoslav (now Dnipro) come to be seen as part of Ukraine? When and how did the idea of the Donbas constituting a part of Ukraine become obvious – especially for the Bolsheviks? This chapter will focus on how these institutional and ideological path-dependencies ultimately determined the "mental geographies", influencing political strategies, and guiding political choices of the actors implicated in the process of delineating the Ukrainian political space.

Imagining a Ukrainian National Space in the 19th Century

The first territorial representations of modern Ukraine appeared in the middle of the 19th century among the intellectual circles of Kharkiv and Kyiv. Those who comprised these groups had already begun to build identities and their loyalties that were distinct from the "Little Russian"[8] or the Russian imperial national project, being predicated, instead on a Ukrainian national idea. Imagining and building a nation in the context of the mid-1800s, also meant imagining its physical territorial form. However, this was not simply a question of defining the geographical limits of the Ukrainian ethnocultural space. Such an undertaking could only be achieved within a political perspective, taking as its goal the placement of Ukraine on the mental map of the progressive intellectual elites who, according to the then popular European Romanticist ideal, needed to first recognize themselves in their people in order to work for its emancipation. Such an approach perfectly exemplified "geographical romanticism"[9]: the use of the ethnographic unity of a contemporary population as a basis to imagine the political space of a nation. The political map of Ukraine would thus be equivalent to its ethnographic map. Such a definition is typical for a stateless nation: when one's identified homelands had long been subjected to an imperial power that denied the historical and cultural subjectivity of its inhabitants, while structuring local economies towards fulfilling the needs of the metropole, the criteria of historical legitimacy or economic rationality hardly offered substantive arguments.

The ideal Ukrainian homeland, however, was not to be found on any political or administrative map of the time. Indeed, on the eve of the First World War, the land populated by ethnic Ukrainians was itself divided between Russia and Austria-Hungary, the latter controlling only the far western regions of present-day Ukraine. The rest of the provinces, which were to form the greater part of the country's future territory, were under Russian rule and held no special status under the tsars. Within this huge, and continuously expanding transcontinental empire, the newly conquered regions were, as a rule, initially placed under the control of governors-general.[10] Once the territories in question were deemed to be sufficiently assimilated, they were then put under a civil administration,[11] becoming a part of the imperial "mainland" and thus blurring any boundary between the metropolis and the colonized peripheries. The Ukrainian regions were also subjected to this practice of integration into the imperial core, which increasingly came to be viewed as a Russian national space by 1900. During this lengthy period, three Governorates-General were created on the territory of present-day Ukraine: Little Russia, with Kharkiv, Chernihiv and Poltava at its center; New Russia and Bessarabia, including the northern coast of the Black Sea and Crimea; and the Governorate-General of Kyiv, grouping the provinces of Kyiv, Volhynia, and Podolia. Although the Governorates-General were gradually abolished, the subdivision of the future Ukraine into three regions remained a *de facto* aspect of the political landscape for years to come.

The February Revolution: Defining the Boundaries of the Nation

In 1917, the February Revolution put an end to tsarist rule; in Ukraine, as in the rest of the former Empire, local soviets (workers councils) and the post-imperial Provisional Government began struggling for power. Mass demonstrations and various people's congresses asking for a wide autonomy for Ukraine also started to multiply as soon as the February Revolution had removed a number of historical obstacles put in place by the former regime.[12] The sudden intensified politicization of the public sphere not only saw social consciousness develop among swathes of the populace who had previously existed outside of state power structures, but also suddenly precipitated numerous forms of national awakening. The Central Rada, an assembly of various Ukrainian progressive political forces, took the initiative of defending and promoting the national claims of the Ukrainian population before the Provisional Government in Petrograd. The definition of Ukraine as a political entity became a more salient issue than ever. However, the new authorities immediately faced a historical conundrum: how to define the borders of an autonomous Ukraine if the only recorded census, dating from 1897, did not include any actual data on the ethnicity of the empire's inhabitants?

Advocates for Ukrainian autonomy considered the Ukrainian people to be all those who had previously indicated "Little Russian" (Ukrainian) as their mother tongue. Logically, Ukraine should therefore comprise territories where this specific part of the population represented the majority.[13] Although Russian largely served as the dominant language of the big cities, especially in the east and south, the Ukrainian-speaking population in the countryside was much more numerous. It should be remembered that Ukrainian society at the time was marked by an opposition between the countryside, Ukrainian and "backward", and the city, centers of Russian imperial domination on the road to modernization. Moreover, those who could be identified as Ukrainian were also the least urbanized ethnic group – being Ukrainian was itself synonymous with being a peasant.[14] Thus, such a division of labor between ethnolinguistic groups made it possible to establish a strong correlation between ethnicity and social position. While Ukrainians may have dominated in a demographic sense, modern political, economic, and civic life in the cities was still the prerogative of Russians, Jews, and Poles. The Ukrainian national movement therefore set itself the task of combating these inequalities, seeing political autonomy as a tool for enabling unhindered development, allowing the Ukrainian nation to emerge from its perceived rural obscurity and enter the sphere of urban modernity where it would finally have its own voice.

Based on this data, the Central Rada drew up a list of provinces that were to be included in the proposed autonomous Ukraine: Kyiv, Volhynia, Podolia, Poltava, and Chernihiv, as well as the eastern and southern provinces of

Kharkiv, Katerynoslav, Kherson, and Tauride.[15] These claims were however not accepted by the Provisional Government in Petrograd, who were determined to keep the industrialized regions to the east and south under the direct control of Russian authorities.

Bolshevik Mental Geographies and the Challenge of the National Struggle

The autonomy of Ukraine and its future territory, subjects much discussed in the Ukrainian political circles of Kyiv, were, however, not a priority for the local militants of the Russian Social Democratic Labor Party, and even less so for its Bolshevik faction (RSDLP(b)). On the one hand, their mental geographies had been shaped by utopian visions of the future: since the ultimate goal of the Bolsheviks was world revolution, the horizons of their political imagination had to be global, not national. On the other hand, their political activities were still limited to the territories of the former Russian Empire, finding fertile ground in the largely Russian and Russified industrial working-class of the major urban centers. In fact, the geographical limits in which the Bolsheviks carried out their activities in 1917 were largely dependent on the networks formed by various soviets. Within the territory of the future Ukraine, there were three such networks in 1917: one at the territory's political center in Kyiv, another in the Black Sea port of Odesa, and the third based in the eastern city of Kharkiv. This division reiterated and recreated the old tsarist administrative structure: instead of seeing Ukraine as a whole, the Bolshevik militants organized themselves into three geographically defined regions. Heorhiy Lapchynsky remembered that the militants of his party were "extremely unprepared to grasp the idea of the unity of Ukraine" and did not ask themselves questions about its possible borders:

> All our previous partisan activity taught us [...] that there were 'three regions' in the 'south of Russia' — Kyiv (*Iugo-zapadnyi krai* or the South-western region), Odesa (the south of the Right bank, Bessarabia, and Crimea), and Kharkiv (Kharkiv, Donbas, Don). [...] We could not even clearly indicate where the borders of the 'Ukrainian Republic' were. Should it, for example, include Odesa, Katerynoslav, Kharkiv, Taurida, or should it be limited to *Iugo-zapadnyi krai*, the Kyiv oblast only?[16]

The mental geography of the militants of the RSDLP(b) in 1917 was thus subject to the inertia of the pre-existing material and ideational structures of the former empire. Revolutionary as they were, the Bolsheviks had not been able to think outside of the imperial geographic paradigm that they had inherited. However, the reality of Ukrainian national mobilization confronted the Bolsheviks with the existing contradiction between the immensity of their political ambitions and the very concrete and local difficulties of a revolution which occurred in a contiguous land empire.

In October 1917, unlike in Petrograd, it was not the Bolsheviks who defeat and overthrow the Provisional Government in Kyiv, but the Ukrainian national movement that then proceeded to consolidate its authority. From then on, any force claiming power over this territory was obliged to position itself in relation to this new context in which the idea of an autonomous or even independent Ukraine becomes more and more popular. However, the Kyiv Bolsheviks did not immediately perceive this fundamental change of paradigm. At the very moment when the Central Rada celebrated its victory, Evgenia Bosch, one of the most respected and trusted activists, declared that the national idea was not popular among Ukrainians since "before the fall of tsarism, it has hardly ever manifested itself".[17] For her, it was "clearly out of the question to speak of any Ukraine", as it was "only a nationalist invention".[18] In reality, not only the Social Democrats, but also the whole urban political environment had been surprised by the extent and speed of the Ukrainian political awakening, whose aspirations had previously been ignored, denied, and even openly derided. Ukrainians, once considered part of a Russian nation, were simply denied a separate voice, and, therefore, were absent from the imagery that dominated among the cultural urban bearers of imperial identity. However, those same Ukrainians had not only become an active subject in the territory's political life, but had even taken power in Kyiv.

Consequently, the Bolsheviks saw themselves as now obliged to address a community whose nationalist demands should not, in principle, be worthy of the interest of a "conscious proletarian".[19] Volodymyr Zatonsky, a prominent member of the Party's local branch, explained that "for the soviets, and thus for the parties of the urban proletariat, both the Bolsheviks and the Mensheviks, Ukraine as such did not exist, because it did not exist for a worker of the city."[20] However, the 1917 revolution in Ukraine had not only been the preserve of the urban workforce, but an expression of political agency by peasantry who were largely Ukrainian. Often wearing the uniform of a soldier, the peasants suddenly emerged from their perceived social obscurity and invaded the cities, irritating the bearers of imperial Russian culture, both socialists and monarchists, who perceived their language as ugly, their culture backward, and their claims pretentious.

However, any political force seriously considering victory in the ongoing regional power struggle could no longer ignore them. The Bolshevik committee of Kyiv even attempted to communicate for the first time in Ukrainian, before the militants realized that only three of them actually knew the language, a state of affairs that certainly gave "a bad impression" and prevented them from engaging with "the masses"[21] as they sought other strategies that could help them "pull" the Ukrainian population "out of the clutches of the Central Rada".[22] They subsequently came to the conclusion that uniting Bolshevik activists and soviets from the south, east, and north of Ukraine, effectively acknowledging the unified territorial limits of Ukrainian autonomy, should be the first step in counteracting the competing political project of the Rada and establish Soviet Russian control over the region. This necessity led activists from the Kyiv RSDLP(b), who considered themselves, above all, "Russian social democrats, from the social democratic party of Russia"[23], to see for the first time the entire Ukrainian ethnic lands as a common political space and culturally coherent whole.

Soviet Ukraine:
An Antidote to Nationalism or a Reactionary Fantasy?

Following a failed attempt at a coup against the First All-Ukrainian Congress of Soviets, the Bolsheviks were chased out of Kyiv by the Central Rada and its military. They subsequently retreated eastwards to Kharkiv, seeking the protection and support of their party comrades who had a much stronger base in this industrial city and could therefore count on the support of the working class, which was more numerous than in Kyiv. The newcomers wasted no time in seeking to convince their comrades to unite and beat the Central Rada at its own game. Under their influence, the Congress of Soviets in Kharkiv, initially conceived as a regional council but promptly reclassified to "All-Ukrainian", declared on December 12, 1917 the creation of a Soviet Ukraine. Tellingly, the name of this state was identical to the one chosen by the Rada: the People's Republic of Ukraine. Concerning territorial claims, the principle was equally clear: "In order to nip in the bud the criminal policy of the Central Rada, which had dared to act in the name of the working masses of Ukraine, the Congress of Soviets considered necessary to assume complete state power in the People's Republic of Ukraine".[24] Thus, the aim was to substitute Soviet Ukraine for that currently under the rule of the Central Rada. However, by proclaiming "their" Ukraine for purely strategic reasons, the Bolsheviks had inadvertently increased the perceived legitimacy of the Ukrainian nation-state idea as it was defined by the national movement, including in its territorial dimension.

Nevertheless, from 1917 to 1922, the party still had several members, if not the majority, for whom "to create Ukraine, even the Soviet one" would be "a reactionary decision".[25] According to the Bolshevik leadership, to give a national form to a state would only mean a "return to the distant past".[26] Founding a republic based solely on the criterion of its relevance within a Marxist economic framework, by contrast, would be rational and therefore progressive. The Soviet Republic of Donets-Kryvyi Rih[27] was a typical example of this approach. Proclaimed by the Bolsheviks in eastern Ukraine in February 1918, it was supposed to be the embodiment of this form of future state organization. By creating an "economic" and not a national republic, Bolshevik militants were convinced that they were defending a truly Marxist vision of the world and of history. The founders of the Donets-Kryvyi Rih Republic even justified their desire to separate the region from Soviet Ukraine in order to join Soviet Russia as indicative of the need to put the resources of Donbas at the service of the "industrial centers of the North", Petrograd and Moscow.[28] In contrast, the existence of a Ukrainian republic, even a soviet one, was perceived as a harmful idea that risked breaking the unity of the economic and cultural bloc inherited from the tsarist era. "We want to join the whole country",[29] insisted the leader of Donets-Kryvyi Rih, Fyodor Sergeev, implying that the whole country was, in essence, the former Romanov Empire and that it was necessary to preserve the integrity of this industrial region as part of the Russian imperial core.

Ultimately, Kyiv Bolsheviks who had found themselves confronting a powerful and organized national movement had begun, in spite of themselves, to see Ukraine as a singular polity. This was not the case for their counterparts in Kharkiv, who faced less direct confrontation from the Ukrainian peasantry while benefiting from the more substantial support of a Russian and Russified workforce. As a result, their respective mental maps did not have to undergo the same process of transformation and cultural realignment. Serafima Hopner, an RSDLP(b) activist in Kateynoslav (now Dnipro), noted that her organization "never recalled" that it was even operating on the territory of Ukraine, perceiving it simply as "the South of Russia". She had subsequently deplored this "most serious political omission" by her party, namely "the ignorance, or rather the complete oblivion regarding the national question", combined with its disregard of peasantry.[30] This confession is symptomatic of the huge imperial blind spot: the two sections of the population whom the Bolsheviks "forgot" when seeking to establish their authority were the same ones whom the former empire had treated as colonized subjects – the peasants and the non-Russians. As progressive as they were in their rhetoric, the Bolsheviks failed to perceive these groups as active subjects instead of objects to be acted upon. By refusing to consider the reality of the peasantry's colonial oppression by the urban-based imperial authorities, which in the Ukrainian case also meant the oppression of an indigenous culture by an imperial one, the Bolsheviks were perpetuating these structural inequalities. Except for a brief period during the mid-1920s, this specific type of "internal" colonialism would remain the persistent feature of Soviet internal politics.

Did Lenin Create Ukraine?

Independent Ukraine was proclaimed on January 22, 1918 by the Central Rada in the context of an armed confrontation with Soviet Russia. Lenin himself had recognized this independence under pressure from Imperial Germany and the other Central Powers, with whom he had recently negotiated a peace agreement at Brest-Litovsk. One of the treaty's key provisions had been the withdrawal of Soviet troops from Ukrainian territory along with the abandonment of Russia's existing territorial claims. In this context, the project of a Soviet Ukraine put forward by the Kyiv Bolsheviks finally found support from the new Russian government, which relocated from Petrograd to Moscow in March 1918. The independence of Soviet Ukraine, which included Kyiv, as well as Kharkiv and Odesa, was proclaimed two weeks after the signing of the peace agreement and gave the local Bolsheviks the opportunity to oppose the armed forces of Germany, Austria-Hungary, and the Central Rada without Soviet Russia being viewed as responsible for their actions. However, the question remains as to why, long after the military defeat of the Ukrainian national forces, the Soviet authorities continued to support the concept of a unitary Ukraine while excluding any possibility for a partition of the Ukrainian political space?

After numerous military defeats, in which the hostility of the local Ukrainian populace played a determining role, the RSDLP(b) became conscious of the power of its social and national aspirations. It soon became apparent that it was not only the mythical *petliurists*[31] but large sectors of the population who were willing to take up arms for the Ukrainian national idea. The Bolsheviks had thus begun to understand that a minimum of respect for Ukrainian sovereignty was not only a useful tool for neutralizing the influence of local nationalists, but a *sine qua non* for the survival of Soviet power, which continued to hold only a precarious sense of legitimacy in those former imperial peripheries where the authority of the central state remained synonymous with colonial oppression. In this respect, the memories of Georgy Lapchynsky are evocative:

> For a long time, even after the proclamation of Ukraine as a soviet republic, some Bolsheviks continued to be followers of a 'theory' according to which a Ukrainian state was a 'fiction' and aimed only at paralyzing the nationalist and petliurist feelings of the petty bourgeoisie. This 'pseudo-internationalism' persisted and was in fact a disguise for Great Russian chauvinism. But no one ever dared to go back and openly oppose the existence of Ukraine as a separate entity.[32]

Thus, even the most intransigent "internationalists" abandoned the idea of partitioning the Ukrainian political space. Instead, they embraced the political map of Ukraine articulated by the Ukrainian national movement; from this point of view, Ukraine consisted of the ethnically Ukrainian lands of which the Donbas was obviously part. By making a concession to the stato-national conception that wanted to match the nation with its territory *de jure*, the Bolsheviks found a way to preserve the *de facto* integrity of the former Russian Empire while also reinforcing their ability to undertake centralized decision-making, guaranteeing the absolute political supremacy of party. It was not therefore the Bolsheviks who "invented" Ukraine: since the end of 1917, Ukraine had imposed itself upon them as a new political reality, including in its territorial dimensions.

Notes

1 Address by the President of the Russian Federation, 21.02.2022, Kremlin.ru: http://en.kremlin.ru/events/president/news/67828.
2 Donbas is a coal basin in eastern Ukraine, a primarily economic region. The use of this term by political actors is often abused and is most often

intended to designate the territory of the Ukrainian oblasts of Donetsk and Luhansk.

3   For example: Pipes, *The Formation of the Soviet Union*; Smith, *The Bolsheviks and the National Question*; Suny, and Martin (eds.) *A State of Nations*; Martin, *The affirmative action empire*; Hirsch, *Empire of Nations*; Smith, *Red Nations*.
4   Friedgut, *Iuzovka and Revolution*; Kuromiya, *Freedom and Terror in the Donbas*.
5   Palko, and Ardeleanu, *Making Ukraine*.
6   Ibid; Rindlisbacher, "From space to Territory".
7   Iefimenko, "Vyznachennia kordonu"; Sluzhyns'ka, "Formuvannia ukraïns'ko-rosiis'koho kordonu".
8   Little Russia was a political and geographical concept, referring mostly to a territory of former Cossack Hetmanate and more generally to the territory and population of modern-day Ukraine. Seen as one of the constituent and subordinate parts of the triune Russian nationality, a Little Russian identity was opposed to Ukrainian identity that insisted on the national distinctiveness of Ukrainians and their equality with Russians.
9   Bilenky, *Romantic Nationalism in Eastern Europe*, p. 81.
10 The governors-general had extraordinary powers, thus compensating for the weakness of the bureaucratic apparatus on the ground. This form of administration was aimed at consolidating tsarist power in the annexed territories.
11 Miller, "The Romanov Empire and the Russian Nation", p. 346.
12 Among the principles that will guide its work, the provisional government indicates "the abolition of all restrictions based on class, religion or nationality". See *Izvestiia*, March 16, 1917. It should be noted that the teaching and publication and Ukrainian language had been prohibited until then.
13 Verstiuk, *Ukraïns'kyi natsional'no-vyzvol'nyi rukh*, pp. 148–154.
14 Krawchenko, *Social Change and National Consciousness*, pp. 1–44.
15 The borders of Ukrainian autonomy claimed by the Ukrainian national movement follow pre-existing administrative boundaries – those of the provinces, even though they were drawn by the tsarist administration in the last century without really taking into account the ethnic composition of the population. For example, Ukrainian peasants constituted the majority of the population in some districts of the neighboring provinces of Voronezh, Kursk or even Grodno. In perspective, referendums were to be held to let the local population choose whether to join the Ukrainian autonomy or to keep the old administrative divisions. On the other hand,

the Central Rada claimed only the mainland part of the Tavria province, considering the Crimean Peninsula as an ethnic territory of the Crimean Tatars, potential allies in the struggle for national emancipation of the non-Russian peoples of the empire.

16   Heorhii Lapchyns'kyi, "Z pershykh dniv vseukraïns'koï radians'koï vlady," *Litopys revoliutsiï*, 5–6 (1927), pp. 48–49.
17   "Oblastnoi s"ezd RSDRP(b). I Vseukrainskoe soveshchanie bol'shevikov. Protokoly," *Letopis' revoliutsii* 5 (1926), p.76.
18   Zatons'kyi, Volodymyr. "Uryvky zi spohadiv pro ukraïns'ku revoliutsiiu," *Litopys revoliutsiï* 4 (1929), p. 141.
19   Lapchyns'kyi, "Z pershykh dniv", p. 49.
20   Zatons'kyi, "Uryvky zi spohadiv", p. 140.
21   Lapchyns'kyi, "Z pershykh dniv", p. 62.
22   *Proletarskaia mysl'*, November 9, 1917.
23   Lapchyns'kyi, "Z pershykh dniv", p. 48.
24   Zamkovoi, Valentin et al. *Bol'shevistskie organizatsii Ukrainy v period ustanovleniia i ukrepleniia Sovetskoi vlasti (noiabr' 1917 – aprel' 1918 gg.): sbornik dokumentov* (Kyiv: Gosudarstvennoe izdatel'stvo politicheskoï literatury USSR, 1962), p. 21.
25   Zatons'kyi, "Uryvky zi spohadiv", p. 163.
26   *Donetskii proletarii*, January 31, 1918.
27   I translated *Donetsko-Krivorozhskaia Respublika* as the Donets-Kryvyi Rih Republic (and not as *Donetsk-Kryvyi Rih*). The adjective "donetskii" here refers to the region of the Donets River basin, not to the city of Donetsk.
28   Myshkis, Khaia. "Materialy o Donetsko-Krivorozhskoi Respublike," *Letopis' revoliutsii* 3 (1928), p. 256.
29   *Donetskii proletarii*, January 31, 1918.
30   Serafima Gopner, "Bol'shevistskaia organizatsiia nakanune i v pervyi period fevral'skoi revoliutsii v Ekaterinoslave," *Letopis' Revoliutsii* 2 (1927), pp. 28–29.
31   Symon Petliura – Commander-in-Chief of the Army and President of the Ukrainian People's Republic (1918–1920), opponent of the Red Army during the Civil War.
32   Lapchyns'kyi, "Z pershykh dniv", p. 51.

Selected Bibliography

Bilenky, Serhiy. *Romantic Nationalism in Eastern Europe: Russian, Polish, and Ukrainian Political Imaginations* (Stanford, CA: Stanford University Press, 2012).

Friedgut, Theodore H. *Iuzovka and Revolution, Volume II: Politics and Revolution in Russia's Donbass, 1869–1924* (Princeton: Princeton University Press, 1994).

Hirsch, Francine. *Empire of Nations. Ethnographic Knowledge and the Making of the Soviet Union* (Ithaca: Cornell University Press, 2005).

Iefimenko, Hennadii. "Vyznachennia kordonu mizh USRR ta RSFRR (1917–1920)". In: *Problemy istoriï Ukraïny: fakty, sudzhennia, poshuky* 20 (2011): 135–176.

Krawchenko, Bohdan. *Social Change and National Consciousness in Twentieth-Century Ukraine* (Basingstoke: Macmillan Press, 1985).

Kuromiya, Hiroaki. *Freedom and Terror in the Donbas: A Ukrainian-Russian Borderland, 1870s–1990s* (Cambridge: Cambridge University Press, 1998).

Martin, Terry. *The Affirmative Action Empire. Nations and Nationalism in the Soviet Union, 1923–1939* (Ithaca: Cornell University Press, 2001).

Miller, Alexei. "The Romanov Empire and the Russian Nation". In: Berger, Stephan/Alexei Miller (eds.) *Nationalizing Empires* (Budapest–New York: Central European University Press, 2015).

Palko, Olena, and Constantin Ardeleanu (eds.) *Making Ukraine. Negotiating, Contesting and Drawing the Borders in the Twentieth Century* (Montreal; Kingston: McGill-Queen's University Press, 2022).

Pipes, Richard. *The Formation of the Soviet Union: Communism and Nationalism, 1917–1923* (Cambridge, Mass.: Harvard University Press, 1964).

Rindlisbacher, Stephan. "From Space to Territory: Negotiating the Russo-Ukrainian Border, 1919–1928," *Revolutionary Russia* 31:1 (2018): 86–106.

Sluzhyns'ka, Ivanna. "Formuvannia ukraïns'ko-rosiis'koho kordonu: dyskusiï i politychni rishennia 20-kh rokiv XX stolittia," in Smolii, Valerii (ed.), *Rehional'naia istoriia Ukraïny. Zbirnyk naukovykh statei*, 7 (2013): 115–126 (Kyiv: Instytut istoriï Ukraïny NAN Ukraïny, 2013).

Smith, Jeremy. *The Bolsheviks and the National Question, 1917–1923* (New York: St. Martin's Press, 1999).

Smith, Jeremy. *Red Nations: The Nationalities Experience in and after the USSR* (Cambridge: Cambridge University Press, 2013).

Suny, Ronald Grigor, and Terry Martin. *A State of Nations: Empire and Nation-Making in the Age of Lenin and Stalin* (Oxford: Oxford University Press, 2001).

Verstiuk, Volodymyr et al. (eds.) *Ukraïns'kyi natsional'no-vyzvol'nyi rukh. Berezen'–lystopad 1917 roku: Dokumenty i materialy* (Kyiv: Vydavnytstvo imeni Oleny Telihy, 2003).

The Territory of Ukraine and Its History

Stephan Rindlisbacher

This short chapter explores the history of modern Ukraine's border-making process from two perspectives: as a matter of foreign policy and as an issue in domestic politics. Indeed, the borders of contemporary Ukraine were ultimately a result of the two world wars, and the great-power negotiations that occurred amidst both global conflicts. However, of equal importance were the internal debates between political elites in the neighbouring Soviet republics. Ukraine's borders thus reflect the broader history of Eastern Europe between 1917 and 1954.

In the chaotic aftermath of the First World War, the Bolsheviks attempted to export their revolution to the wider world. With the help of Ukrainian communists, they created a satellite state in the south, the Ukrainian Soviet Socialist Republic (UkrSSR). At the beginning of 1919, the Russian Socialist Federative Soviet Republic (RSFSR) entered official negotiations with the Soviet Ukrainian government, resulting in a series of border agreements that delineated the territory of Soviet Ukraine according to the pre-existing boundaries of the former Russian Empire's Ukrainian-speaking provinces.

Following a prolonged struggle, Soviet forces eventually prevailed in eastern and central Ukraine. The unfavourable outcome of the war with the neighbouring Republic of Poland, however, led to the Treaty of Riga in March 1921, which saw the UkrSSR secede Galicia and West Volhynia with their Ukrainian-speaking majority. Moreover, while the north-western border with Poland was internationally recognized, the southwestern boundary with Romania remained disputed owing to the latter having occupied and unilaterally annexed Bessarabia during the Russian Civil War. The Soviet-Polish War also saw the first intra-Soviet change of territory in April 1920, with the western parts of the Territory of the Don Army (*Oblast' Voiska Donskogo*) being transferred to Soviet Ukraine. This reshuffling of borders was designed to ensure that the industry of the Donbas (*Donets'kyi basein*) would be managed from a single Soviet republic in order to better coordinate the war effort against Poland.

Border Agreements in the Back Rooms of the Party and State Leadership

The Soviet state with its one-party rule had a distinct power structure. Although the party leadership could order its members in the various state offices to obey direct orders above, the frequent absence of such diktats meant republican and regional politicians often enjoyed a significant degree of agency. Within the Soviet framework, territorial issues were one of the fields where state and party activists could legitimately compete and negotiate if a specific party directive was not already in place. Territorial changes thus often appeared to be open to negotiation, especially in the case of the South Caucasus and Central Asia and the border between the UkrSSR and the RSFSR.

Conversely, party leaders from the RSFSR's North Caucasus region (*Severokavkazskii krai*) had remained unhappy over the transfer of the Donbas industry in 1920. They saw their economic position weakened and thus demanded the port town of Taganrog and the coal mines of Shakhty from Soviet Ukraine. This claim was justified in relation to need to develop the economy of the North Caucasus. On the other hand, representatives of the Ukrainian State Planning Commission and the Ukrainian state administration wanted to correct the border of Ukraine in the north and east in their favour. In addition to this region having a majority Ukrainian population, the need to unify the border area's pre-existing sugar production industry served as a supplementary argument for the Ukrainian side who, like the representatives of the North Caucasus, hoped to improve the economic basis of their home republic.

At the beginning of 1924, the Belarusian Republic was granted a sizable amount of territory that had previously been part of the RSFSR, an act that Ukrainian party representatives interpreted as evidence that the general political mood had sifted in their favour. In April that year, a bilateral UkrSSR-RSFSR border revision commission was formed with Aleksandr Cherviakov, the then head of the Belarusian Republic, appointed as chairman, a role that required him to play the part of nationally unbiased arbitrator. The Ukrainians entered these negotiations with great expectations with their demands extending to parts of the provinces of Kursk, Briansk and Voronezh. In total, these Ukrainian claims included 32.500 square versts (about 37.000 km²) with almost 2 million inhabitants, of which, according to Ukrainian statistics, 65 per cent were Ukrainian-speaking and 35 per cent Russian-speaking.

In mid-July 1924, the Ukrainian side suffered its first bitter political defeat. The Politburo of the Communist Party in Moscow, the supreme ruling body of the Soviet state, decided that parts of eastern Ukraine around the city of Taganrog, as well as parts of the Shakhty, should be incorporated into the RSFSR, illustrating the Politburo's accommodation of the North Caucasus leadership's demands. These were parts of the territories that had only been transferred from the RSFSR to Soviet Ukraine in 1920 with this re-revision being partly justified by the fact that the North Caucasus needed access to a deep seaport and the region was predominantly Russian speaking. The UkrSSR's representatives protested in vain.

At the same time, however, the two RSFSR delegates in the border revision commission had also received instructions from the party leadership that the Ukrainian side should be accommodated wherever the "interests of the RSFSR are not directly affected." Thus, they were advocating for the transfer of the Putyvl county (*uezd*) in the southwest of the Kursk Region to the UkrSSR; the area itself formed a virtual enclave of the RSFSR within Ukrainian territory despite its economy being closely linked to the neighbouring Ukrainian-populated regions. Although the county itself had a majority Russian-speaking population, in this instance it did not matter.

With Cherviakov serving as a decisive influence, the commission opted in favour of the Ukrainian plan that proposed the transfer of the larger territories in the north from the RSFSR. This political decision was similar to the territorial support for Belarus prior in 1924 with the linguistic and economic boundaries better matching the situation on the ground. While sugar production would be under the full direction of Soviet Ukraine, Kursk and Voronezh provinces would still lose crucial economic assets.

However, only a few days later, the politburo intervened again, rejecting any larger territorial revisions in favour of the UkrSSR, arguing that the border revision should only include minor territorial changes. In the end, Ukraine "gained" about 6000 km² inhabited by approximately 300,000 people. This was far less than the 13,000 km² and 500,000 inhabitants, Ukraine had "lost" following the transfer of the territories around Shakhty and Taganrog in the southeast.

Fig. 2–1: The formation of the Russo-Ukrainian border between 1919 and 1928. Courtesy of Stephan Rindlisbacher.

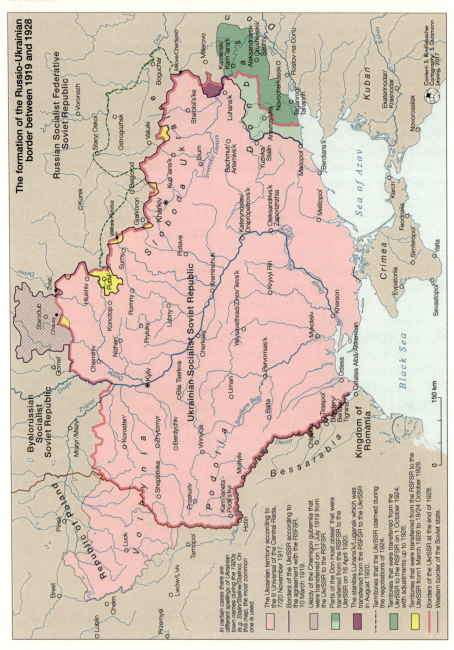

With the politburo's ultimate verdict at the end of 1924, the main lines for the prospective border between the UkrSSR and the RSFSR were set. However, additional fine-tuning took a considerably longer time. At the request of local inhabitants, the beginning of 1925 also marked the start of a series of minor adjustments that attempted to adjust the new boundary in favour of both Soviet republics. However, some cases continued to be disputed.

When Ukrainian intellectuals raised the issue of this unsatisfactory demarcation between the UkrSSR and the RSFSR during a debate with Joseph Stalin in February 1929, the Soviet leader was initially reluctant to address their concerns. However, on being pressed over the issue by his guests, Stalin eventually relented and informed them that: "We have discussed [the border question] several times; but we change borders too often [...]. Far too often we move the borders – this creates a bad impression both inside and outside our country."[1] In doing so, he effectively articulated the general line that would be used when dealing with border issues in the near future, viewing any changes to the Soviet Union's internal borders as nationalistic quarrels that would only lead to conflict while hindering socialist construction and industrialization. As a result, individuals or groups calling for intra-Soviet territorial revisions had to reckon with repression. Consequently, the limited debate and competition around territorial issues among state and party actors was, for a time, brought to an end.

Western Expansion in the Course of the Second World War

In the end, however, Stalin's later foreign policy meant that the borders of Soviet Ukraine did not remain stable. Territorial annexations in the west at the end of 1939 were a direct result of Soviet expansionism in co-operation with Nazi Germany. Shortly before the German attack on Poland, the ideological arch-rivals Hitler and Stalin had come to an agreement, in a secret additional protocol to the Non-Aggression Pact, regarding their countries' respective sphere of interest. Finland, the Baltic states, and eastern Poland, as well as Bessarabia fell into the orbit of the Soviet Union. On September 17th, as the German *Wehrmacht* besieged the now isolated Warsaw, the Red Army invaded eastern Poland. Following a series of staged plebiscites, Eastern Galicia and Volhynia were annexed by the UkrSSR. At first, Soviet forces were welcomed by parts of the population, but this was soon to change due to the imposition of Stalinist policies on society and the local economy.

In June 1940, following the Third Reich's occupation of France, the Soviet government finally called on Romania to cede Bessarabia together with North Bukovina. Faced with the threat of war and the loss of its French ally, the Romanian government acquiesced to Soviet pressure. About two thirds of the former Romanian territories subsequently formed the Moldovan SSR, while the remaining third was annexed by the UkrSSR. Soon after, minor territories alongside the Dniester River were also transferred from the UkrSSR to the Moldovan SSR.

In these newly annexed territories, the Soviet government ordered the rapid collectivization of agriculture with peasant resistance being met with state terror, particularly in western Ukraine. Consequently, German and Romanian troops were also initially welcomed follow the Axis invasion of the Soviet Union in 1941 with local Ukrainian peasants tending to lend their support to Nazi Germany against the Soviets. However, since the German leadership rejected a Ukrainian nation-state, Ukrainian nationalist co-operation soon dissipated. Following the reconquest by the Red Army in 1944, resistance to Soviet power in these western Ukrainian regions was especially well organized and fierce. The territory itself was not fully pacified until well into the 1950s with the guerrilla war in western Ukraine remaining a taboo subject for decades.

In the west, Carpathian Ruthenia also became part of Ukraine in 1945, an area that had previously experienced three changes of rule within 27 years. Until 1918, it had been part of the Hungarian portion of the Habsburg Monarchy before being transferred to the newly established Czechoslovak Republic. During its prolonged dismemberment from 1938 to 1939, however, a significant part of Carpathian Ruthenia was annexed by Hungary. However, with the Axis' defeat in 1945, the Soviet Union then claimed this area for itself leading to its subsequent occupation by the Red Army. The Soviet leadership subjected the region to a special border regime, which severely restricted the inhabitants' freedom of movement. Moreover, although its eastern Slavic-speaking population saw themselves as *rusyny* or *rus'ki*, the Soviet authorities officially defined them as part of the Ukrainian nation. Despite the regime's efforts to weaken traditional identities, the region has therefore maintained a distinct cultural and linguistic position within Ukraine.

A final territorial change in the west of the UkrSSR occurred in 1951 when the Soviet Union and the People's Republic of Poland "exchanged" some 500 km². In the area around the Polish border town of Bełz (today Belz), a coal field had previously been discovered. The Soviet Union wanted to exploit this resource, offering Poland the hilly and war-ravaged region around Ustrzyki Dolne. The Polish government ultimately had to accept this unfavourable deal.

The town of Ustrzyki Dolne itself can be regarded as an example of the brutal population change that took place Eastern Europe during and after the Second World War. In the interwar period, the mixed Jewish-Polish-Lemko shtetl had been part of Poland. Many of its Polish residents were deported after the Soviet occupation in 1939, while the Jewish inhabitants had been sent by the Nazis to the extermination camps. In 1947, the remaining Lemko inhabitants were expelled to Poland by the Soviets. When the area became part of Poland once again in 1951, it was almost deserted.

Crimea and its Historical Belonging

Since the dramatic events of 2014, Crimea has drawn extensive international attention. During the interwar period, the peninsula's territorial affiliation hardly played a role in the intra-Soviet debates on border revisions. At that time, it was characterized by an ethnically heterogeneous population. According to the 1937 census, around 45 per cent of this were Russians, 20 per cent Crimean Tatars, 13 per cent Ukrainians, 5 per cent Jews, and 5 per cent Germans. Additionally, the peninsula also featured small communities of Armenian, Greek and Bulgarian settlers. The Second World War not only brought widespread devastation, but also culminated in a dramatic process of ethnic un-mixing, comparable to what had transpired in Ustrzyki Dolne. During the war itself, many of the peninsula's Jews fell victim to the Holocaust. Following its liberation, the Soviets accused local Germans and Crimean Tatars of having collaborated with the Third Reich and deported these communities to Central Asia. As a result, from 1945 to 1991, the remaining population of Crimea consisted mainly of Russians and Ukrainians.

Ruined and depopulated, the peninsula faced tremendous challenges after 1945 with the most burning economic problem being seasonal drought. However, at the beginning of the 1950s, the State Planning Authority, *Gosplan*, launched a major development project to ensure the irrigation of Crimea. By building a canal several hundred kilometres long, water from the Dnieper River would allow the dry soils of the peninsula to bloom. Advertising brochures even boasted that the canal would make Crimea a "land of plenty". Economically and administratively, it therefore seemed reasonable to transfer the peninsula from the RSFSR to the UkrSSR.

With Stalin's death in 1953, his order that no further internal territorial transfers should take place were quietly dropped, prompting fresh rounds of revisions between the Union Republics. This was further prompted by the increasingly decentralized nature of economic planning with the republics regaining ever more control from Moscow. Against this background, the Supreme Soviet decided in February 1954 to transfer Crimea to Ukraine. In their explanatory statement, state and party leaders pointed to its economic prospects with Kliment Voroshilov, among others, emphasizing that "such a just solution of territorial questions among the republics is only possible under the conditions specific to the Soviet Union. This solution is grounded in economic efficiency and based on the full consent and fraternal cooperation of Soviet peoples."[2] In the press reports as well as in the decision of the Supreme Soviet, the transfer of Crimea was presented as having been solely a matter of economic efficiency and not as kind of "gift" to Ukraine.

After 1954, Crimea's infrastructure became more and more linked to the UkrSSR with pipelines, canals, and electric power grids supplying the peninsula with energy and water from rest of the Republic. The North Crimean Canal, formerly completed in 1976, was a notable example, allowing for extensive agriculture on the peninsula and illustrating the extent to which both Crimea and the Ukrainian mainland could benefit from each other.

The period 1919 to 1954 was crucial to the formation of the Ukrainian state in the sense of territoriality. As this chapter has highlighted, this was ultimately the result of a series of complex negotiations that covered its north, east, and southern boundaries as well as a consequence of westward Soviet expansion during and after the Second World War.

With the collapse of the Soviet Union, Ukraine gained its independence in 1991 with its internationally recognized borders corresponding to those of Soviet Ukraine after 1954. Ukraine's territorial integrity was guaranteed by Russia, the United States, and the United Kingdom by the 1994 Budapest Memorandum in return for Ukraine's renunciation of nuclear weaponry. In the 2000s and early 2010s, Ukraine and Russia also agreed to accurately map and mark a common border, seemingly resolving any future issues between the two for good. In addition, in 2010, the government of Viktor Yanukovych extended the leases for the Russian naval base at Sevastopol' by a further 25 years.

The Russian government saw its geopolitical interests threatened with the violent change of government in Kiev in the spring of 2014. With the stroke of a pen, it ignored the many previous diplomatic guarantees by invading and annexing Crimea and supporting the secessionist republics in eastern Ukraine.

In the case of Crimea and Donbas, since 2014 the war had devastating consequences for both sides. For instance, Ukrainian authorities blocked the North-Crimean Canal and the water access to the peninsula. Crimea is dependent on supplies by sea or via the Kerch-strait-bridge, which had opened in May 2018. Nevertheless, the peninsula suffered heavily from severe water shortages while the coal and steel industries in the Donbas subsequently underwent rapid decline.

After the all-out Russian invasion in February 2022, one of the first things Russian troops did was move to secure the North Crimean Canal's access to the Dnieper River and attempt to redirect the supply of water to the peninsula. Thus, the struggle for control over water and access to industrial assets – or in a broader sense economic issues – would continue to play a significant role in the Russian Federation's endgame.

Notes

1 Stenograph of Stalin's meeting with Ukrainian writers, February 12, 1929, in: *RGASPI*, f. 558, op. 1, d. 4490, l. 19; Leonid Maximenkov, "Stalin's Meeting with a Delegation of Ukrainian Writers on 12 February 1929," *Harvard Ukrainian Studies*, 16:3/4 (1992): 361-431.
2 Kliment Voroshilov, "Address to the Supreme Soviet, February 19," *Pravda*, 27 February 1954, p. 2.

Selected Bibliography

Eschment, Beate and Sabine v. Löwis (eds.) *Post-Soviet Borders: A Kaleidoscope of Shifting Lives and Lands* (London/New York: Routledge, 2022).
Gross, Jan Tomasz. *Revolution from Abroad: The Soviet Conquest of Poland's Western Ukraine and Western Belorussia* (Princeton: Princeton University Press, 2002).
Hirsch, Francine. *Empire of Nations: Ethnographic Knowledge and the Making of the Soviet Union* (Ithaca: Cornell University Press, 2005).
Iefimenko, Hennadii. "Vyznachennia kordonu mizh USSR ta RSFRR," *Problemy istoriï Ukraïny* 20 (2011): 135–176.

Magocsi, Paul R, *With their Backs to the Mountains: A history of Carpathian Rus' and Carpatho-Rusyns* (Budapest/New York: Central European University Press, 2015).

Martin, Terry. *The Affirmative Action Empire: Nations and Nationalism in the Soviet Union, 1923–1939* (Ithaca: Cornell University Press, 2001).

Palko, Olena and Ardeleanu, Constantin (eds.) *Making Ukraine: Negotiating, Contesting and Drawing the Borders in the Twentieth Century* (Montreal: McGill-Queen's University Press, 2022).

Rindlisbacher, Stephan. "From Space to Territory: Negotiating the Russo-Ukrainian Border, 1919–1928," *Revolutionary Russia*, 31:1 (2018): 86–106.

Sasse, Gwendolyn. *The Crimea Question: Identity, Transition, and Conflict* (Cambridge, Mass.: Harvard University Press, 2007).

Constructing Ethnic Identities in Early Soviet Ukraine

Olena Palko and Roman Korshuk

Following the collapse of the Habsburg, Ottoman, and Russian empires, thousands of disparate communities suddenly discovered that they now existed as minorities, often in areas adjacent to their internationally designated homelands. The rights of these various minorities within the borders of the new nation-states were recognised and remained officially under the protection of the League of Nations, from its founding in 1920, to its replacing by the United Nations in 1946. The newly proclaimed Soviet Union, however, did not become a member of the League until 1934, meaning that minorities in this ethnographically diverse area effectively became subject to its domestic and foreign policy considerations. Throughout the 1920s, the Soviet leadership strove to conduct a national minority policy, which would appear to be more generous than the minority treaty requirements, imposed by the League of Nations upon the imperial successor states of central and eastern Europe. In a way, one can say that the Soviet Union in the 1920s developed its policies *vis-à-vis* its western neighbours, particularly Poland, Czechoslovakia, and Romania. In their interwar forms, these three countries possessed large Ukrainian and Belarusian communities, whose sentiments and grievances Soviet leaders wished to use against their respective governments. While Poland, for instance, strove for homogenization and opposed granting its minorities national-cultural rights, the Soviet Union not only declared ethnicity, or rather "nationality" (*natsional'nost'*) as it was called in Soviet discourse, to be a fundamental social category, but also presented ethnic heterogeneity as one of the defining features of Soviet society.

The Soviet Minorities Experiment

The Soviet Union, founded in late December 1922, presided over an extraordinarily diverse population. At the beginning of the 1920s, the Bolsheviks had declared their intention to achieve socialism and national minorities were to play an equal part in the process of its construction. For the first time in history, nationality, or ethnicity (*narodnost'*), became a legally defined category and formed the basis for the administrative (as well as economic) organisation of the new Soviet state. While the 1897 imperial Russian census had offered no direct question on nationality, with imperial demographers defined the ethnic make-up of the empire through a combination of questions on native language, religion and social estate (*soslovie*), the category of *narodnost'* became the key determinant for the first Soviet census of 1926. Moreover, unlike in 1897, the 1926 census was based on presenting nationality as subjective self-determination. As recorded in the survey, 80 per cent of respondents in Soviet Ukraine gave Ukrainian as their nationality, 9.23 identified as Russian, 5.43 as Jewish, 1.64 as Polish, and 1.36 as German. Less numerous were Moldovans, Greeks, Bulgarians, Belarusians, Czechs, Tatars, Gipsies, and Armenians.

Ronald G. Suny and Terry Martin define the 1920s as "the great era of the territorialization of ethnicity" whereby each nationality, no matter how numerically small, was granted the possibility of self-rule in its native language, which extended downward into smaller and smaller territories, the smallest being the size of a single village.[1] Overall, during the 1920s, ethnicity became territorially institutionalized, meaning that every Soviet nationality was provided with a territory of their own, either in the form of a separate, or an autonomous, Soviet republic, national region, or a separate national town or village council (*soviet*).

Soviet Ukraine was the first Soviet republic to implement this reform. This was launched on August 29 1924, by the Council of People's Commissars' (or *Radnarkom*'s) decree "On the formation of national districts and soviets", which resulted in the creation of an intricate system of village soviets (*silski rady*, or *silrady*) throughout Ukraine, the boundaries between which were determined by the ethnic composition of those communities. As Martin notes, the aim of this reform was to create "a maximum possible number of national soviets, which would include in each soviet the maximum possible percentage of each national minority."[2]

By 1929, there were 26 national districts in Ukraine, of which nine were Russian, seven German, four Bulgarian, three Greek, one Polish, and two Jewish. In addition, 1089 national village soviets and 107 town soviets were also established, including some which were formed for the benefit of the territories considerably smaller Swedish and Albanian minorities. Within these national-territorial units, the Soviet state strove to provide access to state institutions, political representation, police and judicial protection, health care, and educational and cultural opportunities delivered in the respective minority language. Moreover, for those individuals of minority origin residing beyond their respective national-territorial units, the state pledged to provide non-territorial autonomy with similar access to services in minority languages and guarantee national rights.

It is not accidental that Ukraine was the first republic to implement this experiment, and later serve as a blueprint for the other Soviet republics. With its multi-ethnic and multi-confessional character, proximity to the western border and previous experience of national movements – both for the Ukrainians and other minorities – Soviet Ukraine was perhaps the only republic in which the wider Union's domestic and foreign concerns mutated and reinforced each other. The generous treatment afforded to both Ukrainians and the so-called western minorities, particularly Poles and Germans, was not only meant to encourage these communities to engage with the rest of Soviet society, but also provide a mechanism to undermine the governments and anti-Soviet propaganda of neighbouring countries.

After Russians and Jews, Poles constituted the largest minority group in Soviet Ukraine. In fact, Ukraine was home to almost half of the Soviet Union's entire Polish population – 476.435 Poles to be precise, most of whom were concentrated in the western provinces of Volhynia, Podolia, and Kyiv. There, as elsewhere in Ukraine, Poles were organized into national soviets; by 1929, 148 Polish national village soviets had been created across Ukraine. In places where the settlement of national minorities had been more concentrated, the creation of separate national regions was also envisaged. Following the official decree of 1922, the first and only Polish national region in Soviet Ukraine was founded in Volhynia province (*okruh*) in 1925, some 120 km east of the Polish border. This new district occupied an area of 650 km^2 with 42,161 inhabitants, out of which 68.9 per cent were recorded as Poles. The centre of this Polish region was in Dovbysh, renamed as Markhlevsk to commemorate the late Polish Bolshevik leader Julian Marchlewski.

The Polish region was established in what was still a socioeconomically backward area; it was far from the railway lines and was still unconnected to the telephone or telegraphy network. The only industry was a ceramics factory, opened in 1840, that had resumed production in 1922. By 1925, the area's population was predominantly peasant, who represented 92 per cent of the total; literacy was low (47 per cent for men and 37 per cent for women); while only 4 per cent of households had been collectivised – the lowest out of all the national units. Within this new administrative unit, Poles received territorial and cultural autonomy with Roman Catholics being permitted to continue their traditional religious practices, albeit under strict party supervision. The region could also boast its own newspaper, *Marchlewszczyzna Radziecka* (*Soviet Marchlewszczyzna*). Moreover, the district had preferential access to state funding to allow for the accelerated modernisation of the region and its population.[3]

The Criteria for Ethnicity

In the historical region of Right-Bank Ukraine – the area with the largest Soviet Polish population– local identities were complex, with entangled language, culture, and religious practices. Unlike the Poles, Ukraine's other minority groups were easier to differentiate: Jews were defined by religion and the common experience of restricted movement; Greeks and Bulgarians by the compact nature of their settlements in the south, and obvious linguistic distinctions; and Germans who, despite being organized around different religious groups and vernaculars, enjoyed a special autonomous status until the 1880s that made them more "recognisable" in cultural and social terms.

By contrast, Poles appeared more ambiguous. Indeed, identities in Western Ukraine were so entangled that it became almost impossible to differentiate a Ukrainian from a Pole. It should be mentioned that this region, prior to the third partition of the Polish-Lithuanian Commonwealth in 1795, had formerly belonged to Poland. Historically, the Polish elites had never stopped opposing the Russian imperial administration, resulting in two major revolts from 1830 to 1831 and 1863 to 1864, which also had found purchase with the local Ukrainian population under the slogan "Our freedom and yours". The imperial administration responded with repressive measures against the Polish population – there were no Polish schools, the use of the Polish language was prohibited. This resulted in the assimilation of the Polish population, with many families switching to Ukrainian or used the mixture of the two.

The imperial legacy posed a great challenge to the Bolsheviks' plans. As demonstrated by the official 1925 inspection of the Polish population in Volhynia region, in Koshelivka village soviet all Catholics regarded themselves as 'Poles', although 70 per cent of them used Ukrainian for everyday communication, whereas in the neighbouring village Baliarka, only 5 per cent used Polish.[4] When asked why people would use Ukrainian instead, some responded that it was a habit and that they did not know that "such freedom for the Polish language existed".[5] Moreover, the same party inspection found that the local population could not differentiate between religion and nationality, with all Catholics being regarded simply as "Poles". For example, in the village of Gorodyshche, in Shepetivka *okruh* only 5 per cent of population could tell *natsional'nost'* from religion, or being Polish from being a Roman Catholic.

The biggest challenge, however, was posed by those "in the middle": the Ukrainian Catholics.[6] For this group, national identity mattered since, depending on classification, they were to be subjected either to Soviet Ukrainization policies (as a titular Ukrainian nation) or the alternative minority policies (as Poles). For the Ukrainian lobby, Ukrainian Catholics were "Polonized by the Catholic Church Ukrainians",[7] whereas for the Polish lobby they were Poles who had been assimilated under the tsarist autocracy.[8] Unfortunately, in the case of Soviet statisticians, these people of ambiguous identity could not exist in two categories at the same time. In this debate, the minority specialists had won. It is safe to suggest that the increase in the number of Poles in Ukraine was due to the re-categorization of those Ukrainian Catholics. In the case of one particular village, Stara Syniava, this change was startling, shifting from 20 Poles and 2006 Ukrainian Catholics in 1924, to 2325 Poles and no Ukrainians in 1925.[9]

As explained by the party officials, before people were afraid of their identity, but "now the Polish population is flourishing thanks to our nationality politics, and the number [in 1925] is 309.800 Poles, 22 per cent of whom are definitely Poles", the latter point referring to those who spoke the Polish language.[10] Consequently, minority specialists worked tirelessly to promote Polish and teach their native language to those categorised as Poles. As mentioned, there were Polish-language schools, reading huts and literacy rooms as well as crash language courses for governmental employees. Pedagogical institutes were also created to prepare teachers and educators while publication in Polish was prioritised.

Motives Behind Ethnic Identification

In the Soviet context, the minority question was particularly sensitive. By reaching out to minorities, Soviet leaders pursued a number of objectives, most pressingly the need to consolidate Soviet rule in ethnically diverse, non-Russian provinces. The arduous experience of the Russian Civil War on the imperial frontiers had itself raised the question of a need for cooperation with local populations. Instead of alienating, or even annihilating, non-Russian elites, the Bolsheviks sought to gain their trust and make them eager contributors to the project of building socialism. In terms of "small western minorities", such as Germans or Poles, there was also an urgent need to shift their loyalties, especially given the support they offered to their kin states during the German occupation of Ukraine in 1918, and the territory's brief occupation by a newly restored Poland in 1920.

To engage minorities in the Soviet state-building project, however, the party needed to overcome a century-long legacy of distrust in central (read: Russian) institutions. As highlighted by Joseph Stalin, in order to make Soviet power "near and dear to the masses of the border regions of Russia", it was necessary to integrate "all the best local people" into the new administration, since "the masses should see that the Soviet power and its organs are the products of their own efforts, the embodiment of their aspirations".[11] The use of native languages was viewed as easing this process of political socialization.

In addition, the war and revolution had left the country devastated. The economy, already damaged through the exertions of the war effort, was ruined. "War Communism" – an emergency economic programme aimed at assisting the Bolshevik military campaign by the nationalization of industries, compulsory labor conscription, and forced grain requisitioning – had only exacerbated the chaos. To fulfil their vision of progress, the Bolsheviks were in dire need of a modernization drive for the country as a whole. However, the modernization of the more backward regions meant standardization and reordering their populations into national categories.

This preferential treatment of minorities had a broader implication. The central party leadership did not stop treating "western national minorities", such as Poles or Germans, with suspicion, especially given the widespread fear of another Polish invasion in the late 1920s. As a consequence, these minorities continued to be closely monitored by the Soviet secret services, which, in turn, reported regularly on the influence that the Polish government continued to exercise over their Soviet co-nationals mainly through their diplomatic services and religious leaders. To prevent minority communities from siding with their 'home' states, the party sought to reduce national discontent, and thereby the potential influence of neighbouring governments in the case of a future war. Particular emphasis was made on poor and middle-income peasants – that constituted the majority of the Polish minority population – who could benefit most from the Soviet modernisation effort.

While fear of foreign invasion was a dominant security concern of the day, an ostentatiously generous treatment of minorities could also provide a positive outlook for the Soviet Union internationally, helping to spread Communism beyond its western borders. In fact, every opportunity was used to contrast the Soviet preferential treatment of its minorities to the assimilatory policies of the Second Polish Republic. At the fifth anniversary of the Polish Markhlevsk region's founding in 1930, Jan Saulevich, the vice director of the Ukrainian Commission of National Minority Affairs, explained that the Polish Region served as an example for workers and peasants just across the border that a proletarian society based on Polish culture was indeed possible. As he elucidated further:

> Situated in the Polish-Ukrainian borderland, the Polish district is a living example of how different the policies in capitalist Poland are; it serves as a constant reminder of the political persecutions of the Ukrainians and Belarusians in Poland; the establishment of the district became one of the main factors to draw and engage the Polish peasant masses into building of socialism, gaining their devotion to the common cause of the Motherland of all the workers – the Soviet Union.[12]

Unravelling the Soviet Dilemma

The Soviet minority experiment was meant to solve the nationality problem once and for all; instead, it created a strong link between ethnic identity, administrative control over territory, access to state funding and, most importantly, land ownership. Thus, the programme only exacerbated existing ethnic tensions. Within less than a decade, the Soviet authorities would come to abandon its strategy of ethnic proliferation and instead start using those state-imposed national categories against their bearers, subjecting entire minority populations to russification and assimilation, ethnic terror, and deportations.

Already on March 5, 1930, the Party Central Committee authorized the deportation of 3000 kulak families from Belorussia and another 15.000 from Ukraine, with the added stipulation being "In the first line, those of Polish nationality."[13] This was followed by the deportation of some 10.000–15.000 Poles from the border regions to mainland Ukraine in 1935–36. A year later, the first wave of Poles from the Zhytomyr and Podolia regions, 36.045 in total, were deported to Kazakhstan.[14] In the wake of the Great Terror, these deportations of ethnic populations intensified and were often accompanied by mass executions. In total, between 1937 and 1938, almost 140.000 Soviet Poles were arrested, of whom 111.000 were executed.[15] Parallel to this, in the so-called "German operation", almost 57.000 ethnic Germans were arrested, of whom almost 42.000 were shot.[16] Both the Polish and German operations provided a model for other national operations organized by the central government. Among them were the Korean, Chinese, Afghan, Iranian, Greek, Bulgarian-Macedonian, Finnish, and Estonian operations.

During the Great Terror, about one-third of the total victims, or 800.000 people, were arrested, deported, or executed on national grounds. These purges escalated even further with the Soviet Union's entry into the Second World War. Almost 82 per cent of Soviet Germans, for example, were deported. Other great waves of deportations unfolded in the southern regions from November 1943 to June 1944, and between July and December 1944, that involved Chechens, Ingush, Crimean Tatars, and at least ten other groups. Following the war's conclusion, yet another round of purges affected populations in the western borderlands, especially in the re-annexed Baltic republics, and newly incorporated Western Ukraine and Belarus.

Scholars have for some time been puzzled by this historical dilemma of the simultaneous promotion and destruction of national identities within the Soviet context. In his seminal work, *Magnetic Mountain*, published in 1995, Stephen Kotkin proposed the view that Stalinism represented its own form of civilisation, being a "progressive modernity".[17] Those scholars who have followed this interpretation, regarded Stalinism as an "Enlightenment" phenomenon, whereby the Soviet political project was founded with the ambition to create a new harmonious society on rational, scientific principles. Accordingly, the Soviet authorities desired to transform the socioeconomic order and refashion wider society. Accordingly, the state was ready to employ unprecedented level of social intervention. In attaining this future socialist utopia, the Soviet authorities also expected the allegiance of their minority populations. These groups would be politically and socially active, eager to contribute to the Soviet modernization effort, and willingly join the Soviet state apparatus; they would, using Kotkin's phrase, "speak Bolshevik", albeit in a variety of national languages. According to Kate Brown, this was reliant upon "the art of persuasion via enlightenment"[18]: a number of cultural, educational, and ideological initiatives were launched that aimed to bring ethnic populations closer to socialism through the means of their native languages.

By the late 1920s, however, the art of persuasion had reached its limit, having never attained the lofty objectives it was meant to fulfil. Although categorized along national lines, as the primary sources suggest, local communities continued to hold fast to their hybrid identities and local cultures, preferring to stay away from the party and ignoring its various initiatives. Moreover, they did not wish to join collective farms and continued to distrust the Soviet regime.[19] Following the Enlightenment perspective, the state resorted to violence in order to accelerate the process of creating a pure community by "excising" those deemed to be obstructing the Soviet state project. In this search for evil, class and ethnicity concurred. Mass deportations from the border zones commenced in the spring of 1930, with many of those targeted as kulaks being repressed only because of their ethnicity.

In his attempt to explain the paradox of this simultaneous pursuit of nation-building and nation-destroying during the Stalinist period, Martin suggests that ethnic terror became an "unintended consequence" of the Soviet modernizing mission. Instead of transcending national identities, the Soviet strategy of ethnic stratification and labelling turned the impersonal category of nationality into a "valuable form of social capital".[20] Those state-imposed national categories started to be used on the ground to voice local interests. The launch of the collectivization campaign also precipitated a mass emigration movement among almost all of the Soviet Union's western national minority communities. Hundreds of Poles fled across the Polish border while others took part in demonstrations demanding the right to emigrate.

These emigration movements became a sign that the Soviet Piedmont Principle, according to which national minorities were meant to draw their brethren from across the border into the embrace of Communism, had failed. Instead, when collectivization and famine threatened their livelihood, Poles and Germans used their national identities to seek help from respective consulates and petition to emigrate, thus repudiating their Soviet fatherland. Such actions reinforced Soviet security concerns and exacerbated the fear of foreign subversion. In addition, there was a violent resistance to collectivization throughout the non-Russian periphery, with the worst peasant uprising taking place in the Polish-Ukrainian border in late February 1930.

Moreover, the Polish minority remained the hardest to collectivize. According to an inspection of the republic's national regions carried out in March 1931, the Polish once lagged far behind other such districts and had the lowest rate of collectivization – some 16.8 per cent (against 4 per cent three years ago), with a 1.8 per cent annual increase during the 1920s (the average rate across Soviet Ukraine being 58.8 per cent by this point).[21] Coupled with the emigration movement, local opposition to collectivization raised questions of the population's perceived loyalty. Consequently, the Soviet authorities responded with the ethnic cleansing of the borderlands and, ultimately, ethnic terror throughout the wider Union.

Eric D. Weitz, a historian of Germany, proposed another approach to understanding the nature of the Soviet ethnic terror under Stalin.[22] In a 2002 *Slavic Review* forum on the topic of race, Weitz argued that Stalin's mass deportations of certain groups during the 1930s and 1940s constituted a "racial politics without the concept of race." Thus, he suggested similarities between the Nazi and Soviet treatment of minority groups. Although the Soviets explicitly rejected the ideology of race, with such (using Stalin's term) "zoological" thinking being a characteristic of the Nazi system and degenerate bourgeois society in general, Weitz argues that traces of racial politics gradually crept into Soviet nationalities policy, especially during the Great Terror and the war period. Certain national groups, who proved to be particularly resistant to socialist appeals, were targeted as "enemy nations" leading to roundups, forced deportations, and resettlement in horrendous conditions. As Amir Weiner put it, "enemy groups previously considered to be differentiated, reformable, and redeemable were now viewed as undifferentiated, unreformable, and irredeemable collectives."[23]

Weitz maintains that race is present when a defined population group is "seen to have particular characteristics that are indelible, immutable, and transgenerational."[24] Race is fate, claims Weitz. As a consequence, certain national groups, targeted as the enemies of socialism, became "racialized" in the sense that their suspect characteristics were seen as psychologically intrinsic to every member of their respective communities and transmitted across the generations. Weitz further maintains that:

> The Soviet drive to remake the very composition of its citizenry, to remove targeted population groups from the social body, to cast certain nations as

pariahs for eternity and to drive them into internal exile, does invite legitimate comparisons with Nazi policies – even though the Soviets themselves explicitly rejected the comparison.[25]

It was this "racial logic" that made Weitz's approach highly controversial. Numerous scholars of the interwar Soviet Union attacked him for obfuscating important differences between the Soviet and Nazi regimes. Prominent among these critics was Francine Hirsch, a renowned scholar of the Soviet nationality question.[26] Although the Soviet regime practiced the politics of discrimination and exclusion, Hirsch rejects the notion that these were committed as part of a programme of "racial politics". In Soviet thought, nationalities, like classes, were conceptualized as sociohistorical groups with a shared consciousness, and not racial-biological groups.[27] Similar to the belief that different classes would eventually disappear under socialism, so to would separate nationalities eventually merge into the Soviet international whole.

The Soviet case presents several important differences to Nazi Germany. First, Soviet experts were tasked with providing scientific evidence for differentiating race and nationality, up to the point that there were two different disciplines dealing with these categories: ethnographers dealt with national cultures, whereas anthropologists were responsible for assessing perceived racial differences. In the process of historical development, both racial and national distinctions would gradually disappear leading to the unification of peoples as new 'ethnohistorical units' – nationalities and nations – based on shared language, culture, and consciousness. While German anthropologists were concerned with "racial purity", their Soviet colleagues described racial mixing as a by-product of sociohistorical development and indicative of an advanced society.[28]

Second, the historiographical focus on race obscures an important aspect of the evolution of ethnic repression in the Soviet Union. At least during the pre-war years, repressive state policies were aimed at specific territories, mainly border regions, where representatives of the so-called western national minorities predominantly lived. The early wave of deportations mainly targeted these politically suspicious segments, but not their communities as a whole. The lists of deportees from villages with "concentrated Polish and German populations" for instance, included "independent peasants who did not fulfil their obligations to the government and those collective farmers [kolhospnyky] who cannot be trusted in the context of the border zone."[29] Once those "harmful elements" were removed, many more minority representatives remained in the region. It is also important to note, that these deportees often still remained within the boundaries of Soviet Ukraine. There were no instances of intentional mass murder targeting populations at the time. The matters changed with the outbreak of the Second World War, when minorities started to be targeted in their entirety and were subsequently deported, mainly to Soviet Kazakhstan, with executions becoming commonplace.

Third, there was an important difference in the way representatives of different nationalities, especially those of "enemy nations", were treated by the authorities. The Soviet regime did not persecute nationalities because of so-called "biological weaknesses", neither did it label particular nationalities as "degenerate races". Instead, they targeted certain peoples for their perceived lack of allegiance and loyalty to the Soviet state, characterizing them as "bourgeois nationalities," "disloyal peoples," and "enemy nations." Respective repressive measures were implemented as a reaction to the threat of nationalism (internally) and fear of foreign intervention (externally), not least due to Poland's attempts to reach out to Poles across its eastern border through the channels provided by the Roman Catholic Church and diplomatic services; or the Third Reich's claims to intervene in the affairs of "ethnic Germans" in the Soviet Union. In addition to Soviet security paranoia, the persistent opposition of certain ethnic minority groups to Soviet policies (collectivization in particular) led to wide-spread concerns that these nationalities could not be "re-invented" as "Soviet" nations, threatening the entire success of the Soviet socialist project.[30]

Moreover, even at the height of the ethnic-based purges, assimilation or re-integration into Soviet society remained possible. It is worth noting, that all former kulaks – regardless of ethnic origin – actually regained their voting rights with the adoption of the "Stalin Constitution" in December 1936.[31] Furthermore, female "special settlers" who married men of other nationalities in the region of resettlement and rejected their old national cultures could be reinstated as Soviet citizens.[32] War provided another possibility to redeem themselves by offering a chance to prove one's loyalty to the Soviet state. Under the official resolution issued in April 1942, former kulaks could undertake military service, with their families being released from the special settlements and receiving new passports. Mass rehabilitation intensified in the post-war years. Weiner maintains that in 1946, the regime removed all limitations imposed on the families of former kulaks who had children serving in the Soviet Armed Forces, were participants in the Great Patriotic War, or received governmental awards. This also applied to women who had married local residents.[33]

While this chapter has no intention of whitewashing the Soviet regime and its numerous crimes against individuals and groups, including ethnic minorities, this brief comparison between the Soviet and Nazi population politics exposes a necessary distinction between states that commit genocide and genocidal regimes. Nazi racial politics resulted in genocide because they endeavoured not just to exclude certain groups from the society but to eliminate their "genetic material" altogether. By contrast, the Soviet regime did not aspire to eliminate its nationalities. Instead, it strove to reinvent its peoples as loyal Soviet citizens and resorted to any means available to achieve this. No doubt, the Soviet regime had the capacity to physically eliminate all members of "selected" nationalities, however, it preferred mass deportations. Having declared the objective to fight any form of nationalism, the authorities initiated a campaign to eradicate the national cultures of targeted ethnic groups: schools were closed down or converted to exclusively using the Ukrainian language, national regions were liquidated, and, most drastically, the populations were forcibly relocated from their historic places of settlement. The Polish district, mentioned earlier in this essay, was reformed in 1935 and split between other administrative units, thus drawing a line to 'Red Polonia' as this experiment was often dubbed.

Instead of searching for similarities between Nazi and Soviet population politics, both should be treated as extreme cases of what James C. Scott dubbed "high modernism", a state's desire for "the mastery of nature (including human nature), and, above all, the rational design of social order commensurate with the scientific understanding of natural laws."[34] As the cases of the Third Reich and the Soviet Union under Stalin demonstrate, "sweeping, rational engineering" of society implemented by a strong, centralized state, and combined with a weak or non-existent civil society, can easily result in societal catastrophes. Nevertheless, state-initiated social engineering, and the violence it necessitates, transcends any ideology or political system. Hence, the Soviet purification drive was comparable not only to that of National Socialism, but also similar to other, non-totalitarian states in 20th-century Europe, such as postwar Poland or Czechoslovakia, or the earlier example of the 1923 population exchange between Turkey and Greece.

Notes

1 Ronald Grigor Suny, *The Revenge of the Past: Nationalism, Revolution, and the Collapse of the Soviet Union* (Stanford: Stanford University Press, 1993), p. 111. Terry Martin, *The Affirmative Action Empire: Nations and Nationalism in the Soviet Union, 1923–1939* (Ithaca: Cornell University Press, 2001).
2 Martin, *The Affirmative Action Empire*, p. 35.
3 *Tsentral'nyi deryhavnyi arkhiv vyshchykh orhaniv vlady Ukraïny* (thereafter: TsDAVO), F.413, op.1, spr. 500.
4 TsDAVO, 413/1/6, ark. 101.
5 TsDAVO, 413/1/6, ark. 102.
6 For the discussion on the problemed posed by the 'so-called' Ukrainian Catholics in Podillia, see: TsDAVO, 413-1-99, ark. 90–96.
7 TsDAVO, 413/1/51, ark. 41.
8 TsDAVO, 413/1/99, ark. 21; 36; 95.
9 TsDAVO, 413/1/99, ark. 90.
10 TsDAVO, 413/1/13, ark. 60.
11 I. V. Stalin, "Politika partii po natsional'nomu voprosu," in *Sochineniia*, Vol. 4, p. 358.
12 Quoted from *Entsyklopediia istoriï Ukraïny*: In 10 Vols (Kyiv: NAN Ukraïny, 2010). Vol.7: 306–307.
13 Martin, "Origins of Soviet Ethnic Cleansing," p. 839.
14 Rubl'ov O., Repryntsev, V. "Represii proty poliakiv v Ukraïni u 1930-ti roky." *Z Arkhiviv VUChK-HPU-NKVD-KGB*. 1/2: 2/3 (1995): 116–156.
15 Petrov, N. V. and Roginskiy, A. B. "Pol'skaia operaziia NKVD 1937–1938 gg," in A. E. Guryanov (ed.) *Represii protiv poliakov i pol'skikh grazhdan* (Moscow: Zven'ya Press, 1997), pp. 37–38.
16 Okhotin, N. and Roginskiy, A. B. "Iz istorii 'nemezkoi operazii NKVD 1937–38 gg." in I. Shcherbakova (ed.) *Nakazanyi narod. Represii protiv rissiiskikh nemzev* (Moscow: Zven'ya Press, 1999), pp. 73–74.
17 Stephen Kotkin, *Magnetic Mountain: Stalinism as a Civilization* (Berkeley: University of California Press, 1995).
18 Brown, *Biography*, 92.
19 Olena Palko, "'Poles of the World Unite': The Transnational History of the 1929 World Congress of Poles Abroad in the Context of Interwar Soviet–Polish Rivalries," *Nationalities Papers* 50:6 (2022): 1143–1163. doi:10.1017/nps.2021.39

20 Terry Martin, "Modernization of Neo-Traditionalism? Ascribed Nationality and Soviet Primordialism," in Sheila Fitzpatrick (ed.) *Stalinism. New Directions*, 348–367 (London/New York: Routledge, 1999).
21 TsDAVO, F.413, op. 1, spr. 552, ark.14.
22 Eric D. Weitz, "Racial Politics without the Concept of Race: Re-evaluating Soviet Ethnic and National Purges," *Slavic Review* 61 (1) (2002): 1–29.
23 Amir Weiner, "Nature, Nurture, and Memory in a Socialist Utopia: Delineating the Soviet Socio-Ethnic Body in the Age of Socialism," *The American Historical Review* 104:4 (1999), p. 1115.
24 Weitz, "Racial Politics," p. 7.
25 Ibid, p. 24.
26 Francine Hirsch, "Race without the Practice of Racial Politics," *Slavic Review* 61 (1) (2002): 30–43.
27 Ibid, p. 30.
28 Hirsch, "Race," p. 36.
29 *Tsentral'nyi deryhavnyi arkhiv hromads'kykh ob'iednan' Ukraïny* (TsDAGO), F1, op.20, spr.6828, ark. 316–317.
30 Hirsch, "Race," pp. 37–38.
31 J. Arch Getty, "State and Society under Stalin: Constitutions and Elections in the 1930s," *Slavic Review* 50, 1 (1991): 18–35.
32 Hirsch, *Race*, p. 41.
33 Weiner, *Nature*, pp. 1132–33.
34 James C. Scott, *Seeing Like a State: How Certain Schemes to improve the Human Condition Have Failed* (New Haven: Yale University Press, 1998), p. 4.

Selected Bibliography

Bemporad, Elissa. *Becoming Soviet Jews: The Bolshevik Experiment in Minsk* (Bloomington: Indiana University Press, 2013).
Brown, Kate. *A Biography of No Place: Ethnic Borderland to Soviet Heartland* (Cambridge, Mass.: Harvard University Press, 2004).
Hirsch, Francine. *Empire of Nations: Ethnographic Knowledge and the Making of the Soviet Union* (Ithaca: Cornell University Press, 2005).
Iakubova Larysa. *Povsiakdenne zhyttia etnichnykh menshyn radianskoï Ukraïny u mizhvoiennu dobu* (Kyiv: Instytut istoriï Ukraïny, 2011).
Martin, Terry. *The Affirmative Action Empire: Nations and Nationalism in the Soviet Union, 1923–1939* (Ithaca, Cornell University Press, 2001).

Nekrich, Aleksandr M. *The Punished Peoples: The Deportation and Fate of Soviet Minorities at the End of the Second World War* (New York: W.W. Norton & Company, 1978).

Palko, Olena. "Debating the early Soviet nationalities policy: the case of Ukraine", in James Harris, Lara Dauds, Peter Whitewood (eds.) *The Fate of the Bolshevik Revolution: Illiberal Liberation, 1917–1941*, 157–172 (London: Bloomsbury, 2020).

Pauly, Matthew D. *Breaking the Tongue: Language, Education, and Power in Soviet Ukraine, 1923–1934* (Toronto: Toronto University Press, 2014).

Suny, Ronald Grigor. *The Revenge of the Past: Nationalism, Revolution, and the Collapse of the Soviet Union* (Stanford: Stanford University Press, 1993).

Street Children in Early Soviet Odesa

Matthew D. Pauly[1]

This is an origins story of the Odesa Comintern Children's Town No. 1. It came to be known in the early Soviet Union for its experimentalism and broad ambition to link the fate of the individual to shared socio-political goals. Origin stories tell us how particular institutions and communities evolved. But they also suggest something about the multi-dimensional character of these communities. As anthropologist Fred Gearing argued in a classic 1958 article: "In a word, a human community does not have a single social structure; it has several. Put otherwise, the social structure of a society is the sum of the several structural poses it assumes around the year."[2] This idea forces us to fight against the grain of established institutional histories of the Soviet Union in which the development of a particular community or establishment is determined by an authority acting from above and the endpoint is presented as preordained.

The Comintern Children's Town was informed by the numerous roles it inhabited, many of which underscored its collectivist orientation: sanctuary, corrective centre, hospital, school, research institution, and political tutor. It was also informed by the various contexts in which it operated: on the edge of empire, in a port city, during the transition from revolution and civil war, and at a time of a tragic famine. Space does not permit a full explication of all these roles, but this children's town was representative of an attachment to the ideal of "the rational institution as a utopia of human transformation and a crucible for new social forms."[3] This was a certainty that predated Soviet Ukraine and had its roots in urban anxieties.

In the late nineteenth century, Russian psychologists developed an epidemiological model to explain the "appearance" and spread of "mental epidemics," coded in ethical terms. These scientists often glossed over the mechanism of transmission, accepting "moral contagion" as fact, and preferring to investigate questions of susceptibility and resistance. After the revolution, scholars continued to reference this idea of a "moral contagion," but no longer because of "irreducible irrationality of human beings."⁴ Rather, it was a corrupting environment that produced the evils of the city, among them juvenile delinquency and hooliganism to which homeless children (*bezprytul'ni*) were particularly prone. Even those previously labelled as "savage" could be redeemed if the correct setting and process was provided.⁵ As Maria Cristina Galmarini-Kabala reminds us, many pre-revolutionary experts "opposed the degenerative theory of child development and instead campaigned to address children with psychological disorders through a curative paradigm."⁶ This was an approach that the Soviet institutions such as the Comintern Children's Town in Odesa aspired to realize.

Genesis

Stories of children who populated Odesa's poorer neighbourhoods and infiltrated its opulent centre to beg, con, and pickpocket fascinated late nineteenth-century and early twentieth-century society in the city and beyond. Delinquent, neglected, and abandoned children represented the city's failures; their existence exposed its corruption and contradictions. The overall count of children cared for in the great variety of municipal shelters at the turn of the century is difficult to discern, but their numbers increased substantially because of the disorder and death introduced by war, revolution, and famine between 1914–1923. Children who came to Odesa seeking solace and sustenance contributed to a daunting 1923 tally of 22,000 dependents in the province's children's homes, slightly less than the republic's highest concentration in the Ekaterinoslav (Dnipro) province.⁷ The problem of children's homelessness was one with a long history that demanded a bold solution.

The 1922 head of the Odesa Provincial Department of Education, Vladimir Potemkin, has left the most complete history of the creation of the Comintern Children's Town, the primary institution meant to refashion "savage" youth. Potemkin credits an early representative of Soviet power in Odesa (and future commissar of education), Oleksandr Shumsky, with laying the groundwork for a large children's settlement. Shumsky imagined it would be housed on the grounds of a former cadet academy and an adjacent dacha complex, renamed Samopomoshch (Russ., Self-Reliance).⁸ In June 1920, the Odesa provincial government, in which Shumsky held a prominent voice, sanctioned the founding of a children's town (*mistechko*), and tasked an interagency body – the Council for the Defense of Children – with logistics. After some study, the council endorsed Shumsky's proposed site.⁹

The town then represented the culmination of a long-held desire to "scientifically" disentangle the problem of children in need of care. However, Potemkin's description also invoked a new form of collectivism. For him, the town embodied "the idea of a harmonious combination of small children's communes."¹⁰ Under the umbrella of a single administrative centre, children housed in a network of children's homes (*dytbudynky*) would work in concert with each other and appointed adults to manage the town's resources and design an educational curriculum. As Andy Willimott has noted, Soviet schools and orphanages often adopted the title "commune," a term that came to be associated with "more than just group association, it also implied an environment, system, or lifestyle devoted to instilling collective values."¹¹ Few in the public objected to this aspiration for shelters. However, it was also a label embraced by university students and workers who sought to establish communal living arrangements in dormitories, factories, and apartments. The founders of the Comintern Children's Town tended to see their charges like the adult communards of Willimott's study saw themselves, "as the advocates of a rational, modern collectivism – the bearers of a proletarian cohesion designed to advance the modern socialist state."¹² While children might not have spontaneously embraced such a role, the town's education was supposed to ensure this political outcome. In fact, the process was erratic. A shortage economy forced regular adjustments and wilful children regularly sought to preserve individual autonomy.

Multiple Structural Poses

The Samopomoshch settlement was a sort of unfinished city garden, established in 1912 for Odesa's aspirational class. The dachas were reportedly well maintained and equipped with all "the comforts, allowed by their owners, representatives of the middle bourgeoisie" (Potemkin identifies captains of shipping, former government bureaucrats, and university professors).¹³ However, two obstacles confronted the organizers of the children's town: a proportion of the dachas were still occupied and there was no sewage system for the settlement. The board worried about the spread of disease and rot because of overflowing cesspools and fungal contamination. The board's proposal imagined a town of up to 2,000 people, but no more. Some members of the Council for the Defense of Children pressed for the transfer of some 10,000 children to the site, but the board resisted. It did not want to create large-scale barracks but sought to reproduce a sort of semblance of domestic "dacha" life. Here perhaps a bucolic vision of communal peace was prioritized over a utilitarian impulse, if only to suggest an improvement over the tsarist past.

A significant pressure was the coming end of the summer; children in makeshift "colonies" on the outskirts of Odesa were threatened with exposure to the cold. Furthermore, according to Potemkin, the city regularly welcomed new arrivals, "children who fell to the earth in their great suffering." Even though health authorities opposed using the Samopomoshch dachas, provincial education and housing officials argued that "whatever shortcomings the settlement would have, the life in it would be incomparably more hygienic and happier than in the slums in which children of poverty must huddle."[14] Housing authorities sanctioned the immediate release of 30 Samopomoshch dachas to the children's town and the eviction of their residents.

Yet another complication was the presence of many Red Army troops on the grounds of the cadet academy in addition to prisoners of war being held in an internment camp. They were here for multiple reasons perhaps, but Odesa's place on the border of the former empire certainly dictated their stationing too. The Soviet government viewed with hostility the occupation of Bessarabia by Romania a short distance away and some Bolsheviks harboured illusions of resurrecting a still-born Soviet republic that had been founded on the territory in 1919.[15] Furthermore, a large number of new troops were expected to arrive, perhaps before their dispatch to the Crimea to oust the remaining forces of White General Pyotr Wrangel in the fall of 1920.[16] In short, the children's town was being created in the midst of the waning days of the civil war. Furthermore, its site was an instrument of revolutionary justice. The creation of the children's town was then an expression of the triumph of rationality, an assumption that became an article of faith for the Soviet educational establishment. But this victory was far from consolidated. It is not surprising then that nothing went according to plan, despite the dictates of local Soviet authorities.

Teetering Forward

The head of the Odesa Provincial Department of Education at the time (and the future Ukrainian deputy commissar of education), Ian Riappo, issued preliminary orders for the transfer of children from Odesa's summer colonies to the imagined town, effectively sanctioning the final creation of the town at this site, regardless of the intervening circumstances. It is not clear what happened to the Red Army troops stationed on the territory, but on September 26, 1920, the internment camp was dissolved and four days later the children's town occupied the cadet academy's headquarters. Multiple children's institutions were placed in the buildings of the academy in a way that reflected the nature of Odesa and evolving Soviet nationalities policy. For example, the former apartment of the director of the academy was granted to a Belarusian school-commune and a Russian kindergarten. A Ukrainian school-commune, Polish school-commune, several other generic schools, and a Ukrainian kindergarten were placed in the former officers' outbuildings. Jewish and Lithuanian school-communes and three children's boarding houses were first assigned buildings in the settlement of Samopomoshch.[17] The previous occupants did not go quietly. The evictees looted the dachas, pulling out windows and doors, and the administrators of the former internment camp took almost all equipment, including workshop tools and even a theatrical stage from the cadet academy.[18] The children's institutions arrived to find nearly empty shelves.

All the attempts of the organizers of the town to prevent these shortcomings, their many requests, petitions, and protests, were in vain. Remarkably, there was no legitimate authority to stop what occurred. The children's town was an attempt to order the disorder of children – corrupted, abandoned, impoverished, and sick – within the boundaries of a single collective space. Yet, it was born in an environment of chaos. The Soviet revolutionary system of justice was supposed to enable its creation, but it was toothless. Provincial authorities had promised to supply the town at the same level as a military field hospital, but assumingly the true military needed these resources more.[19] A so-called surplus commission was tasked with redistributing goods taken from Odesa's mercantile bourgeoisie, but it apparently did not do so effectively or, perhaps equally likely, had hoarded the confiscated goods. The children's town remained poorly supplied – a shortcoming blamed on the poverty of post-civil war Odesa, the looting of state-owned warehouses, and the distance of the town from the city centre (which made the delivery of clothes, bedding, food, fuel, and equipment difficult).[20]

The remaining residents of the Samopomoshch dacha settlement resisted their final eviction, using a technicality of Soviet law to delay their removal. They insisted that the authorities were obligated to ensure their transport to new housing. Several were former shipping officers who appeared to know how to work the bureaucracy. According to Potemkin, these former bourgeoisie turned out to be "magnificent experts in all the compulsory powers of Soviet institutions, from the revolutionary tribunal to the extraordinary commissions."[21] Lastly, at the beginning of 1921, central authorities threatened to throw out the children from the cadet academy to house newly created military-technical courses for the Red Army infantry. Fortunately for the town, this plan was never realized.[22] But the chief challenge was hunger, a problem that increased with the regular addition of new children from the famine-stricken Donbas to the already crowded facility.

Overlapping Competencies

Establishments like the Comintern Children's Town existed to rescue and reform in accordance with the collectivist educational principles shared by conventional primary schools. It was not an institution that received children whom Soviet authorities judged to be most criminal. In October 1922, the Russian People's Commissariat for Internal Affairs (NKVD) issued a new statute that effectively set policy for its Ukrainian counterpart. Its chief objective was to differentiate between institutions responsible for the internment, punishment, or rehabilitation of juvenile delinquents. According to an amendment to the new criminal code approved by the All-Russian Central Executive Committee in June of that year, children as young as fourteen and fifteen could be sentenced by the criminal courts.[23] Others were sent to different types of reformatories, including "correctional houses" and colonies maintained by the Soviet security police, whose new purpose after the promulgation of the statute was to "rehabilitate and reintegrate young offenders."[24] However, they continued to do so imperfectly because their basic orientation remained coercive and punitive.[25] Children judged to be more capable of reform were assigned to children's homes of the kind that made up the Comintern Children's Town.

In Odesa, a juvenile affairs commission overseen by the city government's education department maintained an aptly named "collector" to offer short-term shelter for those apprehended by the police and to sort out who went where. A major problem was what to do with children over the age of 13, whom the children's homes were not obliged to accept. But even young children sent from the collector were viewed with "distrust and caution" by administrators of children's homes, a sentiment that was reciprocated by city authorities. According to a July 1924 Odesa Municipal Education Department report: "Naturally, [these] former pupils of the collector, children with a perverted narcissism, leave the children's homes as a result of this relationship [their unwelcome reception] and take to the street."²⁶ There was perhaps no more damning condemnation of excessive individualism than this charge. Assignment to a children's home by the collector was not unusual and these children were expected to merge into the general population of those not initially detained for criminal behaviour. Mykhailo Kokhansky, the director of the Comintern Children's Town from 1923–1930, justified resistance to the town's collectivist aims on the latent perversion of some, noting in October 1924 that "breakouts [from the town] occur as an exception among the recently arrived children, morally corrupted children with criminal intentions."²⁷

Children from the collector were then present in the children's town and Kokhansky judged them to possess a "criminality" of a different order. Their desire to escape suggested their tendency towards recidivism. But Kokhansky stopped short of saying this. He rather implied that their presence threatened to undo the work of educators in the town as a whole; they were the "exception" that undermined the standard. All children in the town represented a potential "moral contagion" because of their vulnerability to the temptations of the street. Juvenile delinquents of all sorts, and the simply homeless, needed the order that the town provided. Their participation in the town's instruction, it was believed, would provide some immunity, a mechanism to right their lives and safeguard larger Odesa. But importantly the town's administrators folded this impulse into other concerns.

Throughout the early 1920s, the legacy of famine was still felt. Pavlo Ivasevych, a teacher in the town's Ukrainian Home No. 14 (a school-commune and variant of a *dytbudynok*), gives some indication of how this was the case in a 1923 article. He makes clear that the teachers in the town were struggling to adjust to the new environment, to ensure the correct application of educational norms. Like primary schools elsewhere in the republic, schools in the town were to instruct children in the value and practice of group labor and thereby ready them for their generation's common task: the building of socialism. The town's schools enjoyed the advantage of a relatively closed environment, in which teachers might impart these lessons without the interference and distraction of parents whom Soviet educators suspected of retaining outdated, self-centred interests.²⁸ But the pupils' educational pursuit was not trouble-free. What, Ivasevych asks, was the "correct path" to undertake amidst the lingering destruction of "material and pedagogical conditions" in Odesa? He writes: "Imagine the following picture: a hundred hungry, broken, apathetic children who hover near the kitchen, whose conversation is limited to the question of what is for lunch, breakfast, or dinner, or if it is possible to eat weeds?" For Ivasevych, "It was clear to the children that 'no one will set us free,' not God, not the tsar, not a hero, but only their own labor."[29]

The children turned to gardening to sustain their kitchen, naming newly planted vegetable beds after Marx as well as the heroes of the new Soviet state and their children's town. They reportedly took responsibility for the town and thus for their own survival, "every 'child-leader' knows how the whole town, and a single small plant are the shared property of the children's [school-] commune and the result of attention and labor, carefully divided between the children."[30] And they meticulously recorded the growth of every plant. One of the beds of the garden curiously bore the name "little journal," reportedly because of the children's love of this compendium of their labors in the soil. According Ivasevych, the journal was the children's alone: "It is the guide for public criticism, the tribune of social interests of the child, and his simple history."[31] Ivasevych credited authorship of the journal to the rather precociously named "children's scientific collective."

One entry from the journal stridently decried the individualism of class enemies and simultaneously used this understanding to offer a language lesson on the importance of a collective purpose:

> Dear Little Journal! You ask how to say "exploiter" in Ukrainian? This word is foreign, but it is translated into Ukrainian as *"halapas"* [hanger-on] ... For example, in my plant bed there are tall weeds that are no use to anyone but are in fact the opposite – they do harm and make themselves at home, when I water them and not the carrots. Those children who do not do any useful work for our building-commune but live off the work of others are counted as *halapasy*. Goodbye.[32]

Another entry in the children's journal, a poem entitled, *New Path* (*Novyi shliakh*), similarly condemned the oppression of the past, but ended with a celebration of the revolution's achievement for all, especially children:

> And spilled blood for nothing
> Harnessed the people firmly to the yoke
> And still drove with the whip, as if cattle
> The bourgeoisie celebrated bloody banquets
> And beat and punished the people for the truth
> And the poor people suffered quietly

And only furtively damned the torturers

But all the curses did not help –
The unsatisfied bourgeoisie continued to rule
And lies would live a long a time and prosper
And the bourgeois authority made merry despite them
And the workers did not want to live in this way
And they created their proletarian regime
And the path of poverty, which overflowed with tears
All was covered with red flowers. And ardent tears will no long return
And red roses smiled at all.³³

Taken together these entries outlined a form of political education achieved through gardening or labor. Children were instructed to identify the social parasite or weed and focus on an earned future, a time welcomed by red roses – a symbol that invoked the title of the Young Pioneers' periodical, *Chervoni kvity* (Red Flowers). Building socialism was a reciprocal task. The journal "spoke back" to the children in entries made by the teacher, complaining it had not been taken on an excursion to the city, scolding the children humorously for being left outside overnight, or urging children to act upon their talk. It also included jokes that made light of the children's dirty clothes and hunger. The journal was accordingly an expression of a new kind of children's activism. It was this sort of engagement that reportedly allowed children to comprehend their labor, to understand their stake in overcoming such a "cheerless factor" as hunger. The teacher's role was "reduced to an imperceptible helmsman, whose task is not to sink or ground it [the commune metaphorically imagined as a ship]."³⁴

The Promise of Collectivism

The children's collective then determined the fulfilment of duty. Archival information is not nearly as illustrative as Ivasevych's tale, but files recount a continued problem in the Comintern Children's Town with food supply, overcrowding, and truancy.³⁵ What is true is that the multiple poses that the town occupied from its founding come together in this snapshot of Ukrainian Home No. 14. Here were children, sheltered in the sanctuary of a bourgeois dacha, taking classes in military buildings vacated by tsarist cadets and the Red Army, ostensibly improving their physical health and moral fortitude through their labor outdoors and their knowledge through their study, writing, and contributions to a revolutionary institution. And, lest we get too serious, when opportunity presented itself, the children also enjoyed a frolic on the neighbouring Arkady beach. The point is that the children's town by the sea, by the border, and by the threatening and alluring city of Odesa performed all these roles for the children under its protection. The simultaneity of its multiple, overlapping competencies only increased its significance to the young Soviet state, its charges, and to the promise of collectivism.

Children and youth could be "savaged" as well as "savage." The long imperial and Soviet anxiety about the moral contagion that the urban street represented was meant to be resolved by the very range of responsibilities that the Odesa Comintern Children's Town No. 1 embraced. If the initial motivation was containing the threat of juvenile delinquency and vagrancy, activities such as those advocated by Ivasevych recognized that the broader environment inscribed lasting injury on young constitutions. Educators, like Ivasevych, who believed that children could not be morally "defective," would come to be labelled "florists" from the slogan "Children Are the Flowers of Life."[36] In a very real sense, children in the town functioned as their own florists, cultivating themselves as much as vegetal blossoms. Wildness could be tamed, and individual desires subordinated. Within the bustle of activity, the larger "scientific" tension between a children's intrinsic deficits and their victimhood by external, corrupting forces seemed trivial, if not reconciled. And although isolation, correction, and salvation were inherently bound up in the enterprise of the town, they could not be reduced to a singular punitive focus.

Notes

1   "Street Children in Early Soviet Odesa" will appear as "The Savagery of Youth: Odesan Street Children, Public Anxiety, and Collectivist Remedies." In *Proceedings of "The Soviet 'I' and Soviet 'We' Between Ideology and Reality" International Conference, National University of Kyiv-Mohyla Academy*, (forthcoming). It is reprinted with the permission of the editors.
2   Gearing, "The Structural Poses of 18th Century Cherokee Villages," p. 1149.
3   Kelly, *Children's World*, p. 157.
4   Beer, *Renovating Russia*, pp. 191–201.
5   Ibid., pp. 105–106.

6 Galmarini-Kabala, *The Right to Be Helped*, 86–87; Andy Byford, *Science of the Child in Late Imperial and Early Soviet Russia*, pp. 156–157; Caroli, *L'Enfance abondonnée et délinquante dans la Russie Soviétique (1917–1937)*, pp. 35, 38, 188–202.
7 Ball, *And Now My Soul is Hardened*, 283 fn. 229.
8 Potemkin, *Pervyi detskii gorodok imeni Kominterna*, p. 7.
9 For more on the founding of the town, see: Pauly, "Curative Mythmaking," pp. 145–183; Kuz'mych, "Dytiache mistechko im. Kominterna v dokumentakh ta materialakh DAOO ta biblioteky ONIuA," pp. 198–202; Petryshyna and Iurii, "Do istoriï stvorennia pershoho derzhavnoho pozakovoho dytiachoho mistechka v Odesi," pp. 191–197.
10 Potemkin, *Pervyi detskii gorodok imeni Kominterna*, p. 9.
11 Willimott, *Living the Revolution*, p. 45.
12 Ibid., pp. 18, 137.
13 Potemkin, *Pervyi detskii gorodok imeni Kominterna*, p. 9.
14 Ibid., pp. 13–14.
15 King, *The Moldovans*, p. 56.
16 For more on this military campaign, see: Deriabin, *Oktiabr 1920-go*.
17 Potemkin, *Pervyi detskii gorodok imeni Kominterna*, p. 15.
18 Ibid., p. 16.
19 Ibid.
20 Ibid., pp. 17–18. In hungry Odesa, this was not a surprising occurrence. Thefts from warehouses maintained by the American Relief Administration occurred regularly in the former Russian Empire, sometimes with the explicit sanction of Soviet authorities. Patenaude, *The Big Show in Bololand*, pp. 135–140, pp. 191–201.
21 Potemkin, *Pervyi detskii gorodok imeni Kominterna*, pp. 27–28.
22 Ibid., p. 24.
23 Ball, *And Now My Soul is Hardened*, pp. 121–122.
24 Caroli, *L'Enfance abondonnée et délinquante dans la Russie Soviétique (1917–1937)*, p. 297.
25 Ball provides a full description of the great variety of corrective institutions. Ball, *And Now My Soul is Hardened*, pp. 92–93, 96–97, 137, 157, 244. See also: Slavko, *Detskaia besprizornost' v Rossii v pervoe desiatiletie sovetskoi vlasti*, pp. 106–107.
26 *Derzhavnyi arkhiv Odes'koï oblasti (DAOO)*, f. R-1234, op. 1, spr. 8, spr. 82.
27 DAOO, f. R-1234, op. 1, spr. 8, ark. 128.

28　On labor instruction generally in Soviet Ukraine and Russia, see: Pauly, *Breaking the Tongue*; Holmes, *The Kremlin and the Schoolhouse*. On the corrupting influence of the family, see: Kirschenbaum, *Small Comrades*.
29　Ivasevych, "Z zhyttia Ukraïns'koho domu ch. 14 1-ho dyt. horodka Kominterna v Odesi," pp. 28–29.
30　Ibid., p. 29.
31　Ibid.
32　Ibid., p. 30.
33　Ibid.
34　Ibid., pp. 29–30.
35　See, for example: DAOO, f. R-1234, op. 1, spr. 8, ark. 126–127; R-112, op. 1, spr. 488, ark. 30; DAOO, f. R-134, op. 1, spr. 1006, ark. 92–93, 95–96; DAOO, f. R-150, op. 1, spr. 326, ark. 182.
36　Ball, *And Now My Soul is Hardened*, p. 129.

Selected Bibliography

Ball, Alan. *And Now My Soul is Hardened: Abandoned Children in Soviet Russia, 1918–1930* (Berkeley: University of California Press, 1994).

Beer, Daniel. *Renovating Russia: The Human Sciences and the Fate of Liberal Modernity, 1880–1930* (Ithaca: Cornell University Press, 2008).

Byford, Andy. *Science of the Child in Late Imperial and Early Soviet Russia* (Oxford: Oxford University Press, 2020).

Caroli, Dorena. *L'Enfance abondonnée et délinquante dans la Russie Soviétique (1917–1937)* (Paris: L'Harmattan, 2004).

Deriabin, A. (ed.) *Oktiabr 1920-go: poslednie boi russkoi armii Generala Vrangelia za Krym* (Moskva: Reitar, 1995).

Galmarini-Kabala, Maria Cristina. *The Right to Be Helped: Deviance, Entitlement, and the Soviet Moral Order* (Dekalb: Northern Illinois University Press, 2016).

Gearing, Fred. "The Structural Poses of 18th Century Cherokee Villages," *American Anthropologist* 60:6 (1958): 1148–1157.

Holmes, Larry E. *The Kremlin and the Schoolhouse: Reforming Education in Soviet Russia, 1917–1931* (Bloomington: Indiana University Press, 1991).

Kelly, Catriona. *Children's World: Growing Up in Russia, 1890–1991* (New Haven: Yale University Press, 2007).

King, Charles. *The Moldovans: Romania, Russia, and the Politics of Culture* (Stanford, CA: Hoover Institution Press, 2000).

Kirschenbaum, Lisa. *Small Comrades: Revolutionizing Childhood in Soviet Russia, 1917–1923* (New York: RoutledgeFalmer, 2001).

Kuz'mych, Iu. A. "Dytiache mistechko im. Kominterna v dokumentakh ta materialakh DAOO ta biblioteky ONIuA," *Arkhiv. Dokument. Istoriia. Suchasnist': Zbirka naukovykh statei ta materialiv // Pratsi arkhivu Odes'koï oblasti IV* (2001): 198–202.

Patenaude, Bertrand M. *The Big Show in Bololand: The American Relief Expedition to Soviet Russia in the Famine of 1921* (Stanford: Stanford University Press, 2002).

Pauly, Matthew D. *Breaking the Tongue: Language, Education, and Power in Soviet Ukraine, 1923–1934* (Toronto: University of Toronto Press, 2014).

———. "Curative Mythmaking: Children's Bodies, Medical Knowledge, and the Frontier of Health in Early Soviet Odesa." *East/West: Journal of Ukrainian Studies* 9:2 (2022): 145–183.

Petryshyna, L., and A. Iurii. "Do istoriï stvorennia pershoho derzhavnoho pozakovoho dytiachoho mistechka v Odesi," In *Okhorona dytynstva. Dytiache pravo: teoriia, dosvid, perspektyvy: materialy konferentsiï* (Odesa: Iurydychna literatura, 2001).

Slavko, A. A. *Detskaia besprizornost' v Rossii v pervoe desiatiletie sovetskoi vlasti* (Moskva: INION RAN, 2005).

Willimott, Andy. *Living the Revolution: Urban Communes & Soviet Socialism, 1917–1932* (Oxford: Oxford University Press, 2017).

Selfhood and Statehood in Interwar Ukraine: Inventing the "New Man"

Oksana Klymenko and Roman Liubavskyi

In the 1920s and 1930s, authoritarian and totalitarian regimes were established in various European countries. The creation of a "New Man", and methods of total control over all spheres of his life, were central characteristics and necessary conditions for their existence. In the Soviet Union, the New Man's formation was closely intertwined with various projects in the economic sector, such as industrialization, as well as in the social, cultural, and educational spheres via campaigns like Ukrainization or the eradication of illiteracy. According to the Soviet authorities, all these campaigns were aimed at creating a "new ideal world" and a New Soviet Man. Soviet propaganda, which was represented through posters, newspapers, radio, cinema, and other popular mediums, had a significant impact on the New Man's formation.

The "New Man" was a term used by the Soviet authorities to characterize the image of a "real Soviet man", who believed in the idea of revolution, was ready to sacrifice his life for it, actively participated in socialist construction, and obtained education in his free time. In the USSR, there were attempts to explain this term from an ideological point of view. Soviet ideologists of the 1920s and 1930s, particularly Leon Trotsky and Anatoly Lunacharsky, wrote about the New Man in their works.[1]

The Soviet project of creating the New Man through education was complex. It was not only about changing the social and economic conditions of people's lives, but also about changing their habits and lifestyles. To implement these plans, many ideological projects were introduced focusing on the reconstruction of physical spaces, changes to everyday habits, and the mastery of a new model of speaking and remembering. This chapter will consider these processes using several historical examples including socialist city construction, the introduction of new socialist rituals, and new remembrance practices.

Spaces

According to Michel de Certeau, creating a rationally organized space, freed from physical, mental, and political threats to its existence, was one of the prerequisites for implementing utopian urban projects.² The construction of socialist cities next to outstanding industrial facilities during the first five-year plan, such as the Kharkiv Tractor Plant (KhTP, or DniproHES), can be considered one of the most radical projects within New Man education. Indeed, soviet architects were unanimous in their opinion that creating a fundamentally new living space was necessary. However, there was no universal point of reference or detailed view as to how this space would be created; during the 1920s and 1930s, much of this became centred on discussions held between the so-called "urbanists" and "desurbanists". For their part, the Bolsheviks viewed socialist cities as an open field for social experimentation with several projects for creating new cities and towns being developed in the Ukrainian Socialist Soviet Republic during this period.³

Let us consider the socialist city of "New Kharkiv" both as an idea and its construction's implementation. Today, the town space is the centre of the Industrial (1934–2016 *Ordzhonikidzevskyi*) district of Kharkiv, located on the northeastern outskirts of the city with its construction having begun in 1930. It is also known that German and American engineers and architects took part in developing many of these exemplary socialist cities across the USSR, such as Magnitogorsk and Novokuznetsk. However, the study of the State Institute for Urban Design "Dipromisto" documentation makes it possible to establish that, in this case, design work for New Kharkiv was carried out by domestic architects under the guidance of P. Aloshyn.⁴ In the explanatory note to the master plan of the city around KhTP, it was noted that it would not have any housing shortages, unsanitary conditions or any of the other shortcomings characteristic of "old" cities.⁵ The developers believed that to achieve this, it was necessary to abandon the established principles of urban development and create new housing and socio-cultural living conditions.⁶ According to the designers' plan, all KhTP employees would receive apartments in new "housing complexes". Each complex consisted of a set of buildings and premises necessary to ensure the complete "socialization of the individual needs service." According to the project, 36 "housing complexes" were to comprise eight to ten buildings, in which 2548 people would live. These also included a school, a club, a canteen, a kindergarten, and a nursery. It was also planned for the houses to be interconnected by special corridors-bridges at the second-floor level so that residents could visit any of their complex's facilities without having to go outside.⁷ The idea of freeing women from the kitchen was especially key to implementing the desired layout of these apartments. The authors of the project noted that one of the shortcomings of the "old" Kharkiv was the social enslavement of women in the household. According to the general design of the city, there were no kitchens in the apartments, with workers having to instead eat in public canteens.⁸ The program's authors for planning and building up the new city also provided exceptional conditions for cultural recreation among KhTP workers, which were unavailable for employees of enterprises located in Kharkiv.⁹ Each residential complex provided a special hall for cultural and educational events and public meetings. The project also included the creation of an administrative and cultural set, which included an administration building, a theatre, houses of culture, labor, physical culture and sports, cinema and press houses, two hotels, museums, swimming pools, a park of culture, and a football stadium. According to the project, this large number of objects was planned to be erected within ten years.¹⁰

Fig. 2–2: A prospective plan of the apartment block for Traktorobud 3. 1930. TsDAML Ukrainy. F.8, op. 1, spr. 261.
Reprinted with permission.

The project's authors also planned to have all residents of "New Kharkiv" living in multistorey communal buildings. While its construction plan proposed the creation of 288 houses however, only 50 had been built by 1939.[11] Consequently, most KhTP workers did not receive a separate apartment in the 1930s while the area's ongoing housing crisis began to ease only in the mid-1950s. Housing itself consisted of two varieties: one-room apartments for singles and two-room apartments for workers with families. The premises were quite spacious, with high ceilings of 2.9 metres and bathrooms and toilets. However, the construction project's omissions were promptly discovered by those moving in. The KhTP's deputy director Stukota promptly reported to the All-Russian Tractor Association (VATO) that the designers' calculations had turned out to be incorrect: there were more rooms for singles than necessary and not enough apartments for families. As a result, the management of the plant decided to accommodate the families of several employees in rooms designed for only one person.[12] The functional purpose of apartments for singles thus changed, with this problem being repeatedly raised in the pages of the periodical press as KhTP workers' correspondents sent letters to newspaper editorial offices. Thus, the brigadier of the first Komsomol battalion Radkevych sought to inform the public of the challenges faced when seeking to provide the numerous "shock workers" with suitable housing. In a letter to one of the major Soviet periodicals, published in 1932, he claimed that the administration paid attention to him only when it was necessary to fulfil the plan but did not consider his requests to improve living conditions; the author himself lived in the same room with seven other workers and slept on a wooden trestle bed.[13] Therefore, the sanitary and technical qualities of the apartments were reduced due to the excessive number of residents.

It should be noted that these particular workers came from the countryside and gradually acclimatized to urban living conditions, adapting the space within the new apartments to the suit needs of the everyday peasant life to which they had been accustomed. It is worth recalling the case of the plant director, P. Svystun, who reportedly saw a piglet being kept in the bathroom of one of the apartments. In another, the owner had built a stove and chopped wood right on the parquet.[14] Under such conditions, the Bolsheviks' idea for a radical socialist restructuring of life proved impossible to realize as the Soviet authorities failed to change the everyday habits of workers through the specific architectural solutions. Not only did these complex residents not live up to the expectations of the Bolsheviks, they simply adapted many of their "old" everyday practices to better suit their new living space.

Practices

Introducing new revolutionary rituals into everyday life was an essential component of the Soviet policy for forming a New Man. Nevertheless, Party leaders and local cultural workers understood that it would be challenging to displace the various ritualized features of traditional Ukrainian life; for this, it was necessary to offer socialist alternatives such as "red christenings" (*oktiabryny*), or "red weddings". Such measures merit closer study since they represented a critical communication channel between the Soviet government and society. Let us consider these demonstration events, initiated by the leaders of workers' clubs or conscious "Soviet" people, as a cultural product offered to ordinary citizens. One of these events was reflected in the pages of the regional press. On May 11, 1925, the October holidays (*oktiabryny*) appeared as a significant event in the life of the staff of the Second State Confectionery Factory.[15] It is clear that when covering this event, journalists somewhat exaggerated October's importance. However, given the fact that the Soviet authorities advertised the ideas of a new way of life as a cultural trend, such an occasion really could have generated great interest, although the work correspondents reported that participants did not understand the purpose for holding these celebrations.[16] "Red christenings" can be considered a specific form of Soviet public entertainment culture, which was also presented to the citizenry by the authorities. According to correspondents, a large number of working people gathered to watch the ceremony, culminating in the act of filling out a questionnaire for the baby. This action was public, and questions and answers were read aloud to the accompaniment of an orchestra specially invited to attend. Interestingly, in addition to biographical data (name and surname), the questionnaire also required the parents to provide information regarding their social origins and the child's future speciality, which was "chosen" and recorded. The couple then received gifts from the factory committee and the Leninist Communist League of Youth of Ukraine members.[17] "*Oktiabryny*" were another such event, through which the Soviet authorities sought to demonstrate their presence in the social space. The ceremony was filled with semantic codes, the cyphers of which were known to every member of the Soviet society. The first steps of the child's socialization took place in the factory, which testified to the marginalized status of the church within official discourse. The procedure's publicity highlighted, for all those who had gathered, the importance of collectivism as a form of organizing everyday practices. The orchestra, Komsomol guests, and the awarding of parents with prizes reproduced the atmosphere of a solemn holiday.

There is no evidence of how often such events were held. However, analysing these examples makes it possible to understand how the authorities used workers' clubs to demonstrate new social values and spread them through everyday practices. A demonstrative "red wedding", for example, took place on January 15, 1924, in the club for food industry workers. The next day, the city newspaper drew readers' attention to the fact that the ceremony had been held at a club, not a church.[18] Therefore, the authorities attempted to demonstrate the existence of an alternative to sustainable traditions and provided examples of new social relations that were to become role models. Press correspondents portrayed the newlyweds as model citizens who had abandoned established norms and married in a new revolutionary ritual, the wedding itself evoked a solemn meeting of the cultural commission, at which the question of marriage was regarded. The club's management made a welcoming speech, telling the audience about this new way of life's essence and social significance. The newlyweds, who were themselves members of the trade union of food industry workers, were married and pledged to join the ranks of the Communist Youth Union.

Fig. 2–3: Workers club of Shestopark Theatre. New Year's Eve, 1924. Kharkiv Historical Museum. Reprinted with permission.

The Soviet authorities tried to use workers' clubs to demonstrate to workers how the foundations of this new socialist order would be established by introducing them into people's daily lives. Such ideas for this new way of life were put into practice through ceremonial events and public presentations as an ideological product that the authorities offered to "use" in the hope of re-educating society.

Memory

The 1920s and 1930s were a period when various campaigns were introduced across the USSR in order to educate the New Man and establish control over him, including his memory and understanding of the past. Soviet ideologists used memory to form a "new person", which was characterized by a new identity and language, as well as an appropriate attitude towards the state, the team, and workplace.

Soviet commemorative practices in the interwar period were greatly influenced by propaganda, as well as by specially created commissions that were engaged in writing Soviet history: The Commission for the Study of the October Revolution History and the History of the Communist Party, or "Istpart" which was established in the 1920s, and the Commission on the History of the Factories and Plants, abbreviated as the "HFP Commission", founded in the 1930s. Both commissions had a similar structure comprising a central commission in Moscow with branches in each republican as well as local commissions and even ones overseeing individual factories. These commissions included party leaders, historians, and the HFP Commission also employed its own writers, its leading ideologist being the proletarian author Maxim Gorky. In order to write a "correct" version of history, these commissions turned to the collection of memoirs authored by those who had participated in revolutionary events as well as workers.

Both commissions, when collecting these memories, used similar techniques. Istpart collected and recorded memories by organizing so-called "memory evenings" and sending letters of request to members of the Soviet public who had participated in revolutionary events encouraging them to write memoirs and complete questionnaires. Moreover, using these memories, Istpart created the "correct" version of Soviet history based on the class principle, with the October Revolution serving as an important event. In the 1930s, the focus of attention within the politics of memory shifted from the issue of revolution to socialist construction, as the drive toward industrialization was proclaimed and became the Soviet Union's main priority.

Methods for collecting and fixing the memories of socialist construction continued with the traditions initiated by Istpart. These involved holding "memory evenings", individual conversations, and workers writing their memoirs in response to requests from editorial boards. However, there was a significant difference which meant that the workers' memoirs collected by the HFP Commission were to be a primary source for recording the origins of new industrial buildings rather than simply being used as evidence to confirm the Bolshevik version of history. Furthermore, from the beginning of the five-year plans, propaganda actively disseminated information about workers' achievements and records in factories and plants.

Fig. 2–4: *Workers from the Kholodnohirs'kyi raion on 1 May 1923. Kharkiv Historical Museum. Reprinted with permission.*

In addition, it was not only the commissions' influence that was an essential aspect of the formation of the New Man's memory but also the ways in which the authors of these memories, in particular workers, learned to present themselves and narrate their pasts in the "right" way. A key example is the collected autobiographies of the workers of the DniproHES. This appeal to DniproHES is not accidental; after all, Soviet propaganda considered the plant to be a symbol of the first and second five-year plans and one of the most outstanding examples of industrialization in both Ukraine and the wider Soviet Union. Situated near the city of Zaporizhzhia in southeast Ukraine, the construction of the Dnipro Hydroelectric Station lasted from 1927 to 1939 and received its name from its location on the Dnipro, the longest river in Ukraine. The official opening took place in 1932 though some of the facilities had still not been completed by then.

The Commission, engaged in writing the history of DniproHES from 1933 to 1934, paid great attention to the collection of workers' autobiographies and memoirs, sending out personal requests for them to write about themselves and their participation in the construction of this hydroelectric power station. These requests generally concerned those who had moved to another place of work after the power station's completion. Since it was necessary to obtain information only in written form, only forepersons and engineers, rather than the ordinary laborers, were engaged in this process. This was justified by the assumption that those who held the highest positions were educated, unlike much of the regular labor force who remained illiterate, despite the literacy campaign of the 1920s. In addition, all of the authors were male, not female, explained by the fact that men, rather than women, still occupied most leadership positions in Soviet society. Although, as a result of emancipation, some women's brigades were formed, and several well-known female shock workers were employed at DniproHES. As evidenced by the Commission's documents on the history of DniproHES (stored in the State Archive of Zaporizhzhia region), women did not write autobiographies or memoirs. However, many still provided oral testimonies detailing the various roles they had played in the plant's construction.

However, it should be clarified that only those who had started working at DniproHES during the 1920s had to submit a biography. Still, in the 1930s, the Commission collected autobiographies of those who had already worked at other sites. In such a way, the concept of "new Soviet people" was implemented – even the people's past had to correspond to the ideological frame. A worker seeking a position at DniproHES was required to provide an autobiography, which included information about their origins, family, education, and previous places of employment. A special commission was created to verify the information provided in this document and to write relevant requests to the workplaces, where the potential employee claimed to have previously worked.

Such attention to autobiographical information stemmed from the fact that certain social groups were not permitted to work at Soviet industrial facilities. These included "kulaks", priests, and everyone who had belonged to the privileged classes under the previous Tsarist regime, as well as those who participated in the Ukrainian national movement from 1917 to 1921. Soviet propaganda proclaimed that these groups should not be allowed to work at plants and factories because their activities would be aimed at undermining socialist construction. As Sheila Fitzpatrick notes, "Class was a major component of the Soviet identity and the autobiographical picture".[19]

This process of submitting one's autobiography and the attention focused on the workers' pasts was a common practice in all Soviet factories and plants during this early period. Moreover, people were searching for the ideal depiction of their past, influenced by propaganda and observations of what was happening with social groups that could not integrate into Soviet society. Sometimes they constructed their autobiographies subconsciously, copying the propaganda messages they heard. This sometimes led to them incorporating certain clichés *ad hoc*, for example, in order to hide one's "wrong" origin and received their desired job. In this regard, an autobiography might serve a kind of ticket to a brighter future. Olena Stiazhkina clarified some of the ways that ordinary people used to construct their past in the autobiographies, such as seeking to present the "right" origin by placing an emphasis on childhood poverty.[20]

Let us analyse two examples of autobiography from this period. The first was written by Arsenii Zhukov, "the head of the railway transport operation of the right and left banks".[21] The editors personally addressed him with a request to provide his memoirs: "In accordance with your request, now I am reporting my autobiography and outstanding moments of the DniproHES construction".[22] His memoirs have been preserved both in the original version (handwritten) and typewritten, of which there are two printed versions.[23] The texts contain a familiar list of questions such as origin, training, work, and rewards. It is mentioned that he was born into a peasant family but, due to their poverty, when he was three or four years of age he was taken in by another family for educational reasons. It is unknown whether this was the real reason. For instance, it is written that he was unable to remember how much land they had owned, but it is noted that they had had two horses.[24] Considering the second remark, the emphasis on poverty may be somewhat exaggerated since the presence of the indicated number of livestock at the beginning of the 20th century points to what would have represented a reasonably average level of wealth for a peasant family.

The primary attention in the autobiography is given to the description of the DniproHES construction, however, with the author himself seemingly becoming less and less important in his own life story. Indeed, he increasingly appears not even as part of the labor team but as merely an anonymous piece in a mass of people and machines, the details of his personal life and family having been squeezed into the framework of an ideologically necessary plot. Analysing Soviet biographies, Stiazhkina notes that "People wrote their stories, of course, with the goal in mind. First of all, they searched for and wrote a 'correct biography', that is, demonstrating the naivety of class consciousness, true social origin, professional training and individual qualities".[25]

Writing memoirs about the DniproHES construction also served as a tool for teaching a worker to speak of himself primarily as part of a team, not an individual. This idea finds confirmation in autobiography of one Veselago, an engineer from Yaroslavl who also sent his memoirs, dated January 24, 1934, to the DniproHES editorial office:

> The work at DniproHES was so imbued with a collective idea, everyone was so inspired by teamwork that it is challenging for me to single out my role in the common cause. If I take credit for anything, it is the ability to be critical of American technology, the ability to choose what we need, to combine it with Soviet methods of work and to unite the team of workers on the left bank into a friendly family moving towards a common goal. Without suppressing the initiative, but without violating the one-person principle.[26]

The author's attention to the equipment is not incidental since he had previously gone on a business trip to the United States in 1928, in order to study American construction equipment.[27] However, he described his trip quite dryly and entirely without emotion. Veselago focused only on technology, and there were no impressions or judgments about what he had seen in the country that very much belonged to the capitalist world. The author wrote on the subject of this trip as carefully as possible, despite the editorial board members' interest in it. The latter's confirmation is found in the highlighted passages about the journey in one of the variants of the memoir's text.[28] The fact that he was chosen for the trip may indicate his recognized qualifications and, at the same time, his reliability. However, there are some doubts about the latter. At the beginning of his autobiography, he indicates his parents' own occupation as merely being "employees", which was also a kind of cliché and veiled the exact type of work. He had seemingly completed his higher education during the October Revolution, graduating in May 1917 from the Leningrad Institute of Communications Engineers – which indicates the Soviet name for the institute. In addition, he remained non-partisan in 1934.[29] His testimony about military service is also quite cautious, "I was not in military service, I did not serve in any armies"[30], although he would have been 24 years old in 1917. On the one hand, it was a standard phrase that should be written in an autobiography alongside not having any criminal convictions, which he also notes. Conversely, his statement on military service can also be regarded as a signal that in 1917 he had not supported the Bolsheviks' political enemies.

Research into these autobiographies reveals that workers were expected to learn the rules of correct self-presentation as part of a team and within the context of the industrialization campaign. Jochen Hellbeck emphasizes that Soviet workers' self-talk was constantly integrated into the context of nationwide campaigns.[31] However, collected by the Commission for writing DniproHES history autobiographies had the genre of memories. The authors did not just retell their past but had to give the details of their work at DniproHES. As a result, the authors' personalities tended to exist at the periphery while discussion of large-scale construction occupied the central part of their narratives.

We can state that publicity and collectivism, as the New Soviet Man's virtues, were formed as much by the authorities as well as via slogans and popular campaigns, and became embedded in people's daily lives. The authorities tried to present the Soviet project of a New Man as attractive to society in the 1920s and 1930s. They encouraged the introduction of new rites, such as the October (*oktiabryny*) and red weddings, and turned them into a performance, the participants of which received gifts. Utopian ideas for creating a new society therefore became part of everyday Soviet life.

The industrialization and the modernization of society raised the problem of mass resettlement of workers near to their respective enterprises. The so-called "socialist cities" were designed to solve this problem with open spaces, those who lived in these places would supposedly to contribute to assimilating socialist ideals. In order for everyone to eat in the dining room, for example, apartments were designed without kitchens, thus, the private occurrence of a family meal became impossible. Newly constructed socialist cities, such as New Kharkiv, were symbolically opposed to the old ones with the press emphasizing the rationality of their urban space in terms of the absence of a city centre, or a large number of green spaces.

Self-awareness is the main characteristic of a man. The upbringing of the new Soviet person also assumed the assimilation of new (self-)representation practices. Analysis of autobiographies and memoirs shows that people imitated this political canon in their own texts, searching for an ideologically correct version of their biography. The creation of several similar texts thus contributed to one's self-awareness as a Soviet person.

Notes

1 L. D. Trotskii, *Pokoleniie Oktiabria: rechi i statii* (Moscow: Molodaia gvardiia, 1924), p. 260; A. V. Lunacharskii, *Vospitaniie novogo cheloveka* (Leningrad: Priboi, 1928), p. 48.
2 M. De Serto, "Po gorodu peshkom," *Communitas* 5 (2002), p. 82.
3 V. H. Tkachenko, "Budivnytstvo 'Velykoho Zaporizhzhia' v 20–30-ti roky XX stolittia" *Naukovi pratsi istorychnoho fakul'tetu ZDU* 16 (2003), pp. 221–225; M. Alf'orov "Polityka urbanizatsii Skhidnoï Ukraïny u 1920–1939 roky," *Skhid* 1 (2010), p. 77.
4 Tsentral'nyi derzhavnyi arkhiv-muzei literatury i mystetstva Ukraïny (thereafter: TsDAMLM), F. 8, op. 1, spr. 265, ark. 4.
5 Tsentral'nyi derzhavnyi arkhiv vyshchykh orhaniv vlady ta upravlinnia Ukraïny (thereafter: TsDAVO), F. 5, op. 3, spr. 1877, ark. 2.
6 TsDAMLM, F. 8, op. 1, spr. 261, ark. 63.
7 TsDAMLM, F. 8, op. 1, spr. 261, ark. 2.
8 TsDAVO, F. 5, op. 3, spr. 1877, ark. 64.
9 TsDAMLM, F. 8, op. 1, spr. 261, ark. 2.
10 TsDAMLM, F. 8, Op. 1, Spr. 261, Ark. 3.
11 V. Plotnikov, "Pobutove budivnytstvo Kharkivs'koho traktornoho zavodu", *Arkhitektura radians'koï Ukraïny* 5 (1939), p. 15.
12 Rosiiskii gossudarstvennyi arkhiv ekonomiki (RGAE), D. 7620, Op. 1, d. 390, l. 4.
13 RGAE, D. 7620, Op. 1, d. 89, l. 15.
14 Iu. L'vov, *Sled na zemle* (Moscow: Politizdat, 1966), pp. 25–27, 53.
15 "A zachem ego krestit'?", *Khar'kovskii proletarii*, 1925, 11 May, p. 3.
16 Ibid.
17 Ibid.

18 "Ne v tserkve, a v klube (proletarskaia svad'ba)", *Proletarii*, 1924, 16 January, p. 2.
19 Sh. Fitzpatrick, *Sryvaite maski! Identichnosti i samozvanstvo v Rossii XX veka* (Moscow: ROSSPEN, 2011), p. 110.
20 O. V. Stiazhkina, "'Pravyl'na biohrafiia' peresichnoï liudyny 1920-kh rokiv: sposoby konstruiuvannia mynuloho (na materialakh Donbasu)" *Novi storinky istoriï Donbasu: Zb. statei* / hol. red. Z.H. Lykholobova. – Donetsk: DonNU, 2008. – Kn. 15–16, pp. 204–224.
21 Derzhavnyi arkhiv Zaporiz'koï oblasti (DAZO), F. 995, Op. 28, Spr. 37, Ark. 124-zv.
22 DAZO, F. 995, Op. 28, Spr. 37, Ark. 124.
23 DAZO, F. 995, Op. 28, Spr. 37, Ark. 124–125-zv.
24 DAZO, F. 995, Op. 28, Spr. 37, Ark. 124.
25 Stiazhkina, "Pravylna biohrafiia", p. 206.
26 DAZO, F. 995, Op. 28, Spr. 37, Ark. 148.
27 DAZO. F. 995. Op. 28. Spr. 44. Ark. 11.
28 DAZO. F. 995. Op. 28. Spr. 44. Ark. 11.
29 DAZO. F. 995. Op. 28. Spr. 37. Ark. 144.
30 DAZO. F. 995. Op. 28. Spr. 37. Ark. 144.
31 Hellbeck, "Working, Struggling, Becoming", p. 350.

Selected Bibliography

Fitzpatrick, Sheila. *Tear Off the Masks! Identity and Imposture in Twentieth-Century Russia* (Princeton: Princeton University Press, 2005).

Halfin, Igal. *Red Autobiographies: Initiating the Bolshevik Self, Donald W. Treadgold Studies on Russia, East Europe, and Central Asia* (Seattle: Herbert J. Ellison Center for Russian, East European, and Central Asian Studies, University of Washington, 2011).

Hellbeck, Jochen. "Working, Struggling, Becoming: Stalin-Era Autobiographical Texts," *Russian Review* 3 (2001): 340–359.

Hellbeck, Jochen. *Revolution on My Mind: Writing a Diary under Stalin* (Cambridge, Mass.: Harvard University Press, 2009).

Kenez, Peter. *The Birth of the Propaganda State: Soviet Methods of Mass Mobilization, 1917–1929* (Cambridge: Cambridge University Press, 1985).

Stiazhkina, Olena, *Liudyna v radians'kii provintsiï: osvoiennia (vid)movy* (Donetsk: DonNU, 2013).

Liubavskyi, Roman, *Povsyakdenne zhyttia robitnykiv Kharkova v 1920-ti – na pochatku 1930-kh rokiv* (Kharkiv: Rarytety Ukraïny, 2016).

Stalinism and The Holodomor

Daria Mattingly

"Why should we help Spanish people? They did not help us when we starved in 1933!" a Ukrainian collective farmer told grain procurement officials in 1936.[1] This exclamation reveals several things. Firstly, Ukrainian grain was used to help the republicans, whom the Soviet Union supported during the Spanish Civil War. Secondly, 1933 refers to the artificial famine in Soviet Ukraine, known as the Holodomor, that claimed 4 million lives from 1932 to 1933.[2] Finally, despite silencing the fact of the famine, the Holodomor had an enduring presence in the lives of modern Ukrainians.

The Holodomor, which translates as "death by hunger", is a complex phenomenon that includes the 1932–33 famine and the concurrent persecution of the Ukrainian intelligentsia, the political elite, and the Orthodox Church. The sheer scale of the destruction of human life dominates the Holodomor's understanding in Ukraine and western academia in the last forty years. Yet despite the colossal loss of life in peacetime, historical discussion was silenced by the Soviet regime almost until its collapse in 1991. There was no famine relief, no appeal for help to the international community, or even a halt in grain exports. Instead, over several years the Soviet authorities continued to facilitate policies that resulted in people starving to death. Strikingly, even in the western historiography of the Soviet Union, the famine in Ukraine has often been overlooked or located firmly within the context of an all-Soviet famine and cast as a collateral cost of modernization and industrialization, or as part of a broader ideological clash between the Communist authorities and the peasantry.

Conversely, the political roots of the famine in Ukraine could be found not so much in Communist ideology or modernization, but in the events preceding the Holodomor, namely the fall of the Russian Empire and the founding of the Soviet Union itself. Following the February Revolution, the national aspirations of many nations mushroomed across the former empire. Ukrainians were no exception to this development, even if a future Ukrainian state was initially envisaged as existing within a new, federative Russia.[3] However, as the political struggle within Russia intensified and the Bolsheviks seized power, Ukrainian leaders proclaimed independence. Indeed, the overwhelming majority of Ukrainians did not support Bolsheviks and voted for other parties in the elections for the Constituent Assembly.[4] When the Red Army invaded in 1918 to confiscate Ukrainian bread for the workers of Moscow and Petrograd, they were met with widespread resistance.

Amid the civil war in Russia, that broke out at the end of 1917, the effort of the newly established Ukrainian state army, military involvement from Imperial Germany and Poland and offensives carried out by the anti-Bolshevik Whites and various insurgent forces effectively removed Ukraine and its extensive grain production from Russian control for almost two years. Struggling to feed the Russian proletariat, which was the Communists' main support base, at a critical time, Stalin secured bread by using terror in Tsaritsyn, a grain-producing area in South Russia. Yet, the risks of losing Ukraine left an indelible impression on the Bolshevik leadership. While the Reds eventually defeated the Ukrainian forces, and their numerous other adversaries, the war had taught them an important lesson: using terror in procuring grain and controlling food distribution established total control, whereas national movements remained a problem to be resolved.

Upon its founding, Bolshevik Russia faced significant challenges: its economy was in ruins, with widespread famine in the Volga region, and there was little support for the new Soviet regime in the non-Russian republics. Demonstrating a pragmatic approach, Lenin introduced the New Economic Policy that allowed for private initiatives to revive the economy and invited international relief organizations to aid the starving. Alongside this, the Bolsheviks also sought to appease the various national movements with the policy of indigenization by supporting and promoting local languages and cultures. In Soviet Ukraine, indigenization was known as *Ukrainization*. However, neither of these policies could last without further jeopardizing the Kremlin's rule in Ukraine or compromising communist ideology over the long term.

Education in the Ukrainian language and promotion of Ukrainian culture only accentuated the development of a Ukrainian political nation. Considering Ukrainian literature's long history as a public forum without open political debate, Ukrainian writers immediately questioned Moscow's imperial grip on the republic. A prominent author, Mykola Khvyliovy, urged his peers to get "Away from Moscow!"[5] Such expressions raised concerns of the party. Indeed, many modern nations had emerged with the spread of the printed word, so one had to choose carefully what was to be taught, published, or broadcast. Repression against the Ukrainian intelligentsia followed swiftly. Show trials such as that for the Union for the Liberation of Ukraine,[6] with consequent imprisonment and executions, continued well into the 1930s with civil society being effectively destroyed.

Neither did private farming bode well within a Soviet command economy in which there was little room for personal property, especially privately-owned arable land. The collectivization policy sought to create large farms in which land, livestock, and implements were the property of the collective with agriculture itself being centrally managed. Moreover, without any historical precedent, there was no body of expertise who could advise on creating such farms. Instead, village officials and activists, students, civil servants, and workers were recruited to facilitate the policy on the ground using only vague guidelines. In practice, they confiscated property, pressured peasants to join the farms by imposing fines, or threatening them with dispossession. The wealthiest and those opposed to these actions were summarily executed or deported in their hundreds of thousands. Collectivization, from the outset, devolved into mass violence.[7]

Naturally, much of the peasantry resisted. When one's land, implements, and livestock are confiscated; their industrious neighbours, or those critical of Soviet policies, are sent to Siberia or northern Russia; and one is told to work for free for an unelected government, would they be motivated to commit themselves? Some took to arms, and many protested by sabotaging the founding of collective farms, or simply refusing to work. Others voted with their feet by abandoning their farms and villages for the city. The countryside was devastated.

In early 1930, the security services reported to Stalin that there was no Soviet rule in dozens of districts in Ukraine: peasants expelled village officials, took their property back, and stalled the state's sowing campaigns.[8] Resistance to collectivization was fiercer in Ukraine than anywhere else in the Soviet Union, and some local party leaders in Ukraine were hesitant to follow the Kremlin's orders. The republic's rebelliousness must have reminded the Kremlin of the events of ten years prior, posing a security risk, once again, to the wider Soviet project. If collectivization failed in Ukraine, it could just as easily fail in other parts of the country. Moreover, resistance to Soviet policies following displays of defiance by the Ukrainian intelligentsia presented another long-term problem that could see national sentiment smouldering in the countryside, a living reminder of the possibility of a non-Soviet Ukrainian state.

Establishing control over Ukraine manifested in many ways, including the famine. Indeed, all rebellions could be crushed when those rebelling, and their families, had been starved and could no longer resist. Nevertheless, policies addressing the problem of an emergent national movement had to be more lasting.

On a political level, the Communist leadership of Ukraine could no longer be autonomous. The risk of losing Ukraine, as Stalin succinctly put in a 1932 telegram to his representatives, was associated with the republican leadership coming to resembling a parliament or rather "a caricature of a parliament"[9] when they questioned the impossible grain procurement targets that had been set for that year. Indeed, Stalin had even dispatched his trusted envoys, Viacheslav Molotov and Lazar Kaganovich, to push the impossible targets for grain procurement and later to oversee the famine-inducing policies on the ground. In 1933, he subsequently sent another prominent Russian communist, Pavel Postyshev, to assume leadership over the communist party in Ukraine. In such a way control over republican bosses was established during the famine.

In 1932, the Kremlin decided how much grain would be procured in Ukraine over winter 1932–1933. Stalin dismissed all concerns from republican leaders regarding the impossibility of meeting the set targets (these were later lowered but never met). Ukrainian district officials raised similar problems at the III Party conference in Kharkiv in July 1932, but Stalin's envoys, now backed by the republican leadership, simply muted any dissenting voices.[10] As the targets were passed down to the district and village-levels in August, a third of local officials refused to enforce them.[11] While they were replaced with more complacent staff, during the 1932–33 grain procurement campaign that followed, the desertion rates among urban activists in some districts reached 40 per cent, while suicides were not uncommon.[12]

On the ground, village, councils, and collective farm managers organized teams of activists to search farmers' houses for grain. To prevent the starving people from seeking food in the fields, a law prohibiting the theft of socialist property was passed in August 1932. From November, brigades of activists confiscated livestock if no grain could be found, or any other supplies or valuables that could be exchanged for food. On rare occasions when targets were met, collective farms and farmers were given additional targets to meet. Additionally, in late 1932, hundreds of villages and, at times, entire districts were "blacklisted" for failing to meet grain procurement targets. That meant the confiscation of all supplies, including kerosene and matches, which made cooking and preparing food impossible.

In December 1932, another decree prevented peasants from obtaining passports, necessary for purchasing train tickets to escape the famine (collective farmers were not automatically entitled to passports until 1974). Following the directive by the Central Committee of All-Soviet Communist Party (Bolshevik) of 22 January 1933, the borders between Ukraine and Russia and Kuban and Russia were sealed to prevent the victims from leaving the Ukrainian countryside to travel to the other parts of the USSR. Within 50 days of the directive, 219 thousand peasants were detained, most of them returned to the villages they had attempted to escape.[13] All the measures listed above serve as proof of intent to starve the victims by deliberately creating conditions incompatible with life.

Thus, the Soviet authorities were able to dictate who would eat and who would not, demonstrating that resistance would not be tolerated with those who persisted being punished. In March 1933, at the height of the Holodomor, the first secretary of the Central Committee of Communist Party (Bolshevik) of Ukraine Stanislav Kosior wrote to Stalin, informing him that "the famine has not yet taught Ukrainian collective farmers a lesson"[14] and that they were planning additional measures to prolong it into the summer. Understanding no law on socialist property would stop the starving from going into the fields during the summer of 1933, Kosior ordered half a million of armed young people to guard the crops, manning watch towers and undertaking foot and horseback-patrols.[15]

Involving the local population in facilitating the famine translated into establishing a power balance in the villages that lasted until the USSR's collapse. Having proved their loyalty, these local perpetrators subsequently became the village leaders and school masters. For many years after the famine, the victims were obliged to observe them wearing their clothes, using their farming implements, or teaching their children. Most poignantly, no one was punished or faced any consequences for the millions of deaths.

Desperate to survive, people ate grass, berries, mushrooms, herbs, tree bark, acorns, chaff, and other substitutes. Local survival strategies were diverse and heart-wrenching. Mothers took their children to orphanages, hoping they would have a better chance of surviving there while many sold family heirlooms to the newly established chain of state-owned shops, which purchased gold from the rural population. The opening of such a system of shops by the state was possibly eerily coincidental. Some took the last of their valuables across the border to Russia and Belarus, hoping to exchange them for meagre amounts of foodstuffs. As in other severe famines, there were reports of cannibalism.[16] Most victims were buried in unmarked mass graves.

In 1933, local officials organized simple creches where starving children would receive a small, but regular, ration of porridge. This was a lifeline for many with survivors later commenting that the state saved their lives amid the famine. Yet it was the same state that had taken food from them and their parents, creating that very famine. Moreover, while Ukrainians continued to die of starvation throughout the first half of 1933, the USSR proceeded to ship millions of tonnes of Ukrainian grain abroad in hopes of securing more international influence amid the Great depression.[17] The leadership was acutely aware of the situation on the ground yet chose not to help majority of the starving and to export available resources instead.

The famine subsided in the late summer of 1933, when the new harvest was taxed rather than confiscated, and farmers were permitted to keep small private allotments. Millions lost their lives in the meantime with thousands of survivor accounts describing unimaginable trauma. Unable to leave the village, those who remained had to rebuild their lives under the gaze of the officials who had overseen the recent period of starvation. Horrifically, victims were not even allowed to mourn their dead. One even faced accusation of anti-Soviet propaganda for mentioning the famine in public, just like the collective farmer referenced in the opening of this chapter. Stripped of their possessions, or anything that reminded them of life before the famine, Ukrainian peasants became Soviet, or so it seemed.

The man-made character of the famine, accompanied with persecution of non-Soviet Ukrainian intelligentsia and political elite led many scholars to interpret the Holodomor as genocide.[18] Key questions for the historians, however, address the events themselves before establishing pre-existing causal connection between various pieces of evidence. Establishing the intent to destroy Ukrainians as a nation in whole or in part – central point for conceptualising the Holodomor as genocide is a prospect made all the more challenging by the fact that no expression of this exists in the documentation. Stalin did not leave any clear articulation for his motives. The intention can be thus revealed through the policy itself, rather than the pre-mediation of the Holodomor. Intent could be discerned from the actual process of genocide, which was a fluid, complex development rather than a formally defined period of starvation. This could also be shown in response to the famine's emergence as a result of earlier collectivization efforts and grain procurement.

While the famine certainly affected other parts of the Soviet Union, could these areas be described as having already had their borders sealed and certain districts blacklisted, been subjected to proportionally impossible targets, or seen their national intelligentsia and political elite persecuted? Ultimately, political leaders can demonstrate intent via the results of their policies, whether they articulate these intentions or not. Still, regardless of motivation, they are always responsible for the consequences.

Despite the available evidence, many revisionist historians continue to deny not only the intent in the Holodomor but avoid the word 'victims' in describing those who experienced starvation or died as a result of it (which would imply the existence of perpetrators and intentionality). Instead, they discuss 'human cost',[19] thus not distinguishing human acts that led to deaths from occurrences like natural disasters. In the same vein, they interpret the famine as the result of "a poorly conceived and miscalculated policy",[20] "a consequence of the decision to industrialise this peasant country at a breakneck speed"[21] or "a fight to break the anti-Soviet spirit of the peasantry" by Soviet leaders who miscalculated how tough they would be without causing the economically undesirable outcome of mass death.[22] The root of this reluctance can be traced across Slavic studies to the Cold War, when the Soviet Union was juxtaposed with the West. Its unique history and culture were studied and, to some degree, explored with fascination as an alternative to the shortcomings of the West. Therefore, seeking intent in the policies and response to the policies that led to the death of millions presents an epistemological challenge to the Slavists who tend to overlook mass violence nature of collectivisation.

Such an approach, however, ignores the direct mechanisms of the policy. Nobody can survive without food. The argument of an ill-informed leader and a dysfunctional bureaucracy does not stand scrutiny either. We now have unearthed sufficient archival evidence, including correspondence between Molotov, Kaganovich, Stalin and others,[23] to suggest that the leadership was very well-informed and, as the Purges show, deeply involved in processes on the ground. Upon sending Molotov to Ukraine, Stalin telegraphed the former instructions on working with district officials on procurement. These orders were sent down directly from Stalin to those on the ground. To suggest that the Party's General Secretary had been misinformed, brutality was driven from below while blaming a dysfunctional bureaucracy is to ignore ample evidence concerning the mechanisms of a man-made famine.

In fact, in his correspondence with Molotov and Kaganovich, Stalin explains disobedience of the rank-and-file perpetrators of the Holodomor as indicating their possible involvement in the Ukrainian national (*Petliurite*) movement through which they served as agents for Poland. Indeed, there are many references to the 1919 peasant uprising against the Bolsheviks in Ukraine. In the correspondence exchange between the Kremlin and Kharkiv it is stressed that Ukrainian "kulaks are different to those in Russia proper, and they are more cultured,"[24] referring to their political experience accumulated during the Civil War. That is where a link between intent, social, and national, comes to the fore, making Ukraine's 1932–33 famine distinct from the all-Soviet famine that took place from 1931 to 1934.

Finally, not articulating one's intention to kill millions does not imply an absence of intent. The results of the repressive policies point to the goal of starving certain groups with the pursuit of such policies having been a political choice. In his many speeches Stalin expressed desire to improve the lives of ordinary people yet his decisions took lives of millions. In *Dizziness with Success*, he eloquently accuses the rank-and-file perpetrators of having been guilty of the worst excesses while continuing to defend collectivization as a popular policy. His political speeches could not be taken at face value, especially in Soviet history. It is more important to see what was happening in internal correspondence, intelligence reports, and survivor testimonies than to assume the benevolence of their totalitarian leaders based on their party membership.

Brutalising and denial of fundamental rights for the rural population led not only to humanitarian catastrophe but contributed to the very demise of the Soviet Union. Young people strived to leave the countryside by joining the army or seeking-out education and urban-based employment under Brezhnev. Students and workers were sent to the villages to help with sowing or harvesting to address the workforce shortage at the collective farms as collectivized agriculture proved economically unviable. The sheer scale of the Holodomor, however, demonstrated perennial essence of the Russian rule over Ukraine – exploitative and repressive. As Soviet repressive machine fell apart in the 1980s, memories of the Holodomor became the subject of public discussion and academic research in Ukraine, and the role of the Kremlin in organising the famine came to the fore. When the regime was challenged in 1991, Ukraine was one of the first to leave the Union by a popular vote. Upon the collapse of the empire, this time the USSR, the Holodomor became central to the nation-building process in Ukraine and provides for a better understanding of Ukraine's relations with Russia and its Soviet past.

Notes

1   Upravlinnia SBU v Poltavs'kii oblasti, f. R, spr. 15246, ark. 7.
2   Estimations of the number of victims vary, but the dominant consensus among demographers and historians is 3.9 million. See: Jacques Vallin, France Meslé, Sergei Adamets, and Serhii Pyrozhkov "Kryza 1930 rr," in France Meslé and Jacques Vallin (eds.), *Smertnist' ta prychyny smerti v Ukraïni u XX stolitti* (Kyiv: Stylos, 2008), pp. 37–65; Omelian Rudnyts'kyi, Nataliia Levchuk, Oleh Wolowyna, and Pavlo Shevchuk, "Famine losses in Ukraine in 1932 to 1933 within the context of the Soviet Union," in Declan Curran, Lubomyr Luciuk, and Andrew Newby (eds.), *Famines in European Economic History: The Last Great European Famines Reconsidered* (London: Routledge, 2015).
3   According to the Third Universal of the Central Rada of the Ukrainian People's Republic on 20th November 1917. TsDAVOU, f. 1115, Op. 1, spr. 4, ark. 9. Also see Johannes Remy. "'It Is Unknown Where the Little Russians Are Heading to': The Autonomy Dispute between the Ukrainian Central Rada and the All-Russian Provisional Government in 1917," *The Slavonic and East European Review* 95:4 (2017), pp. 691–719. JSTOR, https://doi.org/10.5699/slaveasteurorev2.95.4.0691. Accessed 31 Jan. 2023.
4   Dando, William A. "A Map of the Election to the Russian Constituent Assembly of 1917," *Slavic Review* 25:2 (1966), p. 317.
5   Palko, Olena. "'Away from Moscow': a battle against provincialism in Soviet Ukrainian Literature." *Peripheral Histories?* December 11, 2017, https://www.peripheralhistories.co.uk/post/away-from-moscow-a-battle-against-provincialism-in-soviet-ukrainian-literature. Accessed 31 Jan. 2023.
6   On the SVU trial see, Myroslav Shkandrij and Olga Bertelsen. "The Soviet Regime's National Operations in Ukraine, 1929–1934," *Canadian Slavonic Papers / Revue Canadienne Des*, http://www.jstor.org/stable/23617371. Accessed 31 Jan. 2023.
7   L. Viola, V. Danilov et at., eds. *The War Against the Peasantry, 1927–1930. The Tragedy of the Soviet Countryside* (New Haven: Yale University Press, 2005), p. 148. On collectivization in Ukraine as mass violence see Valerii Vasyl'iev and Lynne Viola, *Kolektyvizatsiia i selians'kyi opir na Ukraïni (lystopad 1929–berezen' 1930)* (Vinnitsa: Logos, 1997).
8   TsDAHOU, f. 1, op. 20, spr. 3191, p. 37.

9   Terry Martin, *The Affirmative Action Empire: Nations and Nationalism in the Soviet Union, 1923–1939* (Ithaka: Cornell University Press, 2001), p. 298.
10 TsDAHOU, f. 1, op. 1, spr. 377, ark. 198, 209.
11 *Holod-henotsyd 1932–1933 rokiv v Ukraïni: The Famine-Genocide of 1932–1933 in Ukraine*, ed. Iurii Shapoval (Kingston, Ontario: Kashtan Press, 2005), pp. 146–211.
12 TsDAHOU, f. 1, op. 1, spr. 395, ark. 147.
13 Stanislav Kul'chyts'kyi, *Holodomor 1932–1933 rr iak genotsyd* (Kyiv: Nash Chas, 2008), p. 310.
14 TsDAHOU, f. 1, op. 20, spr. 6277, ark. 3.
15 TsDAHOU, f. 1, op. 1, spr. 406, ark. 141–142.
16 Warren, Joyce W. and Elissa Bemporad. *Women and Genocide: Survivors, Victims, Perpetrators* (Bloomington: Indiana University Press, 2018).
17 On Soviet exports and Torgsin during the famine see Elena Osokina, *Stalin's Quest for Gold. The Torgsin Hard-Currency Shops and Soviet Industrialization* (Ithaka: Cornell University Press, 2021).
18 Most Ukrainian researchers agree on the Holodomor constituting a genocide, they include, among many others, Stanislav Kul'chyts'kyi, *Holodomor 1932–1933 rr iak genotsyd*; Kul'chyts'kyi, "The 1932–1933 Holodomor in Ukraine within the Context of the Soviet Genocide against the Ukrainian Nation," In Volodymyr Vasylenko and Myroslava Antonovych (eds.) *The Holodomor of 1932–1933 in Ukraine as a Crime of Genocide under International Law*. pp. 74–94 (Kyiv: Kyiv-Mohyla Academy Publisher, 2012); Roman Serbyn, "The Ukrainian Famine of 1932–1933 as Genocide in the Light of the UN Convention of 1948," *The Ukrainian Quarterly* LXII:2 (2006).
19 Christopher Ward, *Stalin's Russia* (London: Edward Arnold, 1993), Chapter 3.
20 Ronald G. Suny, *The Soviet Experiment: Russia, the USSR, and the Successor States* (New York: Oxford University Press, 1998), p. 228.
21 R. W. Davies and Stephen G. Wheatcroft, *The Years of Hunger: Soviet Agriculture, 1931–1933* (Basingstoke: Palgrave Macmillan, 2009), p. 441.
22 Sheila Fitzpatrick, *On Stalin's Team. The Years of Living Dangerously in Soviet Politics* (Princeton: Princeton University Press, 2015), p. 81.
23 On involvement of the top leadership and the mechanism of the famine from the top see Valerii Vasyl'iev, and Iurii I. Shapoval, *Komandyry velykoho holodu: Poïzdky V. Molotova i L. Kahanovycha v Ukraïnu ta Pivnichnyi Kavkaz, 1932–1933 rr.* (Kyiv: Heneza, 2001); Valerii Vasyl'iev, et al. (eds.) *Partiino-radians'ke kerivnytstvo Ukraïns'koï SSR pid chas Holodomoru 1932–1933: Vozhdi*.

Pratsivnyky. Actyvisty. Zbirnyk dokumentiv ta materialiv (Kyiv: Instytut istorii Ukraiiny, 2013); Lynne Viola, "Stalin's Empire," in Timothy Snyder and Ray Brandon (eds.) *Stalin and Europe: Imitation and Domination, 1928–1953* (Oxford: Oxford University Press, 2014), pp. 19–38.

24   TsDAHOU, f. 1, op. 20, spr. 6277, ark. 3.

Selected Bibliography

Applebaum, Ann. *Red Famine: Stalin's War on Ukraine* (New York: Doubleday, 2017).

Klid, Bohdan. *The Holodomor Reader: A Sourcebook on the Famine of 1932–1933 in Ukraine* (Edmonton: CIUS, 2012).

Kulchytsky, Stanislav. *The Famine of 1932–1933 in Ukraine: An Anatomy of the Holodomor*. Translated from the Ukrainian by Ali Kinsella (Edmonton: CIUS, 2018).

Makuch, Andrij and Sysyn Frank E. (eds.) *Contextualizing the Holodomor: The Impact of Thirty Years of Ukrainian Famine Studies* (Edmonton: CIUS, 2015).

Plokhy, Serhii. *The Gates of Europe: A History of Ukraine* (New York: Basic Books, 2015).

Ukrainian Greek Catholics in Search of Ancestry, Belonging, and Identity

Iuliia Buyskykh

From 2015 to 2018, I conducted ethnographic research on religious dynamics and inter-confessional relationships in eastern Poland's Subcarpathia region. This research allowed me to reveal hidden interactions between contradictory memories of local confessional communities, specifically those comprising Roman Catholics, Greek Catholics and Orthodox followers, as well as a sense of belonging to definite places, and religious experience. This, in turn, enabled me to trace mechanisms that demonstrate how religion influences the forging of identities in this region and coexistence between various ethnic and confessional groups. Basing on participant observation, fieldnotes, and interviews, this chapter addresses the interplay of religion, memories, belonging, and identities.

My fieldwork is related to previous anthropological research on religion in southeast Poland, which emphasizes the following: Roman Catholic and Greek Catholic churches in this region have played a crucial role in constructing memories concerning Polish-Ukrainian history on the local level, influencing the relationships between the Polish majority and Ukrainian minority. While conducting my research, I observed how palpable the past seemed to be in the everyday lives of my interlocutors, regardless of their ethnic or religious identity, shaping present day imageries, and relationships.[1] According to Maurice Halbwachs, memory is maintained by the instrumentality of fundamental collective ideas and values, which constitute the "social framework of memory".[2] The main modes of preservation of collective memory are rituals and commemorations sanctifying the continuity of tradition,[3] as well as monuments, museums, and other "sites of memory",[4] reflected in the landscape. Danièle Hervieu-Léger gives an account of religion as representing a *"chain of memory"*, that is, a form of collective memory based on the sanctity of tradition. This continuity of memory "transcends history" and manifests itself in the religious act of recalling a past which "gives meaning to the present and contains the future".[5]

There are two important locations I will focus on in this chapter. The first is a pilgrimage sanctuary known as *Kalwaria Pacławska* ("The Roman Catholic Sanctuary of the Lord's Calvary and the Calvary Holy Mother of God"), which is also a Franciscan monastery. In August 2016 and August 2017, I took part in an interdenominational pilgrimage from Lviv in western Ukraine, to this shrine, organized by the Roman Catholic Church in Ukraine. Kalwaria Pacławska and the neighbouring village of Pacław lie nearly 30 km from Przemyśl and close to the Polish-Ukrainian border. Before the Second World War, this area also featured a well-known Greek Catholic pilgrimage site with a church and a number of chapels, which were subsequently destroyed in the mid-1950s by the Polish communist authorities. Currently there are grassroots attempts by the Ukrainian minority in Przemyśl to commemorate the former Greek Catholic shrine and revive its veneration.

The second location is the mountain of *Zjavlinnia* ("Apparition" in English), near the village of Kormanice, situated 10 km south of Przemyśl and approximately 13 km from Kalwaria Pacławska. Before 1939, this was the site of a Greek Catholic church and a chapel, both of which were also ruined and desecrated by the Polish communist authorities in the mid-1950s. This site was one of the stops on the pilgrimage route to the Greek Catholic pilgrimage site at Kalwaria Pacławska. Since the late 1990s, it has been revived by the efforts of the Ukrainian minority in Poland. There are annual pilgrimages in August from Przemyśl to Zjavlinnia, in which I personally took part in 2018.[6]

Brief Overview of Historical Context[7]

The complexity of interconfessional relations in the region of Subcarpathia goes back to the Union of Brest, which was signed in 1596 between the Ruthenian Orthodox Church (based in the Polish–Lithuanian Commonwealth) and the Holy See to ensure better coexistence between the Roman Catholic and Orthodox Churches and respective local elites on the territories of present-day Belarus, Lithuania, western Ukraine, and eastern Poland. Through this act, the new Uniate (Greek-Catholic) Church appeared. While the Church's administrative structures were to be subordinated to the Vatican, the Byzantine rite would be preserved. Thus, the Greek Catholic liturgy was supposed to be similar to its Byzantine counterpart. Over the following centuries, the liturgy followed by the Greek Catholic Church remained close to the one used in the region's Orthodox churches. Following the three partitions of Poland, in 1808 the eparchies of the original Ruthenian Uniate Church were split between the Austrian Empire, the Kingdom of Prussia, and the Russian Empire. The three eparchies fell under Habsburg jurisdiction were reorganized as the Greek Catholic Church soon after liquidation of the five eparchies that ended up in Russian Empire. Established in 1807, the Greek Catholic Church in the Austrian Empire became the only survivor of the original Uniate church formed through the Brest Union. Consequently, there were many Greek Catholic parishes in Galicia, namely in the Subcarpathia region.

Today, Kalwaria Pacławska is a Roman Catholic site, and the surrounding rural area is inhabited mostly by Roman Catholic Poles. Still, before the Second World War, this area had been more diverse. The history of the Roman Catholic site of worship was researched by the Franciscan priest Józef Barcik, who paid particular attention to the historical coexistence between Greek and Roman Catholics. The history of the Greek Catholic shrine at Kalwaria Pacławska and Pacław had been earlier chronicled by its last rector Josyp Marynowych.[8]

Since the 19th century, both Roman and Greek Catholic pilgrims have seen the hill of Kalwaria Pacławska as their pilgrimage site. The nearest villages were inhabited primarily by Greek Catholics known mostly as *Rusini (Rusyny)*, later to be called Ukrainians, while the Franciscan monastery on the mountain was surrounded by Greek Catholic churches and chapels. Greek Catholics took part in a number of services in the Franciscan Cathedral together with Roman Catholics, with Greek Catholic clergy being granted permission to perform masses. The situation began to change in the late 19th century, however, when both churches' clergies started to compete for parishioners. By the end of the 1880s, the majority of the Greek Catholic inhabitants of Pacław had changed their affiliation to Roman Catholicism and became the parishioners of the Franciscans' Cathedral in Kalwaria Pacławska. In 1867, Greek Catholic priests were no longer allowed to hold services in the Roman Catholic Cathedral. After receiving permission from the Vatican in 1868, the Greek Catholic clergy developed their own pilgrimage site around the church in Pacław. Despite the difference in calendars, Greek Catholic feasts connected with the Marian cult were sometimes celebrated simultaneously with the Roman Catholic feasts. In 1913, the new masonry church in Pacław was consecrated as the "Church of the Dormition of the Mother of God", leading to the development of a significant Greek Catholic pilgrimage site.[9]

This rivalry between Roman and Greek Catholic clergy in Kalwaria Pacławska occurred against the backdrop of several dramatic historical events, such as the First World War, the fall of the Austro-Hungarian Empire, Poland regaining independence in 1918, the Ukrainian-Polish War Eastern Galicia from 1918 to 1919,[10] and the increasingly oppressive policies of the government of the Second Republic of Poland towards its Ukrainian citizens.[11] However, the most crucial reference point for multiple memories and latent tensions between Poles and Ukrainians is the Second World War and its aftermath, when the border between the Soviet Union and communist Poland was delineated with both Polish and Ukrainian underground forces becoming active in Subcarpathia.

Due to various post-war international agreements, constructing the border between the USSR and Poland resulted in a wave of forcible resettlements between 1944 and 1946. Under this process, an estimated 480,000 of the region's Greek Catholic and Orthodox inhabitants were labelled as ethnic Ukrainians, based on their denominational affiliation, and required to relocate to Soviet Ukraine. The remainder, nearly 140,660 Greek Catholic and Orthodox civilians, were resettled in the former German territories acquired by Poland after the Second World War, as well as the northern and western part of the country, under the aegis of "Operation Vistula" in 1947.[12] Simultaneously, Poles, living in the post-war Ukrainian, Belarusian and Lithuanian soviet republics were "repatriated" to Poland. These population shifts were arranged as a part of Poland's post-war communist policy to set up an ethnically homogeneous nation-state and were framed against the wider establishment of new ethnographic frontiers in Europe, which saw the enforced transfers of millions of people. Furthermore, Ukrainians of both denominations, became a national minority, marginalized and stigmatized by the authorities in communist Poland. Such an attitude derived from the application of the collective responsibility to all people of Ukrainian origin for the activities of Ukrainian underground forces against the Polish resistance and civilians in Vohlynia and Eastern Galicia during the war.[13]

In 1946, the so-called "Lviv Council" took place in Lviv, which had already been occupied by the Soviet Union. Under its edicts, prepared by Soviet officials, "the liquidation of the Ukrainian Greek Catholic Church and its amalgamation into the Russian Orthodox Church" was officially mandated. From 1945 to 1946 many priests who refused to collaborate with the government and sign an agreement of "re-union with Orthodoxy" were murdered or sent to the Soviet camps as the Greek Catholic Church was forcible dissolved. Those who managed to survive went underground until 1989. In 1963, the Church was recognized internationally as Ukrainian through the efforts of Yosyf Slipyi, however, in Ukraine itself was only able to re-emergence in the early 1990s.

The key turning point in the revival of the Greek Catholic Church in Ukraine was a demonstration in Lviv demanding its legalization. This took place on September 17, 1989, with thousands in attendance. On October 29, during a service in the Transfiguration Cathedral in Lviv, Father Yaroslav Chukhniy commemorated Pope John Paul II instead of the Patriarch of Moscow and announced his conversion to Ukrainian Greek Catholicism. Following these events, many parishes affiliated to the Russian Orthodox Church followed suit, including those in other cities across Galicia.

In the communist Polish People's Republic, the Greek Catholic Church was also officially prohibited resulting in a number of priests facing persecution. In both countries, the Church was perceived as a threat because of the essential role it had played in the establishment of Ukrainian national identity and national movement on the terrain of former Habsburg Galicia. Some of the priests (22 Greek Catholic and five Orthodox) were sent by Polish communist authorities to the Jaworzno concentration camp in Silesia, southern Poland, having been accused of cooperation with the Ukrainian underground forces.

In 1957, ten years after Operation Vistula, and through the efforts of individual Greek-Catholic priests such as Ivan Dziubyna and Vasyl Hrynyk, new pastorates and parishes began to develop in western and northern Poland, where many Greek Catholics had been resettled. In 1989, Bishop Ivan Martyniak, became the first Greek Catholic to be ordained in Poland since the war and, in 1991, the Przemyśl Greek Catholic Eparchy was restored, covering the entire territory of Poland. In 1996, the Przemyśl-Warsaw Metropolis was formed, which included the Przemyśl – Warsaw Archdiocese and the Wrocław. The Gdańsk Ukranian Greek Catholic Eparchy and the Vistula River were defined as the border of division.

From a theological perspective, and at an institutional level, the Roman Catholic Church and the Greek Catholic Church represent one single Church, subordinate to the Vatican. However, the differences in liturgies and rites create the mistaken impression that they are two different religions. Simultaneously, the Greek Catholic Church in Poland is an independent Church with a Metropolitan Bishop subordinate to the Greek Catholic Church's Ukrainian synod in terms of liturgy and ordination of bishops. The Ukrainian Greek Catholic Church is the largest Eastern Catholic Church in the world. Currently it has approximately 6.5 million members. Within Ukraine itself, the

Greek Catholic Church is the second largest religious organization in terms of number of communities within the Catholic Church. In 2021, the Greek Catholicism in Ukraine is estimated to have 4.5 million adherents across 3495 parishes, while the Greek Catholic Church in Poland counted nearly 55.000 believers within 128 parishes, in 2015. This situation is changing dynamically because of the large influx of Ukrainian workers and especially, because of the recent wave of refugees since the full-scale Russian invasion of Ukraine on February 24, 2022.

"Homecoming" Pilgrimage as a Means of Forging Identity

From 1957 onwards, Greek Catholics in Poland were granted permission to hold liturgies in the Eastern rite. By the late 1950s, those Ukrainians who had gained state permission began to return voluntarily to their regional homelands from western and northern Poland. Both state and local authorities encouraged returning Greek Catholics to attend the newly created Orthodox parishes in Subcarpathia to prevent the creation of grassroots Greek Catholic ones.[14] In a number of cases, Greek Catholics returning from the northwest of Poland discovered their home churches lying in ruins, used as stores, or otherwise converted into Roman Catholic or Orthodox churches, as happened in the villages of Kłokowice and Młodowice near Kalwaria Pacławska. Nowadays, half of these villages are majority Orthodox, although most of the inhabitants are descended from Greek Catholic families, identifying as Ukrainians. The Eastern rite and similarities in liturgy, including its length, bodily engagement, extensive singing, habitual rituals such as lighting candles, recognizable Julian calendar, and the familiar aesthetics of church interiors attracted many of the returnees to Subcarpathia into joining Orthodox parishes, especially if they were held in former Greek Catholic churches. In the majority of cases, people were deeply concerned about belonging to a definite space, animated with divine power, and having "their church" present in the place where they were born and grew up, "where the ancestors' graves are".

For those Greek Catholics and Orthodox resettled to Soviet Ukraine between 1944 and 1946, there was obviously no possibility of visiting "their churches" in Polish Subcarpathia during the communist era. It was after the end of the communist regime in Poland and the fall of the Soviet Union that they and their descendants were able to return across the border. In a number of cases their "homecoming" became a pilgrimage. I see their movement in the broader context of traumatic experience and identity formation, of forgetting and remembering, shared by many groups who perform journeys to their homeland or to the land of ancestors. It has been proven that the phenomena of "roots tourism" and pilgrimage share many features. These pilgrimages contain a process of recovery: family and community memories of displacement, old wounds, and meaningful places. Demands to visit a place influenced by a yearning to connect with one's family history and searching for roots have also been framed as "pilgrimages of nostalgia".[15]

My Greek Catholic and Orthodox interlocutors, residents of Poland and Ukraine who define themselves as Ukrainians in addition to fluid confessional identities, are mostly unrelated to each other and do not maintain relationships beyond the pilgrimage. Nevertheless, they share a common discursive space and participate in cultural practices (including religious) which are closely related. They share emotional ties with particular places and interest in their families' past, connected with the history of the region. I will now address the various modes of "homecoming" pilgrimages performed by Ukrainian Greek Catholics: those who were expelled from Subcarpathia to Poland during Operation Vistula in 1947, only to later return with their descendants and those Ukrainian Greek Catholics and Orthodox who were the offspring of Greek Catholics from the eastern Poland resettled in Soviet Ukraine between 1944 and 1946. These acts of "returning" and the religious experience it generates helps to heal the old wounds rooted in dislocation, expulsion, and the silence of the Soviet era.

Nowadays the site at Kalwaria Pacławska where the Greek Catholic church stood, before being demolished in the 1950s, is private farmland, where the remnants of the church foundations can still be seen. During the Roman Catholic Marian feast of the Assumption, the area is used by pilgrims from Poland who will often pitch tents and park trailers near the very foundations without any knowledge of the local history.[16] There is also a memorial cross on the remnants of the church foundations, erected through the grassroots efforts of the Ukrainian Greek Catholic community in Przemyśl.

Other such form of grassroots pilgrimage seeks to engage with both Ukrainian Greek Catholics from Polish Subcarpathia and Ukrainian Galicia, being the descendants of those expelled from the area during the post-war resettlements. Greek Catholic and Orthodox pilgrims from Ukraine, and members of the Ukrainian Greek Catholic minority from Przemyśl, seem to be completely subaltern in this regional religioscape, dominated, as it is, by the Roman Catholic Church. Despite this, this localized border-shrine allows

Greek Catholics and Orthodox to gain meaningful experiences without having to negotiate for more.

From 2015 to 2017, I attended a Greek Catholic liturgy near the memorial crucifix. This liturgy is not part of the official pilgrimage program organized by the Franciscans, and is not advertised in shrine literature and sermons, being absent in the official Roman Catholic narration. The first time I attended in 2015, a Greek Catholic woman undertaking pilgrimage invited me to this liturgy and, in subsequent years, I followed both Greek Catholic and Orthodox pilgrims journeying to their place of memory. The liturgy was held on August 14th, the last day of the pilgrimage program at Kalwaria Pacławska. After the morning mass in the main cathedral and the general Roman Catholic pilgrimage program, Greek Catholics and Orthodox attended a Greek Catholic mass celebrated by a priest from Mostys'ka, on Ukraine's western border, originally from a family of Ukrainians who were resettled from Subcarpathia in 1946. Taking part in the masses, I observed how deeply my respondents were engaged in the liturgy, and how profoundly touched they were when the priest talked during the sermon about the forcible waves of resettlements from Subcarpathia, and about Greek Catholic priests murdered by the NKVD. After the liturgy pilgrims were crying, kissing the memorial cross, and the priest's vestment.[17]

Those Greek Catholics and Orthodox who took part in this liturgy, engaged in the act of pilgrimage mainly because they had wanted to see the place recognizable from family stories. They called the whole Roman Catholic site "our Kalwaria", highlighting that their grandparents or parents had taken part in Greek Catholic pilgrimages to Kalwaria Pacławska before the Second World War. The Orthodox pilgrims turned out to also be the descendants of Greek Catholic families forced to leave Subcarpathia between 1944 and 1946 and resettled in various regions of Soviet Ukraine. My respondents became acquainted during their pilgrimages to Kalwaria Pacławska. This strong need to attend a place where the church connected to their family stories had once stood, and their desire to take part in their own Greek Catholic liturgy, can be interpreted as an act of commemorating the memory of their ancestors resettled from that area, but also as a way to find their own identities.

Since the revival of the Ukrainian Greek Catholic Church, and the efforts of the Ukrainian minority in Poland to become more visible and regain some of their own community's buildings and churches, there have been attempts to restore the famous pre-war pilgrimage route and site at Kalwaria Pacławska. However, as mentioned above, these efforts proved to be unsuccessful in the face of the national influence wielded by the Roman Catholic Church in

Poland. Therefore, the Greek Catholic clergy, together with active members of the Ukrainian minority in Poland, started to develop a new pilgrimage route in Subcarpathia, connected with a Marian Apparition cult, around mountain of Zjavlinnia. In official narratives of the Greek Catholic Church in Poland, this is presented as a "reborn Ukrainian Kalwaria Pacławska". However, this sacred place is completely unacknowledged within the regional religioscape, being only visible to the Ukrainian Greek Catholic community in eastern Poland.

The mountain of Zjavlinnia is located in a forest not far from Fredropol, the district administrative centre. According to a local legend prevalent among local Greek Catholic and Orthodox Ukrainians, while gathering herbs for her sick mother before the Second World War, a local girl claimed to have seen an apparition of the Mother of God (*Bogorodytsia*) on the mountain. After disappearing, the girl alleged that the *Bogorodytsia* had left her footprints on a stone, from a which spring had started to flow. It was believed that this spring had healing powers, therefore pilgrims going to Kalwaria Pacławska would stop at Zjavlinnia to collect some of the water.[18]

During the Second World War, there was a wooden Greek Catholic church and a chapel near the spring. In 1952, the church was dismantled by the Polish communist authorities, and the wood used for construction in a nearby village.[19] My interlocutor, a Ukrainian Greek Catholic man in his 60s, told me that in the late 1980s, he and his brother, inspired by their fathers' stories about the "healing spring" in the forest and the site of a ruined Marian chapel, went there looking for it. Their parents were resettled from Subcarpathia in 1947 but returned in the 1970s, settling in Przemyśl. They told their sons that the church on Zjavlinnia must have been ruined, however a *"namolene mistse"* (place where generations of people prayed, and performed religious rituals) remained, and was still considered sacred. As Wanner emphasizes:

> In some Orthodox Christian countries, a 'place animated with prayer' (*namolene mistse / namolennoe mesto*) is said to be filled with energy that links individuals to others and to otherworldly powers. [...] Orienting religious practices to such sites circumvents anticipated coercion from clergy and institutions alike, but retains the shared understandings, emotional involvement, and attachments to places these vernacular religious practices breed.[20]

The two brothers claimed to have found the place in the forest where the church once stood and "felt blessed" to discover that a chapel near the "healing spring" still existed. They cleaned up the area around the spring, and with the help of friends started to renovate the chapel. This later became of place of interest to the whole Ukrainian Greek Catholic community in Poland and the revived Church.

For Greek Catholics in Poland the revival of old, abandoned, ruined places of worship became not only a means of religious, but also community, ethnic, and national revival. Understanding the impossibility of building a new church and restoring Greek Catholic pilgrimage to Kalwaria Pacławska, the community of Przemyśl has been reviving the Zjavlinnia sanctuary at a grassroots level since the mid-1990s. The funds for this were collected from the across the Ukrainian minority in Poland, and from diaspora communities in Canada. These mainly consist of Ukrainians and their descendants resettled to northwest Poland in Operation Vistula who had subsequently emigrated to Canada in the early 1990s. Furthermore, in the early 2000s the Greek Catholic Church in Poland was granted official permission to renovate the stone chapel near the spring as well as building a church and a Way of the Cross in the forest.

A one-day pilgrimage from Przemyśl to the mountain of Zjavlinnia has been held since 1995. It is organized annually on August 15 by the Cathedral of St. John the Baptist, which has since functioned as the main church for Greek Catholics in Subcarpathia since 1992. The new church on Zjavlinnia was built and sanctified in 2008. The pilgrimage itself is held at the start of Dormition Fast, preceding the Dormition of the Mother of God (*Uspinnia Bogorodytsi*), which the Ukrainian Greek Catholic Church (including Greek Catholics in Poland) celebrates on August 28, according to the Julian Calendar. From time to time, the pilgrimage is dedicated to a specific date relating to the history of the Ukrainian community in Poland. In 2017, for example, it was devoted to the commemoration of the 70th anniversary of Operation Vistula.

Pilgrimages, in this regard, serve as a means of claiming continuity with a particular place and with the group who share a history of attachment or belonging to it. Sacred sites and restored shrines not only contain memories and therefore history, but also produce history with people and through people, who are engaged in those shrines' revival, restoration, and working to keep those sites alive. In anthropological research on religion, pilgrimage is perceived as a way for individuals and groups to orient themselves in space, time, and history. Greek Catholics and Orthodox converts from Greek Catholic families, both of which represent the Ukrainian minority in Przemyśl and pilgrims coming from Ukraine, seek to reconnect their bonds with denominational, ancestral, and territorial legacies that have become distanced from them due to Soviet-era population transfers and the post-war relocation of state boundaries. Being uprooted, they seek to re-root themselves through pilgrimages and by this find their identity and place in history.

Notes

1. Buyskykh, "Forgive, Forget or Feign".
2. Halbwachs, *On Collective Memory*, p. 47.
3. Hervieu-Léger, *Religion as a Chain of Memory*, pp. 84–89.
4. Nora, *Between Memory and History*.
5. Hervieu-Léger, *Religion as a Chain of Memory*.
6. Buyskykh, "Routes to the Roots".
7. The history of this region is extremely complex, and it is difficult to present it adequately in the relatively short format of an article. Therefore, what is presented is a necessary simplification
8. Marynovych, *Kal'variia Patslavs'ka*.
9. Barcik *Kalwaria Pacławska*, p. 127; Marynovych, *Kal'variia Patslavs'ka*.
10. Zhurzhenko, "The Border as Pain and Remedy"
11. Portnov, *Istoriï dlia domashn'oho vzhytku*, pp. 113–116
12. Snyder, *Bloodlands*, p. 328.
13. Zowczak, *Antropologia, historia a sprawa ukraińska*, pp. 50, 61–62; Baraniecka-Olszewska, "Stereotypes in the Service", p. 95.
14. Litak, *Pamięć a tożsamość*, p. 103.
15. Ioannides, "Pilgrimages of Nostalgia".
16. Bujskich, "Pomiędzy pamięcią a granicą", p. 58.
17. Ibid, pp. 54–59.
18. Pidhirnyi, *Istoriia z'iavlinnia*, p. 45.
19. Ibid, p. 48.
20. Wanner, *An Affective Atmosphere of Religiosity*, pp. 70–71.

Selected Bibliography

Baraniecka-Olszewska, Kamila. "Stereotypes in the Service of Anthropological Inquiry. Pilgrims from Ukraine in the Kalwaria Pacławska Sanctuary," *Ethnologia Polona* 38:2017 (2018): 89–106.

Barcik, S. Józef, OFMConv, *Kalwaria Pacławska* (Warsaw: AK, 1985).

Budz', Kateryna. "Pidpil'ni ukraïns'ki hreko-katolyky i radians'ka vlada: rekonstruktsiia oporu (na prykladi sela Nadorozhna)," *Naukovi zapysky NAUKMA. Istorychni nauky* 169 (2015): 46–51.

Bujskich, Julia. "Pomiędzy pamięcią a granicą: Ukraińska pielgrzymka na Kalwarię Pacławską," *Etnografia Polska* 60 (2016): 43–62.

Buyskykh, Iuliia. "Forgive, Forget or Feign: Everyday Diplomacy in Local Communities of Polish Subcarpathia," *Journal of Global Catholicism* 2:2 (2018): 56–86.

Buyskykh, Iuliia. "Routes to the Roots: The Revival of Greek Catholic Sanctuaries in Eastern Poland," *Journal of Orthodox Christian Studies* 4:1 (2021): 69–91.

Buzalka, Juraj. "Nation and Religion: The Politics of Commemorations in South-East Poland," *Halle Studies in the Anthropology of Eurasia*, vol. 14 (Berlin: Lit-Verlag, 2007).

Coleman, Simon. "Do You Believe in Pilgrimage? Communitas, Contestation and Beyond," *Anthropological Theory* 2:3 (2002): 355–368.

Hałagida, Igor. *Duchowni greckokatoliccy i prawosławni w Centralnym Obozie Pracy w Jaworznie (1947–1949). Dokumenty i materiały* (Warszawa: IPN, 2012).

Halbwachs, Maurice. *On Collective Memory*. Edited, Translated, and with an Introduction by Lewis. A. Coser (Chicago and London: University of Chicago Press, 1992).

Hervieu-Léger, Danièle. *Religion as a Chain of Memory*. Translated by Simon Lee (London: Polity Press, 2000).

Hurkina, Svitlana. "The Response of Ukrainian Greek-Catholics to the Soviet State's Liquidation and Persecution of their Church: 1945–1989," *Occasional Papers on Religion in Western Europe* 34:4 (2014), Article 1: 2–3, http://digitalcommons.georgefox.edu/ree/vol34/iss4/1/

Ioannides Dimitri, Cohen Ioannides Mara W. "Pilgrimages of Nostalgia: Patterns of Jewish Travel in the United States," *Tourism Recreation Research* 27:2 (2002): 17–25.

Lehman, Rosa. "From Ethnic Cleansing to Affirmative Action: Exploring Poland's Struggle with its Ukrainian Minority (1944–89)," *Nations and Nationalism* 16:2 (2010): 287–288.

Litak, Eliza. *Pamięć a tożsamość: Rzymskokatolickie, greckokatolickie i prawosławne wspólnoty w południowo wschodniej Polsce* (Kraków: NOMOS, 2014).

Marynovych, Iosyp. O. *Kal'variia Patslavs'ka* (Przemyśl, 1929).

Nora, Pierre. "Between Memory and History: Les Lieux de Mémoire," *Representations* 26 (1989): 7–25.

Pasieka, Agnieszka. *Hierarchy and Pluralism. Living Religious Difference in Catholic Poland* (New York: Palgrave Macmillan, 2015).
Pidhirnyi B. "Istoriia z'iavlinnia", In O. Pidhirna, V. Pidhirnyj, B. Pidhirnyj, K. Kozak, M. Kozak (eds.) *Z'iavlinnia ta inshi mistsia kul'tu Presviatoï Bohorodytsi.* (Przemyśl, 2005): 45–56.
Portnov, Andrii. *Istoriï dlia domashn'oho vzhytku. Eseï pro pol's'ko-rosiis'ko-ukraïns'kyi trykutnyk pam'iati.* (Kyiv: Krytyka, 2013).
Snyder, Timothy. *Bloodlands: Europe between Hitler and Stalin* (New York: Basic Books, 2010).
The Ukrainian Greek Catholic Church: History (End of 1980s to the Present). 2011: https://risu.ua/en/the-ukrainian-greek-catholic-church-history-end-of-1980s-to-the-present_n52317
Tserkva s'ohodni: https://ugcc.ua/church/history/the-church-today/
Wanner, Catherine. "An Affective Atmosphere of Religiosity: Animated Places, Public Spaces, and the Politics of Attachment in Ukraine and Beyond," *Comparative Studies in Society and History* 62:1 (2020): 68–105.
Zhurzhenko, Tatiana. "The Border as Pain and Remedy: Commemorating the Polish–Ukrainian Conflict of 1918–1919 in Lviv and Przemyśl," *Nationalities Papers: The Journal of Nationalism and Ethnicity* 42:2 (2014): 242–268.
Zowczak, Magdalena. "Antropologia, historia a sprawa ukraińska," *O taktyce pogranicza, Lud* 95 (2011): 45–67.

Crimean Tatars: Claiming the Homeland

Martin-Oleksandr Kisly

Russia's full-scale invasion of Ukraine raised anew the issue of colonial nature of this war and intensified debates on decolonization of Ukraine and its history. Nonetheless, little has been done to discuss the history of the Crimea as of a Russian settler colony.[1] The history of Russian presence in Crimea cannot be comprehensive without considering its indigenous people, the Crimean Tatars, who ever since the annexation of the Crimean Khanate by the Russian Empire in 1783, had been the object of state-driven persecution and discrimination. In this vein, deportation of Crimean Tatars in 1944 should be treated as a high point of the Russian colonial policy in the peninsula. As this chapter intends to show, the history of Crimean Tatars' exile and return is distinctive from other cases of Soviet ethnic deportations, because they not only survived and maintained their connection with the homeland, but also managed to initiate a protest movement, inherently, anti-colonial, and eventually return to Crimea *en masse*.

Deportation

The deportation of the Crimean Tatars began at dawn on May 18th 1944. Soviet soldiers woke up children and their parents without offering any explanations allowing them 15 minutes to pack. In some villages people were simply pushed out of their houses by force and were not allowed to take even food: "Mother managed to take only a pot and the Quran"[2]. Children, women, and the elderly were taken to railway stations where they were loaded into cattle cars. Many children would lose their parents and a lot of families were dispersed while en route to the railway station. Without proper sanitary provision, food, or even medical care in the overcrowded cars, the entire Crimean Tatar population was forced to endure a several-week journey into exile. But not everyone was destined to reach their final destination. The deaths toll were extremely high due to the harsh travel conditions:

> Our car was closed, everyone was squatting, it was impossible to get up. I was thirsty and crying. Dad asked someone for a jar and took some water from a puddle on the floor, but I could not force myself to drink it. Father then began to ask the soldiers who were escorting us to give his child a sip of water. Suddenly water poured from the roof of the car, the adults looked and realized that it was urine: the soldiers standing on the roof were urinating right on our heads ... I don't remember how many days we were on the road. There was not enough air or water, and there was no toilet. People began to die because of hunger and epidemics. The bodies were thrown out at stops or just pushed through the window.[3]

The entire population was deported in three days. Despite the fact that the final destination, according to the "Decree of the State Defense Committee No.5859cc", was the Uzbek Soviet Socialist Republic, where some 151.136 Crimean Tatars were eventually settled, trains carry deportees were also sent to special settlements in the Mari Autonomous Soviet Socialist Republic (that received 8597), and the Kazakh Socialist Soviet Republic (4286). Several oblasts of the of the Russian Soviet Federative Socialist Republic all received deportees from Crimea including Molotov (10.555), Kemerovo (6743), Gorky (5095), Sverdlovsk (3594), Ivanovsk (2800), and Yaroslavl (1059).[4] Overall, the total number of Crimean Tatars deprived of their homeland was approximately 207.111. Between 1944 and 1956, some 49.200 of them died as a consequence of the deportations and the conditions they faced in special settlements with 65.9 per cent of total mortality rate having occurred in the first four years of exile.

As special settlers Crimean Tatars were subject to forced labor, while their rights and freedom of movement were restricted. In particular, there was a ban on leaving the settlement area without the permission of the commandant with the penalty being 20 years of hard labor in a penal camp.[5] Displaced persons also had to visit their commandant's office regularly to check in. However, some Crimean Tatars did attempt to escape. By 1947, a recorded total of 24.524 deportees had fled from their assigned places of settlement with the Soviet authorities only managing to recapture 9917.[6]

The first years of exile were marked by high death tolls caused by starvation, diseases, and acts of oppression committed by the authorities. The lack of proper housing, food shortages, new climatic conditions, absence of basic health-care facilities, and the consequent rapid spread of diseases resulted in severe demographic losses. Almost every family witnessed death as a consequence of starvation or infectious diseases. The Crimean Tatars were also exploited as a source of menial labor. Those sent to the special settlements were involved in industry, coal and uranium mining, chemical production, constructing new hydro-electric stations, and served as workers in various factories. Initially, however, the Soviet government sought to use the Crimean Tatar special settlers as a means of staffing state-run farms, with more than 100.000 being involved in agriculture.[7] Children, too, were obliged to work, especially in the cotton fields of Uzbekistan.

The official reason for deportation, according to the 1944 Decree, was the reported collaboration between Crimean Tatars and the German military during the Third Reich's occupation of Ukraine.[8] Without investigating or clarifying the persons involved in the work of the occupation administrations, the Soviet regime evicted the entire population, including women, children, and the elderly. However, was this the true reason? An entire nation could not have been accomplices of the Nazi regime. In addition, in each Crimean Tatar family at least one male member had fought in the Red Army. Moreover, it should also be noted that Crimean Tatars had participated extensively in the Soviet partisan movement, having represented a fifth of all its combatants in Crimea by 1944.[9] As a result, the civilian population of the Crimean Tatar villages had also suffered significantly at the hands of the German military for supporting the partisans:

> In 1943, the Germans burned down our village, because the population helped the partisans. They gave people 2–3 days to vacate the houses, and then doused them with gasoline and burned them. We moved to the village of Quchuq-Uzen. In April 1944 we returned to our native village and lived there in a hut.[10]

What then, was the actual reason for the deportations? Perhaps, the Soviet authorities sought to punish someone for the state's own military failures in the Crimea, with the Crimean Tatars being a convenient scapegoat. It seems that the most obvious reason were preparations for a potential war with Turkey in the Black Sea region, with Stalin anticipating the need for "cleaning" the territory of its Muslim Turkic-speaking population.[11] It should be noted that a number of researchers draw attention to the genocidal nature of Soviet deportations in general and that of the Crimean Tatars in particular.[12] Indeed, terms such as "ethnic cleansing", "ethnocide", and even "Soviet apartheid"[13] can be found in the literature relating to these deportations. The Soviet Union's mass deportation of Crimean Tatars also signaled the fulfillment of the "de-Tatarization" of the Crimean Peninsula, a process which had started under Tsarist rule following the annexation of the Crimean Khanate by the Russian Empire in 1783.

Fig. 2–5: Father is playing on the violin while his son is dancing Crimean Tatar traditional dance Haytarma. Uzbekistan, the 1950s. Photo by Mustafa Tomak. Courtesy of Nizami Ibraimov archive.

During the 19th century, hundreds of thousands of Crimean Tatars had even emigrated to the neighboring Ottoman Empire. The imperial Russian government had itself encouraged the impoverished Crimean Tatars to leave viewing them as politically unreliable and seeking to turn the peninsula into a settler colony. The 1944 deportations thus cannot be fully understood without reference to earlier bouts of chauvinistic Russian state-policy directed against the Crimean Tatars.[14] The Soviet clearances not only represented a continuation of these earlier imperial policies, but also removed almost all of the societal structures and assets that had allowed the Crimean Tatars to grow and thrive as a distinctive group. Moreover, the Soviet authorities had also succeeded in forging a cultural image of the Crimean Tatars as "traitors" and even sought to dehumanize them. After the evictions, the Crimean Autonomous Socialist Soviet Republic was transformed into a region. Crimean Tatar names were replaced, and their mosques were destroyed; Crimea lost all traces of its indigenous people and became literally Russified in the aftermath of the deportations as the authorities repopulated the peninsula with Russian and Ukrainian settlers.

The deportation of 1944 was supposed to completely remove the Crimean Tatars as a discernable nationality from the demographic map of the world, disrupting their traditional way of life, social structure and cultural institutes. The children of the exiled Crimean Tatars also lost the right to receive an education in their native language. The deportees were themselves expected to assimilate into the cultural milieu of Uzbekistan among the majority Uzbek population. Even Western observers of the time were predicting that the Crimean Tatars would, through assimilation, eventually disappear from history. According to Robert Conquest, these deported peoples became "unnations".[15] By calling them "Tatars" as opposed to their true name – *Crimean Tatars* – the state wiped out the very memory of their presence in Crimea while challenging their indigenous rights and sense of distinctive identity. The removal of the "Crimean" designation also opened the way for assimilation among other groups of "Tatars" and serve to erase all the traces of their presence on the peninsula. Thus the "Crimean Tatars" officially *ceased to exist*, being instead denoted as "citizens of Tatar nationality formerly living in Crimea." Moreover, their removal as "Crimean Tatars" from the official state censuses and renaming to simply "Tatars" also constituted a settler colonial policy aimed at transforming their homeland's indigenous population.[16]

A Point of no Return?

In 1956, a decree issued by the Presidium of the Supreme Council of the USSR released the Crimean Tatars from the special settlements. However, it remained forbidden for them to resettle in the Crimean region. Despite removing the special settlement restrictions, the Soviet government still considered them guilty of treason; Crimean Tatars were given the right to freely travel and settle across the territory of the Soviet Union, but not the Crimean

Peninsula. A memo prepared and issued by the Communist Party's Central Committee in 1956 further argued that Crimean Tatars didn't need to return to Crimea in order to enjoy their rights as Soviet citizens.[17] Thus, unlike other punished peoples, the Crimean Tatars remained deprived of the right to a restored autonomy as well as an opportunity to return to their homeland. Reflecting on the decree, the historian Chantal Lemercier-Quelguejay argued that "In the circumstances, the Crimean Tatars are doomed to be assimilated by the peoples among whom they are now living. Thus, a people with a long glorious and tragic past will disappear finally from history."[18]

The history of the deportation and return of the Crimean Tatars is unique, as they did not receive the right to return and renew their autonomy in 1956, like most "punished peoples". At the same time, they escaped the fate of other unrehabilitated groups: they did not invent a new homeland, as the Soviet Germans had done when they had been deported from the Volga region, Ukraine, and Crimea. Unlike groups such as the Soviet Koreans, who admit that they have become Russified, Crimean Tatars did not remain scattered all over the former Soviet republics. Instead, despite the ban, they sought to return to their homeland during the Soviet era. According to Greta Uehling, "we still lack a very clear understanding of the ways in which forced migrants in the former Soviet Union conceptualize their attachments to place, and the implications of these conceptualizations for the debate concerning people, place, and identity."[19] This raises the question: How did Crimean Tatars managed to return home?

It would be impossible to talk about Crimean Tatars' return without mentioning their connection to the lost homeland. Analysis of memories of deportation suggests that the traumatic loss of the homeland strengthened the exiles' sense of connection to it, with the idea of a return becoming a defining element of Crimean Tatar identity after 1944. Initially, Crimea was perceived as being their lost paradise or promised land. Those Crimean Tatars born in exile learned about the deportations and their lost homeland, primarily within the family circle. Thus, the extended Crimean Tatar families also became communities of memory in which memory and knowledge of the lost homeland and deportation were preserved, reproduced, and spread.

The emergence of this cultural longing to return was also influenced by the image of Crimea as a desirable place to live, as well as return to. Narratives of second generation exiles present an image of Crimea that was created for them by their parents: a fairy-tale homeland, where life flows harmoniously. The desire to return was rooted in this sense of harmony. From their exile, older generations of Crimean Tatars had constructed an image of a lost homeland as a place with incredible landscapes and plentiful resources.

The idea of returning as a process that would inevitably take place in the future, despite all the historical obstructions, was also formed in exile. For example, one of my interviewee, Ediye, as a child heard from her father that he would definitely bring his family home.[20] This image of Crimea also manifested as a call to leave everything and return to the homeland illegally. Such an aspiration to return also carried a sense of biological imperative through with Crimean Tatars came to understood themselves as an essential part of the homeland with their exile having severely ruptured this connection. Uehling mentions that some members of the second generation had even espoused a metaphysical theory that the molecules of the Crimean-grown fruits their parents had eaten eventually became a part of their bodies.[21] Thus, the notion of returning itself must be considered as an idea or ideology arising among the deported Crimean Tatars under the influence of hopes, dreams, or fantasies about relating to their homeland.

Return

After 1956, a Crimean Tatar national movement emerged with the goal of demanding state-organized mass return to Crimea and the restoration of the Crimean Autonomous Soviet Socialist Republic as a vehicle for national autonomy. The national movement was itself engaged in nonviolent resistance with almost the entire community participating. As a result of large-scale petition campaign, a new decree was issued on September 5th, 1967, according to which the collective charges against the Crimean Tatars were dropped. However, as it later transpired another resolution was also issued on the same day, according to which the Crimean Tatars were still forbidden from returning to their homeland.[22] It was ultimately this decree that provoked a process of reverse exodus with about 10.000 Crimean Tatars returning to their homeland between 1967 and 1978. Thousands undertook a journey into uncertainty together with elders who dreamed of dying in their native land, and children who had never seen Crimea, but had accepted the dream of it from their parents.

The returnees would first arrive into Simferopol, the administrative center of the Crimean oblast, and immediately seek to claim their right to live in the homeland. The parks and squares of the city were promptly occupied by groups of protesting Crimean Tatars who were waiting for an appointment with the local authorities in order to get some form of legal clarification. As they were not permitted to book hotel rooms, the streets of Simferopol subsequently became their temporary home. The human rights activist Petro Grigorenko, who came to Crimea in the summer of 1968, later wrote in his memoirs that the train station, airport, and city squares were filled with Crimean Tatars who "besieged" the Soviet and local party authorities. Grigorenko drew particular attention to the fact that Crimean Tatar families, many with small children in their arms, typically found themselves being forced to sleep on open ground in various public spaces.[23]

Fig. 2–6: *The Karabash family in central park of Simferopol, 1968. From the family archive.*

This strategy of return, which I term "through the front door", represented a form of direct action that lasted approximately a year. During this period, only 111 Crimean Tatars received a permit allowing them to relocate back to the peninsula. For others, however, it soon became apparent that they were not welcome in Crimea.

An additional resolution was issued on September 5, 1967, stating that the Crimean Tatars would be permitted to live anywhere within the Soviet Union, but only "in accordance with current legislation on the employment and passport regime". In practice, this meant that newcomers needed to register for a residence permit, for which they were required to have a job. However, without registration they could not apply for employment in the area they wished to live. This vicious circle had been deliberately created in order to prevent the Crimean Tatars from returning to their homeland. Nevertheless, many sought to circumvent this by heading to the smaller villages in the northern steppe region of Crimea, where they had a better chance of receiving a permit from the local authorities, or at least remaining unnoticed.[24]

In addition to creating obstacles for obtaining a residence permit, which was also required in order to purchase property, the authorities resorted to forced evictions. Police raids against Crimean Tatars were mostly conducted in the middle of the night, with officers forcing open doors and windows and dragging the residents, including women and children, to waiting vans, beating and tying the men's hands and feet. Once again, there was no opportunity to collect personal belongings and valuables were usually stolen by the police officers. Indeed, an evicted family could even find themselves be left at an empty railway station in the middle of the steppe without money. Such forced removals served as a form of re-traumatization, reminding older members of the deportations of 1944, and received the name "repeated deportation".[25]

Fig. 2–7: Forced eviction from Crimea, the 1970s. From Gulnara Bekirova's archive.

Nevertheless, this new wave of evictions from Crimea did not stop the Crimean Tatars from seeking to return again, with some families being forcibly removed three or more times. One of my informants, Abdripi, remembers that on returning to the Crimea in 1969, his family was forcibly evicted from peninsula in less than a month. Having collected a sufficient amount of money, they made a second attempt to return in 1975, during which his father was again accused of violating the passport regime and ordered to leave. He instead hid himself in the family home's closet every time the local policeman came to check.[26] However, not all those Crimean Tatars evicted from the peninsula succeeded in their efforts to return. As a result of such evictions, many began to form diaspora communities on the territory of the neighboring Kherson and Krasnodar regions. These new areas where evicted Crimean Tatars settled subsequently became places of transit or *spaces in between*, situated between exile and homeland.

Concluding this practice of return did not guarantee registration or protection against eviction, however, some Crimean Tatars did manage to purchase a house, register themselves, and find employment. Between 1967 and 1978, about 10.000 Crimean Tatars returned to their homeland in this way.[27]

The growing number of returnees provoked a strong reaction from the Soviet authorities. In 1978, the "Resolution of the Council of Ministers of the USSR" legalized forced evictions from Crimea, seeking to ensure that everything occurred "according to the law". The resolution forbade the sale of houses to Crimean Tatars, imposing sanctions on homeowners. Moreover, while those Crimean Tatars who had been forcibly evicted were previously able to return to their properties, this became impossible after 1978 as houses purchased by Crimean Tatars were demolished following the owners' removal. The adopted resolution was aimed only at Crimean Tatars.[28] This act suspended the return process for almost a decade. Such aggravation of the situation in Crimea also led to increased political persecution of Crimean Tatars and even led to several high-profile suicides, among which was the self-immolation of Musa Mamut in 1978.

Fig. 2–8: Musa Mamut funeral. From the book Reshat Dzhemilev, ed., Zhivoy fakel: samosozhzhenie Musy Mamuta (New York: Fond Krym, 1986).

With the start of *perestroika*, Crimean Tatars' migration back to Crimea resumed in 1987. This process was expedited by several events that took place in 1989 forcing former deportees to flee Uzbekistan for Crimea *en masse*. Notably among these was the Fergana Massacre, in which Uzbek nationalist mobs attacked the local Meskhetian Turkish community, themselves historic deportees from Georgia. Alongside the Meskhetian Turks, the Crimean Tatars who lived near the epicenter of the conflict became refugees. Elvira, one of my informants, recalls that in 1989 there was a feeling that Crimean Tatars would become the next target for nationalist violence.[29]

At the end of 1989, two documents were adopted, which met the requirements of the Crimean Tatars, albeit only partially. On November 14th, the Supreme Council of the USSR declared its intention to restore the rights of repressed peoples by law, approving the summary of the state commission on the problems of Crimean Tatars on the 28th. The document recognized the right of the Crimean Tatar people to return to their historical homeland and restore national integrity. Thus, the central government legitimized their right to return, prompting the start of a mass repatriation process.

Fig. 2–9: "Homeland or Death". Crimea, 1990. Photo by Valeriy Miloserdov.

Return entails an emplacement process, which means inventing or reinventing homeland because of the impossibility of returning to the past. A bitter taste of a promised land and everyday struggle for their rights made the Crimean Tatars face new challenges. During their absence Crimea was totally russified in every sense. After the collapse of the Soviet Union Russia preserved its influence on the peninsula. Upon repatriating to their native land, Crimean Tatars was involved in a struggle for their political rights and land. Local elites, former party nomenclature, maintained existing hierarchies in Crimea. As such, Crimean Tatars lacked the resources and institutions for restoration of their sovereignty. Unsatisfied claims of indigenous people, to a certain extent, was a cause of Russian occupation of Crimea in 2014.

Fig. 2–10: *"Here will be our home, son!". Crimea, 1991. Photo by Rifat Yakupov.*

Conclusion

The deportation of the Crimean Tatars represented the culmination of a colonial policy directed towards indigenous people of Crimea. Crimean Tatars were expected to assimilate into Uzbekistani society and disappear as a nation. Instead, they not only preserved their connection to the homeland while in exile but forged a modern form of Crimean Tatar identity. The long-term intention to return to Crimea endured, despite the ban. Thus, the Crimean Tatars national movement was anti-colonial by its very nature. The process of reverse migration by Crimean Tatars should thus be seen as a complex system intertwined with strategies for maintaining ties with Crimea from exile, different practices of return, and the emplacement process. Upon arriving back in their native land, Crimean Tatars found themselves in the position of being a colonized indigenous people in a settler colony, having returned to an area now dominated by Russian culture and a Russian-speaking population.

Notes

1. Rorry Finnin, "Why Crimea Is the Key to Peace in Ukraine," *Politico*, January 13, 2023, https://www.politico.com/news/magazine/2023/01/13/peace-ukraine-crimea-putin-00077746?fbclid=IwARotNIjTAuYM7OyTTg_ellplnqGGxroS4k_qlBqfW7pZcdgUbb5wwj-cmCU
2. Refat Kurtiev, ed., *Deportatsiia krymskikh tatar 18 Maia 1944 goda. Kak eto bylo. Vospominaniia deportirovannykh.* Vol. 2 (Simferopol: Odzhak, 2005), p. 151.
3. Ibid., p. 72.
4. Gulnara Bekirova, *Piv stolittia oporu: Krymski Tatary vid vyhnannia do povernennia (1941–1991 roky). Narys politychnoï istoriï* (Kyiv: Krytyka, 2017), p. 101.
5. Aleksandr Yakovlev, ed., *Stalinskie deportatsii, 1928–1953* (Moscow: Materik, 2005), p. 563.
6. J. Otto Pohl, "The deportation of the Crimean Tatars in the context of settler colonialism," *Uluslararasi Suçlar ve Tarih* 16 (2015), p. 57.
7. Brian Glyn Williams, *The Crimean Tatars. From Soviet Genocide to Putin's Conquest* (Oxford: Oxford University Press, 2016), p. 107.
8. Yakovlev, *Stalinskie deportatsii*, p. 497.
9. Williams, *The Crimean Tatars*, p. 94.
10. Kurtiev, *Deportatsiia krymskikh tatar*, Vol. 1, p. 67.
11. Williams, *The Crimean Tatars*, p. 97.
12. Robert Conquest, *The Nation Killers: The Soviet Deportation of Nationalities* (London: Macmillan, 1970); Mustafa Edige Kirimal, "Complete Destruction of National Group as Groups: The Crimean Turks," in *Genocide in the USSR: Studies in Group Destruction*, eds. Nikolai Deker and Andrei Lebed (New York: Scarecrow Press, 1958); Norman M. Naimark, *Stalin's Genocides* (Princeton: Princeton University Press, 2010).
13. Terry Martin, "The Origins of Soviet Ethnic Cleansing," *The Journal of Modern History* 70:4 (1998): 813–61; Brian Glyn Williams, "Hidden Ethnocide in the Soviet Muslim Borderlands: The Ethnic Cleansing of the Crimean Tatars," *Journal of Genocide Research* 4/3 (2002): 357–73; J. Otto Pohl, "Soviet Apartheid: Stalin's Ethnic Deportations, Special Settlement Restrictions, and the Labor Army: The Case of the Ethnic Germans in the USSR," *Human Rights Review* 13 (2012): 205–24.
14. Pohl, "The deportation," p. 57.
15. Conquest, *The Nation Killers*, p. 67.

16 Maksym Sviezhentsev, and Martin-Oleksandr Kisly, "Race in Time and Space: Racial Politics Towards Crimean Tatars in Exile, Through and After Return (1944–1991)," *Krytyka*, June 2021, https://krytyka.com/en/articles/racial-politics-towards-crimean-tatars.
17 Nikolai Bugay, ed., *Prinuditel'noe pereselenie krymskikh tatar: put' k reabilitatsii (materialy i dokumenty)* (Moscow: Akvarius, 2015), pp. 64–66.
18 Lemercier Quelquejay, "The Tatars of the Crimea, A Retrospective Summary," *Central Asia Review* 16:1 (1968), p. 25.
19 Greta Uehling, "Thinking about place, home, and belonging among Stalin's forced migrants: A comparative analysis of Crimean Tatars and Meskhetian Turks," in Tom Trier (ed.) *Meskhetian Turks at a crossroads: Integration, repatriation, or resettlement?* (London: Global Book Marketing, 2007), p. 610.
20 Ediye M., 1963. Interviewed by the author, 12 August 2015.
21 Greta Lynn Uehling, *Beyond Memory: The Crimean Tatars' Deportation and Return* (New York: Palgrave Macmillan, 2004), p. 115.
22 Bekirova, *Piv stolittya oporu*, pp. 197–203.
23 Petro Grigorenko, *V podpolye mozhno vstretit tolko krys* (New York: Detinets, 1981), p. 635.
24 Martin-Oleksandr Kisly, *Crimean Tatars' return to the homeland in 1956–1989* (PhD diss., National University of Kyiv-Mohyla Academy, 2021), p. 121.
25 Ibid., p. 127.
26 Abdripi S., 1962. Interviewed by the author, 2 August 2015.
27 Oleg Bazhan, ed., *Krymski tatary, 1944–1994: Statti, documenty, svidchennia* (Kyiv: Ridnii krai, 1995), pp. 240–241
28 Bekirova, *Piv stolittya oporu*, p. 241.
29 Elvira A., 1962. Interviewed by the author, 9 January 2014.

Selected Bibliography

Bekirova, Gulnara. *Piv stolittia oporu: Krymski Tatary vid vyhnannia do povernennia (1941–1991 roki). Narys politichnoï istoriï* (Kyiv: Krytyka, 2017).
Fisher, Alan W. *The Crimean Tatars* (Stanford: Hoover Institution Press, 1978).
Jobst, Kerstin Susanne. *Geschichte der Krim. Iphigenie und Putin auf Tauris* (Berlin, Boston: De Gruyter Oldenbourg, 2020).

Kisly, Martin-Oleksandr. "Post-Traumatic Generation: Childhood of Deported Crimean Tatars in Uzbekistan." *International Crimes and History* 16 (2015): 71–93.

O'Neill, Kelly. *Claiming Crimea: A History of Catherine the Great's Southern Empire* (New Haven: Yale University Press, 2017).

Pohl, J. Otto. "The deportation of the Crimean Tatars in the context of settler colonialism." *International Crimes and History* 16 (2015): 45–69.

Sviezhentsev, Maksym, and Martin-Oleksandr Kisly. "Race in Time and Space: Racial Politics Towards Crimean Tatars in Exile, Through and After Return (1944–1991)," *Krytyka*, 2021, https://krytyka.com/en/articles/racial-politics-towards-crimean-tatars.

Uehling, Greta Lynn. *Beyond Memory: The Crimean Tatars' Deportation and Return* (New York: Palgrave Macmillan, 2004).

Williams, Brian Glyn. *The Crimean Tatars. From Soviet Genocide to Putin's Conquest* (Oxford: Oxford University Press, 2016).

III. Sovereignty Regained:
Ukraine in the Post-Soviet Age

Primary Sources

Declaration of State Sovereignty of Ukraine (1990)
Passed by the Verkhovna Rada of the Ukrainian Soviet Socialist Republic

Kyiv, July 16, 1990

The Verkhovna Rada of the Ukrainian SSR,

- Expressing the will of the people of Ukraine;
- Striving to create a democratic society;
- Acting on the need of comprehensive guarantees of human rights and freedoms;
- Respecting national rights of all nations;
- Caring for the full-fledged political, economic, social, and spiritual development of the people of Ukraine;
- Recognizing the necessity to develop a constitutional state;
- Aiming to establish the sovereignty and self-rule of the people of Ukraine;

PROCLAIMS
State Sovereignty of Ukraine as supremacy, independence, integrity, and indivisibility of the Republic's authority within the boundaries of its territory, and its independence and equality in foreign relations.

I. Self-Determination of the Ukrainian Nation

The Ukrainian SSR as a sovereign national state develops within the existing boundaries to exercise the Ukrainian nation's inalienable right to self-determination.

The Ukrainian SSR protects and defends the national statehood of the Ukrainian people. Any violent actions against the national statehood of Ukraine undertaken by political parties, non-governmental organization, other groups or individuals shall be legally prosecuted.

II. Rule of the People

Citizens of the Republic of all nationalities comprise the people of Ukraine. The people of Ukraine are the sole source of state authority in the Republic. The absolute authority of the people of Ukraine is exercised directly through the Republic's Constitution, as well as via people's deputies elected to the Verkhovna Rada and local councils of the Ukrainian SSR. Only the Verkhovna Rada of the Ukrainian SSR can represent all the people. No political party, non-governmental organization, other group or individual can represent all the people of Ukraine.

III. State Power

The Ukrainian SSR is independent in determining any issue of its state affairs. The Ukrainian SSR guarantees the supremacy of the Constitution and laws of the Republic on its territory. State power in the Republic is exercised on the principle of its division into legislative, executive, and judicial branches. The Prosecutor General of the Ukrainian SSR, appointed by the Verkhovna Rada of the Ukrainian SSR, and responsible and accountable only to it, has the highest authority in the oversight of the precise and uniform application of law.

IV. Citizenship of the Ukrainian SSR

The Ukrainian SSR has its own citizenship and guarantees each citizen the right to retain citizenship of the USSR. The citizenship of the Ukrainian SSR is acquired and lost on the grounds determined by the law on citizenship of the Ukrainian SSR. All citizens of the Ukrainian SSR are guaranteed the rights and freedoms stipulated by the Constitution of the Ukrainian SSR and standards of international law recognized by the Ukrainian SSR. The Ukrainian SSR guarantees equal protection of the law to all citizens of the Republic regardless of their origin, social or economic status, racial or national identity, sex, education, language, political views, religious beliefs, type and character of occupation, place of residence or other circumstances. The Ukrainian SSR regulates immigration procedures. The Ukrainian SSR cares for and undertakes measures to protect and defend the interests of the Ukrainian citizens beyond the Republic's borders.

V. Territorial Supremacy

The Ukrainian SSR has the supremacy over all of its territory. The territory of the Ukrainian SSR within its existing boundaries is inviolable and cannot be changed or used without its consent. The Ukrainian SSR is independent in determining the administrative and territorial system of the Republic and the procedures for establishing national and administrative units.

VI. Economic Independence

The Ukrainian SSR independently determines its economic status and secures it by law. The people of Ukraine have the exclusive right to control, use and direct the national resources of Ukraine. The land, its interior (mineral wealth), air space, water and other natural resources found on the territory of the Ukrainian SSR, the natural resources of its continental shelf and exclusive (maritime) economic zone, and all economic and scientific-technical potential created on the territory of Ukraine are the property of its people, the material basis of the Republic's sovereignty, and is used to meet material and spiritual needs of its citizens. The Ukrainian SSR has the right to its share of the all-union wealth, especially in all-union gemstone and hard currency stocks and gold reserves, which were created through the efforts of the people of the Republic. Issues concerning the all-union property (joint property of all republics) are solved through agreements between the republics entitled to the above property. Businesses, institutions, organizations, and objects belonging to other states and their citizens, and international organizations may be located on the territory of the Ukrainian SSR and may use the natural resources of Ukraine in accordance with the laws of the Ukrainian SSR. The Ukrainian SSR independently establishes banking (including a foreign economic bank), pricing, financial, customs, and tax systems, develops a state budget, and, if necessary, introduces its own currency. The highest credit institution of the Ukrainian SSR is the national bank of Ukraine accountable to the Verkhovna Rada of the Ukrainian SSR. Businesses, institutions, organizations, and manufacturing companies located on the territory of the Ukrainian SSR pay a fee for the use of land and other natural and labor resources, and deductions from their foreign currency earnings, and pay taxes to local budgets. The Ukrainian SSR guarantees protection to all forms of ownership.

VII. Environmental Safety

The Ukrainian SSR independently determines procedures to organize nature protection on the territory of the Republic and procedures for the use of natural resources. The Ukrainian SSR has its own national committee for protection of the population from radiation. The Ukrainian SSR has the right to ban construction and to halt the operation of any businesses, institutions, organizations, and other objects that threaten environmental safety. The Ukrainian SSR cares about the environmental safety of its citizens, about the gene pool of its people, and about its young generation. The Ukrainian SSR has the right to compensation for the damages to the environment of Ukraine brought about by the acts of union authorities.

VIII. Cultural Development

The Ukrainian SSR is independent in solving issues associated with science, education, as well as cultural and spiritual development of the Ukrainian nation and guarantees all nationalities living on the territory of the Republic the right to free national and cultural development. The Ukrainian SSR guarantees national and cultural recovery of the Ukrainian nation, its historical consciousness and traditions, national and ethnographic characteristics, and functioning of the Ukrainian language in all spheres of social activity. The Ukrainian SSR strives to meet national and cultural, as well as spiritual and linguistic needs of the Ukrainians living outside the Republic's borders. National, cultural, and historical values located on the territory of the Ukrainian SSR belong exclusively to the people of the Republic. The Ukrainian SSR has the right to return into the ownership of the people of Ukraine its national, cultural, and historical values found outside the borders of the Ukrainian SSR.

IX. External and Internal Security

The Ukrainian SSR has the right to its own armed forces. The Ukrainian SSR has its own internal armies and bodies of state security subordinated to the Verkhovna Rada of the Ukrainian SSR. The Ukrainian SSR determines procedures for military service by citizens of the Republic. Citizens of the Ukrainian

SSR perform their military service, as a rule, on the territory of the Republic, and cannot be used for military purpose beyond its borders without the consent of the Verkhovna Rada of the Ukrainian SSR. The Ukrainian SSR solemnly declares its intention of becoming a permanently neutral state that does not participate in military blocs and adheres to three nuclear free principles: to accept, to produce and to purchase no nuclear weapons.

X. International Relations

The Ukrainian SSR, as an international law subject, maintains direct relations with other states, enters into agreements with them, exchanges diplomatic, consular and trade representatives, and participates in the activity of international organizations to the full extent necessary for effective guarantees of the Republic's national interests in political, economic, ecological, informational, scholarly, technical, cultural, and sports spheres. The Ukrainian SSR acts as an equal participant in international affairs, actively promotes the reinforcement of general peace and international security, and directly participates in the general European process and European structures. The Ukrainian SSR recognizes the prevalence of general human values over class values and the priority of generally accepted standards of international law over the standards of the domestic law. Relations of the Ukrainian SSR with other Soviet republics are built on the basis of agreements concluded on the basis of the principles of equality, mutual respect, and non-interference in internal affairs. The Declaration is the basis for a new constitution and laws of Ukraine and determines the positions of the Republic for the purpose of international agreements. The principles of the Declaration of the Sovereignty of Ukraine are used for preparation of a new union agreement.

Originally published on the Website of the Verkhovna Rada of Ukraine's website: http://static.rada.gov.ua/site/postanova_eng/Declaration_of_State_Sovereignty_of_Ukraine_rev1.htm. *Public Domain.*

Home is still possible there...

Kateryna Kalytko

Home is still possible there, where they hang laundry out to dry,
and the bed sheets smell of wind and plum blossoms.
It is the season of the first intimacy
to be consummated, never to be repeated.
Every leaf emerges as a green blade
and the cries of life take over the night and find a rhythm.
Fragile tinfoil of the season when apricots first form
along with wars and infants, in the same spoonful of air,
in the stifling bedrooms or in the cold, from which the wandering
beg to enter, like a bloom of jellyfish, or migratory blossoms.
The April frost hunts white-eyed, sharp-clawed,
but the babies have the same fuzzy skin for protection.
What makes them different is how they break
when the time comes for them to fall, or if they get totally crushed.
Behind the wall a drunken one-armed neighbor
                                 stumbles around his house,
confusing all the epochs, his shoulder
bumps into metal crutches from WWI,
                                 a Soviet helmet made of cardboard,
and the portrait of a man with a glance like a machine gun firing
and hangers for shirts, all of them with a single sleeve.
So they will fall and break into pieces and fates
branches parted, fruit exposed to the winds.
The neck feels squeezed, in the narrow isthmus of the throat
time just stands still and mustard gas creeps through the ditches.
All of this is but a forgotten game we play in the family backyard,
hiding amongst the laundry that hangs outside

       the world becomes more fragile at each moment,
                    and when you suddenly embrace
       through the cloth — you don't know who it is,
                    and whether you've lost or found.
       And the swelling parted body of war intrudes into a blossoming heart
       because we didn't let it enter our home on a cold night to warm itself.

Translated from the Ukrainian by Olena Jennings and Oksana Lutsyshyna.

Originally published in Oksana Maksymchuk and Max Rosochinsky (eds.) Words for War: New Poems from Ukraine, with an introduction by Ilya Kaminsky and an afterword by Polina Barskova (Boston, MA: Academic Studies Press; Cambridge, Mass.: Harvard Ukrainian Research Institute, 2017). Reproduced with permission.

Matvey Vaisberg, The Wall [Stina] (2014)

Matvey Vaisberg, Painting from The Wall cycle (2014). Reprinted with the artist's permission

Conversation Pieces

Between the Holodomor and Euromaidan: In Search of Contemporary Ukrainian National Identity

David Marples, in conversation with Manuel Férez Gil

David R. Marples is a Distinguished University Professor of Russian and East European History, University of Alberta. He is the author of sixteen single-authored books, including *Understanding Ukraine and Belarus* (2020), *Ukraine in Conflict* (2017), *Our Glorious Past: Lukashenka's Belarus and the Great Patriotic War* (2014), and *Heroes and Villains: Creating National History in Contemporary Ukraine* (2008). He has published over 100 articles in peer-reviewed journals. He has also edited four books on nuclear power and security in the former Soviet Union, contemporary Belarus, and Ukraine. At the University of Alberta, he received the J. Gordin Kaplan Award for Excellence in Research (2003) and the University Cup in 2008. In 2009, he was Visiting Fellow for the Wirth Institute at the Department of Contemporary European History, University of Innsbruck where he taught a course on Ukraine and Belarus as EU Border Countries. In 2013, he was Visiting Fellow at the Slavic and Eurasian Center, Hokkaido University, Japan.

Manuel Ferez: *Your study and publications on Russia and Eastern Europe are very extensive. To start the interview, we would like to know how you, a Canadian professor, became interested in these topics.*

David Marples: I have no family background in eastern Europe. My interest began as an undergraduate at the University of London. I had run out of courses for my History degree and opted for a couple at the School of Slavonic Studies. The first was in person on Imperial Russia and the second was a directed study with Dr. Martin McCauley. It sparked my interest in the area, and in the Soviet Union, and I never really looked back. Initially, I moved from the

UK to Canada to work with a Professor from Ukraine, Ivan Lysiak-Rudnytsky. He introduced me to the Canadian Institute of Ukrainian Studies and its Director, Manoly R. Lupul. Rudnytsky was the supervisor of my MA thesis, and moved me firmly in the direction of Ukraine. I had been advised earlier, however, that our generation was producing too many Russian specialists and that it would be wiser to start to study one of the national republics of the USSR. Ukraine seemed the obvious choice. My PhD supervisor at Sheffield, Everett M. Jacobs, was the most influential figure in my early career, an American from Boston of Jewish background.

M.F.: *Your Ukraine-related publications include three books that I found very important "Understanding Ukraine and Belarus" (2020), "Ukraine in Conflict" (2017) and "Heroes and Villains: Creating National History in Contemporary Ukraine" (2008). I would like to start with the theme of creating the contemporary national history of Ukraine. What are the central elements in this identity? How do you think the Russian invasion and aggression (2014-present) has impacted the development of this Ukrainian national identity?*

D.M.: Ukraine inherited the Soviet legacy and after independence there was no obvious direction either for the teaching of history or understanding the past. For some years, the country's path was ambivalent. By the early 1990s, the Famine of 1933 was already being elevated as an event that defined the identity of modern Ukraine, namely suffering at the hands of a regime based in Moscow. At a conference in Kyiv in 1990, it was referred to as an act of Genocide. Ukrainian focus on the famine had been evident to me from my second visit to Ukraine in 1989. Prior to late 1987, it was officially denied to have happened at all. While such revelations were taking place, independent Ukraine continued to honour the victims and victory of the "Great Patriotic War." Even in 2003 Kharkiv, the History Museum was featuring an exhibition of the Holodomor on one floor and the liberation of the city on the other. School textbooks were equally muddled.

The Famine-Holodomor was gradually elevated to be the most important historical marker for modern Ukraine. The process began under the presidency of Leonid Kuchma, but reached its peak during the 2005–10 presidency of Viktor Yushchenko. The memory of the Famine had been largely preserved by the Ukrainian Diaspora in the West, particularly on its major anniversaries. Western publications, sponsored by Ukrainian institutions, included Robert Conquest's 1986 book *The Harvest of Sorrow* and the collection *Famine in Ukraine*

1982-83, edited by Roman Serbyn and Bohdan Krawchenko. Yushchenko opened the Holodomor Memorial in Kyiv, which contains books of memory from the affected oblasts of Ukraine and an elaborate monument in the shape of a candle. It stands on the hill overlooking the city, alongside the Great Patriotic War Museum and the Pecherska Lavra monastery.

Yushchenko began a world tour to push the policy of the Ukrainian Famine as a Genocide, which was accepted by some, though far from all Western countries. In 2008, the Ukrainian Parliament accepted the decree on the same topic, but with a bare majority as a large portion of MPs abstained from voting. The focus on the Famine, and with Moscow (and particularly [Joseph] Stalin, [Lazar] Kaganovich and [Viacheslav] Molotov) as the perpetrator placed Russia in the position of "the other" in Ukrainian historical memory. The Russians, including then president Dmitry Medvedev, angrily rejected the theory, arguing that the famine was more widespread than the borders of Ukraine, and had affected equally the Volga Region and (two years earlier) Kazakhstan, at that time part of the Russian Republic.

If the Western Diaspora initiated the campaign and caused it to be rooted in Ukraine itself, it has not remained static. In particular, the Holodomor Research and Education Consortium (HREC), sponsored by Ukrainian businessman James C. Temerty, has been very active in conferences, publications, and school and higher education curricula. Key centres of research are the Ukrainian Research Institute at Harvard University and the Canadian Institute of Ukrainian Studies in Edmonton and Toronto, with programs funded by Temerty. The result to date has probably been "preaching to the converted" though the publication of the book *Red Famine* by Anne Applebaum in 2017 may also have been influential among Western readers. Whatever its benefits, HREC is a political entity that adheres to a certain view of the famine and for that reason I have reservations about its influence.

The choice of the Famine as the foundation stone of modern Ukraine signified that national suffering with Ukrainians as victims was more important than national achievements. The choice of the name Holodomor (death by hunger) was similar to that of the Holocaust, the destruction of European Jews during the Second World War, which was the obvious marker for comparison. Yushchenko led the way in inflating the number of famine victims to 7 and then 10 million—current research conducted by demographers suggests that the most likely figure was 3.9 million on the territories that comprised Ukraine in 1991. Thus, at the level of state propaganda, the Holodomor resulted in more victims than the number of Jews who died in the Holocaust, the event that largely defined the word Genocide. It was a rewriting of the past that reached a new level in the "cult of competitive suffering."

While the Famine has been a divisive issue in Ukrainian-Russian relations, it is not the only event in the 20th century to have escalated tensions decades later. The legacy of the Organization of Ukrainian Nationalists (OUN) and Ukrainian Insurgent Army (UPA) continues to elicit widespread debate as to their impact on modern Ukraine and place in national identity building. I described the discussions among scholars in my book *Creating National History in Contemporary Ukraine*, and concluded that they were fruitful and well informed. Unfortunately, however, the topic of extreme Ukrainian nationalism became heavily politicized well before Russia attacked Ukraine in 2022.

First, however, a little background for the reader. The OUN was founded in 1929 in interwar Poland, on the roots of the Ukrainian Military Organization. Noted for extremist actions against Polish officials in the heavily Ukrainian populated region of southeastern Poland, it split into two wings in 1940: an older group under Andrii Melnyk and a younger one under Stepan Bandera. Though both played roles during the Second World War, it is the OUN-B that has been the focus in recent times. Bandera himself played a peripheral role during the war, spending most of the time under arrest in the German concentration camp at Sachsenhausen near Berlin, but he has remained a symbol for the far-right in modern-day Ukraine. In the Ukrainian Diaspora, he remains a controversial but influential figure.

In October 1942, the Ukrainian Insurgent Army was founded during the German occupation of Poland. Led by OUN member Roman Shukhevych, who had played a role in the German auxiliary police in occupied Ukraine and Belarus, it carried out ethnic cleansing of millions of Poles the following spring in Volhynia. After the Soviet army advanced into the western regions of Ukraine, UPA carried out a desperate battle to prevent the reestablishment of Soviet rule that lasted into the late 1940s and early 1950s. Shukhevych was killed in a skirmish with Soviet security forces near Lviv in 1950.

About the time *Creating National History* was published, Yushchenko made both Bandera and Shukhevych "heroes of Ukraine." The move represented a belated attempt to restore their popularity toward the end of a fairly disastrous presidency and was reversed after the 2010 presidential elections when Viktor Yanukovych was victorious. Neither that election or the various parliamentary elections suggested that extreme nationalism of the OUN variant had much influence in Ukraine by 2010. More important is the intervention of the state in historical memory and identity building. The Famine and the OUN had been advanced as two platforms offering yardsticks to follow. For Bandera and Shukhevych, Communism was the enemy and Ukrainian independence the goal. The fact that neither played a role in the latter's eventual attainment was largely forgotten. This focus on the 20th century was aways going to be divisive. Ukraine slowly began to reject its Soviet-era identity but the question with what to replace it was a difficult one.

M.F.: *Among the recent events that happened in Ukraine, the EuroMaidan revolution is undoubtedly one of the most important. You published with Frederick Mills "Ukraine´s Euromaidan: Analyses of a Civil Revolution in Ukraine", in that sense could you share your perspective on what happened on Maidan and how it has been incorporated into the Ukrainian national narrative.*

D.M.: The uprising that began in Kyiv's Maidan in November 2013 went through several phases that were not always closely related. It began as a protests against President Yanukovych's decision not to sign an Association Agreement with the European Union. That stage lasted until the end of November. Initially, support was very broad, and the demonstration was peaceful, but it was broken up by force on the night of November 30 and December 1, and thereafter a new stage began.

The second stage incorporated a lot of elements: in general, there was disgust as the overt corruption of the Yanukovych government and that of the president personally. On January 1, there was a large march through the Maidan to commemorate the birth of Stepan Bandera, the OUN leader, which symbolized perhaps that the far-right was taking a more active role. By early 2014, Russian-speaking nationalists of the Right Sector had joined in. Some protesters were armed, but the majority remained peaceful. In February, the confrontation between the Maidan protesters and the Berkut police on the government side became more violent. It culminated in the shooting of demonstrators by snipers, operating from the roofs of surrounding buildings. No definitive identification of these snipers has ever surfaced.

Euromaidan became known as the "Revolution of Dignity" and those who died as martyrs for the cause of a Ukraine moving away from Russia and the Soviet era. Support for the uprising divided Ukrainian society. It was heavily backed by western Ukraine and most of Kyiv, but opposed in the east and parts of the south. It ended with the departure of Yanukovych and the election of a new government. It was not the first such mass protest in the Maidan but it was the most decisive. The Orange Revolution was not a revolution in the sense that it did not replace the government or the existing structure. Russia's choice, Yanukovych duly became president in the next election in 2010. But in 2014, the protesters rejected the mediation of Europeans and the ruling Regions Party dissolved. Everything would be different thereafter. It was a decisive change.

M.F.: *What are the effects of Euromaidan on the Ukrainian society?*

D.M.: After Euromaidan, Ukraine was at war. Crimea was annexed by Russia, and Russian-backed governments took over parts of the Donbas region, including the two major cities Donetsk and Luhansk. Russia had not formally invaded these regions but backed them materially and with weapons. They survived Ukraine's "Anti-Terrorist Operation" (ATO) of the summer of 2014 solely because of Russian support. In 2015, Ukraine issued four Memory Laws, which outlawed the Communist Party and several other far left parties. Communist symbols were banned, and the names of towns, streets, and smaller settlements derived from the Soviet era were changed to more appropriate Ukrainian names.

Perhaps most seriously, one of the laws made it an offence to denigrate the dignity of "fighters for Ukraine of the 20th century," with a list of names that included Bandera and Shukhevych. All those who had worked for the Soviet structure were excluded, including even those who had brought about Ukraine's declaration of independence in 1991, such as the first president Leonid Kravchuk. Lenin statues had been mostly toppled during the Euromaidan protests. Those remaining were now removed as well as statues to other figures of the Communist era. An anti-corruption committee was established. Within a few years, the Ukrainian Orthodox Church declared independence from its Moscow counterpart. The army was also gradually reformed and more decisively separated from its Soviet era, severing links between Ukrainian and Russian officers.

One should not exaggerate changes to the political structure or in removing corruption. Ukraine's first post-Maidan president was an oligarch and one of the co-founders of the Regions Party, Petro Poroshenko. Though he espoused the new principles and adopted nationalist rhetoric, he did not separate himself from his business or embark on a radical policy to eliminate corruption in society. Ukraine became poorer in the period 2014–19, replacing Moldova as Europe's poorest country. But the outer appearance of society changed, the gap between Ukraine and Russia widened. Armed nationalist groups were initially purged and then allowed to roam the streets of Kyiv and other cities. Some attacked LGBT parades and gypsy camps.

The divisions in society remained. Petty scandals occupied society. Ukraine was becoming more democratic but there were deep scars. Prospects for joining the EU receded as a result of the corruption, and there was no consensus on NATO membership. But the outer appearance was transformed.

M.F.: *Ukraine, its history, culture and identity, has occupied a rather marginal space in the curricula of Latin American universities. Current events drew the world's attention to Ukraine. As an expert on Ukraine, how to approach Ukraine without falling into the sensationalism of the media and in a way that allows us to place it in a broader perspective: democratization, Europeanization and liberalization of the post-Soviet space.*

D.M.: First of all, Ukraine needs to be removed from the neo-colonial Russian context and treated as a separate entity with its own history and culture. Ukrainians have clearly been recognized as an ethnic group meriting their own state for the past century, and they were the largest group not to receive their own state from the Paris Peace Treaties that ended the First World War in 1918. By numbers alone, a country of over 40 million people merits individual scrutiny.

Second, Ukraine has a rich, multicultural history that needs to be examined beyond its ethnic context. For much of its history, the lands that make up Ukraine today were part of foreign empires and controlled from outside Kyiv or Kharkiv (or for that matter, Lviv). Thanks to a very active Diaspora, there is a tendency for world governments to look at Ukraine from a very western Ukrainian or Galician perspective, with overemphasis on Ukrainian nationalism and the "heroes" of the Second World War. Such stress does not reflect Ukraine as a whole, as reflected in the 2019 election that brought Volodymyr Zelensky to power. Most Ukrainians want democracy, but they also support moderation and toleration. They struggled in part because of the longevity of the Communist legacy that resulted in former Communists occupying high offices for so many years: Kravchuk, Kuchma, and others. Ukrainians are an integral part of Europe. They always have been. Possibly the roots of East Slavic states like Russia and Belarus can be traced back to the Kyiv state of the tenth century. It is still debated. But by the 21st century, there were clear differences between Ukraine and its east Slavic neighbours.

The third point pertains to academia. For generations, scholars focused on Russia and believed that by studying Russia they understood Ukraine. It is a fallacy. Thanks to social media, many experts on Russia are today expressing their views on Ukraine as a closely related entity. The war in Ukraine is considered by some as a "local" Russian affair. There is no understanding of the separate evolution of Ukraine, its traditions and culture, outside the general milieu of Greater Russia. Likewise, there is no recognition among such scholars of Ukrainian sovereignty and right to pursue its own path. Instead, they speak of the follies of NATO expansion, or the machinations of the United States as causes of the current war – following directly the rhetoric of Vladimir Putin and Sergei Lavrov.

It will take a generation to eradicate such influences despite the fact that self-determination of nations was one of the original Wilsonian principles in which post-First World War settlements were elaborated. None of this is to suggest that Ukraine does not have problems or is a unified society. It does and they have not been nullified by the war, but they need not be the prime focus while Ukraine is being subjected to such barbarities during the Russian assault.

M.F.: *The book you edited entitled "The War in Ukraine's Donbas. Origins, Contexts, and the Future" has just been published. It seems to me a very important issue that must be addressed beyond the politicized narratives established by Russia and her propaganda and understand the Donbas within the Ukrainian processes. Please tell us a little about the book and why it is important for the readers to approach this topic through serious and academic publications like yours.*

D.M.: The book arose from a conference I organized at the University of Alberta. I realized that there were wide disparities among scholars as to why war developed in the Donbas and that in many ways the area is quite different from other regions of Ukraine. Even in the Soviet period there was a distinct Donbas identity that is neither Ukrainian nor Russian. I gathered about 20 scholars, including some local ones, with others from Ukraine, United States, Japan, and Russia. Not everyone I invited could come, but the selection was ideal. We covered Euromaidan and its aftermath, the start of the war, the Donetsk People's Republic, refugees and displaced persons, economic issues, and some suggestions for ways to end the war.

Today, much of our information about the world comes from social media. But it has meant that many non-experts gain a voice, and some of them have little knowledge of the subject area. I think the chapters in this book are all offered by scholars from the area or with a deep understanding of the Donbas. The book avoids polemics and propaganda and explains how the Donbas war originated and why it has lasted so long. I accepted the premise that Russia played a major role but argued that it was not the only factor in explaining the protracted conflict. Certain conditions existed that made separatism more likely. And there was the recent memory of Yanukovych, the former governor of the region, who filled his Cabinet with appointees from Donetsk in the government of 2010. There are so many corroborating elements: declining industries, mafia gangs, corruption, political clans, and the like.

M.F.: *It is difficult and irresponsible to predict what will happen with the Russian war and invasion of Ukraine, but it would be interesting if you could tell us what the post-conflict scenarios could be not only for the future of Ukraine but for that of Russia, its civil societies and political elites.*

D.M: It is difficult for sure. I should say at the outset that I consider the attack on Ukraine to be the greatest mistake of Putin's political career. It was poorly thought out and the army was ill prepared for the drive on Kyiv. The war has cost Russia dearly. If Russia loses the war and is forced to give up its occupied territories in the south (excluding Crimea) and the east, then I think it will cost Putin his position as president. At worst, it could lead to separatist movements within the Russian Federation and the disintegration of the state. But let is consider some possibilities.

a) A stalemate situation mediated by foreign powers such as Turkey and Israel would weaken Ukraine and lead to the loss of further territories to Russia. It would not preclude further wars and any future Ukrainian government based on such mediation would be weak and short-lived. The future of the Ukrainian state would always be in doubt and post-Putin Russia governments would likely try to expand occupied territories in the future.

b) A complete Russian victory is unlikely as long as Ukraine is backed by Western powers with weapons and credits. But Putin could complete the occupation of the Donbas and then seek an armistice on the grounds that Russia had achieved its main goals. In turn, a settlement based on these acquisitions would bring down the current Ukrainian government. Russia in my view would need to step up conscription and change its current dependence on raw recruits and career soldiers, co-opted from the poorest strata of society, particularly from non-Russian republics. The existence of the so-called Donetsk and Luhansk People's Republics increases the chances of success along these lines. Like a) above, this outcome would create huge problems for the future of the Ukrainian state.

c) A complete Ukrainian victory may be the most unlikely outcome given the comparative weakness of Ukraine compared to Russia, and the wide disparity in numbers and resources. But it is the only outcome that could offer the possibility of a lengthy period of peace for Europe. Ukraine would regain all the territories it possessed in 1991, with the exception of Crimea. I can think of no obvious way Ukraine could retake Crimea without a navy of any size and with Russia controlling the Black Sea. And it may not be a desired outcome anyway, since Crimea is a difficult appendage that requires a constant supply of water and food. Moreover, the Russian presence in Crimea precludes any easy integration within Ukraine. It was provided as a symbolic gift by the Russian Republic in 1954 with no anticipation that Ukraine would gain independence less than four decades later. One could argue that it is also not part of Russia given its Tatar (not to mention Greek) heritage, but Russians make up most of the population. Thus, my recommendation to Ukraine in the event of a complete land victory would be to relinquish Crimea on a permanent basis.

In the event that Russian forces are driven out of Ukraine, then I think Ukraine will need significant help to rebuild its towns and villages destroyed by missiles and warfare. It will also require more protection than it gained in 1994 when it gave up its nuclear weapons. Ultimately, that protection would require NATO membership. It is as vulnerable as the Baltic States, for example.

On a global level, changes need to be made to the United Nations, which has proved powerless in the event of a major 21st century European war. The Security Council cannot remain in its present form since there is no possibility of preventing a Russian veto, just as in the past the United States and China could also limit its functioning during international crises in which they played key roles. I don't think it should be abolished. It is the only such body in place. But a Security Council based on the victors of the Second World War no longer makes sense. A rotation between major nations makes more sense but one would need to determine how to define the word "major."

First Published on 9 September 2022. This interview first appeared in Spanish on https ://orientemedio.news.

Works cited

Applebaum, Ann. *Red Famine: Stalin's War on Ukraine* (New York: Doubleday, 2017).
Conquest, Robert. *The Harvest of Sorrow: Soviet Collectivization and the Terror-Famine* (Oxford: Oxford University Press, 1986).
Marples, David. *Heroes and Villains: Creating National History in Contemporary Ukraine* (Budapest, New York: Central European University Press, 2008).
Marples, David, and Frederick Mills (eds.). *Ukraine´s Euromaidan: Analyses of a Civil Revolution in Ukraine* (Stuttgart: ibidem Press, 2015).
Marples, David. *Ukraine in Conflict: An Analytical Chronicle* (Bristol: E-International Relations, 2017).
Marples, David. *The War in Ukraine's Donbas. Origins, Contexts, and the Future* (Budapest, New York: Central European University Press, 2022).
Marples, David. *Understanding Ukraine and Belarus: a Memoir* (Bristol: E-International Relations, 2020).
Serbyn, Roman, and Krawchenko, Bohdan (eds.). *Famine In Ukraine 1932–1933* (Edmonton: Canadian Institute of Ukrainian Studies, 1986).

Ukraine: Between National Security and the Rule of Law

Maria Popova, in conversation with Manuel Férez Gil

Maria Popova is Jean Monnet Chair and Associate Professor of Political Science at McGill University in Montreal. She holds a BA in Spanish Literature and Government from Dartmouth College and a PhD in Government from Harvard University. She has lived and conducted research across Eastern Europe and Eurasia and its various regime incarnations – from growing up in Bulgaria before 1989, through interviewing judges and lawyers in Russia and Ukraine for dissertation research in the 2000s, to her current attempt to disentangle real from fake anti-corruption efforts in Bulgaria, Romania, and Ukraine. Popova's work explores the intersection of politics and law in the region, specifically the rule of law, judicial reform, political corruption, populist parties, and legal repression of dissent. Popova's book, *Politicized Justice in Emerging Democracies* (2012), won the American Association for Ukrainian Studies prize for best book in the fields of Ukrainian history, politics, language, literature and culture. Other work appears in *Europe-Asia Studies, Problems of Post-Communism, Journal of East European Law*, and *Daedalus*. Popova's research is broadly interdisciplinary and has made it into volumes edited by historians (*Beyond Mosque, Church and State: Alternative Narratives of the Nation in the Balkans*, 2016) and sociologists (*A Sociology of Justice in Russia*, 2018).

Manuel Ferez: *Thank you very much for talking to us. Please tell us about yourself, your biography, studies and professional work.*

Maria Popova: I grew up in Bulgaria in the 1980s, witnessed the collapse of communism as a teenager, and was among the first wave of students from the post-Communist region, who got full scholarships to study at American universities. I graduated from Dartmouth College in 1997, worked for a year in Washington DC, during which I developed a keen interest in the politics of the former Soviet Union as a research assistant to Anders Aslund and Martha Olcott – two leading academic/think tank specialists on Russia, Ukraine and Central Asia– and then headed to Harvard University where I completed a PhD in political science in 2006. I have since taught political science at McGill University in Montreal, Canada. I have done extensive field research in both Ukraine and Russia since the late 1990s, but as Russia's authoritarian regime became increasingly repressive, it got harder to do research on the courts there.

M.F.: *Your research is focused on the rule of law, political corruption and legal repression of dissent in the post-Communist region.*

M.P.: My research broadly focuses on courts and democracy in the post-Communist region. I have written about judicial independence and judicial reform in Russia, Ukraine, and Bulgaria. I have written about how courts can influence the electoral process and outcome through registration cases and how they affect media freedom through defamation cases. I have also written about the politics of prosecuting grand corruption.

M.F.: *Before approaching the issue of Ukraine from these perspectives, could you tell us a little about the dynamics of ex-communist countries in these areas, how to combat corruption, improve the rule of law and transparency in this space.*

M.P.: My research suggests two broad conclusions. First, there is no institutional silver bullet that improves rule of law, reduces corruption, and increases transparency. We cannot create well-functioning, impartial judiciaries through institutional engineering – best practices such as life tenure for judges, a Supreme Judicial Council in charge of judicial careers and financing, institutional insulation of the judiciary from the political branches are often either insufficient or, sometimes, counterproductive in producing the desired outcomes – impartial courts that uphold the rule of law. Instead, it is more important to have the right people in positions of power, both in the judiciary and in the political branches, people who are motivated to improve the rule of law, people who believe in independent and impartial courts and bring about change. Second, political regime matters a lot. Establishing the rule of law in an authoritarian regime is a chimera. As messy as democracies can be, sustained political competition slowly and gradually brings about positive change in terms of independent courts, which can constrain incumbents and maintain regime openness.

M.F.: *Much has been said about Ukraine due to the Russian invasion and occupation of its territory but little about the progress that Ukraine has made in combating corruption, democracy and the rule of law. At what point did the country begin to take action in this regard and what were its main motivations?*

M.P.: The big divergence between Russia and Ukraine as political regimes started after the Orange Revolution in 2004. The success of the popular mobilization against corruption and electoral fraud created an important precedent that helped Ukraine consolidate a competitive regime where actors accepted that they cannot reimpose autocracy – civil society would not allow it. This does not mean that corruption was immediately brought under control and the rule of law took root immediately. This has been a slow and painstaking process.

M.F.: *Ukraine's pro-European aspirations also have a relationship with the country's internal political processes and the search for better governance. Tell us about the EU-Ukraine relationship in this regard and how the Kyiv government has benefited from it.*

M.P.: The 2014 Maidan revolution provided another boost to anticorruption and rule of law efforts. As it became increasingly clear to the majority of Ukrainians, Ukraine's survival depended on its pro-European course, and this underscored that rule of law and anticorruption are top items on the reform agenda. The assistance of international partners and the efforts of domestic civil society activists together provided significant pressure on politicians to pursue judicial reform and anticorruption. In 2019, [Volodymyr] Zelensky won the presidency precisely on a promise to do even more in these areas than his predecessor Poroshenko. The ball has been rolling in the right direction, though more remains to be accomplished.

M.F.: *Your book "Politicized Justice in Emerging Democracies" won the American Association for Ukrainian Studies prize for best book in the fields of Ukrainian history, politics, language, literature and culture. Please tell us about the book, specially about why it is important to understand the concept of "politicized Justice" when we talk about young democracies.*

M.P.: The book compares the degree of politicization of the courts in Russia and Ukraine in the late 1990s and early 2000s and ten years after its publication, the title is somewhat embarrassing – while Ukraine did become a democracy, Russia is anything but. The core contributions of the book, however, have withstood the test of time. Sustained political pressure on courts in politically salient legal cases – or politicized justice – is an enduring feature of politics not just in young democracies, but increasingly in old ones as well. Just note former president [Donald] Trump's attacks on the legal system that is now looking into his potential malfeasance. Secondly, subsequent research in other contexts around the world has confirmed my finding that intense political competition could, under some circumstances, create an incentive for politicians to increase their control over the judiciary, rather than pull back and respect it as a neutral arbiter. As politicians in competitive regimes face imminent loss of power, they tend to lean on the courts more in order to try to achieve their political goals before their time is up.

M.F.: *Rule of law is a very important aspect in the development of a democracy. How would you assess the situation in Ukraine in relation to this issue? Could you give us some examples of positive and negative steps.*

M.P.: Ukraine has made significant strides towards the rule of law since 2014. It has adopted massive legislative changes aimed at bringing both the legal codes and the structure of the Ukrainian judiciary in line with best practices recommended by the Venice Commission of the Council of Europe. New institutions such as an Anti-Corruption investigative body, prosecution, and court, a revamped High Council of Justice, a judicial ethics commission have been established with sustained advice and involvement by both international partners and civil society activists. Despite all the legislative activity and innovation, however, it seemed that change was slow to come in the informal institutions that shape the interaction between the presidential administration and the judiciary. Both [Petro] Poroshenko and Zelensky engaged in informal pressure and influence and had point people for the judiciary in their administrations who wielded significant power. Remember, for example, how in Zelensky's much-discussed conversation with Trump (when the latter tried to blackmail him to open an investigation into Hunter Biden), Zelensky assured Trump that the prosecutor general is "his person". The common complaint by rule of law activists was that political incumbents were implementing judicial reform measures reluctantly and trying to circumvent them through informal channels. It seems that the war has injected the necessary political will for rule of law in the presidential administration. A very positive development from mid-

August 2022 is that the Ukrainian parliament appointed a leading civil society activist, Roman Maselko, to the High Council of Justice.

M.F.: *Russian aggression and invasion of Ukraine will have many negative effects on the country, in fact the Russian occupation and invasion already extends for more than eight years. How can a young democracy like Ukraine deal with this situation? How high is the risk of setbacks in Ukrainian democracy if Russian invasion and aggression persists?*

M.P.: Ukrainian democracy has endured and even strengthened despite Russia's aggression. It has strengthened because democracy has become the only game in town – for Ukrainians, Russian autocracy is such a vivid nightmare that they would never accept steps domestically towards consolidation of power around an authoritarian leader. The risks to Ukrainian democracy come from the need to balance civil and political rights with national security. It's a familiar debate in democracies, old and new, how to ensure that valid national security concerns don't lead to undue limits on individual rights? The question is particularly acute in Ukraine as the country faces the very real problems of treason and collaboration by local officials and political figures with the Russian aggressor, as well as information warfare coming from Russia in the form of disinformation campaigns. The key to dealing successfully with these threats without eroding Ukrainian democracy would be to strengthen the rule of law by enhancing the trust and legitimacy of the judiciary, which would need to develop an impartial process for adjudicating complex cases. This issue is a source both of vulnerability and of great opportunity for Ukraine. If the process goes well, Ukraine will have a rule of law breakthrough moment, which will put the country on great footing for decades to come. Another risk to Ukrainian democracy comes from the endurance of oligarchic networks of political corruption, which erode trust in the state and enhance inequality. Before the war, civil society was strongly mobilized to push an anticorruption agenda. Since February, the issue has deservedly taken a back seat to strengthening state capacity to maintain the war effort. The key to Ukrainian democracy's future development will be restarting anticorruption efforts and continuing Ukraine's trajectory towards cleaner politics.

M.F.: *The relationship with the European Union is a central pillar in Ukraine's foreign policy. As an academic working on Ukraine, what do you think will be the medium and long-term scenario of the EU-Ukraine relationship?*

M.P.: The achievement of candidate status in June of this year was a watershed moment in Ukraine's history. After vacillating the Ukrainians are now united in their goal and belief that their future as an independent nation depends on European integration. Thus, there will be considerable political will to undertake the necessary reforms to achieve this goal. Hopefully, on the EU's side there would be enduring understanding that European security and lasting peace depend primarily on bringing Ukraine into the European family and working to contain Russia as long as it remains an imperialist autocracy with aggressive designs on its neighbours.

First published on 12 September 2022. This interview first appeared in Spanish on https://orientemedio.news.

Works cited

Popova, Maria. *Politicized Justice in Emerging Democracies* (Cambridge: Cambridge University Press, 2012).

Analytical Articles

Society in Turbulent Times: The Impact of War on Ukraine

Anna Chebotarova

On February 24, 2022, Russia launched a full-scale multi-front invasion of Ukraine. This date marks the beginning of a new phase in a protracted Russian-Ukrainian military conflict that has been raging with varying intensity since 2014. The strength and effectiveness of the Ukrainians' military fightback came as a surprise to many politicians and analysts. Before the full-scale invasion, many predicted the Ukrainian army's rapid collapse from the technically and numerically dominant adversary. The societal resilience and resistance to the Russian attack have been unprecedented, particularly in the eastern and southern parts of Ukraine. A wave of peaceful protests has since swept through the newly occupied, predominantly Russian-speaking regions. Hundreds of residents in the cities of Kherson, Henichesk, and Melitopol rallied with Ukrainian flags against the invasion, often in the presence of Russian tanks and soldiers. Indeed, military and societal responses to the 2022 Russian attack were much more potent than in Crimea and Donbas eight years prior.

Whereas earlier sociological research has labelled the Ukrainian identity as "ambivalent",[1] the surveys in the war-time period have provided solid empirical evidence of tectonic shifts in Ukrainian self-perceptions and geopolitical orientations. Comparing the situation in the early and recent months of the Russian-Ukrainian War, Serhii Kudelia[2] explains Ukraine's weakness in 2014 as a function of four primary deficiencies: lack of political legitimacy, defensive capacity, societal cohesion, and support from the international community. Over the next eight years, as the author shows, the situation in Ukraine has improved significantly in all four dimensions.

In this short essay, I will outline what effects the ongoing war – both protracted military conflict since 2014 and the full-scale Russian invasion in 2022 – has so far had on Ukrainian society and public opinion. The empirical data comes from three waves of surveys on Ukrainian regionalism, conducted by the University of St. Gallen from 2013 to 2017 (N=6000)[3] and an Info Sapiens survey (N=1000) commissioned by the international research project VALREF[4] only months after the full-scale Russian invasion in April 2022. Additionally, I will use the data from several other opinion surveys conducted in Ukraine before and after the beginning of the Russian-Ukrainian war.

Ukrainian Ambivalence

Ukraine's post-Soviet history began with the unified democratic choice of its people. In a December 1991 referendum, 90.3 per cent approved the Act of declaration of Ukrainian independence, with a clear majority across all the oblasts (administrative regions). Since then, Ukraine has faced multiple challenges. Implementing market reforms on the ruins of the former Soviet planned economy was complicated by efforts to build new state structures and accommodate the diversity of ethnolinguistic, religious, and cultural groups into a viable and coherent national community. Institutional weakness, a conflictual political system, and chaotic privatization of state-owned assets resulted in the formation of oligarchic clans that originated from the Soviet nomenklatura. Very quickly, corruption and inequality became significant structural issues. One of the questions that perplexed researchers concerned the mechanisms behind enduring political pluralism in Ukraine, as opposed to post-Soviet Russia and Belarus, which were rapidly falling into authoritarianism. Lucan Ahmad Way[5] offered – for instance – an impactful concept of "pluralism by default" to explain the peculiarities of Ukraine's political system in the first decades of independence. As the author argued, such pluralism emerged from state and party weakness and the contradictory nature of Ukraine's nation-building projects. Therefore, political competition endured not because political leaders were especially democratic or because institutions or societal actors were particularly strong but because the government was too fragmented and the state too weak to monopolize political control.[6]

For a long time, the tension between Soviet-nostalgic and new Ukrainian nation-building projects yielded a balancing act in Ukrainian politics and society. The notion of "ambivalence" denotes a state of having polarized emotions about the same object (emotional ambivalence) or expressing mutually exclusive ideas (intellectual ambivalence) and decisions (volitional ambivalence). In the Ukrainian case, this concept was consistently developed by sociologist Eugene Golovakha,[7] who demonstrated that social ambivalence, essentially a parallel orientation towards mutually exclusive values and ideas, has been a characteristic feature of Ukrainian society in the first decades of independence. One of the examples could be simultaneous popular support for market economy and socialism, the celebration of both Soviet and new Ukrainian national holidays, or parallel orientations towards both Russia and the European Union. According to Golovakha, ambivalent consciousness plays the role of a "double-edged sword" for society in transition. On the one hand, it shields individuals from the psychological trauma of radical social changes and protects a community from dramatic clashes. On the other hand, ambivalent consciousness, as an unstable balance of two opposing cultures, cannot last long without destructive social and psychological consequences.

The ambivalences and contradictions in Ukrainian society were usually regarded as firmly divided by region and language. Such attitudes and orientations have indeed differed across Ukraine, particularly along the East-West axis.[8] However, the fueling of these differences had become politically and socially toxic by 2004 when competition in Ukraine's presidential elections came to revolve around regional cleavages. By the outbreak of the Orange Revolution in November of that year, Ukrainian ambivalence had evolved into an antagonistic phase, primarily because of its instrumentalization for political gains.

The Flickering War

The Euromaidan and the subsequent annexation of Crimea became a turning point in the history of independent Ukraine. In March 2014, right after the annexation of the Crimean Peninsula, Russia-backed separatist protests arose in the Donetsk and Luhansk oblasts of Ukraine (Donbas region) and across Southern and Eastern Ukraine. Proclaiming the Donetsk and Luhansk People's Republics (the so-called DNR and LNR), armed groups seized government buildings. These events subsequently fueled the Russian-Ukrainian military conflict, which has smoldered – with various degrees of intensity – until the full-scale invasion in 2022. It is estimated that during this protracted phase, approximately 14 000 people were killed, among whom 3400 were civilians.[9] Even in periods of relative calm following the Minsk II peace settlement, around a dozen Ukrainian soldiers were still being killed every month. As of late 2021, the overall number of people displaced internally (IDPs) was approaching one million. Moreover, those who became IDPs preferred to settle in the eastern part of the country – in Ukraine-controlled parts of Donbas and the adjacent regions – not far from the homes they were forced to abandon and the loved ones left behind.[10]

Nevertheless, before 2022, wider Ukrainian society had slowly learned to live with this low-key war, while coverage of the fizzling conflict gradually faded in the international media. Generally, societal preference towards conflict resolution followed peaceful negotiations and compromise scenarios (Fig. 3–1), yet 25 to 30 per cent of Ukrainians supported the idea of fighting until the total victory of the Ukrainian army counter-offensive Anti-Terrorist Operation (ATO).

Fig. 3–1: Distribution of desirable solutions for the Donbas Conflict ("Ukrainian Regionalism" Survey, University of St. Gallen, 2015–2017)

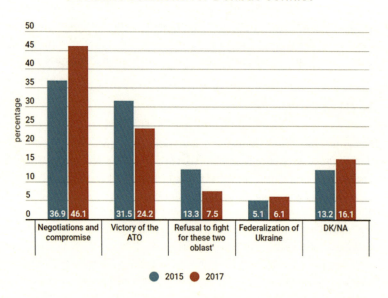

The attitudes towards the Minsk II agreement, signed back in 2015, diverged across Ukrainian society. While 42 per cent favored its implementation, 32 per cent agreed that Ukraine should follow the agreement only if the other sides do so, with 15 per cent opposing the idea altogether. There was a reasonable apprehension that Russia would use the Minsk agreements to infiltrate and strengthen its influence on Ukraine's domestic and foreign policy, endangering Ukraine's sovereignty.[11]

Since 2014, the non-government-controlled areas of Donetsk and Luhansk oblast and Crimea have been a "blind spot" for Ukrainian sociologists. Owing to various safety protocols and methodological considerations, the surveys were commonly conducted only in the regions and areas controlled by the Ukrainian state.[12] At the same time, some scholars have carried out quantitative and qualitative research in the non-government-controlled areas (NGCAs). Despite methodological challenges, one tendency in such surveys is apparent: the longer people lived on the territories outside Ukrainian political control, the deeper the value, geopolitical and attitudinal gap with the rest of Ukraine became. Thus, as the 2017 ZOiS survey showed,[13] the majority of inhabitants of Ukrainian-controlled Donbas (65 per cent) firmly opted for the reintegration of NGCAs into the respective oblast, while most of the respondents in the so-called DNR and LNR supported special autonomy for the "republics" – either within Ukraine (35 per cent) or even Russia (33.1 per cent).[14] The differences with the rest of Ukraine became even more striking. According to a May 2017 survey, only 18.2 per cent of DNR and LNR residents supported the idea of Ukraine joining the European Union, while this share in government-controlled Ukraine reached 53 per cent. Since its arrival in March 2020, the COVID-19 pandemic has only exacerbated the rupturing of this delicate fabric of social ties, as the level and possibilities of direct contact between occupied and non-occupied territories have decreased dramatically. The crossing through the "checkpoint" with Crimea or the "contact line" separating the conflict-affected people residing in the government-controlled areas (GCAs) and the NGCAs of Eastern Ukraine has been severely limited. This has prevented hundreds of thousands of people from accessing essential services and maintaining connections with the other side.

For Ukraine at large, different tendencies have been prevalent. As several scholars note, political changes unleashed by the Euromaidan victory and Russia's aggression in 2014 have replaced societal ambivalence and confrontation with the consolidation of Ukrainian national identity. The Maidan, the annexation of Crimea and the beginning of the war in Donbas led to a patriotic mobilization and a substantial shift in Ukrainian politics. A significant part of the electorate with pro-Russian sympathies was left out of political participation, which led to the homogenization of the Ukrainian political and cultural field.

The regional polarization that characterized the preceding decade has almost disappeared from the electoral map. In post-Euromaidan presidential elections, the winning candidates (Petro Poroshenko in 2014 and Volodymyr Zelensky in 2019) received majority support almost in all oblasts across the country (Fig.3-2).

Fig. 3–2: The Results of 2nd ballot of Presidential elections in Ukraine by winning candidate per oblast (2010; 2019)

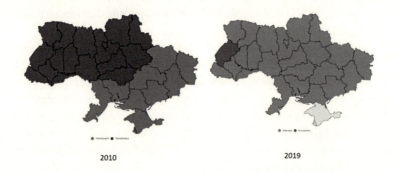

2010　　　　　　　　　　2019

Thus, while the social distance towards Crimea and the NGCAs of Donbas has been growing, the protracted military conflict has increased cohesion and unity in government-controlled Ukraine. Many scholars have described this new sense of Ukrainian nationalism as becoming predominantly civic – being more tolerant and inclusive toward citizens from various ethnolinguistic and religious background.[15] Others brought attention to cultural trends of Ukraine becoming "more Ukrainian",[16] the othering of Russophone Ukrainians, the polarizing discourses in post-Euromaidan society, and new mechanisms of "civic" exclusion.[17]

Fig. 3-3: *The dynamics of feeling proud for being a Ukrainian citizen, 2002-2020, Ukrainian Society: Sociological Monitoring Survey.*[18]

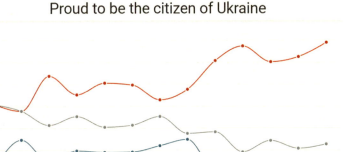

The share of respondents who did not feel proud to be citizens of Ukraine has decreased three times during the first phase of the Russian-Ukrainian War – from almost 25 per cent in 2013 to 8.4 per cent in 2020 (fig.3-3). One might also notice three "spikes" in the rising curve of pride in being Ukrainian citizens – 2005 (after the Orange Revolution), 2014–15 (following the Euromaidan and the beginning of the Russian-Ukrainian conflict) and 2020 (following Volodymyr Zelensky's victory in the 2019 Presidential elections). Even though societal attitudes towards the Orange Revolution and the Euromaidan varied significantly across different regions, both events have ignited faith in the power of joint actions and more positive future perspectives of Ukraine. Indeed, Zelensky's landslide victory marked a moment of overwhelming societal optimism (albeit short-lived). The 2019–20 opinion polls show that for the first time in a decade, the share of respondents satisfied with their lives exceeded the percentage of those dissatisfied (40 per cent to 36 per cent). In their recent book, *The Zelensky Effect*, Olha Onuch and Henry Hale explore the sources and mechanisms behind the popularity of a politician that reflected and expressed "the hopes and frustration of Ukraine's first 'Independence generation' as well as [...] civic duty, the importance of Ukraine's diversity, and the common quotidian experiences that bound Ukrainians together".[19]

The growing confrontation motivated many Russophone Ukrainians to redefine their national belonging as Ukrainian. Yet this tendency could already be observed among Russian speakers before the war. As the "Ukrainian Regionalism" survey shows, already in 2013, 82.9 per cent of respondents declared they were Ukrainians (this share was higher than 60 per cent in all oblasts except Crimea). Prior to the Euromaidan and the war, 59 per cent of Russian speakers and 89 per cent of bilinguals identified as Ukrainians, while in 2017, these numbers were already 66 per cent and 92 per cent, respectively. As of 2017, over 60 per cent said their native language is Ukrainian, while the share of declared Russian speakers has decreased (from 21.2% in 2013 to 11.4% in 2017). At the same time, using Ukrainian and Russian in communication with various social groups took different constellations, with the growing popularity of Ukrainian in both personal and professional realms (Fig. 3–4).

Fig. 3–4: Predominant language of communication with various groups, 2017 ("Ukrainian Regionalism" Survey, University of St. Gallen).

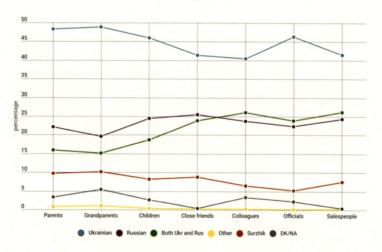

The outbreak of the Russo-Ukrainian War caused a tectonic shift in Ukrainian ambivalence towards the country's geopolitical choice. If earlier opinions were divided between the desire to join the EU and the alliance with Russia, after 2014, this fork became the opposition between EU membership and retaining a non-aligned neutral status. Between 2013 and 2017, support among Ukrainians to join the EU nearly doubled – while support to join a union that includes Russia decreased by five times.

Fig. 3–5: *Preferable geopolitical choice, 2013–2017, Ukrainian Regionalism Survey*

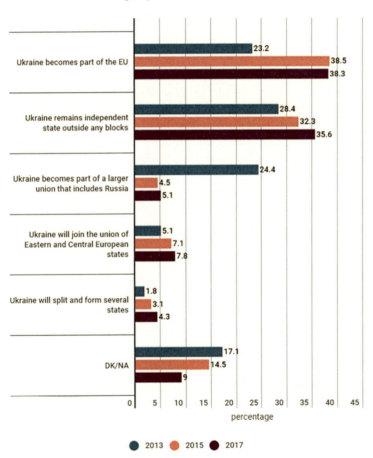

Until recently, the perspectives of accession to NATO remained a regionally divisive question. While the overall support has grown from 18 per cent in 2013 to 45.1 per cent in 2017, it was still significantly lower in south-eastern Ukraine, particularly among Russian speakers and the representatives of the older generation. Only after the full-scale invasion did the support for joining NATO soar to an unprecedented 83 per cent across Ukraine.

Nation-Building to the Sound of Sirens

Surveys conducted before the full-scale Russian invasion revealed that only 19 per cent of Ukrainians estimated its likelihood as high[20]. Yet, when it did happen, Ukrainians reacted with remarkable cohesion and solidarity. According to the VALREF survey conducted in April 2022, 70 per cent of respondents claimed they were prepared to take up arms to defend Ukraine, while 94 per cent reported either being ready to help the Ukrainian army or already engaging in supportive activities (such as financial donations or volunteering). The volunteer movement and grassroots networks, developed over the years of confrontation in Donbas, have been activated with renewed vigor. In the first weeks of the war, people in the newly occupied territories showed their attachment to Ukraine by organizing demonstrations with Ukrainian flags, which were then brutally dispersed by the Russian military. For the first time, the share of people who thought that things in the country were going in the right direction was five times higher than those who held the opposite view (76 per cent to 15 per cent in March), remaining as high as 82 per cent in December 2022. Finally, support for President Zelensky has tripled, reaching an unprecedented 93 per cent.[21]

Such cohesion is not unique, and we may witness the classical "rally-round-the-flag" effect (a concept introduced by political scientist John Mueller in 1970). This phenomenon is typically characterized by a sharp increase in patriotism and public support for national leaders during war or security crises. The durability of such consensus for almost a year at the time of writing makes the Ukrainian case quite remarkable. Thus, since May 2022, the percentage of respondents who deny the possibility of Ukraine's territorial concessions has only grown (from 82 per cent to 85 in December 2022), even if it may prolong the war.[22]

The war has already taken an enormous toll on Ukraine, causing a demographic crisis and the displacement of millions of Ukrainians internally and abroad. It has also led to significant economic problems as millions lost their jobs and were forced to flee their homes. According to a report from the World Bank, in 2022, Ukraine experienced a tenfold increase in poverty due to war.[23] The number of military and civilian casualties has not yet been precisely calculated but is estimated in the tens of thousands. The wailing of air raid sirens has become a constant soundtrack of Ukrainian daily life as Russia continues its brutal attacks on critical energy infrastructure to demoralize the civilian population. At the same time, the overwhelming majority continue to believe in an eventual Ukrainian victory (over 90 per cent as of August 2022) and brighter perspectives for the country's post-war future.[24] This unifying aspiration became a coping strategy – an emotional "anesthesia" that helps Ukrainians resist and endure exceptionally difficult circumstances. For the majority of respondents (55 per cent), Ukraine's victory would mean expelling Russian troops from the entire territory and restoring the country's pre-war borders (as of 2014).[25] The success of such a scenario would inevitably pose the challenges of reintegration and transitional justice in regions that have been under Russian influence and control since 2014.

Even though the war currently remains ongoing, and the outcome is unknown, February 24, 2022, marked a new tragic milestone in Ukrainian nation-building and its radical separation from the "Russian world." The Russian invasion's brutality, which includes the destruction of residential areas and genocidal mass violence against civilians, is only likely to expedite this separation. The full-scale invasion further strengthened anti-Russian tendencies in Ukrainian identity politics. Along with limiting access to Russian media and social networks, introducing language quotas and measures aimed at separating the Ukrainian Orthodox Church from the Moscow Patriarchate, the politics of spatial and cultural "derussification" has been gaining momentum in Ukraine. The drive to distance the country from the aggressor state is widely supported in the society under attack. However, the internal tensions around the Russophone Ukrainian culture and the "language question" among Ukraine's Russian speakers will likely pose a challenge to the long-term resilience and cohesion of a society traumatized by war.

Conclusion

Since the proclamation of independence, Ukrainian society has evolved from ambivalence through internal confrontation to growing social unity and solidarity. The latter trend was significantly accelerated by the external threat from Russia since 2014, which left Crimea and part of Donbas out of Ukrainian political control. Popular identification with the Ukrainian state and the growing salience of Ukrainian identity has been a persistent phenomenon exacerbated by the war. The sense of national pride that waxed and waned with every new revolution has now become a clear unifying trend in a defiant society.

Ultimately, the brutality of Russian aggression has caused Ukrainians to redefine their national identity on three main pillars: the rejection of the "Russian world", belief in an impeding victory of Ukraine and a brighter postwar future, as well as aspirations to integrate with the West. Societal unity in the face of aggression has been unprecedented and persistent, but internal cleavages may re-emerge as Ukrainians feel the growing human and economic costs of war. Prolonged violent conflict makes keeping the balance between protecting national security and defending democratic values a challenging task. Moreover, given the importance of restoring the territorial integrity of Ukraine within its pre-war borders, strategies for reintegrating Crimea and Donbas have yet to be developed, as the experience of occupation had an alienating effect on these regions.

Notes

1. Ievhen Holovakha, "Osoblyvosti politychnoï svidomosti: Ambivalentnist' suspil'stva ta osoblyvosti," *Politolohichni Chytannia* 1 (1992): 24–39
2. Serhiy Kudelia, "The Ukrainian State under Russian Aggression," *Current History* 121:837 (2022): 251–57, https://doi.org/10.1525/curh.2022.121.837.2 51.
3. "Ukrainian Regionalism Surveys: Methodology," accessed December 31, 2022, https://www.uaregio.org/en/surveys/methodology/.
4. "National Values and Political Reforms in Post-Maidan Ukraine – Department of Literature, Area Studies and European Languages," accessed December 31, 2022, https://www.hf.uio.no/ilos/english/research/projects/valref/index.html.
5. Lucan Way, *Pluralism by Default: Weak Autocrats and the Rise of Competitive Politics* (Baltimore: John Hopkins University Press, 2015).
6. Way, *Pluralism by Default*, p. 5.
7. Holovakha, "Osoblyvosti politychnoï svidomosti"

8   Ulrich Schmid and Oksana Myshlovska (eds.), *Regionalism without Regions: Reconceptualizing Ukraine's Heterogeneity*, Leipzig Studies on the History and Culture of East Central Europe, vol. 5 (Budapest; New York: Central European University Press, 2019).
9   "Conflict-Related Civilian Casualties in Ukraine" (UN Human Rights Monitoring Mission in Ukraine, January 27, 2022), https://ukraine.un.o rg/sites/default/files/2022-02/Conflict-related%20civilian%20casualties %20as%20of%2031%20December%202021%20%28rev%2027%20January %202022%29%20corr%20EN_0.pdf.
10 "Internal Displacement Monitoring Center: Country Profile Ukraine," IDMC, accessed December 31, 2022, https://www.internal-displacement .org/countries/ukraine.
11 Duncan Allan, "The Minsk Conundrum: Western Policy and Russia's War in Eastern Ukraine," *Chatham House – International Affairs Think Tank* (blog), May 20, 2020, https://www.chathamhouse.org/2020/05/minsk-conundr um-western-policy-and-russias-war-eastern-ukraine-0/minsk-2-agree ment.
12 Olexiy Haran, Maksym Yakovlyev, and Maria Zolkina, "Identity, War, and Peace: Public Attitudes in the Ukraine-Controlled Donbas," *Eurasian Geography and Economics* 60:6 (2019): 684–708, https://doi.org/10.1080/1538721 6.2019.1667845.
13 Gwendolyn Sasse, "The Donbas – Two parts, or still one?," accessed December 31, 2022, https://www.zois-berlin.de/publikationen/the-donbas-two-parts-or-still-one.
14 Ibid.
15 O. V. Haran' and Maksym Yakovlyev (eds.), *Constructing a Political Nation: Changes in the Attitudes of Ukrainians during the War in the Donbas*, Second edition (first English-language edition) December 2017; first edition March 2017 (in Ukrainian) (Kyiv: Stylos Publishing, 2017); Volodymyr Kulyk, "National Identity in Ukraine: Impact of Euromaidan and the War," *Europe-Asia Studies* 68:4 (2016): 588–608, https://doi.org/10.1080/0966813 6.2016.1174980; Grigore Pop-Eleches, "Revolutions in Ukraine: Shaping Civic Rather Than Ethnic Identities," *PONARS Eurasia* (blog), February 22, 2018, https://www.ponarseurasia.org/revolutions-in-ukraine-sha ping-civic-rather-than-ethnic-identities/; Nadiia Bureiko and Teodor Lucian Moga, "The Ukrainian–Russian Linguistic Dyad and Its Impact on National Identity in Ukraine," *Europe-Asia Studies* 71:1 (2019): 137–55, ht tps://doi.org/10.1080/09668136.2018.1549653.

16. Dominique Arel, "How Ukraine Has Become More Ukrainian," *Post-Soviet Affairs* 34:2–3 (2018): 186–89, https://doi.org/10.1080/1060586X.2018.1445460.
17. Oleg Zhuravlev and Volodymyr Ishchenko, "Exclusiveness of Civic Nationalism: Euromaidan Eventful Nationalism in Ukraine," *Post-Soviet Affairs* 36:3 (2020): 226–45, https://doi.org/10.1080/1060586X.2020.1753460.
18. Valerii Vorona and Mykola Shul'ha (eds.), "Ukraïnske suspil'stvo: monitorynh sotsial'nykh zmin," *30 Rokiv Nezalezhnosti* 22:8 (2021).
19. Olga Onuch and Henry Hale, *The Zelensky Effect* (London: C Hurst & Co publishers ltd., 2022).
20. "Dynamika otsinky viis'kovoï zahrozy (16–17 liutoho 2022)," accessed January 2, 2023, http://ratinggroup.ua/research/ukraine/dinamika_ocenki_voennoy_ugrozy_16-17_fevralya_2022_g.html.
21. "Sociological Group 'Rating'," accessed January 3, 2023, https://ratinggroup.ua/en/.
22. Anton Hrushets'kyi, "Dynamika hotovnosti do terytorial'nykh postupok dlia iaknaishvydshoho zavershennia viiny: rezultaty telefonnoho opytuvannia, provedenoho 4–27 hrudnia 2022 roku," accessed January 2, 2023, https://kiis.com.ua/?lang=ukr&cat=reports&id=1167&page=1.
23. Andrea Shalal, "World Bank Says Ukraine Has Tenfold Increase in Poverty Due to War," *Reuters*, October 15, 2022, sec. Europe, https://www.reuters.com/world/europe/world-bank-says-ukraine-has-tenfold-increase-poverty-due-war-2022-10-15/.
24. "Den' Nezalezhnosti Ukraïny: shcho obiednuie ukraintsiv i yak my bachymo peremohu na shostomu misiatsi viiny," accessed January 3, 2023, https://dif.org.ua/article/den-nezalezhnosti-ukraini-shcho-obednue-ukraintsiv-i-yak-mi-bachimo-peremogu-na-shostomu-misyatsi-viyni.
25. "Den' Nezalezhnosti Ukraïny."

Selected Bibliography

D'Anieri, Paul J. *Ukraine and Russia: From Civilized Divorce to Uncivil War* (Cambridge: Cambridge University Press, 2020).

Haran', O. V., and Maksym Yakovlyev (eds.) *Constructing a Political Nation: Changes in the Attitudes of Ukrainians during the War in the Donbas*. December 2017.

Kulyk, Volodymyr. "National Identity in Ukraine: Impact of Euromaidan and the War," *Europe-Asia Studies* 68:4 (2016): 588–608.

Kuznetsova, Irina, and Oksana Mikheieva. "Forced Displacement from Ukraine's War-Torn Territories: Intersectionality and Power Geometry," *Nationalities Papers* 48:4 (2020): 690–706.

Minakov, Mikhail, Heorhij Kasjanov, and Matthew Rojansky (eds.) *From "The Ukraine" to Ukraine: A Contemporary History, 1991–2021* (Stuttgart: ibidem Verlag, 2021).

Onuch, Olga, and Henry Hale. *The Zelensky Effect* (London: C Hurst & Co publishers ltd., 2022).

Schmid, Ulrich, and Oksana Myshlovska (eds.) *Regionalism without Regions: Reconceptualizing Ukraine's Heterogeneity*. Leipzig Studies on the History and Culture of East Central Europe, vol. 5. (Budapest; New York: Central European University Press, 2019).

Way, Lucan. *Pluralism by Default: Weak Autocrats and the Rise of Competitive Politics* (Baltimore: John Hopkins University Press, 2015).

Wilson, Andrew. *Ukraine Crisis: What It Means for the West* (New Haven: Yale University Press, 2014).

Competing Identities
of Ukraine's Russian Speakers

Volodymyr Kulyk

In the first decade after the breakup of the USSR, both local and Western experts believed that Russians and Russian speakers might endanger the social stability or even the territorial integrity of the newly independent states they had found themselves in. Even in countries such as Ukraine, where the Russians seemed to be culturally close to the titular population, most authors did not believe that this minority would put up with nationalizing policies allegedly pursued by the majority-dominated state. The Russians' resistance was considered inevitable in view of their distinct ethnocultural identity and a strong interest in preserving it.

Two decades after those analyses, it is quite clear that this view was mistaken. Instead of successfully mobilizing in defence of their group interests, Ukraine's Russian-speakers have lost much of their distinct ethnocultural identity which should have driven such mobilization. In the face of the Russian aggression of 2014, most Russian-speakers, even in the seemingly pro-Russian east-southern regions, allied with their fellow citizens rather than their linguistic 'brethren' across the border. As the analysis below will demonstrate, their spectacular choice in favour of Ukraine was based on inconspicuous changes in their ethnonational identity over the previous years. Rather than forming into a community distinguished by its main language, they had gradually been transformed from Soviet people into Ukrainians – without drastic changes in their language practice. While most of them remained primarily Russian-speaking, this is not how they would define themselves.

Making Sense of People Speaking Russian

In many publications of the early post-Soviet years, ethnic Russians in Ukraine and other former republics were viewed as clear-cut groups with a strong ethnic identity, or even parts of one dispersed group which was often referred to as the "new Russian diaspora".[1] People who had been registered as Russians by "nationality" in the last Soviet census of 1989 were assumed to constitute a real social collectivity strongly attached to their "ethnic homeland". Such perceptions not only arose from the essentialist thinking of the time but also from the political reality of the early 1990s. Accordingly, studies of the Russian "diaspora" focused on the potential for destabilizing protests against their new states of residence which was believed to be related to the size, demographic characteristics, and the degree of political organization of the group as well as to its treatment by the "host" state and the "ethnic homeland".[2] This conflict-centred approach to post-Soviet ethnopolitical processes soon received a boost in Rogers Brubaker's influential conceptualization of these processes as a triadic relationship between a particular "nationalising" state, the Russian minority on its territory, and the Russian state supporting its ethnic "kin" across the border.[3] In this inherently conflictual relationship, the Russians seemed more likely to rebel or emigrate than accept their minority status, let alone assimilate.

Later, scholars came to recognize the inadequacy of treating the post-Soviet Russians as a diaspora, of which Russians in Ukraine formed a homogenous part clearly distinct from the Ukrainian majority. Andrew Wilson was one of the first to emphasize that "questions of national identity in Ukraine cannot be understood via a crude contrast between 'Ukrainians' as the eponymous state-bearing nation and 'Russians' as a diaspora group of the Russian Federation".[4] The rejection of the majority-minority contrast was facilitated by a growing awareness among scholars dealing with Ukraine that in this post-imperial society "nationality" is not necessarily the most politically relevant of all ethnocultural characteristics. As a result of the Soviet regime's ambiguous nationalities policies, millions of people embraced Russian as their main language but most of them retained their ethnic self-designation as Ukrainians. Accordingly, there was a large discrepancy between ethnicity and language, meaning that the ethnic and linguistic boundaries between the two main groups did not coincide. Dominique Arel and Valeri Khmelko argued that post-Soviet Ukrainian society was better described as consisting not of two but of three groups: the Ukrainian-speaking Ukrainians, the Russian-speaking Ukrainians and the (overwhelmingly Russian-speaking) Russians.[5] Moreover, they demonstrated that the census data on "native language" greatly underestimated the discrepancy between ethnicity and language since many people had arguably interpreted that question as pertaining to ethnonational background or loyalty rather than linguistic practice.

In another important publication of the time, Paul Pirie emphasised that any categorisation including an unambiguous designation of "nationality" was inadequate in a society where "inter-ethnic marriage, language usage and urbanisation are all factors which contribute to mixed self-identification".[6] Therefore, many people identified with both ethnic groups, most frequently the Ukrainian and Russian ones, or did not have a stable identification with any of them, which often led to the preference for some pan-ethnic identity (in the 1990s this usually meant Soviet). Such ambiguous and unstable identifications were particularly widespread in eastern and southern Ukraine with its high level of urbanization, mixed marriages, and the predominant use of the Russian language by people of all "nationalities".

The realisation of ambiguous lines between the two main groups and a tremendous regional variation in their relationship with each other led scholars to reconsider the likely ethnopolitical consequences of the presence of large numbers of Russians and Russian-speakers in post-Soviet Ukraine. First and foremost, a mismatch between ethnicity and language meant that key ethnopolitical actors were not always sure what group they should seek to mobilize and represent. Simply put, Russophone Ukrainians could be seen as a "vital swing group" that the Russian-speaking entrepreneurs did not want to lose to the Ukrainian nationalist parties.[7] For the Russian-speaking elites of the east and south, downplaying ethnicity in favour of language or some other unifying characteristic would mean a huge increase in the size of "their" group. Moreover, given strong local and/or regional identities in certain parts of the country and particular economic interests of the regional elites, it was no wonder that "local political parties use[d] pan-ethnic boundary markers in order to maximise their potential appeal" and that the "imagined community" that their discourse implied and (re)produced was regionally specific rather than country-wide.[8]

While most of the early studies of Ukraine's Russians and Russian speakers focused on their *political* response to the post-Soviet reality, in the following years scholars became increasingly interested in their *cultural* response. In his study of the Russian-speakers in Ukraine and three other post-Soviet states, David Laitin sought to assess their readiness to assimilate into the newly dominant culture and/or adjust their ethnolinguistic identities. Laitin concluded that in Ukraine, similarly to Kazakhstan and in contrast to Latvia and Estonia, Russian speakers expected no significant gains from linguistic assimilation which, therefore, could not reach such a scale in society as to become irreversible. He argued that ethnic Russians and those titulars who had been linguistically assimilated under the USSR soon after its disintegration came "to see themselves – in conglomerate terms – as a 'Russian-speaking population'".[9] Laitin failed to admit that Russian-speakers might seek to retain their accustomed language without making it a cornerstone of their identity or that they might change their language behaviour in some aspects without "tipping" into full-fledged assimilation. Moreover, as his analysis focused on comparison between different post-Soviet countries, his research downplayed the different dynamics in different regions within a certain country and the different preferences of ethnic Russians and Russian-speaking titulars within his alleged conglomerate.

An impressive regional differentiation had by then been demonstrated by Ian Bremmer (1994) in a study of the political and cultural preferences of ethnic Russians in three Ukrainian cities. In Kyiv and Lviv most Russians seemed to opt for integration into the titular-dominated society but in Simferopol, the capital of the Russian-dominated Crimean autonomy, they sought to retain their accustomed linguistic environment and wanted political conditions that would ensure it. Jan Janmaat found similar differences in his study of Russian-speaking schoolchildren in Kyiv, Lviv, Odesa, and Donetsk which focused on the cultural response to Ukrainianization policies in education.[10] In addition to a regional differentiation between the patterns of integration in the first two cities and retention in the latter two, Janmaat also detected a remarkable contrast between preferences of mixed couples and "purely" ethnic Russian families in predominantly Ukrainian and Ukrainian-speaking Lviv, with the former increasingly opting for assimilation and the latter preferring retention.

In the following decade, many authors revealed considerable regional differentiation in Russian-speakers' behaviour in both micro- and macro-analyses of language and identity processes. In particular, some micro-level studies found that Russian-speakers in different parts of Ukraine had come to feel Ukrainian based on their country of residence and citizenship, even if many of them also felt Russian based on their origin and/or accustomed language. Against the background of the traditional ethnolinguistic definition of Ukrainian identity in Lviv, these "new Ukrainians" saw the Ukrainian nation "rather as a civic community of compatriots, based on common feelings of belonging to the nation, land and loyalty to the state".[11] In the predominantly Russian-speaking city of Odesa, the increased salience of civic Ukrainian identity paradoxically led to its projection onto the established ethnic categorization of "nationality", so that people considered themselves Ukrainian in both senses. This contributed to the blurring of the very categories of "Ukrainian" and "Russian" which people nevertheless considered meaningful. At the same time, this Ukrainian identity did not necessarily involve assimilation into the Ukrainian language or even its addition to one's active, day-to-day repertoire; a *positive attitude* to the perceived national language was often deemed more important. While in Lviv, young Russian-speakers felt the need to speak Ukrainian outside of their minority circle, to their peers in Kharkiv such adaptation seemed unwarranted and artificial.[12]

On a macro-level, survey-based studies confirmed the observed reality of the unabated prevalence of Russian, which meant that most people who used to rely on it at the outset of independence continued to use it exclusively or predominantly and pass it on to their children, in flagrant discrepancy with their increasingly Ukrainian ethnolinguistic identity.[13] Moreover, examinations of the factors determining Ukrainian citizens' political and cultural attitudes demonstrated that the region of residence was at least as strong a predictor as – in many cases, much stronger than – language use, native language, and nationality. This pointed to an essential heterogeneity of the populations defined by these characteristics.[14] In one study specifically designed to verify Laitin's argument about the salience of Russian-speaking identity, Lowell Barrington found that among people speaking Russian all or part of the time, the attachment to the self-designation as a "Russian-speaker" was much weaker than to those defined by citizenship and ethnicity.[15] He also confirmed that ethnicity and region matter more than language in determining individual identities. In his conclusion: "As a result, there appears to be no single, unifying label that the Russian-speakers have found and accepted. Their status as a unified 'identity group' is, consequently, ambiguous at best".[16] It is this study that I primarily build on in examining identity preferences of people speaking mostly Russian, seeking to demonstrate that most of them have acquired a salient Ukrainian identity without abandoning their accustomed language.

Competing Identifications of Russian-Speakers

My analysis of changes in ethnonational identifications among the Ukrainian population is based on three nationwide surveys conducted by the Kyiv International Institute of Sociology (KIIS) at various times before and after the Euromaidan protests and the Russian aggression of 2014. These surveys were conducted in February 2012, September 2014, and February 2017. Since the annexed Crimea and the occupied parts of the Donbas became inaccessible to Ukrainian sociologists after 2014, I excluded respondents from those territories in the earlier surveys in order to make the data comparable. Therefore, statistically significant changes in characteristics presented in the tables reflect changes in popular perceptions rather than in the territories controlled by the Ukrainian government. Broadly speaking, significant differences are those exceeding 3 per cent.

The first question inquired about primary self-designation ("Who do you consider yourself primarily?") and provided a list of alternatives related to territorial entities of varying scales. The comparison of responses from the two most distant surveys, 2012 and 2017, reveals diachronic changes in the relative salience of people's attachment to Ukraine vis-à-vis its competitors on both the sub- and supra-national levels, in particular a transformation brought about by Euromaidan and the war. Table 1 demonstrates the relative salience of various territorially defined identities for those respondents who said that they spoke only or predominantly Russian in their everyday lives – against the background of the Ukrainian population as a whole. Moreover, the Russian-speakers' responses are presented not only for Ukraine as a whole but also for its two geographical "halves", one encompassing the west and the centre and the other the east and the south, with vastly different shares of predominantly Russian-speaking people and different histories of their residence on the respective territories.

The table's figures clearly demonstrate that both the Ukrainian population as a whole and its predominantly Russian-speaking part in particular became increasingly attached to their country of residence and thus inclined to identify themselves primarily in national terms. At the same time, among Russian speakers this identification is less predominant than among those people using primarily Ukrainian or the two languages equally, while identification with their respective localities remains stronger than in the other linguistic groups. Moreover, the gap between the Russian-speaking populations of the two geographical halves of the country not only persists but grows wider. In the west and centre, the Russian-speaking minority increasingly resembles the Ukrainian-speaking majority, while in the east and south the Russian-speaking majority lags behind in its identification with the Ukrainian state and nation. This gap vividly demonstrates the crucial importance of the regional dimension of identity processes in Ukraine.

Table 1: Responses to the survey question: "Whom do you consider yourself primarily" (February 2012 and February 2017, in %)

	2012				2017			
	All respondents	Russian speakers			All respondents	Russian speakers		
		All	West and Centre	East and South		All	West and Centre	East and South
Citizen of Ukraine	54.8	43.6	52.2	41.4	66.2	57.5	68.9	53.2
Resident of locality	27.6	28.1	21.2	29.9	23.8	28.5	23.9	30.3
Resident of region	8.1	12.8	6.2	14.5	4.3	6.1	0.6	8.1
Resident of the post-Soviet space	2.7	6.0	7.1	5.7	1.1	2.4	0.6	3.1
European	2.5	2.7	5.3	2.1	1.3	1.7	2.8	1.3
Citizen of the earth	2.8	5.3	8.0	4.6	3.0	3.5	2.8	3.8
Hard to say	1.5	1.5	0.0	1.8	0.2	0.3	0.6	0.2

The second question compared Ukrainian identity not only with other territorial identifications but also with widespread identifications of other kinds including those defined by gender, religion, occupation, ideology, ethnicity, and language. Unfortunately, this question was only included in the September 2014 survey so we can analyse post-Euromaidan priorities but not the evolution for the years of independence (see Table 2). When asked which of the listed twenty words best characterize them, being allowed to choose no more than three, respondents indicated their identification as "Ukrainians" more frequently than any other, even though the characteristic "man/woman" was almost as popular. Although the specific meaning of the word "Ukrainian" for a particular respondent remains unclear, whether civic, ethnic, or some combination thereof, the fact is that this self-perception is extremely salient in today's Ukraine. It is no wonder that people indicating their nationality as Russian were much less inclined to think of themselves as Ukrainians than those declaring Ukrainian nationality. More surprisingly, one in eight of self-designated Russians also considered it important to identify as Ukrainian, implying that the latter identification was for them primarily civic, and the former primarily ethnic. For all respondents using mainly Russian in everyday life, their identification as Ukrainians turned out to be much more salient than that as Russian-speakers, in a clear repudiation of the above-mentioned predictions of the formation of a distinct Russian-speaking community. While less inclined to identify as Ukrainians than those speaking predominantly Ukrainian or both languages equally, most Russian speakers primarily identified themselves not in terms of language but rather in terms of gender, locality, or religion.

Similarly to the previous question, the two halves of Ukraine differed considerably in the identification priorities of their residents, particularly among those who usually spoke Russian. In the west and centre, Russian speakers were much more inclined to identify as Ukrainians than in the east and south where, in contrast, local and regional identifications were more prevalent. Not only were differences between the geographical parts commensurate with those between the two linguistic groups, but also inter-regional differentiation was more pronounced in the Russian-speaking group than the Ukrainian-speaking one. Perhaps most remarkably, even in the south-eastern part of the country people speaking predominantly Russian were more likely to think of themselves as Ukrainians than Russian-speakers or Russians, notwithstanding a strong emphasis by those regions' elites on the Russian language and culture as a crucial element of their distinct identity.

Table 2: Responses to the survey question: "Which of the words listed below best characterises you? If it is hard for you to choose one, indicate a few but not more than three main characteristics" (September 2014, in per cent; shown are figures only for twelve options that turned out to be most popular among all respondents)

	Ukraine			West + Centre		East + South	
	All respondents	Russian nationality	Russian speakers	Russian speakers	Ukrainian speakers	Russian speakers	Ukrainian speakers
Orthodox	26.4	27.3	28.2	23.5	24.4	29.9	30.7
Man/woman	44.1	49.2	48.4	45.2	35.2	49.5	57.9
Worker	5.0	8.3	5.8	1.8	3.2	7.2	3.9
Resident of my city/village	27.7	20.3	26.6	16.9	27.0	29.9	34.7
Greek Catholic	2.7	0	0.3	1.2	5.8	0.0	0.0
Ukrainian	50.9	12.0	27.2	35.5	68.5	24.3	73.3
Intelligentsia	2.8	3.0	3.4	2.4	2.6	3.7	2.7
Russian	2.2	25.8	6.3	6.0	0.0	6.3	0.0
Resident of my region	14.4	16.5	17.4	7.8	13.5	20.7	6.7
Pensioner	11.9	20.5	10.5	7.8	10.4	11.5	25.3
Patriot	7.5	2.3	5.2	7.2	9.5	4.5	14.7
Russian-speaker	2.7	11.3	6.9	10.8	0.1	5.3	0.0

It should be noted, however, that the increasing "Ukrainianness" of the Russian-speaking part of Ukraine's population means that most of these people do not cease to be Russian-speaking when becoming (more) Ukrainian. Indeed, the share of those using predominantly Russian in their everyday life decreased only marginally for the first three decades of independence, not least because young people, while knowing the Ukrainian language better due to its increased use in education, did not speak it more than older generations who had been raised and schooled under the Soviet regime.[17] Although more Ukrainian appeared in certain domains such as education, public administration, and family communication, in other practices the Soviet-induced predominance of Russian persisted or even increased, perhaps most importantly in the workplace and the media. Euromaidan and the war, while stimulating attachment to Ukrainian as the perceived national language and alienation from Russian as the perceived language of the aggressor, did not convince a considerable part of Ukraine's population to suddenly change their language practice. Although many people who used to speak almost exclusively Russian seemed to be more willing to use some Ukrainian, at least in certain practices, by no means did this change amount to a full-fledged switch from one language to the other, which would then be reflected in responses to the survey question on everyday language. The surveys of 2012 and 2017 show virtually identical distributions of respondents by the language they primarily use in everyday life, both in Ukraine as a whole and in each of its geographical halves. Public discourse, in particular social media, provided numerous examples of both individual declarations of abandonment of the irreparably tainted language and objections to perceived infringements on the right to use it.[18] Between these two extremes, most Russian speakers continued to rely on their accustomed language without commenting on this choice, thus manifesting their perception thereof as being perfectly normal. This has only changed after Russia's full-blown invasion of Ukraine in February 2022.

Explaining the Low Salience of Russian-Speaking Identity

Perhaps the main factor contributing to the low salience of Russian-speaking identification is a lack of clear boundaries between Russian-speaking people and the rest of Ukraine's population. What seems unambiguous in survey data using one of the more or less arbitrary criteria for defining "Russian speakers", proves to be messy in real life, where both language practice and ethnolinguistic identity are anything but clear-cut. Most people in today's Ukraine use both Ukrainian and Russian in their everyday lives, albeit to greatly varying degrees, and very many, 21 per cent by self-designation in the 2017 survey, combine the two languages more or less equally. Moreover, even among those who speak predominantly Russian, many still consider Ukrainian to be their native language; in the 2017 survey, this share was 13 per cent, while a further 36 per cent claimed to have two native languages. Whether this choice is informed by ethnic origin, the idea of Ukrainian as the national language for all citizens, or other considerations, people care about their perceived native language no less than the language they usually speak – as clearly demonstrated by their preferences regarding the language situation and language policy which many surveys have inquired about.[19] Such a discrepancy between ethnolinguistic identity and language practice was an outcome of Soviet policies that promoted identification among Ukrainians with the Ukrainian nation and "its" language, on the one hand, and a reliance on Russian as the main language of social mobility and inter-ethnic unity, on the other. After the proclamation of independence, this discrepancy persisted and even increased as ever more people identified as Ukrainians without speaking much of the eponymous language.[20] As the above analysis has demonstrated, the tendency became stronger after the Maidan and the outbreak of war, hence the discrepancy grew even greater.

For one particular aspect of ethnolinguistic diversity to become much more salient than others, the state, or some other influential actor, would have to emphasize this aspect in their policies and discourses. Over three decades of independence, however, the Ukrainian state has mostly refrained from such an emphasis, even if it has prioritised the Ukrainian language and thus given some advantages to its speakers. The promotion of Ukrainian, usually far from aggressive, did not result in any systematic discrimination against speakers of Russian, most of whom could still use their preferred language in the workplace, when communicating with public servants, and in other practices.[21] Even in education, where a shift toward Ukrainian was perhaps the most perceptible, most of those who wanted their children to be taught in Russian (and this by no means included all the people who spoke mainly Russian themselves) had, until very recently, no problem finding schools or classes which could provide such services. To be sure, many Russian-speakers considered themselves, or people like them, to be discriminated against, and their share was higher than among those speaking mainly Ukrainian. However, this asymmetrical view of discrimination had much to do with the former group being accustomed to enjoying the full range of communicative practices in their preferred language, a custom that the latter group had never had a chance to acquire. Yet, even at the peak of the promotion of Ukrainian under President Viktor Yushchenko, 57 per cent of Russian-speaking respondents in a 2006 survey by the sociological centre *Hromadska Dumka* stated that they had never encountered manifestations of language-based discrimination against

Russian-speakers, while only 13 per cent claimed that they had encountered such manifestations quite often.[22]

Related to the lack of large-scale discrimination against Russian-speakers is a strong presence of political actors (seen as) representing the interests of this constituency. Having the full scope of political rights, Russian-speaking citizens were able to elect politicians to positions within local councils, the national parliament, and sometimes even the presidency who they hoped would protect their right to use their preferred language. The best-known example of such a language-related vote was the victory of Leonid Kuchma in the presidential election of 1994, thanks to overwhelming support by Russian-speakers, much of which was predicated on his campaign promise to elevate the legal status of Russian.[23] Although, upon election, Kuchma refused to take steps to guarantee the uninhibited use of Russian in all social domains, Russian-speaking voters repeatedly brought enough Russian-friendly candidates to parliament who then managed to block the most radical Ukrainianization measures during the presidencies of Kuchma and Yushchenko. Moreover, these votes eventually ensured the victory of Viktor Yanukovych who launched a counteroffensive against Ukrainianization, culminating in the passing of a new language law in 2012 that elevated the status of Russian, thereby legalising its actual prevalence in most social domains. This victory, as well as the earlier successes of Yanukovych's party in the parliamentary elections of 2006 and 2007, stemmed from a mobilization of Ukraine's eastern and southern constituencies by the anti-Orange elites who emphasized proximity to Russia and the reliance on the Russian language as those regions' core values.[24] While obviously detrimental to identification with Ukraine as a whole, this mobilization did not prioritize linguistic identity but regional and local ones, thus not only contributing to their prevalence in the east and south but also to the alienation of these regions' residents from their compatriots in the west and centre, which also meant disunity of the Russian-speaking population nationwide. Moreover, in seeking power across the entirety of Ukraine, rather than just its eastern and southern parts, Yanukovych and his associates had to balance their support for the Russian language with a recognition of the value of Ukrainian, just as their opponents mostly refrained from explicit de-legitimization of Russian and its speakers. Indeed, no major party ever presented itself as representing only one of the two main language groups or geographical halves of the country, even if some came to be widely seen as such. The lack of institutionalization of ethnolinguistic differences was no less important for national unity than the representation of different groups in power bodies and their influence on policymaking.

While politicians kept the fragile balance between the interests of Ukrainian- and Russian-speakers, members of both alleged groups increasingly perceived themselves as Ukraine's citizens or simply Ukrainians due to their participation in many practices prioritizing this identity, from education to traveling with a Ukrainian passport to watching Ukrainian sport teams compete with foreign ones. By the second decade of independence, this identification prevailed in both of the main language groups and in all macro-regions of Ukraine, even if the anti-Orange mobilization somewhat undermined its strength among the Russian-speakers of the east and south. The outbreak of war with Russia in 2014 brought Ukrainian citizens a new experience of defending one's country and/or expecting an attack by a foreign army, an experience that was widely claimed to have increased both identification with Ukraine and alienation from Russia. As a result, even in these regions, people predominantly speaking Russian by no means thought of themselves primarily as Russian-speakers or Russians, two identifications whose combined popularity in the 2014 survey did not exceed that of their self-perception as Ukrainians. In the west and centre, the prevalence of Ukrainian identification was much stronger. Both the great regional variation of Russian-speaking identification and its low salience compared to the Ukrainian one clearly demonstrates that there is no unified Russian-speaking identity group, just people outside of Russia who continued speaking primarily Russian. After February 2022, many of them found it problematic to continue speaking Russian, a language which they came to associate with the enemy.

Acknowledgment

The 2012 survey was funded by a grant awarded to me by the Shevchenko Scientific Society in the USA from the Natalia Danylchenko Endowment Fund. The 2014 survey was made possible by a grant awarded by the Canadian Institute of Ukrainian Studies, University of Alberta, from the Stasiuk Family Endowment Fund. The 2017 survey, designed in collaboration with Henry Hale, was funded from our research budgets at George Washington University and Yale University, respectively.

Notes

1. Shlapentokh, *The New Russian Diaspora*.
2. Kolstoe & Edemsky, *Russians in the Former Soviet Republics*; King & Melvin, *Nations Abroad*.
3. Brubaker, *Nationalism Reframed*.
4. Smith et al., "Rethinking Russia's post-Soviet diaspora," p. 121.
5. Arel & Khmelko, "The Russian Factor and Territorial Polarization".
6. Pirie, "National identity and politics", p. 1079.
7. Smith et al., "Nation-Building in the Post-Soviet Borderlands," p. 119.
8. Smith & Wilson, "Rethinking Russia's post-Soviet diaspora," p. 855.
9. Laitin, *Identity in Formation*, p. 33.
10. Janmaat, *Nation-Building in Post-Soviet Ukraine*.
11. Polese & Wylegala, "Odessa and Lvov or Odesa and Lviv", p. 798.
12. Sovik, *Support, Resistance and Pragmatism*.
13. Kulyk, "Soviet nationalities policies".
14. Barrington & Faranda, "Reexamining region, ethnicity, and language in Ukraine"; Kulyk, "Language identity, linguistic diversity".
15. Barrington, "Russian-Speakers in Ukraine and Kazakhstan".
16. Ibid., p. 152.
17. Kulyk, "The demography of language practices".
18. Kulyk, "Language and identity in Ukraine after Euromaidan".
19. Kulyk, "Language identity, linguistic diversity".
20. Kulyk, "Soviet nationalities policies".
21. Kulyk, "The demography of language practices".
22. Kulyk, "Language policy in Ukraine".
23. Arel & Khmelko, "The Russian Factor".
24. Kulyk, "Language policies and language attitudes"; Kulyk, "Language policy in Ukraine".

Selected Bibliography

Arel, D. and Khmelko, V. "The Russian Factor and Territorial Polarization in Ukraine," *The Harriman Review* 9: 1–2 (1996): 81–91.

Barrington, L. "Russian-Speakers in Ukraine and Kazakhstan: 'Nationality,' 'Population,' or Neither?" *Post-Soviet Affairs* 17:2 (2001): 129–158.

Barrington, L. & Faranda, R. "Reexamining region, ethnicity, and language in Ukraine," *Post-Soviet Affairs* 25:3 (2009): 232–256.

Bremmer, I. "The politics of ethnicity; Russians in the new Ukraine," *Europe-Asia Studies* 46: 2 (1994): 261–283.

Brubaker, R. *Nationalism Reframed: Nationhood and the National Question in the New Europe* (Cambridge: Cambridge University Press, 1996).

Janmaat, J. G. *Nation-Building in Post-Soviet Ukraine: Educational Policy and the Response of the Russian-Speaking Population* (Amsterdam: University of Amsterdam, 2000).

King, C. & Melvin, N. *Nations Abroad: Diaspora Politics and International Relations in the Former Soviet Union* (Boulder, CO, Westview Press, 1998).

Kolstoe, P., with a contribution from Edemsky, A. *Russians in the Former Soviet Republics* (Bloomington, Indiana University Press, 1995).

Kulyk, V. "The demography of language practices and attitudes in Ukraine," *Harvard Ukrainian Studies* 29: 1–4 (2007): 295–326.

Kulyk, V. "Language policies and language attitudes in post-Orange Ukraine," in: Besters-Dilger, J. (ed), *Language Policy and Language Situation in Ukraine: Analysis and Recommendations*, pp. 15–55 (Frankfurt et al.: Peter Lang, 2009).

Kulyk, V. "Language identity, linguistic diversity, and political cleavages: Evidence from Ukraine," *Nations and Nationalism* 17:3 (2011): 627–648.

Kulyk, V. "Language policy in Ukraine: What people want the state to do," *East European Politics and Societies* 27: 2 (2013): 280–307.

Kulyk, V. "Soviet nationalities policies and the discrepancy between ethnocultural identification and language practice in Ukraine,", in: Beissinger, M. and Kotkin, S. (eds), *The Historical Legacies of Communism in Russia and Eastern Europe*, pp. 202–221 (Cambridge: Cambridge University Press, 2014).

Kulyk, V. "Language and identity in Ukraine after Euromaidan," *Thesis Eleven* 136:1 (2016): 90–106.

Laitin, D. D. *Identity in Formation: The Russian-Speaking Populations in the Near Abroad* (Ithaca and London, Cornell University Press, 1998).

Pirie, P. S. "National identity and politics in Southern and Eastern Ukraine," *Europe-Asia Studies* 48:7 (1996).

Polese, A. and Wylegala, A. "Odessa and Lvov or Odesa and Lviv: How important is the letter? Reflections on the 'Other' in two Ukrainian cities," *Nationalities Papers* 36: 5 (2008): 787–814.

Shlapentokh, V., M. Sendich, and E. Payin. *The New Russian Diaspora: Russian Minorities in the Former Soviet Republics* (Armonk, NY and London, M.E. Sharpe, 1994).

Smith, G., and A. Wilson. "Rethinking Russia's post-Soviet diaspora: The potential for political mobilisation in eastern Ukraine and north-east Estonia," *Europe-Asia Studies* 49: 5 (1997): 845–864.

Smith, A., V. Law, A. Wilson, A. Bohr, and E. Allworth. *Nation-Building in the Post-Soviet Borderlands: The Politics of National Identities* (Cambridge: Cambridge University Press, 1998).

Søvik, M. B. *Support, Resistance and Pragmatism: An Examination of Motivation in Language Policy in Kharkiv, Ukraine* (Stockholm: Stockholm University, 2007).

The Donbas: A Region and a Myth

Oleksandr Zabirko

While the entire world was looking with horror at the ongoing war in Ukraine, there was still one country in Europe where the word "war" was not mentioned in the official media: the Russian Federation. In the official parlance of the Kremlin, the undisguised Russian invasion of Ukraine was referred to as a "special military operation to defend the Donetsk and Luhansk People's Republics" or simply a "special operation in the Donbas." The supposed goal of this operation was to "demilitarize and denazify Ukraine" in order to prevent the imminent "genocide of the population of the Donbas."[1] Since Ukraine controlled about two-thirds of the Donetsk and Luhansk administrative regions prior to the start of the Russian military onslaught on February 24, 2022, the genocide allegation, coupled with Russia's recognition of "people's republics" within the administrative boundaries of Ukrainian territories, became a "veritable" reason for war.

Distorting and obfuscating the truth has long ago become an essential part of the Russian leadership's political repertoire. Without adhering to this perfidious rhetoric, it is nevertheless worth taking a closer look at the construct of the "Russian-speaking people of the Donbas" – after all, for more than eight years the Donbas has been the scene of a fierce struggle between the Ukrainian armed forces and the (pro-)Russian "people's militias" from Donetsk and Luhansk. But what actually is Donbas and who are its inhabitants?

Territory and History

The Donets Basin (*donetskii basein* in Russian), or Donbas for short, was originally not a topographical, political, or cultural term, but primarily a geological one. It refers to the coal deposits in the basin of the river Siverskyi Donets, which, since the late 19th century, enabled the rapid growth of local heavy industry. Thus, the territorial affiliation of Donbas, or rather the defining of certain localities and areas as being part of the Donbas, was decided based on what lay several hundred meters below ground. Therefore "historical Donbas" includes not only the Russian-speaking agglomerations of Donetsk and Luhansk, but also the Ukrainian agricultural regions, the Greek and Tatar settlements on the coast of the Sea of Azov, and even parts of Rostov Oblast in what is now the Russian Federation.

In terms of topography, the Donbas belongs to a steppe area that used to be called the "wild field", essentially a no man's land. This reputation saw it attract those seeking greater freedoms, leading to the wild field becoming a free, Cossack steppe land. Even after the free steppe was conquered, the frontiers closed, the Zaporozhian Cossackdom abolished, and the Don Cossacks incorporated into the Russian Empire, the metropolis' hold on this former frontier region remained weak, while the people's free spirit died hard. Moreover, while industrial development from the latter half of the 19th century onward, certainly tightened the grip of the Russian imperial administration over this sparsely populated area, it also opened the region to massive levels of migration, thereby recreating the former frontiers in a symbolic sense.

The prerequisites for the formation of the Donbas as an industrial hub arose in the late 18th century and were closely connected to the geopolitical interests of the Russian Empire in the Black Sea area. After a series of successful wars against the Ottoman Empire, and the forceful liquidation of the Crimean Khanate as an independent Tatar state in 1783, Russia seized the Northern Black Sea coast and launched an ambitious project of building new seaports and strengthening its navy. These ambitions required a solid industrial base, therefore the vast reserves of coal discovered as early as 1721 in the territory of present-day Donbas acquired new value. In 1795, by decree of Empress Catherine II, the authorities started the construction of the Luhansk iron foundry and established new coal mines in Lysychia Balka, now the town of Lysychansk.

These first islets of industrial society in what is now the Donbas had a somewhat paradoxical nature, combining advanced technology and a modern pioneering spirit with the archaic social structures of the Russian state. Both the mines and factory where subject to a severe regime of military discipline, where workers were basically treated like soldiers. Their whole life was regulated by the "mining statute", which generally followed the norms of the army statute: officials were given military ranks, while military courts observed and enforced labor discipline, punishing workers for even the slightest offence.

Furthermore, this industrialization and technological development required foreign capital and knowledge, which were welcomed by the Russian authorities, but ultimately altered the perception of the former "wild field" by adding new facets and new tensions to the area. While the colonial practices of British, French, German, and (especially) Belgian entrepreneurs in the Donbas resulted in the region being nicknamed "the white Congo",[2] rapid industrial growth also fueled hopes of a "New America" arising in the East European prairies. This optimistic expectation was famously pronounced by Aleksandr Blok in his eponymous poem.[3] Unsurprisingly, the free steppe was not free for everyone. Pernicious ethnic tension and severe economic exploitation were facts of life, yet this reputation did not discourage people from seeking freedom and fortune in the Donbas.

Despite the influences of Western urban culture, the dual military-civic structures of the newly founded industrial settlements became a distinct feature of pre-Soviet Donbas and arguably forged the peculiar political culture of this mining region, which would persist over the subsequent decades and survive different state formations and political regimes.

At the core of the region's path dependent trajectory, one may identify the socio-political and cultural characteristics of stone coal as a natural resource, which facilitates certain types of production and social structures. In culture and literature, resources are often associated with certain models of political order and domination: cotton production, for example, is associated with slavery (as in the southern United States), and grain cultivation with serfdom (as in the Russian Empire). In this sense, coal mining can also be considered a culture-forming phenomenon.

However, the idea of coal mining areas as regions that decisively promoted the emergence of the first "mass democracies", famously postulated by Timothy Mitchell in his book *Carbon Democracy* (2013), is not as easily established when looking at the development of the Donbas. Although one can find clear and frequent references to the miners' and workers' strong sense of communal solidarity, one looks in vain for the image of a consolidated, institutionalized democracy or an open society. Similarly, the role of social-democratic ideology or trade unions remained marginal and was often overshadowed by the region's supposed affinity to various forms of political radicalism and authoritarian rule. Arguably, the Donbas never managed to produce any political organization or movement that would fit into Western historical framework. According to Hiroaki Kuromiya, "class" and "nation," the two major political concepts that arose in reaction to the Enlightenment, did not necessarily apply to the politics of the Donbas.⁴ Leon Trotsky's claim that "One can't go to the Donbas without a gas mask", best describes the noxious political history of the region: everyone from Moscow to Kyiv and every political party from the far-right to Marxists seems to have gotten burned politically in this region.

In the early 1920s, the Donbas was often perceived as the laboratory for the creation of the Soviet "new man" and a motor for a profound social transformation – an attitude famously captured in Dziga Vertov's avant-garde movie *Enthusiasm* (1931). However, already in the late 1920s this transformation was firmly anchored within the totalitarian policies of Stalinism, which turned the Donbas into a testing ground for "rapid industrialization", the "collectivization of agriculture", and the "aggravation of the class struggle".⁵ While the region's rural population was decimated by the 1932–33 Holodomor (or the Great Famine), the infamous Shakhty Trial of 1928, the first show trial of the Stalin era, heralded the beginning of the "purges" in industry. The launch of the so-called Stakhanovite movement in 1935 also placed Donbas coalmining at the very center of the all-Soviet campaign intended to increase worker productivity in all segments of industry and agriculture, turning it into a trope within state ideology and the perceived epitome of Soviet identity.

The rise of coal and steel production in the Donbas reached its climax in the late 1960s and 1970s and was followed by rapid decline in the early 1980s due to the increasing role of oil and gas both in the global economy and Soviet exports. This resulted in the mining sector becoming increasingly dependent on state support, precipitating a long period of stagnation culminating in a wave of miners' strikes from the late 1980s into the 1990s – in the wake of Ukrainian independence. The transition towards a capitalist economy only accelerated the economic and social decline of the region's historically mono-industrial towns. Moreover, since the 2000s, the growing socio-economic tensions in the Donbas "re-activated" issues of language and identity, thus making its Ukrainian-Russian dualism susceptible to political manipulation.

Languages and Identity

The Russian-speaking population of the Donbas, which sits at the core of Putin's contemporary war rhetoric, is by no means a "natural", but rather a hybrid historical phenomenon. Like most other Ukrainians, the people of the Donbas are largely bilingual, with Russian clearly dominating everyday communication. However, Russian as a high variety (i.e. the language variety, which has a higher prestige and is used for official purposes) was ultimately established in the Donbas only after the Second World War as a result of both state-sponsored Russification, particularly in the sphere of education, and the growing difference between urbanity and rusticity in Soviet Ukraine. During this period, the Ukrainian language was largely considered the language of the rural areas. As a consequence of the forced urbanization and industrialization of the Donbas, it often came to be perceived as a sign of cultural and social backwardness with those who moved to the cities and towns tending to switch to Russian in the public sphere and retain their use of Ukrainian only when communicating with relatives.

Nevertheless, the Ukrainian element has always been a constitutive part of regional identity, even though its role had often been downgraded to the level of folklore. For instance, in the popular Soviet musical comedy "The Young Years" (*Gody molodye*, 1959), which takes place in the Donbas and Kyiv, all the characters speak Russian, but all the songs are performed in Ukrainian.

The image of an industrial "melting pot" facilitated a regional attitude of national indifference, which under the conditions of Soviet cultural and education policies, could only mean its further Russification. Indeed, while this tendency could also be observed across wider Soviet Ukraine, intellectual resistance against this state of affairs is associated, first and foremost, with Ivan Dzyuba, a philologist from Donets'k, who in his 1965 book *Internationalism or Russification?* directly addressed and criticized the Communist Party leadership for its policy on nationalities. Although Dzyuba articulated his criticism from a Marxist standpoint, he was still sentenced to five years in prison in 1972. Despite this, Dzyba and other prominent dissidents from the Donbas, such as the poet Vasyl' Stus or the human-rights activist Oleksa Tykhyi, undoubtedly contributed to the image of the Donbas as a place of dissidence within Ukrainian culture, constantly challenging the official Soviet monopoly.

Like other coal and steel regions, such as Germany's Ruhr valley or Poland's Upper Silesia, today's Donbas can probably be described as a translocal entity: an area that has no clear administrative or natural boundaries, and only gains contours and solidity through various narratives, such as those found in literature and film – and often through a nostalgic retrospective. Since Soviet times, industrial culture and the working man's ethos have been a source of collective pride and cornerstones of local identity, which blurred ethnic, religious, or ideological boundaries. However, since the 1970s, most of the mines, factories, and machinery have hardly been modernized or restructured, having continued to be exploited until their imminent collapse. As a typical old industrial region, the Donbas has inherited its economic base from the early era of industrialization with its inflexible large-scale enterprises as well as a high industrial density coupled with below-average economic growth. Against this background, the memory of the Soviet era mutated into a myth of the "golden age" in which the region was still considered the engine of the wider Soviet economy. It was precisely this mythology that made the local population particularly receptive to Russia's neo-imperial propaganda.

Separatism and Beyond

In 1991, the overwhelming majority of the Donbas population voted for Ukrainian independence. Yet, when the Soviet Union collapsed, the Donbas immediately became the most troublesome spot for Kyiv. The problem was not just that the Donbas had a large Russian population, or that it was highly Russified linguistically and culturally, but rather the exaggerated political ambitions of the regional elites and the incompatibility of the old industrial structures with the rules of the new capitalist economy.

On the other hand, after the fall of communism in 1989–91, the Donbas often became an object of deliberate "othering" by the Ukrainian political and cultural elites precisely because of its historical and structural peculiarities, thus serving as contrasting foil for the nation-building practices of the new state. Being often portrayed as a reservation of the collective Other or as a "sick" and "ugly" part of the Ukrainian national body, the Donbas was now obliged to adapt to an unsettled, subaltern status.

Before 2014, however, there was no pronounced cultural, let alone political, separatism or irredentism in the Donbas. Although Russia's meddling in local politics intensified after Ukraine's Orange Revolution in 2004, and the region soon became the electoral stronghold of the pro-Russian "Party of Regions" (and its leader Viktor Yanukovych), this remained firmly anchored in the all-Ukrainian context, with separatist and secessionists agenda still a marginal feature. The population on both sides of the Russian-Ukrainian border was convinced that this border should be passable for people and goods in both directions. Faced with a geostrategic choice between Europe and Russia, the Donbas residents probably did not reject the pro-European, democratic aspirations of the Ukrainian Euromaidan movement as such. Rather, they rejected the entire premise through which such a geopolitical choice had to be made in the first place.

According to the results of a poll conducted by the Kyiv International Institute of Sociology in the spring of 2014 – before the active military clashes commenced – only one-third of the population of the Donetsk and Luhansk regions supported the idea of stronger affiliation with Russia. Another third favored a broader level of autonomy for the Donbas within the Ukrainian state, while roughly the remaining third wanted to preserve the status quo. In 2014, the pseudo-referendum on the creation of the two independent "people's republics" in the territory of Donbas was held by pro-Russian activists within the context of a regional power vacuum and the overall confusion that followed the, by then, ex-President Yanukovych's escape to Russia. Moreover, the referendum only took place in a few cities (mainly in the Donetsk agglomeration) without independent election observers, therefore it remains unknown what proportion of the population actually participated in this "state-building event".

Similarly, one can hardly speak of a Russian "popular uprising" in the region. The maximum number of participants in the pro-Russian rallies in Donetsk, a city with over a million inhabitants, was about 30.000 to 35.000 people, with the total number who stormed administrative buildings and subsequently participated in units of the "people's militia" only being about 1.500 to 2.000. While the participation of Russian citizens in the hostilities in these territories has become the subject of heated debate since the outbreak of the conflict, the glorification of Russian "volunteers" and their participation in the fighting in eastern Ukraine is increasingly proving to be a leading theme of literary productions, being expressed in numerous published texts with an almost touching directness and simplicity. An illustration of this is provided by the anthology *Vybor Donbassa* ("The Choice of the Donbas"). Published in 2017, the volume, which is full of contributions by writers from Yaroslavl, Moscow, Orenburg, Chelyabinsk, and other Russian cities, makes it clear that the supposed "Donbas choice" was predominantly made outside the Donbas.[6]

Indeed, long before the events of 2014, some prominent Russian authors had already envisaged a war in the Donbas as both a trigger for major changes in Russian society and as the pivotal moment for Russia's reemergence as a global power. For instance, Zakhar Prilepin's *Terra Tartara*, a "prophetic" essay published in 2009, predicted mass uprisings starting in Russia shortly after the outbreak of a war in Ukraine:

> There were some problems with one of [our] country's former colonies, the land of Ukraine, where, somehow, slowly and gradually, a civil war broke

out, with West fighting East. (...) Of course, it was necessary to do something about it, since all over the country volunteer units were beginning to organize themselves. Easily crossing the state border, they were vanishing into the vast open spaces of Ukraine.[7]

Having acquired military experience in the "Ukrainian Civil War", numerous Russian volunteers are returning to Russia to resume their fight for the national cause on the "home front". Similar scenarios are proposed in various novels that explore a forthcoming war in Ukraine written between 2003 and 2010 by authors from the Donbas: Fedor Berezin, Georgii Savitskii (both from Donetsk) and Gleb Bobrov (from Luhansk). Bobrov's novel *The Era of the Stillborn* (2008), Berezin's *War 2010: The Ukrainian Front* (2009), and Savitskii's *Battlefield Ukraine. The Broken Trident* (2009) all characterize the Ukrainian state as a "stillborn" geopolitical anomaly, which will give way to the rise of a new Eurasian empire, or even the re-established USSR. In all these texts, Ukraine in general, and the Donbas in particular, turn into a battleground and the place where the fable of Russia's imperial recovery begins. Unsurprisingly, all of these writers have seized the opportunity to take an active part in the war in the Donbas, grasping the chance to become the heroes of their own stories.

What unites this body of anti-Ukrainian literature, written both by Russian and the local authors, is the geo-political function attributed to the Donbas as a borderland region. As the much-desired imperial renaissance of Russia is obstructed by social atomization and corruption, the new imperial community is imagined as extending beyond the borders of the Russian Federation. Thus, the revival of the Russian state starts with the rescue of "compatriots" living in the Donbas. Rogers Brubaker defines this kind of political attitude as "transborder nationalism of the external national homeland", but while for Brubaker the typical goals of this sort of nationalism are to "promote the welfare, support the activities and institutions, assert the rights, and protect the interests of one's own ethnonational kin in other states",[8] in Russian patriotic literature it is frequently applied in order to deny the very existence of those states. Indeed, the territories themselves are describes as attributable to Russia since they are already inhabited by a Russian-speaking population.

Caught in the Russian neo-imperial dreams, the Donbas not only became the site of the largest military contestation in Europe since the Second World War but is also currently experiencing an unprecedented wave of urbicides, through the deliberate destruction of urban areas by the Russian artillery, and the expulsion of the local population. Moreover, the identity of the Donbas as a region with distinct, recognizable features has already become questionable. In the Russian geopolitical imagery, the area is now firmly anchored within the historical brand of *Novorossiya* (literally "New Russia") as well as within the concept of *russkiy mir*, or the Russian world. Both concepts intrinsically deny the region's cultural and ethnic diversity, reducing it to an area unequivocally attributed to the Russian sphere of political and cultural uniformity.

In Ukraine, however, the question of whether the Donbas deserves recognition as a distinct region remains, at least, debatable. Already in 2021, Oleksiy Danilov, the Secretary of the National Security and Defense Council and the former mayor Luhansk, pointed out that the word "Donbas" does not appear in official Ukrainian state documents and should therefore be abandoned altogether in favor of the more politically correct and neutral-sounding names of the local oblasts (administrative regions) Donetsk and Luhansk.[9] This bureaucratic logic notwithstanding, the term itself remains ubiquitous in the language of Ukrainian literature and media.

Yet, even if the future of the Donbas remains contested and obscure, its physical and symbolic survival today seems only possible within the boundaries of the pluralist and democratic Ukrainian state.

Re-Imagining Ukrainian Donbas

The growing interest in the Eastern borderlands, with the purpose of overcoming the country's supposed East-West divide, was a visible trend in the Ukrainian literature of the 2000s resulting in some notable shifts in Ukraine's imagined geography. Although in many literary texts the Donbas still features as the realm of collapsing Soviet industry and corrupted national consciousness, other depictions that sought to present the region's symbolic re-integration into the Ukrainian cultural sphere, proved far more productive and successful.

Serhiy Zhadan, a writer from the East, has particularly distinguished himself in this respect. In his novel *Voroshylovhrad* (2010), Zhadan follows the development of a young city dweller who unexpectedly becomes the heir to a run-down petrol station located somewhere in the Donbas, in the middle of the eastern Ukrainian "transit landscape". The new owner tries to come to terms with this unexpected and undesired property; however, he soon recognizes the no-man's land of the Donbas steppe as his "own place" and learns how to defend it against the intrigues and attacks of the local oligarchs and their mafia networks. Today, it is tempting to interpret this plot as a metonymy for Ukraine's coming to terms with the neglected and largely troublesome region on its eastern border, however, Zhadan's text, full of lyrical intermezzos and allegoric motives, escapes such straightforward parallels to the current geopolitical reality. In fact, the words "Ukraine" or "Russia" are not even mentioned in his novel.

Zhadan sticks to this strategy of deliberate poetic obfuscation of political realities in his more recent novel *Internat* (2017), which directly addresses the Russian military onslaught in the Donbas after 2014. In the book, the author describes an inner transformation of the protagonist, Pasha, as a result of his direct confrontation with the war. While trying to rescue his nephew from an orphanage in the occupied territory, Pasha gradually reconsiders his apolitical attitude and his self-selected role as an outsider. The hellish experience of travelling through his occupied hometown (recognizable as Debaltseve, the site of a major battle between Ukrainian army and Russian paramilitary units in 2015) forces Pasha to acknowledge his indifferent and apolitical attitudes as the fertile ground for the ongoing war. At the end of the story, an apathetic "Donbas dweller" turns into a self-conscious citizen who takes responsibility for his decisions and cares for those in need.

Instead of focusing on the issues of state or nation building, in both novels Zhadan pursues communitarian ideals of social cohesion and demonstrates mechanisms of solidarity, which function within the small communities of friends, relatives, and neighbors. Against this background, the proletarian ethos and the collectivist ideals of a coal-mining region no longer appear as the relics of the Soviet past but allow for the symbolic re-integration of the Donbas into the Ukrainian national project. Of course, this re-integration cannot be reduced to the writings of a single author. Other Ukrainian writers and poets such as Volodymyr Rafeenko, Evgeniya Belorusets, Andrey Kurkov, and Iya Kiva have also developed their own approaches for dealing with this war-torn region. Although it is hardly possible to reduce their literary discourses to a common denominator, one may still observe a poetic resemanticization of the Donbas in these contemporary Ukrainian publications (written both in the Russian and Ukrainian languages). Here the Donbas features as the terrain of historical anomie, where periods of radical political transformation and sheer violence trigger a constant feeling of anxiety over the perceived lack of social norms and moral standards, yet this uninviting terrain can still be treated with compassion and sympathy. Thus, in contemporary Ukrainian poetry, the former realm of the collective Other is often transformed into a nostalgic or melancholic landscape of abandoned industrial sites and collapsing architecture, evoking feelings of loss, decay, and sorrow.

In times of war, however, the decay is usually perceived not as a gradual and slow process, which invites the reader to undertake contemplation and reflection. Instead, it becomes synonymous with artillery barrages and air raids, and therefore is often presented as a quick and painful decomposition of the entire region or as the sudden and unexpected collapse of the life-worlds of its inhabitants. In her poem *Decomposition* (2014) Lyuba Yakimchuk, a poet from Pervomaisk, in the Luhansk oblast, summarizes this traumatic experience as follows:

> nothing changes on the eastern front
> well, I've had it up to here
> at the moment of death, metal gets hot
> and people get cold
> don't talk to me about Luhansk
> it's long since turned into hansk
> Lu had been razed to the ground
> to the crimson pavement
> my friends are hostages
> and I can't reach them, I can't do netsk
> to pull them out of the basements
> from under the rubble (...)
> there's no poetry about war
> just decomposition
> only letters remain
> and they all make a single sound – rrr
> Pervomaisk has been split into pervo and maisk
> into particles in primeval flux
> war is over once again
> yet peace has not come (...)
> I stare into the horizon
> it has narrowed into a triangle
> sunflowers dip their heads in the field
> black and dried out, like me
> I have gotten so very old
> no longer Lyuba
> just a –ba

Since 2014 not only the political future of the Donbas, but its sheer existence as recognizable regional entity remains opaque. On the one hand, after eight years of military contestation it is becoming increasingly clear that the area does not represent a consolidated communal or regional structure but is rather a terrain with multiple splits and ruptures. The ongoing war certainly changes the self-perception and the regional identity of the people on both sides of the frontline. The geopolitical "decomposition" caused by the Russian aggression against Ukraine is mirrored and amplified here by myriad smaller splits within local communities and even families. The spirit of war nurtures old wounds and opens new ones.

On the other hand, it is obvious that the semantics of the word "Donbas" have expanded beyond the mere denomination of the old coal-basin and the corresponding industrial sites. It became a synonym for political instability, economic decay, but also for the remarkable solidarity and stubborn resistance. With the former geopolitical periphery becoming more and more central, the tenacity of the Donbas is perhaps that of a myth, rather than that of a certain area. This is the myth about a harsh terrain populated by simple and undemanding inhabitants, who live by simple rules and stick together against all odds. Or as Serhiy Zhadan (2011) puts it:

> Everything that you make with your hands, works for you.
> Everything that reaches your conscience beats
> in rhythm with your heart.
> We stayed on this land, so that it wouldn't be far
> for our children to visit our graves.
> This is our island of freedom,
> our expanded
> village consciousness.
> (...)
> because, man, as long as we're together,
> there's someone to dig up this earth,
> and find in its warm innards
> the black stuff of death
> the black stuff of life.

Notes

1. Putin, Vladimir (2022): *Obrashchenie prezidenta Rossiiskoi Federacii "O provedenii spetsial'noi voyennoi operatsii"* [Adress of the President of the Russian Federation "On conducting a special military operation"], 24 February 2022, http://kremlin.ru/events/president/news/67843 (28 December 2022).
2. Lazans'ka, *Istoriia pidpryemnytstva*.
3. Blok, Aleksandr, *Sobranie sochinenii v vos'mi tomakh. Tom 3: Stikhotvorieniia i poemy, 1907–1921* (Moskva: Gosudarstvennoe izdatel'stvo khudozhestvennoi literatury, 1960), pp. 268–270.
4. Kuromiya, *Freedom and Terror in the Donbas*, p. 335.
5. Ibid, pp. 119–166.
6. See Bobrov, *Vybor Donbassa*.
7. My translation (O.Z).
8. Brubaker *Nationalism Reframed*, p. 5.
9. Oleksii Danilov, "V Ukraïni nemaie slova "Donbas", *Ukraïns'ka Pravda*, 24 March 2021, https://www.pravda.com.ua/news/2021/03/24/7287714/ (28 December 2022).

Selected Bibliography

Berezin, Fëdor. *Voina 2010: Ukrainskii front* (Moskva: Eksmo, 2009).

Blok, Aleksandr. *Sobranie sochinenii v vos'mi tomakh. Tom 3: Stikhotvorieniia i poemy, 1907–1921* (Moskva: Gosudarstvennoe izdatel'stvo khudozhestvennoi literatury, 1960).

Bobrov, Gleb (ed.): *Vybor Donbasa. Literatura narodnykh respublik* (Lugansk: Bol'shoi Donbass, 2017).

Bobrov, Gleb. *Epokha mertvorozhdennykh* (Moskva: Eksmo, 2008).

Brubaker, Rogers. *Nationalism Reframed: Nationhood and the National Question in the New Europe* (Cambridge: Cambridge University Press, 1996).

Kuromiya, Hiroaki. *Freedom and Terror in the Donbas: A Ukrainian-Russian Borderland, 1870s-1990s* (Cambridge: Cambridge University Press, 1998).

Lazans'ka, Tamara I. *Istoriia pidpryemnytstva v Ukraïni* (Kyiv: Institut Istoriï Ukraïny NAN Ukraïny, 1999).

Mitchell, Timothy. *Carbon Democracy: Political Power in the Age of Oil* (London: Verso, 2013).

Prilepin, Zakhar. *Terra Tartara. Ėto kasaetsia lichno menia* (Moskva: AST, 2009).
Savitskii, Georgii. *Pole boia Ukraina. Slomannyĭ trezubets* (Moskva: Eksmo, 2009).
Yakimchuk, Lyuba. Decomposition, translated by Oksana Maksymchuk and Max Rosochinsky, in: *Words for War: New Poems from Ukraine*, (2014) https://www.wordsforwar.com/decomposition (28 December 2022).
Zhadan, Serhiy. *Internat* (Chernivtsi: Meridian Czernowitz, 2017) [in English translation: *The Orphanage*, translated by Reilly Costigan-Humes and Isaac Stackhouse Wheeler, Yale University Press, 2021].
Zhadan, Serhiy. The Mushrooms of Donbas, translated by Virlana Tkacz and Wanda Phipps, in: *Poetry International Rotterdam*, 2011) https://poetryinternationalweb.org/pi/site/poem/item/19472/THE-MUSHROOMS-OF-DONBAS (28 December 2022).
Zhadan, Serhiy. *Voroshylovhrad* (Kharkiv: Folio, 2010). [in English translation: *Voroshilovgrad*, translated by Isaac Stackhouse Wheeler and Reilly Costigan-Humes, Dallas: Deep Velum, 2016).

Towards Gender Equality in the Ukrainian Society

Tamara Martsenyuk

Gender equality has been one of the values of democratic societies for more than 50 years. Its declaration as a value implies the achievement of an equal position for both women and men in all spheres of life in society through the legal provision of equal rights and opportunities and the elimination of gender discrimination. It also infers an application of temporary special measures aimed at eliminating the imbalance in the opportunities of women and men in exercising equal rights.

These ideas should be put into practice by building sustainable institutional support for gender equality: the equal involvement of women and men in various spheres of public life, such as family, politics, security and defense; taking into account the needs of different categories of the population, such as women and men of different ages, marital status, region of origin, or states of health; counteracting gender stereotypes and gender violence; and expanding awareness-raising activities and a culture of gender equality.

In Ukraine, a lot has been done over the last 30 years to draw attention to the topic of gender equality and human rights in general. Firstly, a national mechanism for ensuring gender equality has been developed. Back in 2005, the Law of Ukraine "On ensuring equal rights and opportunities for women and men" was adopted. Ukraine also became the first post-Soviet country to adopt a law against domestic violence in 2001. The work of the executive authorities tasked with overseeing these policies is coordinated by the Government Commissioner for Gender Policy. These are all components of so-called "top-down" approach regarding the regulation of gender equality.

Secondly, bottom-up approach (grass root activism) is also important, especially through the work of women's feminist movements that fight for equal rights. This chapter will take a closer look at the process that has led to the formation of the women's movement in Ukraine and its role in ensuring gender equality in Ukrainian society.

The Women's Movement in Ukraine: A Brief History of Visibility

Feminism as an organized women's movement and cultural tradition, emerged in Ukraine during the 1890s. *Tovarystvo ruskikh zhenshchin* [The Association of Ukrainian Women], founded in 1884 in Stanislav (now Ivano-Frankivsk) by the writer and feminist Natalia Kobrynska (1855–1920), is historically considered the first women's organization. In 1887, the first Ukrainian women's almanac *The First Wreath* was published by Kobrynska together with the Ukrainian publisher, writer, and civil activist Olena Pchilka. Additionally, through her *Women's Library* collection, Kobrynska also published other works for women, written by women. However, the largest women's organization in Halychyna (Galicia), and the Ukrainian lands in general, was the Union of Ukrainian Women. During the 1930s, this organization was headed by another well-known activist of the women's movement, the journalist and writer Milena Rudnytska (1892–1979).

"History Without Women" is the title of the introduction to Martha Bohachevsky-Chomiak's book *Feminists despite themselves: women in Ukrainian community life, 1884–1939*. This work, is considered to be the first thorough study of the women's movement in Ukraine, particularly during the second half of the 19th and first half of the 20th centuries. As the researcher indicates in an interview: "Women tried to do something practical everywhere. But women's work is very exhausting, and it turns out that you do what you have to do, and then there is neither energy nor desire to sit down and write: this is my concept, this is what I did." Therefore, the researcher indicates that so-called "pragmatic feminism" was inherent to that period.

During Soviet times, the dominant position was occupied by the gender construct of the working mother. Martha Bohachevsky-Chomiak indicates that the women's issue in the USSR remained a purely social and political issue in which soviet women were integrated into society through active participation in the economy. Bohachevsky-Chomiak points out that "woman's rights merge with the duties of a mother, and a woman does not exist as a self-contained unit. There is a woman in the service of the state, which she did not build." At a time when nearly one hundred percent of women worked full-time, the state was responsible for raising children. Motherhood was considered almost the greatest duty to the state while the role of the father was marginalized.

A large number of women's non-governmental organizations have existed in Ukraine since the 1990s. According to data from the State Statistics Committee, as of 2000, there were about a thousand registered women's non-governmental organizations in Ukraine. However, these organizations have never become mainstream in terms of membership and women's participation in their activities, comprising only 4 per cent of all non-governmental organizations.

It is interesting to note, however, that even in the 1990s, along with more traditional women's organizations, such groups were still being established and were not afraid to include the word "feminism" in their titles. In particular, it is worth singling out the non-governmental organization "Progressive Women" Vinnytsia Feminist Society, which was founded in 1995 under the leadership of Natalia Kozlova and is still operating today.

Since the 1990s, most Ukrainian women's organizations, with the exception of scientific or educational gender centers, have focused their activities on resolving social problems that are considered exclusive to women. These include the protection of motherhood and childhood, providing assistance to disabled children, and support for low-income single mothers. At the same time, several women's organizations within the Ukrainian diaspora that, in addition to traditional "women's issues", such as the preservation of the Ukrainian language and culture, seek to defend ideas such as the dignity and inviolability of women, compliance with international standards in the field of human rights, and adherence to the rule of law. Key to this was founding of the Toronto-based World Federation of Ukrainian Women's Organizations (WFUWO) in 1948, which unites 31 organizations from 21 countries on four continents. The activities of WFUWO, particularly in recent years, have also concerned the following topics as drawing attention to gender-based violence, involving women in peace-making processes, and the role of men in ensuring equal rights and opportunities.

Feminism as a theme in post-Soviet studies originated in the field of literary studies. Regarding the development of the topic of feminist discourse in literature, it is worth mentioning the figure of Solomiia Pavlychko (1958–1999), a professor at the University of Kyiv-Mohyla Academy and one of the founding members of the feminist seminar at the Institute of Literature of the National Academy of Sciences of Ukraine. The seminar had a rather informal format: in addition to Pavlychko, researchers interested in the topic included Tamara Hundorova, Vira Ageieva, and Nataliya Shumylo.

The results of this intellectual circle's research have proven to be quite fruitful. Examples of their more prominent works include the following: *Women's Space: Feminist Discourse of Ukrainian Modernism* (2003) by Vira Ageieva and *Femina Melancholica: Sex and Culture in Olha Kobylianska's Gender Utopia*

(2002) by Tamara Hundorova. Equally important is the work of the literary critic, writer, and director of the Center for Gender Studies Nila Zborovska (1962–2011), notably *Feminist Reflections. At the Carnival of Dead Kisses* (1999).

The writer Oksana Zabuzhko is another notable example, having authored one of the first feminist novels in Ukrainian literature, *Fieldwork in Ukrainian Sex* (1996), as well as *Notre Dame d'Ukraine: A Ukrainian Woman in the Conflict of Mythologies* (2007), which explores a female author working within a colonial culture. Similarly, in 2004, the writer Yevgeniya Kononenko published a feminist collection of short stories *Prostitutes Get Married, Too* (2004). The poetess, literary critic and journalist Liudmyla Taran is another prominent cultural figure who has published various interviews with Ukrainian feminists active during the 1990s, as well as editing the collection *Woman as a Text. Emma Andievska, Solomiia Pavlychko, Oksana Zabuzhko. Fragments of Creativity and Contexts* (2002).

In the 21st century, feminist topics are gradually overcoming certain fears that were once prevalent in Ukrainian society, resulting in greater visibility in the various spheres of social life such as language, art, educational institutions, and civic initiatives. Feminist initiatives are also becoming more diverse and face greater debate around a number of "classic" issues within the movement for equal rights and opportunities: prostitution and sex work, women's labor rights in the military and the militarization of society, the involvement of transwomen in the feminist movement, the feminization of poverty and the financial hardships vulnerable groups of women often face, and women's involvement in politics and gender quotas.

Ukraine's International and National Obligations to Ensure Gender Equality

Women's feminist organizations have actively participated in the development of the policy of equal rights and opportunities, taking into account the best international practices. To date, Ukraine has ratified the main international treaties in the field of human rights and regulatory documents: the Universal Declaration of Human Rights, which states that all human beings are born free and equal in dignity and rights; the International Covenant on Civil and Political Rights and the Optional Protocol to it; the International Covenant on Economic, Social and Cultural Rights; The Convention on the Elimination of All Forms of Discrimination Against Women (CEDAW), which calls for comprehensive development and progress for women in order to guarantee them human rights and fundamental freedoms on an equal basis with men, and various other UN Human Rights treaties. In addition, Ukraine also joined the Beijing Declaration and Platform for Action, adopted and localized the UN Sustainable Development Goals for the period 2016 to 2030.

Ensuring equal rights and opportunities for women and men is an important area of activity for the Council of Europe (CoE), of which Ukraine is a member. The CoE itself follows a number of basic documents concerning issues of the equal rights and opportunities: the *Convention for the Protection of Human Rights and Fundamental Freedoms* (adopted by the CoE in 1950 and ratified by Ukraine in 1997), the "Declaration of the Committee of Ministers of the Council of Europe on the Equality of Women and Men (1988)", the "Convention of the Council of Europe on preventing and combating violence against women and domestic violence (also known as the Istanbul Convention of 2011)", and the "Recommendation of the Committee of Ministers of the Council of Europe to member states on preventing and combating sexism (2019)". In particular, the Declaration of the Committee of Ministers of the Council of Europe on the Equality of Women and Men states that "in modern society there is de jure and de facto inequality between women and men." Therefore, member states of the CoE should work on developing their gender policies to change the situation. In addition, the CoE's Gender Equality Strategy 2018–2023 has also been adopted, with its members expected to focus on achieving six goals. The Government of Ukraine is advancing in the fulfilment of these goals with the help of the State Social Program to ensure equal rights and opportunities. Moreover, in the summer of 2022, the 2011 Istanbul Convention, which is "the most comprehensive international instrument for combating violence against women and domestic violence in its many forms," was finally ratified.

Equally important are Ukraine's European integration intentions, especially those concerned with ensuring gender equality. Human rights, democracy, and the rule of law are declared as core values for the European Union. Regarding gender equality policy, the European Commission applies a so-called "dual approach": implementing the policy of "gender mainstreaming" and initiating special measures. Gender mainstreaming involves the (re)organization, improvement, establishment, and evaluation of political processes in such a way that participants in the political decision-making process adopt a gender approach in all areas of politics and at all stages. Special measures in gender policy at the EU level include legislation, information and educational campaigns, and financial programs. The aim of these measures is to resolve particular problems, such as the gender pay gap and lack of representation of women in certain areas of employment. Ukraine is also trying to apply this dual approach in its own gender policy.

Ukraine has also confirmed its commitments to promoting gender equality by joining the Global Partnership for the Promotion of Gender Equality, known as the *Biarritz Partnership*: an initiative of the G7 countries with the participation of UN Women that works to develop an action plan to implement the commitments of the Government of Ukraine within the framework of this international initiative. The UN Security Council's Resolution 1325 "Women, Peace, Security" is an important document for strengthening the involvement of women in the processes of achieving peace and post-conflict reconstruction. This resolution stipulates that UN member states should develop national action plans for its implementation. In 2020, the Cabinet of Ministers of Ukraine approved the National Action Plan for the Implementation of the UN Security Council's Resolution 1325 "Women, Peace, Security" for the period up to 2025.

The international community constantly monitors the situation regarding the provision of equal rights and opportunities. The "Global Gender Gap Report", prepared by the World Economic Forum, measures the size of the gender gap in four important areas of inequality between men and women: economic participation, education level, political representation, and health care. In 2021, Ukraine took 74th place out of 156 studied countries. In the Ukrainian case, the country was recorded as performing especially poorly in regard to political representation, specifically women's participation in the decision-making process, for which it was ranked 97th. Accordingly, it is important to reduce these gender gaps, especially in the area of women's access to decision-making processes.

Since the declaration of independence in 1991, the idea of equal rights and opportunities for women and men has been increasingly viewed in Ukraine as a key priority. For example, according to Article 24 of the Constitution of Ukraine, "there shall be no privileges or restrictions based on race, colour of skin, political, religious and other beliefs, sex, ethnic and social origin, property status, place of residence, linguistic or other characteristics." The Law of Ukraine "On ensuring equal rights and opportunities for women and men" (2005) also includes definitions of concepts such as equal rights and opportunities for women and men, gender-based discrimination, positive action, and sexual harassment. Article 3 of the Law states:

> State policy on ensuring equal rights and opportunities for women and men is aimed at establishing gender equality; prevention of gender-based dis-

crimination; application of positive actions; prevention and counteraction of gender-based violence, including all manifestations of violence against women; ensuring equal participation of women and men in making socially important decisions; ... protection of society from information aimed at discrimination on the basis of gender.

In order to implement the various international and national obligations aimed at ensuring equal rights and opportunities, Ukrainian civil society has becoming increasingly active, including women's feminist organizations. As an example, it is worth mentioning the activities of the Public Council on Equal Opportunities Caucus under the Verkhovna Rada of Ukraine (VRU). The mission of the Public Council is to promote ideas of gender equality and support the policy of ensuring equality for women and men through discussion, analysis of draft laws, development and presentation of expert opinions and proposals. It is also involved in advocacy and conducting informational events in order to establish an independent, democratic, Ukrainian state and a strong and independent civil society that can provide equal opportunities for each person for development and self-fulfilment.

Initiatives implemented by the Public Council in recent years have included the campaign to "Uncover the truth about violence" in support of the Istanbul Convention, the online marathon "Time of Women's Leadership", together with the public alliance "Political Action of Women", an educational campaign and monitoring project "#vyborybezsexyzmu [electionsWITHOUTsexism]". This focused on preventing discrimination against female candidates and allowing for fair contests during the local elections of 2020 that were free of sexism, threats, bullying, and institutional pressure (appeals to political parties were published). In collaboration with various women's non-governmental organizations, the "#KvotyZamistKvity [QuotasInsteadofFlowers]" campaign to support gender quotas in legislation during the women's march (held on March 8, 2019), while also campaigning under VRU to support gender quotas in electoral legislation, termed "Women in power – women in the Rada".

Successes of the Ukrainian Women's Feminist Movement in Building Gender Equality

Over the past few years, many feminist academic and grassroots events, particularly the annual March for Women's Rights held on March 8, have taken place in various cities across Ukraine encompassing different generations and different types of women's organizations and public male feminists. International organizations actively support these initiatives, for example, UN Women and the *HeforShe* campaign. It is worth noting the visibility and activity of women at EuroMaidan in 2013 and 2014. In addition to the barricades, this included a large number of activities, in which women were actively involved. These included care work, distributing information, logistics (such as running the Euromaidan-SOS hotlines), as well as providing legal aid, medical and psychological assistance, safe transportation, working with mass media, and educational provision through schemes such as Maidan Open University and Maidan library. Women were also active in security roles such as *Automaidan*, *Varta v likarni* [Guard in the hospital], *Varta shvydkoyi dopomogy* [Ambulance Guard], and as community guards alongside fundraising for victims and volunteer support schemes. Moreover, the end of the protests did not lead to the end of this support work. Nadia Parfan's online initiative *Half the Maidan: Women's Voice of Protest*, for example, continued to attract attention, and was accompanied by a number of campaigns on the Maidan and elsewhere. The journalist Kristina Berdynskykh also launched the project *There are people. Warm stories from the Maidan* to talk about the "ordinary" people of the protest space while journalist and human rights activist Iryna Vyrtosu was responsible for compiling *Maidan. Women's Affairs* a published collection of interviews with 17 heroines from the protests and descriptions of the dozens of women's initiatives that took place. Through this, it can be seen that women "made the revolution" on an equal footing with men, rather than merely "helped" them make it.

The "Invisible Battalion" campaign provided an opportunity to recognize the role of women in the war, resulting in the granting of labor rights to women working in the Armed Forces of Ukraine (ZSU). As a result of the joint efforts of the women's veteran movement, women's groups based within Ukrainian military formations and female parliamentary deputies, the campaign led to the adoption of Law No. 2523 "On amendments to certain legislative acts of Ukraine on ensuring equal rights and opportunities for women and men in the Armed Forces of Ukraine and other military formations". In 2016, women gained access to nearly 100 combat military positions that were previously available only to men. In November 2017, the campaign's activities were brought to wider public through the documentary *Invisible Battalion*. In other words, recent years have seen greater attention being paid to the issue of gender equality in the military and the role of women in the ZSU itself. There has also been a gradual increase in the number of women in the ZSU and military institutions of higher education. As of July 2022, about 57,000 women serve in the armed forces together with volunteers from territorial communities, of whom about 32,000 are engaged in active war zones. Overall, the number of servicewomen in the ZSU has effectively doubled since 2015 with women also gaining greater access to military education.

The role of women in Ukrainian national history has also received increasing recognition. This has been especially well documented by the unique Gender Museum in Kharkiv, the Museum of the Women's Movement in Lviv, and the Ukrainian Association for Researchers in Women's History.

Gender-based violence is one of the main topics in the women's struggle for equal rights. A recent example was the *#IAmNotAfraidToSayIt* campaign, which was initiated by the feminist activist Nastya Melnychenko, and drew special attention to the issue of sexual violence with a flash mob organized under *#IAmNotAfraidToSayIt* taking place offline. In Kyiv and other cities, particularly Dnipro, Lviv, Chernivtsi, and Zaporizhzhia, other public events were held under the *#IAmNotAfraidToDoIt*. Similarly, Anastasia Salnykova, an activist for the human rights organization *Natural Rights of Ukraine*, that deals with issues relating to motherhood, and a public health researcher, organized a flash mob under the *#ItIsTimeToSayIt* against obstetric violence as part of the International Day for the Elimination of Violence against Women during which women shared their stories and examples of problem resolving.

In recent years, much has also been done in Ukraine to combat gender inequality in education and to spread best practices for ensuring equal rights and opportunities for women and men. The community of responsible teachers *EdCamp* has been particularly proactive in organizing meetings and events on the topic of combating discrimination and ensuring gender equality. In Kharkiv, the NGO *Krona* implemented a gender educational experiment. The *HeForShe* solidarity movement for gender equality developed by UN Women, launched a student project to combat stereotypes and discrimination, *HeForShe* University Tour. These are just a few examples of successful practices for spreading the value of gender equality in education.

Professional critical human rights education is especially important for promoting gender equality. The master's program in Gender Studies, Gender Studies Courses, a Network of Gender Education Centers, countering gender stereotypes and sexual harassment at the university level, the relevant policy at the Kyiv-Mohyla Academy are all examples of achievements in this area.

Within the political sphere, gender quotas were introduced to overcome the barriers and stereotypes faced by women in, or seeking, public office. During the last local elections of 2020, the project *Elections Without Sexism* was launched and resulted in several lawsuits. Consequently, by 2022, the share of women in the Verkhovna Rada reached 20 per cent.

Mass media is no less important area in the struggle for equal rights and opportunities. *Povaha* [Respect] is a campaign against sexism against women that focuses on the media, public and political communications. Its work includes the website *povaha.org.ua*, public events, the development of the women's expert database *Ask a Woman*, and a number of video blogs distributed via social media. It has also advocated for greater discussion on sexism in Ukraine via open letters, responses to the appeals of female readers, and providing instance commentary on current news and events. Contributors to *povaha.org.ua* website itself include various professional female researchers, journalists, bloggers, and authors.

It is worth noting the following challenges of ensuring gender equality. These include a continuing culture of sexism among politicians and public figures and the fact that security and defense sector does not always perceive women as specialists. There is also an ongoing lack of success stories regarding rights violations lawsuits, such as the sexual harassment case brought against the military by Valeria Sikal. Gender equality in the labor market represents another important challenge in the fight for equal rights that requires greater attention alongside the sustainability of international projects and the successful cooperation of different generations of activists.

However, the greatest challenge remains, unsurprisingly, the ongoing Russo-Ukrainian War and its consequences for both women and men. As of May 30, 2022, the number of Ukrainian refugees reached 6,801,987 with 83 per cent of forced migrants being women. According to the UN Women report:

> With the closure of schools and the high demand for volunteer work and the absence of men, the burden of unpaid work that women are forced to do, has significantly increased. The departure from the principles of gender equality is already evident in the conditions of a long crisis. The war increases unemployment among the entire population, which is likely to push women into unprotected informal sectors of the economy and lead to increased poverty.

Humanitarian aid will be needed to meet the needs of women, men, girls and boys who find themselves in vulnerable situations and belong to various marginalized groups, especially members of the Roma community, the elderly, and people with disabilities. It is necessary to support women-led organizations and organizations that protect the rights of women and have been involved in the response, by providing financial resources and strengthening their voice on national and international platforms.

Experts point to the importance of providing displaced women and men with vocational training and livelihood opportunities, taking into account changing gender roles, as well as reducing the burden of home schooling by encouraging families to redistribute care work. Despite the war, the issue of gender equality is always timely. And women's feminist organizations in Ukraine are doing much to achieve it.

Translated from Ukrainian by Olha Chyzmar.

Selected Bibliography

Bochachevsky-Chomiak, M. *Feminists despite themselves: women in Ukrainian community life, 1884–1939* (Toronto: CIUS Press, 1988).

Hankivsky, O., & Salnykova, A. (eds.). *Gender, politics, and society in Ukraine* (Toronto: University of Toronto Press, 2012).

Kis, O. Survival as Victory: *Ukrainian Women in the Gulag* (Cambridge, Mass.: Harvard University Press, 2021).

Khromeychuk, O. "Experiences of women at war: Servicewomen during WWII and in the Ukrainian Armed Forces in the Conflict in Donbas," *Baltic Worlds* 4 (2018): 58–70.

Martsenyuk, T., and S. D. Phillips. "Talking About Sexual Violence in Post-Maidan Ukraine: Analysis of the Online Campaign# IAmNotAfraidToSayIt," *Sexuality & Culture* 24:2 (2020): 408–427.

Martsenyuk, T., G. Grytsenko, and A. Kvit. "The 'Invisible Battalion': Women in ATO Military Operations in Ukraine," *Kyiv-Mohyla Law and Politics Journal* 2:2 (2016): 171–187. DOI: 10.18523/kmlpj88192.2016-2.171-187

Onuch, O., and T. Martsenyuk. "Mothers and daughters of the Maidan: Gender, repertoires of violence, and the division of labour in Ukrainian protests," *Social, Health, and Communication Studies Journal*, 1:1 (2014): 105–126.

Phillips, S. D. *Women's social activism in the new Ukraine: development and the politics of differentiation* (Bloomington: Indiana University Press, 2008).

Rubchak, M. J. (ed.). *Mapping difference: the many faces of women in contemporary Ukraine* (New York; Oxford: Berghahn Books, 2011).

Zabuzhko, O. The "Death of Don Juan: Modernism, Feminism, Nationalism–Rethinking Ukrainian Literature." *17th Annual JB Rudnyckyj Distinguished Lecture.* Thursday, November, 19 2009.

The Art of Misunderstanding

Kateryna Botanova

In front of me sat a grey-haired woman with a quiet, slightly hesitant voice. She had contacted me through mutual friends in Tbilisi, where she had recently organized a project. Her foundation had worked for a long time in the South Caucasus and 'other conflict regions', encouraging 'mutual understanding through art'. It now wanted to expand to Ukraine, 'due to the current conflict'.

It was 2017. I had recently moved to Switzerland after twenty years of cultural practice in Ukraine. Maybe this was my chance to do important and useful work with a foundation that had been established by a Swiss diplomat known, in particular, for having participated in negotiating the Minsk agreements.

The woman, let's call her Dina, was a lecturer at the Zurich University of the Arts. She wanted, quite rationally, to start with research: to visit places 'in or close to the conflict zone', talk to the locals, hear their needs. Overall, the program was already clear: there would be a few master classes by Swiss musicians, dancers, and performers, some work would be done in schools or with young artists, some help would be given to refugees, and some art exchanges might take place. In short, the arts would be put to the service of peace-making and dialogue. This is how the foundation worked for five years in Abkhazia, an unrecognized break-away region of Georgia, as well as in the border regions of Georgia and neighboring Armenia. Dina was especially proud of the projects in Abkhazia: the region is very poor and even getting past the heavily guarded border was almost impossible.

I tried to explain to her that Ukraine is nothing like Abkhazia. There is no 'conflict', there is a Russian-instigated war of occupation that had already been raging for three years. I could hardly believe I had to explain all this to a person who should have known what was happening in Ukraine and in the South Caucasus first-hand. 'You cannot imagine how rich and vibrant cultural life is in the south-east of Ukraine, even close to the 'conflict line',' I said; 'how much has happened since 2014, how many initiatives and people connect this region with other parts of the country. We will have to listen to local cultural activists very carefully if we want to do something that will actually make sense.' Dina looked at me with a mixture of sadness and sympathy.

That autumn, she and I traveled to Severodonetsk, Sloviansk, Kramatorsk, Dobropillia, Bakhmut and Mariupol. In Kyiv we met with several cultural activists, some of whom had been forced to flee eastern Ukraine. Others were based in the capital but were working with partners in the east. A few months later, Dina prepared a funding application to the Swiss Agency for Development and Cooperation (SDC) for a project that, in addition to workshops for schoolchildren from the 'grey zone' along the conflict line, focused on handicraft workshops for women from the areas controlled, and not controlled, by the Ukrainian government. Over a period of eight months, women from both sides of the military border that divided the Donetsk region would meet in Mariupol, weave or embroider something under the guidance of Swiss artists, and talk about peace.

The SDC rejected the project, largely because of concerns for the security of people. Dina returned to building dialogue in the South Caucasus, paid for by the Swiss government and various philanthropists. I was left with memories of incredible people and cities, the true value of which I understood only this year, after some of them almost disappeared.

***

Most Ukrainian cultural activists have faced similar attitudes from their western European colleagues at least once since 2014: a desire for reconciliation together with a patronizing attitude towards Ukrainian positions. As unpleasant as it was before, it is now simply unbearable.

Invitations to participate in panel discussions, to attend workshops or submit artworks to joint exhibitions, to publish texts in a collection, to take part in a film festival are regular occurrences – a frantic wave of well-intentioned invitations with no end in sight. Most of these gestures of goodwill are invitations to enter dialogue with Russian cultural actors. They are generally not motivated by solidarity and empathy, but rather the belief that it is within the cultural field that dialogue and reconciliation between the aggressor society and the society under attack should take place. Only occasionally do these events involve people from countries and contexts with similar experiences of prolonged aggression, resistance, and struggle for identity: from Palestine, Syria, Afghanistan, Bosnia-Herzegovina, Kosovo and elsewhere. During the first nine months of the war, just one panel I spoke on included someone from another conflict zone: a curator from Bosnia. It was a particularly warm and important conversation.

Since the beginning of the full-fledged aggression that broke out on 24 February 2022, the Ukrainian cultural community has been actively looking for a solution to the problem of 'compulsive reconciliation', trying to tread the thin and sometimes dangerous line between preserving one's dignity and the need to retain the interest and attention of western cultural institutions, media and platforms where one can talk about the war in Ukraine. I doubt a general solution exists: each situation is unique and must be dealt with separately.

However, there are several approaches that seem very important when talking about the arts and reconciliation. One of them is to borrow from feminist rhetoric phrases like 'no means no', 'my body (country) my choice' and 'nothing about us without us'. In seeking to defend not their position but the right to have a position, Ukrainian cultural activists are turning to the tools of an emancipatory discourse that challenges the patriarchal power determining whose voices are important and whose are not; who has the right to decide what happens to their bodies and who does not.

By using a feminist vocabulary designed to defend female subjectivity and the agency of the female body, Ukrainian cultural activists express the collective corporeality of war: its terrifying physical presence, its threat to each and every person, and the sense of community as a single organism, when the death or injury of even complete strangers echoes with intense pain.

When it comes to the conditions for ending the war, for demilitarization or understanding violence, the international feminist community is far from unanimous in its support of Ukrainian women's voices and positions. Yet this emancipatory rhetoric has proven quite effective in the international artistic environment, which is generally sensitive to injustice, de-subjectivation and segregation.

But perhaps the most important feature of this defence of Ukrainian subjectivity is that it is directed not at the aggressor, but a 'third party' – a concerned observer who has taken on the mantle of 'arbitrator', a role that has always been theirs to assume.

The war in Ukraine is exposing the epistemological power of the global West (or North). This is the power to name and legitimize, to hold up a 'gold standard' of democracy, of social and political institutions, of histories and even traumas. It is the power to evaluate the development of other societies not on their own terms, but against a universal measure. It is the power to instrumentalize the cultural fields and the arts, a power so firmly established that attempts at reflection and resistance become almost impossible.

But there is another effective, though much less common approach that Ukrainian cultural activists have used in their artistic works and in public discussions. It entails entering the pacifist discourse but, instead of accepting forced dialogue or compulsive reconciliation, choosing disagreement; voicing one's own position without fear of criticism or conflict. This is not just a radical assertion of one's agency which defies the evaluator and their judgments. It is also the start of a much-needed discussion about the sources of the belief in art as the territory of reconciliation and the power systems that keep this belief in place.

***

Like other former Second World countries, Ukraine was the beneficiary of western cultural policy already applied to the Third World since the 1960s. Having lost much of its grip over its former colonies, the global West returned in the form of international development agencies, of which European cultural institutions often formed a part. Global corporations and mining companies were also a part of these aid packages. Financial assistance to young democracies was motivated by a mixture of guilt, national security concerns, and the promotion of business interests. Development logic gave back power to the 'white man', this time in the nobler garb of helper and mentor who alone possessed knowledge of the architecture of society, governance and the economy. The development logic was ruthlessly practical, stipulating that all societal functions should be efficient, subject to assessment and evaluation. Culture was no exception.

Under the guidance and financial support of the West, culture lost its meaning and autonomy, its ability to be a system of relations in which liberation, awareness and subjectivity can grow. It was losing its utopian, visionary potential, becoming disconnected with the society to which it belonged, as well as its needs, traditions and challenges. The main function of culture, from Zimbabwe to Senegal, from Nigeria to Colombia, became to reduce inequality, alleviate poverty and, above all, promote social cohesion and reconciliation.

Reconciliation ranged from conflicts between indigenous peoples and the descendants of colonizers; between former masters and servants; between different ethnic groups and communities (and their cultures) which 'historically' (a euphemism for 'the decision of the former metropole') found themselves in the same country; between victims of genocides and the perpetrators and their descendants; between those who protested against corrupt or criminal local authorities and their legitimate and unwavering representatives.

Countless Western (or Northern) cultural peacemakers visited (and still do) the Global South with workshops and lectures, masterclasses, and summer schools. They taught children and adults, amateurs, and professionals how to find common ground and inner peace through the arts. They organized joint choirs and even orchestras, advised museums, libraries and universities. They were not necessarily detached from reality, although sometimes it was not clear what the reality was. For decades, even local cultural and social activists had been thinking in terms of 'underdeveloped democracies' that were essentially corrupt and in need of 'inequality reduction' and 'conflict prevention', unconsciously borrowing from a vocabulary imposed from above.

In the 1990s, this wave of aid reached eastern Europe and the former Soviet Union. Another batch of young democracies needed mentoring, especially after the Yugoslav Wars. Although culture only came into focus later during the 2000s, it was still approached as an instrument of belated education or enlightenment, as a way to stitch together the tattered social fabric of individual societies, if not whole regions. After the Maidan Revolution and Russian occupation of Crimea and parts of eastern Ukraine in 2014, calls for reconciliation and mutual understanding grew exponentially.

I am not saying that it is the forms and methods of support that constitute the problem. Rather, it is the epistemological system on which this support is based. The 'development logic' behind the instrumentalization of culture assumes that the development of societies is a standardized linear process. It stipulates that the world is divided into the fully developed societies of the Global North and those that are somewhere *en route*. Development epistemology is based on forms of knowledge and social interaction inherent to these 'successfully developed' societies.

This system of knowledge and its carriers – those who make key decisions and those who monitor the processes of their execution – are *a priori* external to any development processes in the societies of the former third and second worlds. In this system, there is no place for ethnic conflicts, nationalisms, memory wars or real wars; for annexations, revolutions, *coups d'état*, identity conflicts (or identities in general) or culture wars. Any conflict is a glitch that needs to be repaired, reconciled, *dialogued*. Which is where culture and the arts come in.

***

In his lecture 'Planetary consciousness and the possible future of culture',[1] Achille Mbembe talks about the different systems of knowledge and contexts in which culture exists outside the standardized utilitarian framework. Freed from its externally imposed functionality, culture provides 'vital energy for various forms of writing, constituting archives, performing identity, thinking, remembering'.

Culture that resonates with its own society, that is in tune with it, chooses forms of remembering, living through trauma, expression of identities and social interaction that are necessary and within reach at any given moment. It can choose reconciliation or dialogue, but it must be the choice of its constituents. It can choose and use dialogue not for reconciliation, but as a form of cognizance, learning, and, exposing ignorance, misunderstandings, or conflicts. This was at the core of the intense process of cultural exchange in and with eastern Ukraine after 2014.

What Ukrainian cultural actors started in 2014 was a process of cultural emancipation as a way of comprehending the reality here and now; a dream of different possible futures. It was a process of decolonization of knowledge and representation. It was the articulation of the maxim 'nothing about us without us' in the language of culture.

After the beginning of the full-scale invasion, Ukrainian art assumed the role of radical decolonizer of culture in general. By resisting imposed pacification and forced reconciliation, Ukrainian artists are reclaiming the power of arts to bear witness, to preserve reality, to be present. For over nine months, they have been saying that art is not about understanding, and certainly not understanding between the aggressor and those who are defend their right to life and existence.

Responding to the open letter of Russian artist Dmitry Vilensky, Ukrainian artist Nikita Kadan wrote:

> I have no use for words that do not save lives. For now, I prefer to stick with my own experience, with collecting knowledge about the crimes that are being committed before my very eyes. My thoughts are not with recovering 'the territory of dialogue'; my thoughts are with recovering the occupied territory.[2]

This article was first published in English in Eurozine (2 January 2023) and in Polish in Dwutygodnik (original in Ukrainian) and has been provided by Eurozine (www.euro zine.com) © Kateryna Botanova / Dwutygodnik / Eurozine. Reproduced with permission.

Notes

1. Achille Mbembe. Planetary Consciousness and Possible Future of Culture. 10 December 2021. https://www.youtube.com/watch?v=8fI3-6fjkqc (Accessed 22 December 2022.).
2. On Words That Do Not Save Lives. An open letter by Ukrainian artist Nikita Kadan. Artterritory. 3 October 2022. https://arterritory.com/en/visual_arts/topical_qa/26363-on_words_that_do_not_save_lives (Accessed on 22 December 2022.).

Selected Bibliography

Biedarieva, Svitlana (ed.) *Contemporary Ukrainian and Baltic Art. Political and Social Perspectives, 1991–2021* (Stuttgart: ibidem-Verlag, 2021).

Bodrozic, Natasa, Kateryna Botanova, Nora Galfayan, et al. (eds.) *Imagining the Public. The Status and Challenges of the Independent Cultural Actors in Armenia, Georgia, Moldova and Ukraine*. A SPACES publication. 2014.

Cooper, Frederick. "Modernizing Bureaucrats, Backward Africans, and the Development Concept," in: Frederick Cooper and Randall Packard (eds.) *International Development and the Social Sciences: Essays on the History and Politics of Knowledge* (Berkeley: University of California Press, 1997).

Lozhkina, Alisa, and Konstantin Akinsha. *Between Fire and Fire. Ukrainian Art Now*. Exhibition catalogue. (2019).

Mbembe, Achille. *Out of the Dark Night. Essays on Decolonization* (New York: Columbia University Press, 2021).

Sarr, Felwine. "Reopening Futures", in: Achille Mbembe and Felwine Sarr (eds.) *The Politics of Time. Imagining African Becoming* (Cambridge: Polity Press, 2023).

Tsymbalyuk, Darya. "Academia must recentre embodied and uncomfortable knowledge" *Nature Human Behaviour* 6 (2022): 758–759.

The Territory Resists the Map
Geolocating Reality and Hyperreality
in the Russo-Ukrainian War

Roman Horbyk

Some time ago it became quite fashionable to speak of a "conflict of narratives". The militaristic terminology was diverse and quite broad. Thinkers, scholars, and practitioners spoke about wars of narratives, wars of interpretation, clash of representations, and even narrative battles. I would refrain from providing obvious references – suffice it to say that I myself partook of this trend through my own contribution, "Narratives at War".[1] The idea behind it was simple: apart from bombs and tanks, words and texts are also wielded as weapons, and in this our 21st century the emphasis often shifts to the latter. Today – when no longer words and texts – bombs and tanks litter all of Ukraine, and the world customarily decries the lack of dialogue – I would like to look at it differently: war as a form of dialogue and communication in the first place.

And I would be merely following in the footsteps of one of the greatest authorities on the subject, Carl von Clausewitz, who famously defined war as continuation of politics by other means. His idea is usually interrupted here with a period. However, after that period, Clausewitz continued:

> Do political relations between peoples and between their governments stop when diplomatic notes are no longer exchanged? Is war not just another expression of their thoughts, another form of speech or writing? Its grammar, indeed, may be its own, but not its logic.[2]

What the great strategist tried to say here, is that the logic of war belongs to politics or, to be more precise, that war is governed by political logic. In this sense, it is really only a continuation of politics. What makes war different is its grammar: the exchanges of volleys, the turns of phrase, or returns of fire.

War does not merely involve representation. It is intimately, inseparably intertwined with it, wired by it. War *is* representation, to use the well-expounded philosophical pun involving communicative and political meanings. The clashing armies are words that form sentences in the dialogue of war. They stand for the polities that send them into battle against each other and, by extension, they stand for the nations whose flags they carry, much like national football teams. Perhaps here lies the root of the idea of shared responsibility that Ukrainians tend to extend to all Russians. We know that the genocidal war crimes committed by rank-and-file Russian soldiers in Bucha, Irpin', Hostomel', Mariupol', Volnovakha, Motyzhyn, Chernihiv, Kharkiv, Nova Basan', Kherson, Bakhmut, Soledar, Kreminna, and countless other towns and villages are the expression of a widespread hatred shared by a broad cross-section of the Russian population – we know this better than anyone because we are the object of that hatred. And, speaking from my own personal experience of being under a missile strike, I can testify that it does feel like a rhetorical act, a very powerful one roughly signifying that, "your presence in the world is unwanted, to the extent that we are ready to take extreme measures from a great distance to ensure this, mobilising all of our military skills, scientific knowledge, technical excellence, industrial complex, culture and ideology".

As an extreme act of dialogue, the writing of war involves many other representation forms. One of such tools inherent to modern war is the map. Warfare is determined by space and time, is dependent on manoeuvre, and as such requires spatial awareness. Yet it is with the arrival of scientific cartography and industrial warfare, impossible without large-scale intricate coordination, that wartime maps became indispensable, either as a representation of the actual situation on the ground desired to be as detailed and objective as possible – or as a summary of a plan, an algorithm to be enacted by the army, and a representation of the desired situation to be achieved through it.

Such was the situation of advanced, industrial, modern warfare. However, towards the end of the Cold War, a new tendency began to emerge. Non-state or para-state actors entered the stage bringing with them the concept of "new wars" – bloody conflicts between weak paramilitary groups, such as those in the former Yugoslavia. Meanwhile, the West achieved the so-called "Revolution in Military Affairs", or RMA, that favoured "those who fully exploit and operationalize the latest technological developments".[3] The result was a series of wars between completely unequal combatants, such as the Gulf War, or insurgencies.

It was the Gulf War that prompted Jean Baudrillard to famously conclude that "it did not take place".[4] What he meant is that the war was not so much a war as a mere extermination of inferior Iraqi forces while, as experienced by global audiences via mass media, it had very little to do with actual developments on the ground but was rather a collection of spectacular images that created a simulated version of it. It was not a war but a simulacrum thereof.

A simulacrum is a key concept that can even explain current Russia's war on Ukraine and why it turned out so unexpectedly. In Baudrillard's writings, it is defined as a representation that has no relation to reality whatsoever. It represents something that does not exist. It is not simply a misrepresentation; it is a representation that has completely and aggressively broken up with reality. Baudrillard begins his explanation of the concept of simulacrum with a fable by Jorge Luis Borges in which the Empire embarks on creating a map of its territory so detailed that it ends up covering everything on a one-to-one scale, devouring that territory in the process:

> It is nevertheless the map that precedes the territory – precession of simulacra – that engenders the territory and if one must return to the fable, today it is the territory whose shreds slowly rot across the extent of the map.[5]

This is the postmodern idea that Russia's intellectual milieux were so fascinated by for three decades. It became the motherboard on which Russian society itself has run. It cries out from Viktor Pelevin's sophisticated novels and from the crudity of Pervyi Kanal's most heinous fabrications. It has become a mantra for Vladislav Surkov's intellectual travesties and the leading doctrine of the Russian Ministry of Foreign Affairs, the notorious MID (*Ministerstvo inostrannykh del*). There is no reality at all, there is only a sum of contradictory perceptions. Perceptions can be tampered with and thus change reality. Moreover, tampering with perception is the only way to change reality (which does not exist anyway). There is no truth and objectivity is not just impossible but is even undesirable as an ideal. Everything is relative, and what does not seem so, must be relativized. Nothing is true and everything is possible, to quote the ingenious title of Peter Pomerantsev's book on Russian television.

It was television – Baudrillard's unmistakably "favourite" medium – that created the world for ordinary Russians and populated it with endearing and threatening figures. Aggressive and emotionless Baltic nationalists. Stupid Central Asians. Lazy and cunning Ukrainians. Bloodthirsty Banderites. Azov battalion Nazis. Decadent fags from Gayropa. All conspiring to corrupt Mother

Russia and rob it of the last remnants of Soviet glory. And good-natured, all-forgiving Russians led by a stalwart leader against this motley crew of delinquents and degenerates. All these were visualized with believable images, some of which may have been staged but many undoubtedly true, inserted into the frame of the narrative I have just outlined, and connected with each other, all pointing in one direction. Thus, the real and fictional were smoothly blended into the hyperreal, "the model of a real without origin or reality".[6] And thus, Russians lost the ability to distinguish between reality and the simulation of reality.

During the military buildup for the invasion, simulation was mobilized and deployed with full force. In February 2022, the Winter Olympic Games broadcasts were interspersed with heartbreaking reports from the Russian-occupied eastern Ukraine, populated with the simulated entities of the so-called "Donetsk and Luhansk people's republics". Dramatic footage of explosions, the sound of cannonade, agitated voiceovers, and even an evacuation of the local population, followed. When checked with independent sources, the picture looked absurdly different: it is Ukraine that was shelled, and many of the evacuees were driven only to the edge of their town and then told to go home by foot. In fact, it was an exercise in creating a Hollywood version of reality.

And then spoke Putin himself. On February 21st, he addressed his television audiences with a speech lasting over an hour. He insisted that Ukraine and other post-Soviet states were an artificial creation by Lenin and the Bolsheviks, that they were thus fake while Russia was perennial and real. Putin held that Ukraine – once again, unlike Russia – was corrupt in a unique, unheard-of way, and that this country, perhaps the only state in the world, apart from Israel, whose president and prime minister were for a while both Jewish, was filled with ethnic and xenophobic nationalism. He said that Ukraine was being militarized in preparation for a military attack on Russia, a nuclear power with a superiority of military numbers many orders of magnitude greater than that of its western neighbor. He also alleged that Ukraine is mired in extreme and ever-growing poverty.

It is possible to fact-check this speech, no doubt. But what would remain after this fact-checking? Perhaps only the atmosphere of hatred and thinly veiled threats, that I, as a Ukrainian in Kyiv at the time, felt with extreme clarity. It was the only point during the entire crisis that I genuinely felt fear.

As sad and unjust as it sounds, had Russia won an easy victory, the world would have remembered Putin's simulacrum as truth. Not just that: Putin would have *made* his simulacrum into truth. And this was a simulacrum that was meant to replace reality. It was a map projected onto the actual territory of Ukraine with the intention to replace it. Before, and during the early days of, the invasion, Russian television talk shows discussed maps that illustrated various visions of Ukraine's post-war destiny. While admitting the flexibility of their goals, all of them entailed a division of the country into several parts. Some were to be absorbed into Russia, others would be kept as puppet buffer territories leaving only the few westernmost regions as a rump Ukrainian state the size of Estonia, and a convenient object to continue projecting simulacra onto. The territory had to be altered to match the map that they had in mind. This was to be done in particular, through the necropolitics of genocide.[7]

So, Russian soldiers launched their missiles and went into Ukraine armed with this map that they had to make a reality, like an expedition corps in the darkest days of colonialism. Essentially, this was the moment when the postcolonial approach to Russo-Ukrainian relations has been fully and finally vindicated. Russia was now openly behaving as an imperialist conqueror, and Ukraine has left its postcolonial condition and engaged in a very concrete anti-colonial struggle that could certainly inspire a 21st century sequel to Franz Fanon's *The Wretched of the Earth*.

But it also became a moment when something unexpected happened. Something that became a turning point: the simulated map has met the territory it sought to modify with brutal violence. The soldiers met an army that, in spite of alleged corruption, did not fall apart and run away as had happened in Afghanistan. They met towns that, despite the narrative of poverty and degradation, instilled in Russian soldiers an irresistible urge to loot everything from flatscreen TVs to lingerie, because those towns had living standards these soldiers could never dream of at home. And, most importantly, they faced a land and a nation that in spite of everything they had been told was real and genuine and not at all willing to give up.

It is here that we part with Baudrillard and the postmodernist hall of mirrors and enter something new. For the first time in our contemporary era, we are witnessing a true war waged between combatants that turned out to be comparable. It is no longer the Gulf War butchery of an inferior enemy or a murky "new war" of clandestine insurgents and illegal organizations. For the first time we saw reality fight back against hyperreality. This reality itself became the ultimate and the best possible fact-checking of Putin's speech and the map he handed out to his nation. And, oh what a surprise, we got to see that the real is real.

In the current Russian invasion of Ukraine, part of the Russo-Ukrainian War that has been raging since 2014, the map was meant to precede the territory, but in fact the map no longer precedes the territory. On the contrary, the map recedes before the territory. The key statement in this great dialogue of war, in the writing of war, has been the Ukrainian response to the Russian statement: "Nothing is true and everything is possible", is met with "Some things – ourselves included – are true and not everything is possible, certainly not our new colonization".

I can also see this in the empirical aspects of my current research project where I study how the Ukrainian military has used mobile phones on the frontline in Eastern Ukraine. This frontline now extends throughout the entire country. The results I and other scholars of media and technology use, such as Olga Boichak and Tanya Lokot, have collected reveal how modern technologies and their infrastructures blend into activism and grassroot self-mobilization. While my focus lies on the military uses, I could see how mobile phones and the networks of base stations serve to fill gaps in the military infrastructure. Back in 2014, Ukraine had no secure and reliable military communication system, prompting soldiers to turn their civilian phones into one, despite the risks. This subsequently became a network that has supported Ukrainian resistance.[8]

So, it is no wonder that the Russian army made it one of its priority targets. Russians have developed sophisticated radioelectronic warfare systems, such as the Leer 3 that launches two drones and can suppress mobile communication up to 100 kilometers away. It is capable of creating fake, virtual base stations that imitate your operator and can siphon data off your phone while also making it disseminate false messages and malware. We saw them in use during protests in Belarus and Kazakhstan, where they successfully subverted mobile communication for days and thus suppressed protest coordination. It was only logical to see them in Ukraine. From interviews with refugees from Irpin', Kherson, Mariupol' and other areas, that I conducted in Lviv in March and April 2022, while working as a volunteer with a medical and psychological service at the train station, a picture of the Russian tactic arises. First, they try to destroy physically through shelling as many base stations as possible. The population is forced into shelters and cellars with weak, or no, signal. Then they activate their radioelectronic devices that suppress the remaining signal, this typically happens around 9 am and lasts through the day. At night, the signal improves and allows at least some communication. Another solution for civilians is to climb the top floors of high-rise buildings to catch a signal from the more remote base stations but this comes with extra risks. It is this "radiosilence" from the occupied areas that allows mass killings such as those in Bucha and Mariupol to happen in the quiet. It is a tool of genocide and Russian necropolitics.

However, the territory and the infrastructure it hosted do fight back even here. The Armed Forces of Ukraine have greatly increased their communication capacity. The Russians, by contrast, turned out to be lacking in it to such extent they must resort to using civilian mobile phones with Ukrainian simcards looted from the population. As a result, they fall prey to the lack of infrastructure they themselves destroyed and to Ukrainian wiretapping, resulting in a permanent flood of recorded conversations with their families where shocking subjects are discussed such as looting, rapes, summary executions, and other war crimes. Reportedly due to the use of civilian phones, a lot of senior Russian officers, including generals, have been killed. And, in many cases, technicians working for Ukrainian mobile operators have risked their lives to repair the damaged infrastructure as quickly as possible.

The Russian dictator put his society into a hall of crooked mirrors where they spent so much time that they started believing their crooked representations. The map to replace the territory was confused with the map to represent the territory – and no wonder Russians came armed with outdated, Soviet era maps rather than the high-tech navigation that Ukrainians are using. As we observe this spectacular breaking of these crooked mirrors, I would like to end with a question. The Ukrainian resistance was met with surprise not only in Russia but here in the West as well. Western media and academia have created their own simulacra of both Russia and Ukraine to which us experts were often too tolerant. What will be the responsibility of those who have made and spread these simulacra? And what will be the new paradigm for understanding Ukraine, Russia, and Eastern Europe that we need so much now? What will we see when the last shards of the shattered mirrors hit the ground?

Notes

1 Horbyk, "Narratives at War."
2 Clausewitz, *On War*, p. 252.
3 Jordan et al, *Understanding Modern Warfare*, p. 53.
4 Baudrillard, *The Gulf War*
5 Baudrillard, *Simulacra and Simulation*, p. 1.

6   Ibid.
7   Mbembe, "Necropolitics."
8   Horbyk, "The war phone."

Selected Bibliography

Baudrillard, Jean. *Simulacra and Simulation* (Ann Arbor: University of Michigan Press, 1994).

Baudrillard, Jean. *The Gulf War Did Not Take Place* (Bloomington: Indiana University Press, 1995).

Boichak, Olga. "Digital War: Mediatized Conflicts in Sociological Perspective." In: Rohlinger, Deana A. & Sarah Sobieraj (eds). *The Oxford Handbook of Digital Media Sociology*, pp. 511–527 (Oxford: Oxford University Press, 2021).

Clausewitz, Carl von. *On War*. Trans. by Michael Howard and Peter Paret (Oxford: Oxford University Press, 2007).

Horbyk, Roman. "Narratives at War: Representations of Europe in News Media of Ukraine, Russia and Poland during Euromaidan." In: Fornäs, J. (ed.). *Europe Faces Europe: Narratives from Its Eastern Half*, pp. 93–132 (Bristol: Intellect, 2017).

Horbyk, Roman. "'The war phone': Mobile communication on the frontline in Eastern Ukraine," *Digital War* 3 (2022): 9–24.

Jordan, David, James D. Kiras, David J. Lonsdale, Ian Speller, Christopher Tuck and C. Dale Walton. *Understanding Modern Warfare* (Cambridge: Cambridge University Press, 2016).

Lokot, Tetyana. *Beyond the Protest Square: Digital Media and Augmented Dissent* (Lanham: Rowman & Littlefield Publishers, 2021).

Mbembe, Achilles. "Necropolitics." In: Morton, Stephen & Stephen Bygrave (eds). *Foucault in an Age of Terror*, pp. 152–182 (London: Palgrave Macmillan, 2008).

Afterword. Let Ukraine Speak

Integrating Scholarship on Ukraine into Classroom Syllabi

John Vsetecka

In her keynote address on April 8, 2022, at the British Association for Slavonic and East European Studies (BASEES) conference, Dr. Olesya Khromeychuk – noted historian of Ukraine – asked those in attendance to consider where Ukraine was on their mental maps. The surprisingly difficult question she posed was a reminder about the chronic lack of visibility of Europe's largest country and its 40 million citizens. The talk was more than just an encouragement to know and learn about Ukraine, it was an academic call to arms that tasked Western academics with confronting their own biases toward Ukrainian history, language, and culture. The continued risk of neglecting Ukraine, she warned, was that "If Ukraine does not exist on these mental maps, its existence on the actual map of the world will continue to be at risk."[1]

The threat of erasing Ukraine from maps, both mental and literal, became real once again on February 24, 2022, when Russia renewed its years-long war against Ukraine by dropping bombs and launching ground attacks across the country. The war has highlighted the crisis of Ukraine's representation in college and university classrooms in the West, causing many academics to reconsider what they know about Ukraine and how they teach about the country – if they teach about it at all. For too long, Western academia put Ukraine on the periphery, preferring to engage with histories of Moscow instead of Kyiv. In language departments, Russian language courses are privileged over Ukrainian ones. And "great" Russian writers like Dostoevsky and Tolstoy continue to be taught while Franko and Shevchenko remain shelved.

As we look ahead to the next academic year and begin to construct syllabi, we need to ask ourselves, "Can Ukraine speak?" This question borrows from the thinking of Gayatri Chakravorty Spivak, who asked what powers and voice colonial populations have under the foot of empires and imperial rule. In many ways, Ukraine has been treated as a colony of Russia throughout its history. The late historian Tony Judt wrote in his monumental tome *Postwar* that "For much of its history as a Soviet republic, Ukraine was treated as an internal colony."[2] Today, Ukraine remains free and independent, even as it fights against Russian colonial ambitions and Vladmir Putin's dictatorial efforts to exert control over its land.

What is the responsibility of instructors and professors in all of this? Simply put, we need to let Ukraine speak.

The colonial privileging of Russia is a problem that the academy in the West has been slow to acknowledge. Many historians of the Soviet Union, for example, built careers around being "Russianists" despite the geographical makeup of the Soviet Union consisting of fifteen different republics. Some have started to interrogate this tendency. Dr. Lewis Siegelbaum's recent essay on his career as a Russian historian, "Bumping Up Against Ukraine as a Historian of Russia," is one example. Despite Siegelbaum's best intentions, scholars of Ukraine have read his piece against the grain, noting that it standardizes a belated treatment of Ukraine. The piece unintentionally forefronts the problem of non-Ukrainianists suddenly becoming "experts" on a country that others have studied for their entire careers. Historians of Ukraine know all too well that it has been, in fact, them who have been "bumping up against Russia" for much of their careers. A determined group of scholars around the world have long advocated for the importance of Ukrainian studies. This essay introduces scholarship by experts on Ukraine to college and university instructors who are not Ukraine specialists but seek to more fully include Ukraine in various courses. This article offers suggestions for integrating scholarship about Ukraine into your syllabi for the coming year. By including works on Ukraine, you will help elevate knowledge about the country in your classrooms and become an active participant in helping students put Ukraine on their mental maps.

Where to Begin? Putting Ukraine on Students' Mental Maps

Regardless of what subject you are teaching, I suggest beginning any discussion of Ukraine with Olesya Khromeychuk's article "Where is Ukraine? How a western outlook perpetuates myths about Europe's largest country." This piece is adapted from Khromeychuk's keynote lecture at the 2022 BASEES conference.[3] This reading lends itself to reflective discussions with students about their perceptions and understanding of Ukraine. This reading could facilitate an in-class icebreaker activity or be used for a take home assignment in which students are given time to write a short reflection about how they understand Ukraine and where they see it physically in the world. The reading would also pair nicely with a quick map exercise where students are handed a blank map of Europe and asked to mark all those countries that they think are part of Europe, leading to a discussion about what "counts" as Europe and what does not. Map exercises on the first day of class can be an effective way to challenge students' understanding of geography and to acquaint them with areas and countries that they will encounter later in the semester.

If you're digitally inclined, I suggest using the *MAPA: Digital Atlas of Ukraine* tool from the Harvard Ukrainian Research Institute.[4] The interactive and multi-layered map can be configured by users to address themes of history, language, culture, population, religion, and statistics. This cross-disciplinary tool can be used in courses ranging from GIS and geography to digital humanities and allows students to work with Ukrainian topics in an interactive and engaging format.

For scholarship that expounds on the complex history of cartography and Ukrainian borders, look to Dr. Steven Seegel. His first book, *Ukraine under Western Eyes: The Bohdan and Neonila Krawciw Ucrainica Map Collection*, contains nearly 100 maps that will be useful for those interested in cartographic representations of Ukraine. His other two books, *Mapping Europe's Borderlands: Russian Cartography in the Age of Empire* and *Map Men: Transnational Lives and Deaths of Geographers in the Making of East Central Europe* will also be of interest to those wishing to learn more about maps and the people behind them. Kate Brown's *A Biography of No Place: From Ethnic Borderland to Soviet Heartland* is a must-read book about shifting borderlands and the people who inhabit them, and works well in lower and upper-level undergraduate classrooms.

General Historical Overviews of Ukraine

In July 2021, Putin crafted a historically distorted and incorrect essay titled "On the Historical Unity of Russians and Ukrainians" that asserted Russians and Ukrainians are one people.[5] The essay was a justification for existing Russian attitudes and actions toward Ukraine, and it served as a precursor for another speech he made on February 21, 2022, that presented Russia's argument for an all-out invasion on February 24. In linking the histories of Russia and Ukraine, Putin denied Ukrainian history and nationhood. However, Ukraine has its own history that is different, and separate from, that of Russia's. The following recommendations will help you and your students understand this history more comprehensively.

To help orient your students with the history of Ukraine, start with Mark von Hagen's provocatively titled article, "*Does Ukraine Have a History?*" in the journal *Slavic Review*. After that, turn to Serhy Yekelchyk's *Ukraine: Birth of a Modern Nation*, which is a highly readable history of Ukraine that is broken into eleven convenient chapters that each cover a specific period of Ukraine's history. No matter the time period you teach, this book offers short, digestible chapters that cover everything from Kyivan Rus (beginning in the late 9th century) to independence (1991). All of these will work well with undergraduate students.

If you are teaching more advanced courses, you can assign Serhii Plokhy's *Gates of Europe: A History of Ukraine*, which offers a comprehensive overview of Ukraine's history in a longer format. This book may be better suited for an upper-level undergraduate course or graduate seminar where students have time to take a deep-dive into Ukrainian history and politics. Another possibility is Faith Hillis' *Children of Rus': Right-Bank Ukraine and the Invention of a Russian Nation*. This book is best suited for graduate seminars on nationalism, Russia, Ukraine, and eastern Europe.

Another solid overview of Ukrainian history is Ivan L. Rudnytsky's *Essays in Modern Ukrainian History*. This collection is particularly well suited for assigning short reading excerpts to students. For an example, see how Professor Timothy Snyder of Yale University utilized the collection in his class called "The Making of Modern Ukraine."[6] Snyder's own work, *The Reconstruction of Nations: Poland, Ukraine, Lithuania, Belarus, 1569–1999*, offers a valuable assessment of Ukrainian history from 1569 to 1981 in about 100 pages in part two of the book. This, too, can be broken up into weekly readings for students. I also recommend Paul Robert Magocsi's *A History of Ukraine: The Land and its Peoples* and Orest Subtelny's book by the same name for further overviews of Ukrainian history.

Understanding Russia's War on Ukraine in Historical and Contemporary Perspective

With the ongoing war, it seems necessary to read Ukraine's history closely and in connection to contemporary events. Serhy Yekelchyk helps link past and present in the revised and updated second edition of his book, now titled *Ukraine: What Everyone Needs to Know*. If you are looking to assign shorter opinion pieces that speak to these same issues, try this one from *The New Yorker*, "Vladimir Putin's Revisionist History of Russia and Ukraine," where Serhii Plokhy breaks down critical moments in Ukraine's history in a discussion with journalist Isaac Chotiner.[7] For a discussion about the importance of Ukraine and its history in a global context, use Ukrainian historian Yaroslav Hrytsak's opinion piece, "Putin Made a Profound Miscalculation on Ukraine," in the *New York Times*.[8] This piece from *NPR*, "From Stalin to Putin, Ukraine is still trying to break free from Moscow," succinctly puts Ukraine's struggle with Russia into a longer historical perspective.[9]

Courses on contemporary history or international relations, as well as courses that use a now/then lens will especially want to include works that address what is happening in Ukraine today. Political scientist Paul D'anieri's *Ukraine and Russia: From Civilized Divorce to Uncivil War* is very useful for understanding Russian-Ukrainian relations since the collapse of the Soviet Union. It is especially relevant for instructors of political science, international relations, diplomacy, and recent history. You might also consider utilizing the podcast "The history and evolution of Ukrainian national identity" produced by *The Conversation* that examines the history and evolution of Ukrainian national identity by Ukraine experts Dominque Arel, Olga Onuch, and Volodomyr Kulyk.[10]

It will be important to remind your students that February 24, 2022, was not the start of Russia's war on Ukraine; rather, it was a violent uptick in a war that has been raging for more than eight years. Essays from *The War in Ukraine's Donbas: Origins, Contexts, and the Future*, edited by David Marples, elaborate on the history of the war in Ukraine's east. For a short, but personal, account of the war from a female and civilian perspective, I highly recommend Olesya Khromeychuk's *A Loss: The Story of a Dead Soldier Told by His Sister*. This book is an excellent addition to any syllabus that addresses Ukraine since 2014 because of its short length and highly readable prose.

Finally, I recommend works of fiction that are set in Ukraine since 2014. Try Andrey Kurkov's *Grey Bees*, which is a story of about Russia's war on Ukraine as experienced by a beekeeper in the war's grey zone. I also suggest Serhiy Zhadan's The Orphanage. The book follows a Ukrainian language teacher who sets off through the war zone to get to his nephew who lives in an orphanage in occupied territory. Both books make the war in Ukraine palpable to students and expose them to Ukrainian literature.

Highlighting 20th Century Ukraine in European History Courses

This section provides readings about Ukraine that can be incorporated into classes, both lower-and upper-division, on 20th-century Europe. The sections below cover events such as Ukraine's 1917, the 1932–33 Holodomor and the wider interwar period, WWII, and the postwar period through independence.

Ukraine's 1917 and the Formation of the Soviet Union

Students are often introduced to this period through the 1917 Russian Revolution, with Ukraine left out of the narrative. In reality, Ukraine experienced its own version of this revolution, and the repercussions of these events led to the Ukrainian War of Independence that lasted from 1917 to 1921. To learn more about this period, I suggest assigning chapter three from George Liber's *Total Wars and the Making of Modern Ukraine, 1914–1954*. Liber provides a detailed overview of this period that highlights the main points of 1917 and its impact on Ukraine through WWII. Other accessible options include Mark von Hagen's essay "The Ukrainian Revolution of 1917 and why it matters for historians of the Russian revolution(s)" in the online journal *EuroMaidan Press*,[11] and Serhii Plokhy's "Ukraine in the Flames: '1917 in Kyiv,'"[12] a short essay on the Harvard Ukrainian Research Institute's website.

The Interwar Period

This section covers the major events that took place in the interwar period in Soviet Ukraine. The paragraphs below offer suggested readings that cover contested nationalities policies, language, and culture. Especially important is the last part of this section that discusses the 1932–33 famine, now known commonly as the Holodomor, that killed millions of Ukrainians in only two years.

A process called *korenizatsiia* (indigenization or nativization) sought to integrate diverse, non-Russian national cultures into their respective Soviet republics in an attempt to reverse a longer trend of Russification. The larger aim was to appeal to different nationalities and offer them buy-in to the idea of a greater Soviet identity, which leaders hoped would take precedent over national interests and allow them to strengthen Soviet power. For a good overview of the incorporation of nationalities in the Soviet Union, look to Fran Hirsch's *Empire of Nations: Ethnographic Knowledge and the Making of the Soviet Union*, which is broken up into three parts that could be easily assigned as excerpts. Matthew

Pauly's book, *Breaking the Tongue: Language, Education, and Power in Soviet Ukraine, 1923–1934*, details the complexity of *korenizatsiia* in Ukrainian-language schooling. You can also watch an interview with Matthew Pauly about his book,[13] and listen to a podcast about the book on the New Books Network.[14]

If an article-length piece is more accessible for your students, try George Liber's article, "Korenizatsiia: Restructuring Soviet nationality policy in the 1920s."

Other valuable works on Soviet Ukraine and the cultural politics and history of this period are available from Olena Palko and Mayhill Fowler. Palko's *Making Ukraine Soviet: Literature and Cultural Politics under Lenin and Stalin* challenges center-periphery dynamics by focusing on the development of Ukraine's cultural projects. Fowler's *Beau Monde on Empire's Edge: State and Stage in Soviet Ukraine* is a cultural history of theater and the arts in Soviet Ukraine. You can watch her speak about her book at the HURI Seminar in Ukrainian Studies,[15] and you can read an interview I did with her about her work on Ukraine on H-Ukraine.[16]

The interwar period in Soviet Ukraine was also marked by periods of extreme violence, famine, and genocide. Perhaps the most significant event in this period was the 1932–1933 man-made famine known as the Holodomor (meaning "death by hunger"), which was accompanied by the destruction and suppression of Ukrainian language, culture, and religion by the Soviets in what is now considered by many experts to be an act of genocide against Ukraine. The literature on the topic is vast, so I recommend utilizing the resources from the Holodomor Research and Education Consortium,[17] which has put together a list of translated sources and articles on the topic that privilege Ukrainian voices.[18]

I also suggest using Norman Naimark's very student-friendly book, *Stalin's Genocides*. Chapter four is a short overview that works well with undergraduate students. Stanislav Kulchytsky's *The Famine of 1932–1933 in Ukraine: An Anatomy of the Holodomor* is an important book on the subject by a leading Ukrainian expert who brings together thirty years of research into a short, accessible volume. The Canadian Institute of Ukrainian Studies Press at the University of Alberta has published a number of short, edited volumes on the Holodomor; selected chapters are available on the Internet.[19] *The Holodomor Reader*, a collection of primary sources in English translation, may be especially useful in history courses. For instructors who like to utilize different forms of texts, including comics and illustrations, consider assigning part one of Igort's *The Ukrainian and Russian Notebooks: Life and Death under Soviet Rule*. Finally, Anne Applebaum's *Red Famine* and the intro chapter of Timothy Snyder's *Bloodlands* are useful for upper-level courses as they offer extensive secondary treatment of the famine.

For transnational histories of Ukraine in the interwar period, look to Nadia Zavorotna's *Scholars in Exile: The Ukrainian Intellectual World in Interwar Czechoslovakia*, which details the lives of the Ukrainian intelligentsia abroad. Those who are interested in architecture, design, and industrialization projects in the Soviet Union will enjoy Christina Crawford's recent book about the Kharkiv Tractor Plant (among other Soviet industrial sites) and its transnational connections, entitled *Spatial Revolution: Architecture and Planning in the Early Soviet Union*, and see my short interview with her about her work on H-Ukraine.[20]

WWII, the German Occupation, and the Holocaust

WWII and the Holocaust are subjects often taught from a Western perspective that leaves little room to understand the experience of those in the East. Although many books have been published on the Soviet Union and the war that foreground Russia, there were millions of Ukrainians who served in the Red Army and millions of Ukrainians died during the German occupation of Ukraine in the 1940s. The first phase of the Holocaust, known as the "Holocaust by Bullets," was carried out in Ukrainian lands, therefore it is crucial to integrate Ukrainian experiences and narratives into courses on this subject.

Jennifer Popowycz penned a compelling overview of the "Holocaust by B ullets" in Ukraine on the website of The National WWII Museum in New Orleans. It describes how mobile killing units, made up of the German SS, German army, and local collaborators, murdered Jews in Ukraine. This piece introduces students to a perspective of the Holocaust that is taught less often. For more extensive treatment, see Wendy Lower's *Nazi Empire-Building and the Holocaust in Ukraine* and *The Ravine: A Family, A Photograph, A Holocaust Massacre Revealed* or Karel C. Berkhoff's *Harvest of Despair: Life and Death in Ukraine under Nazi Rule*.

The literature on the Jewish experience in Ukraine during this time period is extensive and offers unsettling accounts of violence, collaboration, and mass killing. Jeffrey Veidlinger's brief history of Babi Yar in *The Conversation* is a useful overview of the horrid killing that took place in the center of Kyiv in September 1941.[21] Veidlinger's most recent book, *In the Midst of Civilized Europe: The Pogroms of 1918–1921 and the Onset of the Holocaust*, gives a valuable pretext that helps articulate the earlier killing of Jews by peasants in Ukraine, and could serve as an optional reading for your syllabus. His earlier work, *In the Shadow of the Shtetl: Small-Town Jewish Life in Soviet Ukraine*, may also be of interest due to the author's use of oral history that recounts the Jewish experience of returning home after WWII. Ola Hnatiuk's *Courage and Fear* works well in an upper-level classes as an insightful account of WWII experiences among Jewish, Polish, and Ukrainian populations in Lviv. Other relevant titles include Amelia Glaser's *Jews and Ukrainians in Russia's Literary Borderlands: From the Shtetl Fair to the Petersburg Bookshop* and A. Anatoli (Kuznetsov's) *Babi Yar: A Document in the Form of a Novel*, which documents Kuznetsov's witnessing of Nazi war crimes in Kyiv.

An assessment of this period is incomplete without a discussion of collaboration between some Ukrainians and German occupiers. Useful works to consult on this difficult topic are John-Paul Himka's *Ukrainian Nationalists and the Holocausts: OUN and UPA's Participation in the Destruction of Ukrainian Jewry, 1941–1944* and Tarik Cyril Amar's *The Paradox of Ukrainian Lviv: A Borderland City between Stalinists, Nazis, and Nationalists*. For a shorter account of this history, look to Masha Gessen's article in *The New Yorker*.[22]

Another WWII event that often escapes WWII coverage in the classroom is the 1944 deportation of the Crimean Tatars, which resulted in ethnic cleansing and cultural genocide. An article on Al Jazeera gives a good overview of the deportation and the meaning it embodied when Russia annexed Crimea in 2014.[23] Karina Korostelina elaborates further on the same topic and addresses attempts to repatriate Crimean Tatars and the continued discrimination they face. To explore how poetry and literature helped break the silence surrounding the deportation of Crimean Tatars, consider Rory Finnin's recent book, *Blood of Others: Stalin's Crimean Atrocity and the Poetics of Solidarity*.

Postwar Ukraine and Chornobyl

Two important works highlight the effects of WWII that lingered long after the war. Oksana Kis's *Survival as Victory: Ukrainian Women in the Gulag* is an anthropological study that privileges Ukrainian women's voices and details the experience of life in Soviet forced labor camps of the 1940s and 1950s. Filip Slaveski's *Remaking Ukraine after World War II: The Clash of Local and Central Soviet Power* explores local Ukrainian populations fighting back against Stalinist practices after the war.

One of the better-known events in Soviet Ukraine's history is the Chornobyl nuclear disaster that occurred in April 1986. The HBO series *Chernobyl* that debuted in 2019 reinvigorated the public's interest in this dark event, and it brought widespread attention to Ukraine.[24] Students often express strong interest in this topic and there are multiple excellent readings to choose from. Kate Brown's *Manual for Survival: An Environmental History of the Chernobyl Disaster* is part history, part ethnography, and part detective story. It is a gripping read that students will not want to put down. Serhii Plokhy's *Chernobyl: The History of a Nuclear Catastrophe* is another historical account of the subject that is worth considering for its minute-by-minute recounting of the history of the nuclear disaster. No reading list on Chornobyl would be complete without Svetlana Aleksievich's *Voices from Chernobyl: The Oral History of a Nuclear Disaster* Picador, which highlights the human aspect of the nuclear disaster. This can pair well with either Brown or Plokhy.

Independence

Any of the readings on the Chornobyl disaster pair well with Serhy Yekelchyk's chapter "From Chernobyl to the Soviet Collapse" in *Ukraine: Birth of a Modern Nation*, which can be used to teach students about the demise of the Soviet Union and Ukraine's independence in 1991. Selections from Tamara Hundarova's *The Post-Chornobyl Library: Ukrainian Postmodernism of the 1990s* are also very useful for understanding decolonization in Ukraine and the efforts of Ukrainians to liberate themselves from a Soviet past.

Understanding 21st Century Ukraine

New scholarship on a variety of Ukrainian topics have highlighted feminist and queer perspectives, race, and music, while others have addressed the Revolution of Dignity. World history courses or contemporary events classes should include the 2013–2014 Revolution of Dignity (also known as Euromaidan). One option is to have students read an entry in the online edition of the Encyclopedia Britannica to get familiar with the revolution,[25] and pair it with selections from either Marci Shore's *The Ukrainian Night: An Intimate History of Revolution* or Mychailo Wynnyckyj's *Ukraine's Maidan, Russia's War: A Chronicle and Analysis of the Revolution of Dignity*, which provide different scholarly analyses of the revolution.

A variety of university courses will benefit from recent works that address topics ranging from LGBTQ, feminist and human rights in Ukraine, to drug use and disease, to music, culture, and race. Emily Channell-Justice's edited collection, *Decolonizing Queer Experience: LGBT+ Narratives from Eastern Europe and*

Eurasia, contains essays on activism, resistance, and resilience in post-socialist spaces, including one chapter on Ukraine. Jessica Zychowicz's *Superfluous Women: Art, Feminism, and Revolution in Twenty-First Century Ukraine* is a more extensive treatment of the experiences of artists, feminists, and queer activists in Ukraine. This book could be used in courses on activism/social movements, human rights, or the history of revolutions.

Other studies focus on subjects such as drug use, music, and race. Jennifer Carroll's remarkable study of drug use in Ukraine, *Narkomania: Drugs, HIV, and Citizenship in Ukraine*, is a must-read for anyone studying or teaching about substance use, HIV, and citizenship in post-Soviet spaces. On the subject of music, Maria Sonevytsky's new book, *Wild Music: Sound and Sovereignty in Ukraine*, is a beautiful ethnography about the ways that various forms of music in Ukraine contribute to, and re-imagine, Ukrainian culture. Adriana Helbig's Hip Hop Ukraine: Music, Race, and African Migration reveals interracial encounters among African students, migrants, and workers in Ukraine. Pair this book with more recent events surrounding the treatment of Africans in Ukraine as a result of the current war. Char Adams discusses African students' efforts to organize their own war relief efforts[26] and Monika Pronczuk addresses the barriers that many Africans faced when trying to flee the war in Ukraine.[27]

Further Resources in Lieu of a Conclusion

If you find only one thing in this article that works for your future classes, it will be significant because you are working to let Ukraine speak. The recommendations in this article represent a small fraction of what is available.

In addition, consider the following resources:

- The Harvard Ukrainian Research Institute has a very helpful guide titled "Teaching and Studying Ukraine: List of Resources".[28] Emily Channell-Justice and I contributed to this resource compilation during the onset of the COVID-19 pandemic to provide online tools to help instructors teach about Ukraine.
- For podcasts on books in Ukrainian studies, turn to New Books Network and their section on Ukraine.[29] Experts in the field interview authors whose books are about Ukrainian topics, and these audio resources are useful for keeping up with new literature in the field and hearing directly from authors themselves.

- H-Ukraine (part of the larger H-Net platform) shares and collects recent scholarship, teaching resources, interviews, and other material related to the academic study of Ukraine. It is free to subscribe to H-Ukraine, and announcements get sent directly to your inbox.[30]

Thank you for reading this guide. I appreciate your efforts to make Ukraine visible in your classes and put the country on students' mental maps. Studying Ukraine is more important than ever.

First published as John Vsetecka, "Let Ukraine Speak: Integrating Scholarship on Ukraine into Classroom Syllabi," Clio and the Contemporary, clioandthecontemporary.com, *3 July 2022. Reproduced with permission from Clio and the Contemporary.*

Notes

1. Olesya Khromeychuk, "Where is Ukraine? How a western outlook perpetuates myths about Europe's largest country," *Royal Society for Arts Journal* 2 (2022), p. 29.
2. Tony Judt, *Postwar: A History of Europe since 1945* (New York: Penguin, 2005), p. 648.
3. Dr Olesya Khromeychuk (Ukrainian Institute London), BASEES 2022 Keynote Lecture, 8 April 2022. https://www.youtube.com/watch?v=CJthJb1tKoY. Accessed on 17 January 2023.
4. *MAPA: Digital Atlas of Ukraine*, https://gis.huri.harvard.edu/.
5. Vladimir Putin, "On the Historical Unity of Russians and Ukrainians" https://en.wikisource.org/wiki/On_the_Historical_Unity_of_Russians_and_Ukrainians. Accessed on 17 January 2023.
6. Timothy Snyder, "The Making of Modern Ukraine": https://networks.h-net.org/system/files/contributed-files/habsburg-syllabi-making-modern-ukraine.pdf. Accessed on 17 January 2023.
7. "Vladimir Putin's Revisionist History of Russia and Ukraine", Serhii Plokhy in conversation with Isaac Chotiner. https://www.newyorker.com/news/q-and-a/vladimir-putins-revisionist-history-of-russia-and-ukraine. Accessed on 17 January 2023.
8. Yaroslav Hrytsak, "Putin Made a Profound Miscalculation on Ukraine". https://www.nytimes.com/2022/03/19/opinion/ukraine-russia-putin-history.html. Accessed on 17 January 2023.

9   Greg Myre, "From Stalin to Putin, Ukraine is still trying to break free from Moscow". https://www.npr.org/2022/01/31/1076012108/from-stalin-to-putin-ukraine-is-still-trying-to-break-free-from-moscow. Accessed on 17 January 2023.
10 "The history and evolution of Ukrainian national identity", https://theconversation.com/the-history-and-evolution-of-ukrainian-national-identity-podcast-179279. Accessed on 17 January 2023.
11 Mark von Hagen, "The Ukrainian Revolution of 1917 and why it matters for historians of the Russian revolution(s)", https://euromaidanpress.com/2017/09/15/ukraines-1917-1921-statehood-and-why-it-matters-for-historians-of-the-russian-revolution/?__cf_chl_tk=9qBZe4HsA5hc33rQ.GLaDtW6rvqCz1t1WsvguuQHm.Q-1655314729-0-gaNycGzNCGU. Accessed on 17 January 2023.
12 Ukraine in the Flames: "1917 in Kyiv" by Serhii Plokhii, https://huri.harvard.edu/news/ukraine-flames-1917-kyiv-serhii-plokhii. Accessed on 17 January 2023.
13 UkeTube Ukrainian Video: "Language, Education & Power in Soviet Ukraine, 1923–1934," Matt Pauly. https://youtu.be/qOdZPL1-DJY. Accessed on 17 January 2023.
14 New Books Network. Matthew Pauly, Breaking the Tongue. Language, Education, and Power in Soviet Ukraine, 1923–1934. Nov 15, 2016. https://newbooksnetwork.com/matthew-pauly-breaking-the-tongue-language-education-and-power-in-soviet-ukraine-1923-1934-u-of-toronto-press-2014. Accessed on 17 January 2023.
15 HURI Seminar in Ukrainian Studies. Mayhill Fowler: "Beau Monde on Empire's Edge: State and Stage in Soviet Ukraine", https://www.youtube.com/watch?v=q_LhxK1Mm7c. Accessed on 17 January 2023.
16 John Vsetecka, H-Ukraine Spotlight: Interview with Mayhill Fowler, https://networks.h-net.org/node/4555727/discussions/5886088/h-ukraine-spotlight-interview-mayhill-fowler. Accessed on 17 January 2023.
17 *Holodomor Research and Education Consortium*, https://holodomor.ca/.
18 *Holodomor Research and Education Consortium*, https://holodomor.ca/resources/further-reading/translated-academic-articles/.
19 Canadian Institute of Ukrainian Studies: https://www.ciuspress.com/?s=Holodomor&v=1ee0bf89c5d1. Accessed on 17 January 2023.
20 John Vsetecka, H-Ukraine "Spotlight" Interview with Christina Crawford. https://networks.h-net.org/node/4555727/discussions/7904172/h-ukraine-spotlight-interview-christina-crawford. Accessed on 17 January 2023.

21 Jeffrey Veidlinger, "A brief history of Babi Yar, where Nazis massacred Jews, Soviets kept silence and now Ukraine says Russia fired a missile." https://theconversation.com/a-brief-history-of-babi-yar-where-nazis-massacred-jews-soviets-kept-silence-and-now-ukraine-says-russia-fired-a-missile-178574. Accessed on 17 January 2023.
22 Masha Gessen, "The Holocaust Memorial Undone by Another War." https://www.newyorker.com/magazine/2022/04/18/the-holocaust-memorial-undone-by-another-war. Accessed on 17 January 2023.
23 Michael Colborne, "For Crimean Tatars, it is about much more than 1944." 19 May 2016. https://www.aljazeera.com/features/2016/5/19/for-crimean-tatars-it-is-about-much-more-than-1944.
24 Chernobyl. HBO.2019. https://www.hbo.com/chernobyl.
25 "The Poroshenko Administration," Encyclopedia Britannica. https://www.britannica.com/place/Ukraine/The-Poroshenko-administration. Accessed on 17 January 2023.
26 Char Adams, "How African students in Ukraine are leading their own rescue efforts." 2 March 2022. https://www.nbcnews.com/news/nbcblk/black-african-students-ukraine-are-leading-rescue-efforts-rcna18531.
27 Monika Pronczuk, "Africans Say Ukrainian Authorities Hindered Them from Fleeing." 1 March 2022. https://www.nytimes.com/2022/03/01/world/europe/ukraine-refugee-discrimination.html.
28 "Teaching and Studying Ukraine: List of Resources. https://huri.harvard.edu/teaching-resources-list.
29 New Books Network, Ukrainian Studies: https://newbooksnetwork.com/category/peoples-places/ukrainian-studies.
30 H-Ukraine: https://networks.h-net.org/h-ukraine.

Bibliography

Aleksievich, Svetlana. Voices from Chernobyl: The Oral History of a Nuclear Disaster (London: Picador, 2006).

Amar, Tarik Cyril. *The Paradox of Ukrainian Lviv: A Borderland City between Stalinists, Nazis, and Nationalists* (Ithaca: Cornell University Press, 2015).

Anatoli A. (Anatoly Kuznetsov). *Babi Yar. A Document in the Form of a Novel; New, Complete, Uncensored Version* (New York: Farrar, Straus and Giroux, 1970).

Applebaum, Anne. *Red Famine: Stalin's War on Ukraine*, First United States edition. (New York: Doubleday, 2017).

Berkhoff, Karel C. *Harvest of Despair: Life and Death in Ukraine under Nazi Rule* (Cambridge, Mass.: Belknap Press of Harvard University Press, 2004).

Brown, Kate. *A Biography of No Place: From Ethnic Borderland to Soviet Heartland*, 1. Harvard Univ. Press paperback ed (Cambridge, Mass. London: Harvard University Press, 2005).

Brown, Kate. *Manual for Survival: A Chernobyl Guide to the Future*, First edition (New York: W. W. Norton & Company, 2019).

Carroll, Jennifer J. *Narkomania: Drugs, HIV, and Citizenship in Ukraine* (Ithaca: Cornell University Press, 2019).

Channell-Justice, Emily (ed.) *Decolonizing Queer Experience: LGBT+ Narratives from Eastern Europe and Eurasia* (Lanham: Lexington Books, 2020).

Crawford, Christina E. *Spatial Revolution: Architecture and Planning in the Early Soviet Union* (Ithaca: Cornell University Press, 2022).

D'Anieri Paul J. *Ukraine and Russia:From Civilized Divorce to Uncivil War*, 1st ed. (Cambridge: University Press, 2019).

Finnin, Rory. *Blood of Others:Stalin's Crimean Atrocity and the Poetics of Solidarity.* (Toronto: University of Toronto Press, 2022).

Fowler, Mayhill C. *Beau Monde on Empire's Edge: State and Stage in Soviet Ukraine* (Toronto: University of Toronto Press, 2017).

Glaser, Amelia. *Jews and Ukrainians in Russia's Literary Borderlands: From the Shtetl Fair to the Petersburg Bookshop*, Northwestern University Press Studies in Russian Literature and Theory (Evanston, Ill: Northwestern University Press, 2012).

Hagen, Mark von. "Does Ukraine Have a History?" *Slavic Review* 54:3 (1995): 658–73, https://doi.org/10.2307/2501741.

Helbig, Adriana. *Hip Hop Ukraine: Music, Race, and African Migration*, Ethnomusicology Multimedia (Bloomington; Indianapolis: Indiana University Press, 2014).

Hillis, Faith. *Children of Rus': Right-Bank Ukraine and the Invention of a Russian Nation* (Ithaca: Cornell University Press, 2013).

Himka, John-Paul. *Ukrainian Nationalists and the Holocaust: OUN and UPA's Participation in the Destruction of Ukrainian Jewry, 1941–1944*, Ukrainian Voices Vol. 12 (Stuttgart: ibidem Verlag, 2021).

Hirsch, Francine. *Empire of Nations: Ethnographic Knowledge & [and] the Making of the Soviet Union* (Ithaca: Cornell University Press, 2005).

Hnatiuk, Aleksandra. *Courage and Fear* (Boston: Academic Studies Press, 2019).

Hundorova, Tamara. *The Post-Chornobyl Library: Ukrainian Postmodernism of the 1990s* (Boston: Academic Studies Press, 2019).

Igort et al., *The Ukrainian and Russian Notebooks*, First Simon&Schuster hardcover edition (New York: Simon & Schuster, 2016).

Khromeychuk, Olesya. "Where is Ukraine? How a western outlook perpetuates myths about Europe's largest country," *Royal Society for Arts Journal* 2 (2022): https://www.thersa.org/globalassets/pdfs/journals/rsa-journal-issue-2-2022.pdf.

Khromeychuk, Olesya. Foreword by Andrei Kurkov, *A Loss: The Story of a Dead Soldier Told by His Sister* (Stuttgart: ibidem Press, 2021).

Kis', Oksana Romanivna. *Survival as Victory: Ukrainian Women in the Gulag*, Harvard Series in Ukrainian Studies 79 (Cambridge, Mass.: Harvard University Press, 2020).

Korostelina, Karina. "Crimean Tatars From Mass Deportation to Hardships in Occupied Crimea," *Genocide Studies and Prevention: An International Journal* 9: 1 (2015), https://doi.org/<p>http://dx.doi.org/10.5038/1911-9933.9.1.1319</p>.

Kul'chyc'kyj, Stanislav. *The Famine of 1932–1933 in Ukraine: An Anatomy of the Holodomor* (Edmonton: CIUS Press, 2018).

Kurkov, Andrey. *Grey Bees*. Translated by Boris Dralyuk (Dallas: Deep Vellum Publishing, 2022).

Liber, George. "Korenizatsiia: Restructuring Soviet Nationality Policy in the 1920s," *Ethnic and Racial Studies* 14:1 (1991): 15–23, https://doi.org/10.1080/01419870.1991.9993696.

Liber, George. *Total Wars and the Making of Modern Ukraine, 1914–1954* (Toronto: University of Toronto Press, 2016).

Lower, Wendy. *Nazi Empire-Building and the Holocaust in Ukraine* (Chapel Hill (N.C.): University of North Carolina Press, 2005).

Lower, Wendy. *The Ravine: A Family, a Photograph, a Holocaust Massacre Revealed* (Boston: Houghton Mifflin Harcourt, 2021).

Lysiak Rudnytsky, Ivan. *Essays in Modern Ukrainian History* (Edmonton: Canadian Institute of Ukrainian Studies, 1987).

Magocsi, Paul R. *A History of Ukraine: The Land and Its Peoples*, 2nd, rev.expanded ed., repr. ed. (Toronto: University of Toronto Press, 2012).

Marples, David R. *The War in Ukraine's Donbas: Origins, Contexts, and the Future* (Budapest: Central European University Press, 2022).

Motyl, Alexander J. and Bohdan Klid. *The Holodomor Reader: A Sourcebook on the Famine of 1932–1933 in Ukraine* (Toronto: Canadian Institute of Ukrainian Studies Press, 2012).

Naimark, Norman M. *Stalin's Genocides: Human Rights and Crimes against Humanity* (Princeton: Princeton Univ. Press, 2012).

Palko, Olena. *Making Ukraine Soviet: Literature and Cultural Politics under Lenin and Stalin* (London; New York: Bloomsbury Academic, 2021).

Pauly, Matthew D. *Breaking the Tongue: Language, Education, and Power in Soviet Ukraine, 1923–1934* (Toronto: University of Toronto Press, 2014).

Plochij, Serhij Mykolajovyč. *Chernobyl: History of a Tragedy* (London: Allen Lane, 2018).

Plokhy, Serhii. *The Gates of Europe: A History of Ukraine* (London: Allen Lane, 2015).

Seegel, Steven. *Map Men: Transnational Lives and Deaths of Geographers in the Making of East Central Europe* (Chicago: The University of Chicago Press, 2018).

Seegel, Steven. *Mapping Europe's Borderlands: Russian Cartography in the Age of Empire* (Chicago: The University of Chicago Press, 2012).

Seegel, Steven. *Ukraine under Western Eyes: The Bohdan and Neonila Krawciw Ucrainica Map Collection*, Harvard Series in Ukrainian Studies (Cambridge, Mass.: Harvard University Press, 2013).

Shore, Marci. *The Ukrainian Night: An Intimate History of Revolution* (New Haven: Yale University Press, 2017).

Siegelbaum, Lewis H. "Bumping Up Against Ukraine as a Historian of Russia," *Region* 10:1 (2021): 137–52.

Slaveski, Filip. *Remaking Ukraine after World War II: The Clash of Local and Central Soviet Power*, New Studies in European History (Cambridge: University Press, 2021).

Snyder, Timothy. *Bloodlands: Europe between Hitler and Stalin* (New York: Basic Books, 2010).

Snyder, Timothy. *The Reconstruction of Nations: Poland, Ukraine, Lithuania, Belarus, 1569–1999* (New Haven, CT: Yale University Press, 2003).

Sonevytsky, Maria. *Wild Music: Sound and Sovereignty in Ukraine*, Music/Culture (Middletown, Connecticut: Wesleyan University Press, 2019).

Subtelny, Orest. *Ukraine: A History*, 4th ed. (Toronto: University of Toronto Press, 2009).

Veidlinger, Jeffrey. *In the Midst of Civilized Europe: The Pogroms of 1918–1921 and the Onset of the Holocaust*, First edition (New York: Metropolitan Books, Henry Holt and Company, 2021).

Veidlinger, Jeffrey. *In the Shadow of the Shtetl: Small-Town Jewish Life in Soviet Ukraine* (Bloomington, Ind: Indiana University Press, 2013).

Vynnyc'kyj, Mychajlo. *Ukraine's Maidan, Russia's War: A Chronicle and Analysis of the Revolution of Dignity*, Ukrainian Voices Vol. 1 (Stuttgart: ibidem-Verlag, 2019).

Yekelchyk, Serhy. *Ukraine: Birth of a Modern Nation* (New York: Oxford University Press, 2007).

Yekelchyk, Serhy. *Ukraine: What Everyone Needs to Know*, Second edition (New York: Oxford University Press, 2020).

Zavorotna, Nadia. *Scholars in Exile: The Ukrainian Intellectual World in Interwar Czechoslovakia* (Toronto: University of Toronto Press, 2019).

Zhadan, Serhii. *The Orphanage*, A Margellos World Republic of Letters Book. Translated by Reilly Costigan-Humes, and Isaac Stackhouse Wheeler (New Haven: Yale University Press, 2021).

Zychowicz, Jessica. *Superfluous Women: Art, Feminism, and Revolution in Twenty-First-Century Ukraine* (Toronto: University of Toronto Press, 2020).

Contributing Authors

Fabian Baumann is an SNSF Postdoc Mobility fellow at the Research Center for the History of Transformations, University of Vienna. Having studied in Geneva, Saint Petersburg, and Oxford, he earned his doctorate at the University of Basel in 2020. His most recent publication is an article titled "Nationality as Choice of Path: Iakov Shul'gin, Dmitrii Pikhno, and the Russian-Ukrainian Crossroads," published in *Kritika: Explorations in Russian and Eurasian History*. His book *Dynasty Divided: A Family History of Russian and Ukrainian Nationalism* is forthcoming with Northern Illinois University Press, an imprint of Cornell University Press. Baumann's research interests include the history of nationalism, empire, and the family, as well as Russian-Ukrainian relations in the imperial and Soviet periods.

Boris Belge is an SNSF Ambizione post-doctoral research fellow at the University of Basel. His project "Managing Trade" investigates infrastructure and economic practices in the port of Odesa (1794–1905). His first book, *Klingende Sowjetmoderne. Eine Musik- und Gesellschaftsgeschichte des Spätsozialismus* was published in 2018 by Böhlau Verlag. He also co-edited, together with Martin Deuerlein, *Goldenes Zeitalter der Stagnation? Perspektiven auf die sowjetische Ordnung der Brežnev-Ära* (Tübingen 2014). Belge's research interests include trade, the economic and maritime history of Ukraine and imperial Russia, and the social and cultural history of late socialism.

Kateryna Botanova is a Basel-based cultural critic, curator, and writer from Kyiv, Ukraine. She writes on decoloniality, solidarity, and care with a special focus on artistic practices and societal dynamics in the Global South, Eastern Europe, and Ukraine, in particular. Botanova is a co-curator of multidisciplinary biennial Culturescapes (Basel, Switzerland) and an editor for its published anthology collections. Between 2010 and 2015, she was a director of the Center for Contemporary Art in Kyiv and founder and editor-in-chief of the online magazine *Korydor*. She is a member of PEN-Ukraine.

Iulia Buyskykh is a historian and socio-cultural anthropologist affiliated with the Institute of History of Ukraine, National Academy of Sciences of Ukraine and the Centre for Applied Anthropology, an NGO based in Kyiv. She previously held a post-doc at the Institute of Ethnology and Cultural Anthropology, University of Warsaw (2015 – 2016). Buyskykh spent the academic year of 2019–2020 at Pennsylvania State University as a Fulbright scholar. Her research interests include lived religion (Christianity) in post-communist Ukraine and Poland, inter-confessional relationships, memory and border studies, Polish-Ukrainian shared history, ethics, and empathy in qualitative research.

Anna Chebotarova is a sociologist and a research fellow at the Department of Literature, Area Studies, and European Languages at the University of Oslo, Norway. She is currently engaged in the international project "National values and political reforms in post-Maidan Ukraine". Chebotarova previously worked as a coordinator for the "Ukrainian Regionalism: a Research Platform" project at the University of St. Gallen (Switzerland). She is also affiliated with the Center for Urban History in East-Central Europe (Lviv, Ukraine).

Manuel Férez Gil is a PhD candidate in the Department of Sociology at the Alberto Hurtado University in Santiago de Chile. His doctoral research is focused on the identity of the Sephardic Jews in Chile. Férez Gil has edited and compiled five academic works, among which are *Estos son los Kurdos, análisis de una nación* (Porrúa, 2014) and *Una mirada a la Turquía contemporánea* (Universidad Anáhuac, 2016). He specializes in the study of ethnic, religious and linguistic minorities from the Middle East and the Caucasus and their emigration processes to Latin America.

Roman Horbyk is a Senior Lecturer at Örebro University (Sweden). He is a media researcher working mainly on fake news, media and war, history of media and culture, primarily in Eastern Europe. He defended two dissertations, the first one in Kyiv focussing on illustrated press in the 1920s Weimar Republic and Soviet Ukraine and the second on at the Södertörn University (Sweden), focusing on media power in representations of Europe in Ukraine, Russia and Poland during Euromaidan (2017). His current research project deals with how mobile phones are used by Ukrainian soldiers and civilians at war. He has worked as a journalist and is active as a playwright and screenwriter, including for *Pryputni* (2017).

Olesya Khromeychuk is a historian and writer. She has taught the history of East-Central Europe at the University of Cambridge, University College London, the University of East Anglia and King's College London, and has written for *The New York Times*, *The New York Review of Books*, *Der Spiegel*, the *Los Angeles Review of Books*, *Prospect* and *The New Statesman*. Khromeychuk is the author of *The Death of a Soldier Told by His Sister* (2022) and *"Undetermined" Ukrainians. Post-War Narratives of the Waffen SS "Galicia" Division* (2013). She is currently the Director of the Ukrainian Institute London.

Oksana Klymenko is a Senior Lecturer at the National University of "Kyiv-Mohyla Academy". Her primary research interest includes Ukrainian history in the 20th century, memory studies, Soviet society, gender studies, and labor history. In 2016, Oksana held a fellowship at the University of Giessen (Gießener Zentrum Östliches Europa). In 2018, she received the Dissertation Research Grant from the US-based Shevchenko Scientific Society and from 2021 to 2022 she was Visiting Fellow at the Institute for Human Sciences in Vienna (Austria).

Roman Korshuk is an Assistant Professor of Political Sciences at the Faculty of Philosophy at Taras Shevchenko, National University of Kyiv. He has authored numerous publications on ethnology and the history of national movements in Ukraine and Western Europe.

Volodymyr Kulyk is a Head Research Fellow at the Institute of Political and Ethnic Studies, National Academy of Sciences of Ukraine. He has also taught at Columbia, Stanford, and Yale Universities, Kyiv Mohyla Academy and the Ukrainian Catholic University as well as having held research fellowships at Harvard, Stanford, University College London, the University of Alberta, the Woodrow Wilson Center, and other Western scholarly institutions. His research fields include the politics of language, memory, and identity as well as political and media discourse in contemporary Ukraine as well as language policies in multilingual countries across the world. He is the author of four books and more than 80 articles and chapters published in Ukrainian and

Western journals and collected volumes. His latest book is *Movna polityka v bahatomovnykh kraïnakh: Zakordonnyi dosvid ta ioho prydatnist' dlia Ukraïny* (Language Policies in Multilingual Countries: Foreign Experience and Its Relevance to Ukraine; Kyiv: Dukh i Litera, 2021).

Martin-Oleksandr Kisly is a historian of Crimea and the history of the Crimean Tatars with a focus on the Soviet and post-Soviet periods. Born in Simferopol, Crimea, he defended his PhD dissertation entitled *Crimean Tatars' Return to the Homeland in 1956–1989* at the History Department of the National University Kyiv-Mohyla Academy. In 2017, Kisly was a Fulbright Scholar at the University of Michigan, Ann Arbor, and has held a number of research fellowships, most recently at the Institute for Human Sciences (IWM) in Vienna. His research interests include (but are not limited to): oral history, memory, trauma, identity, migration and colonialism. He is also one of the authors of the online course "Crimea: History and People".

Roman Liubavskyi is an Associate Professor of History and Deputy Dean for Research at Kharkiv National V. N. Karazin University. His scholarly interests include Soviet history, the history of everyday life, and urban studies. Roman is the author of the monograph *Everyday Life of Kharkiv Workers in the late 1920s and early 1930s* (in Ukrainian). He also took part in the international scientific project "Practices of self-representation of multinational cities in the industrial and post-industrial age", which was implemented with the support of the Kovalsky Program and the Program for the Study of Modern Ukraine of the Canadian Institute of Ukrainian Studies of the University of Alberta (Edmonton, Canada).

Tamara Martsenyuk is an Associate Professor at the University of Kyiv-Mohyla Academy (Kyiv, Ukraine), and a visiting scholar at the Free University of Berlin and Leuphana Universität Lüneburg (Germany). Her main research fields and interests include issues such as social inequalities, sociology of gender, and women's activism. She is the author of more than 100 scientific works, several journalistic articles, and textbook and monograph chapters, including *Gender for all. A Challenge to Stereotypes* (2017), *Why You Shouldn't Be Afraid of Feminism* (2018), and *Guardians of the Galaxy: Power and Crisis in a Man's World* (2020). Martsenyuk is also a keen advocate of public sociology: the idea that science and research should be used for the sake of social changes, and is constantly involved in various international research or teaching projects.

Daria Mattingly is a lecturer in European history at the University of Chichester in the United Kingdom. She received her doctoral degree from the University of Cambridge where she taught Soviet and Russian history as a Leverhulme Early Career Fellow. Daria completed her MA in Russian History at the University of Bristol and studied philosophy at Kyiv Shevchenko University in Ukraine. Having previously provided research assistance to Anne Applebaum for her book on the 1932–33 famine in Ukraine, Daria is currently finishing her own monograph on the identifiable and memorial traces of the rank-and-file perpetrators of the Holodomor.

Vladyslava Moskalets is a historian and researcher at the Ukrainian Catholic University, and the Center for Urban History in Lviv, Ukraine. She received her PhD in 2017 at the Jagiellonian University. She was a Fellow at the Institute for the History of Polish Jewry and Israel-Poland Relations (March-May 2016), and a Fulbright Scholar Fellow (2018–2019) at the Northwestern University, Chicago. Since 2016, Moskalets has been teaching courses related to Ukrainian and Jewish history of the 19th century, consumption history, and Hebrew. She is currently Senior lecturer at the Department of History of the Ukrainian Catholic University, and coordinator of the Jewish Studies program.

Olena Palko is an Assistant Professor at the University of Basel. She was awarded her PhD from the University of East Anglia in 2017 and previously held the position of Leverhulme Early Career Fellow at Birkbeck College, University of London. She is the author of *Making Ukraine Soviet. Literature and Cultural Politics under Lenin and Stalin* (Bloomsbury Academic, 2021) and a co-editor of *Making Ukraine: Negotiating, Contesting, and Drawing Borders in Twentieth Century* (McGill Queens University Press, 2022). Her research interests lie in the field of early Soviet cultural history and the interwar history of Eastern Europe.

Matthew D. Pauly is an Associate Professor of History at Michigan State University. He is the author of *Breaking the Tongue: Language, Education, and Power in Soviet Ukraine* (University of Toronto Press) – which has just been released in a paperback edition – as well as numerous journal articles and book chapters on early Soviet nationalities policy, education, and childhood in the Russian Empire and Soviet Ukraine. He has won grants for his research from the US Fulbright Program, International Research & Exchanges Board, American Councils for International Education, Shevchenko Scientific Society, and Canadian Foundation for Ukrainian Studies.

Hanna Perekhoda is a PhD student and graduate assistant at the University of Lausanne. Her current research focuses on how the institutional and ideological structures of empire and those of the nation-state determined mental geographies, influenced political strategies, and guided the choices of political actors involved in the process of delimitating the Ukrainian political space from 1917 to the 1920s. Her main areas of interest are the new imperial history, the historical sociology of the Bolshevism, and nationalism studies centered on the non-Russian peripheries of the Russian Empire and the Soviet Union. She is a co-editor of the volume *L'invasion de l'Ukraine. Histoires, conflits et résistances populaires* (Paris, Editions la Dispute, 2022).

Stephan Rindlisbacher is a researcher at the Center for Interdisciplinary Polish Studies at the European University Viadrina in Frankfurt (Oder), where he examines processes of territorialization in the early Soviet Union. He is the author of *Living for the Cause: Vera Figner, Vera Zasulich, and the Radical Milieu in Late Imperial Russia* (2014, in German) and has published extensively on the early Soviet period. His latest book is an edited documentary collection *Our Work with the Masses Is Not Worth a Kopeck...: A Document Collection on German and Polish Rural Soviets in Ukraine During the NEP, 1923–1929*, co-edited with Frank Grelka (Harrassowitz Verlag, 2021).

Oleksii Sokyrko is an Associate Professor of History at Taras Shevchenko National University of Kyiv. His research interests cover early modern Ukrainian military and social history and everyday life from the 17th to the late 18th centuries, as well as Early Modern Ukrainian and East European comparative studies. He is the author of five scholarly monographs, among which are *Culinary Journey through the Hetmanate. Secrets and Mysteries of Od Ukrainian Cuisine of the mid-17th – 18th centuries* (Kyiv, 2021, in Ukrainian) and *Guarding the Mace. Court Troops of the Ukrainian Hetmans in the Mid-17th – Second Half of the 18th Century* (Kyiv, 2018 in Ukrainian). Sokyrko is currently working on another monograph exploring military and state institutions in the Cossack Hetmanate.

John Vsetecka is a PhD Candidate in the Department of History at Michigan State University where he is finishing a dissertation on the aftermath of the

1932–33 famine (Holodomor) and the 1946–47 famine in Soviet Ukraine. During the 2021–2022 academic year, John was a Fulbright Scholar in Kyiv, Ukraine. He is also the founder and a current editor of H-Ukraine (part of the larger H-Net platform), which shares and promotes academic and scholarly content related to the study of Ukraine.

Oleksandr Zabirko studied Literature and Linguistics at the University of Luhansk (Ukraine) and the University of Duisburg-Essen (Germany). He is currently a researcher at the Slavic Department of the University of Regensburg. His major fields of research are literary models of spatial and political order, contemporary literature(s) from Russia and Ukraine, and fantastic literature in general. His most recent publication is a monograph *Literarische Formen der Geopolitik: Raum- und Ordnungsmodellierung in der russischen und ukrainischen Gegenwartsliteratur* ("Literary Forms of Geopolitics: The Modelling of Spatial and Political Order in Contemporary Russian and Ukrainian Literature") (Münster, 2021).

Editorial

The book series **New Europes** aims to provide a new understanding of Europe's past and present in the face of current crises such as Russia's war against Ukraine, climate change, the post-pandemic recovery, and the rise of new forms of authoritarianism. These challenges call for multidisciplinary, transnational, historical and critical approaches to existing paradigms for thinking about Europe. The editors encourage authors to revisit established narratives of European, national and subnational histories, to correct the neglect of geographical areas such as Eastern Europe in general studies of Europe, and to seek out new methodologies for interpreting documentary evidence. Books in the series are accompanied by richly commented selections of primary sources for independent study, alongside co-authored as well as single-authored books on topical issues. Edited by a group of scholars from History, Political Science, Gender Studies, and Literary Studies, the series aims to serve three sets of readers: the general public interested in contextualising present conflicts; readers seeking to deepen their expertise of modern European society in global contexts; and those involved in education at the level of schools as well as higher education, looking for inspirations and approaches in research and teaching of European history.

The series is edited by *The University of New Europe*, represented by Jan C. Behrends, Dina Gusejnova, Alexander Etkind, Mykola Makhortykh, Andrea Pető, Ellen Rutten, Dorine Schellens, and Philipp Schmädeke.

U   N   E

The University of New Europe

Advisory board: Ayşe Gül Altınay, Aleida Assmann, Gruia Bădescu, Paul Betts, Halyna Hryn, Ilya Kalinin, Bill Kissane, Pavel Kolář, Eva Michaels, Olena Palko, Luisa Passerini, Andryi Portnov, Ksenia Robbe, Jay Winter, Vasily Zharkov, and Tatiana Zhurzhenko.

Historical Sciences

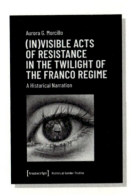

Aurora G. Morcillo
(In)visible Acts of Resistance in the Twilight of the Franco Regime
A Historical Narration

January 2022, 332 p., pb., ill.
50,00 € (DE), 978-3-8376-5257-4
E-Book: available as free open access publication
PDF: ISBN 978-3-8394-5257-8

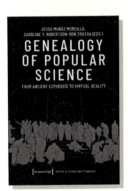

Jesús Muñoz Morcillo, Caroline Y. Robertson-von Trotha (eds.)
Genealogy of Popular Science
From Ancient Ecphrasis to Virtual Reality

2020, 586 p., pb., col. ill.
49,00 € (DE), 978-3-8376-4835-5
E-Book:
PDF: 48,99 € (DE), ISBN 978-3-8394-4835-9

Monika Ankele, Benoît Majerus (eds.)
Material Cultures of Psychiatry

2020, 416 p., pb., col. ill.
40,00 € (DE), 978-3-8376-4788-4
E-Book: available as free open access publication
PDF: ISBN 978-3-8394-4788-8

All print, e-book and open access versions of the titles in our list are available in our online shop www.transcript-publishing.com!

Historical Sciences

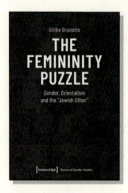

Ulrike Brunotte
The Femininity Puzzle
Gender, Orientalism and the »Jewish Other«

September 2022, 236 p., pb., col. ill.
45,00 € (DE), 978-3-8376-5821-7
E-Book:
PDF: 44,99 € (DE), ISBN 978-3-8394-5821-1

Andreas Kraß, Moshe Sluhovsky, Yuval Yonay (eds.)
Queer Jewish Lives Between Central Europe and Mandatory Palestine
Biographies and Geographies

January 2022, 332 p., pb., ill.
39,99 € (DE), 978-3-8376-5332-8
E-Book:
PDF: 39,99 € (DE), ISBN 978-3-8394-5332-2

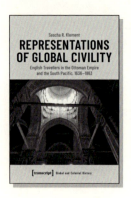

Sascha R. Klement
Representations of Global Civility
English Travellers in the Ottoman Empire and the South Pacific, 1636–1863

2021, 270 p., pb.
45,00 € (DE), 978-3-8376-5583-4
E-Book:
PDF: 44,99 € (DE), ISBN 978-3-8394-5583-8

All print, e-book and open access versions of the titles in our list are available in our online shop www.transcript-publishing.com!